WHEN

AMERICA

FIRST MET

CHINA

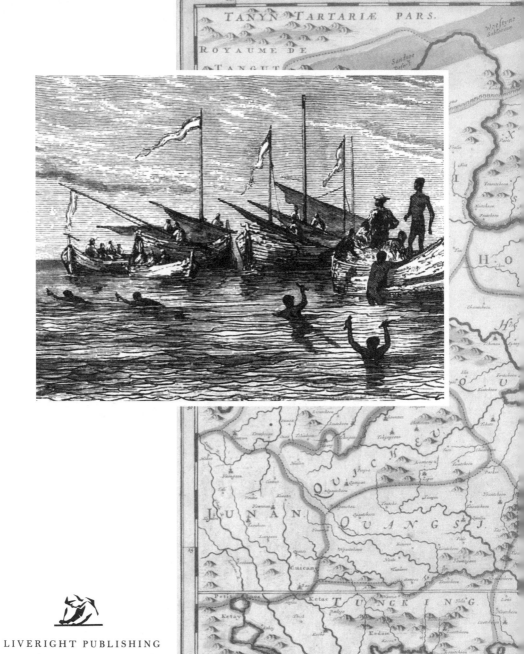

LIVERIGHT PUBLISHING
CORPORATION
A DIVISION OF
W. W. NORTON & COMPANY
NEW YORK · LONDON

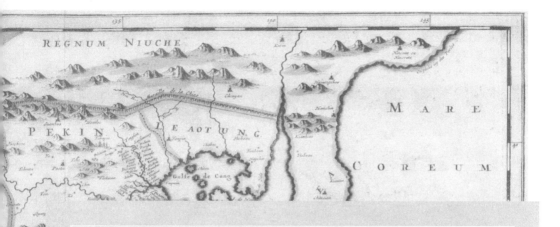

WHEN AMERICA FIRST MET CHINA

AN EXOTIC HISTORY of TEA, DRUGS, AND MONEY IN the AGE of SAIL

Eric Jay Dolin

For information about permission to reproduce
selections from this book, write to Permissions,
Liveright Publishing Corporation,
a division of W. W. Norton & Company, Inc.,
500 Fifth Avenue, New York, NY 10110

For information about special discounts for bulk purchases,
please contact W. W. Norton Special Sales
at specialsales@wwnorton.com or 800-233-4830

Manufacturing by Courier Westford
Book design by Barbara M. Bachman
Production manager: Anna Oler
Maps by David Cain

LIBRARY OF CONGRESS CATALOGING-IN-PUBLICATION DATA

Dolin, Eric Jay.
When America first met China : an exotic history of tea, drugs,
and money in the Age of Sail / Eric Jay Dolin. — 1st ed.
p. cm.
Includes bibliographical references and index.
ISBN 978-0-87140-433-6 (hardcover)
1. United States—Commerce—China—History—18th century.
2. United States—Commerce—China—History—19th century.
3. China—Commerce—United States—History—18th century.
4. China—Commerce—United States—History—19th century.
I. Title.
HF3128.D65 2012
382.0973051—dc23
2012016598

Liveright Publishing Corporation
500 Fifth Avenue, New York, N.Y. 10110

www.wwnorton.com

W. W. Norton & Company Ltd.
Castle House, 75/76 Wells Street, London W1T 3QT

1 2 3 4 5 6 7 8 9 0

To Penny, Ron, and Sage

CONTENTS

A NOTE ON THE TEXT

THE ROMANIZATION OF CHINESE WORDS HAS CHANGED OVER TIME. The older Wade-Giles system has been replaced by pinyin, which is now the official romanization system used in China, and by modern scholars and journalists. *When America First Met China* uses pinyin for personal and place names, giving the Wade-Giles equivalent in parentheses on the first use of each. The only exceptions to this rule are Western names that are firmly entwined with the history of the China trade, and that are familiar to Westerners. These include Canton, Whampoa, Peking, Macao, Lintin, Nanking, Kowloon, Hong Kong, the Yangtze River, and the Pearl River. For these the pinyin equivalent will appear in parentheses on first use.

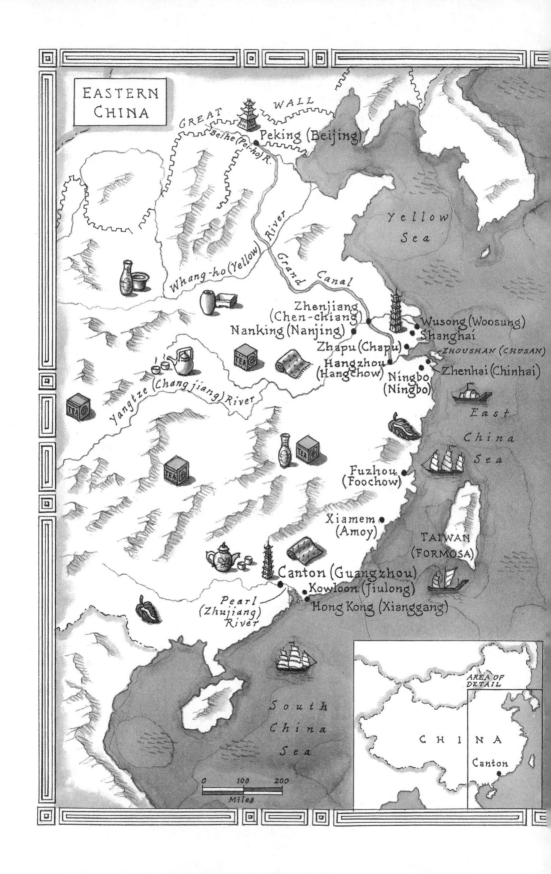

EASTERN
CHINA

GREAT WALL

Beihe (Pei-ho) R.

Peking (Beijing)

Yellow
Sea

Whang-ho (Yellow) River

Grand Canal

Zhenjiang
(Chen-chiang)
Nanking (Nanjing)

Zhapu (Chapu)

Wusong (Woosung)
Shanghai

ZHOUSHAN (CHUSAN)

Hangzhou
(Hangchow)

Ningbo
(Ningbo)

Zhenhai (Chinhai)

Yangtze (Chang jiang) River

East
China
Sea

TEA

Fuzhou
(Foochow)

Xiamem
(Amoy)

TAIWAN
(FORMOSA)

Canton (Guangzhou)
Kowloon (Jiulong)
Hong Kong (Xianggang)

Pearl
(Zhujiang)
River

South
China
Sea

0   100   200
Miles

AREA OF
DETAIL

CHINA

Canton

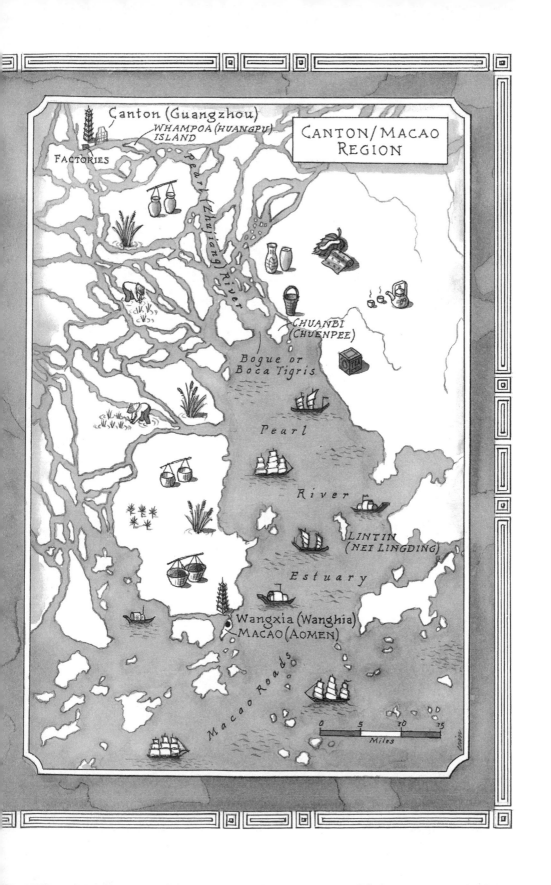

Canton (Guangzhou)
WHAMPOA (HUANGPU) ISLAND
FACTORIES

Pearl (Zhujiang) River

CANTON/MACAO REGION

CHUANBI (CHUENPEE)

Bogue or Boca Tigris

Pearl

River

LINTIN (NEI LINGDING)

Estuary

Wangxia (Wanghia)
MACAO (AOMEN)

Macao Roads

0   5   10   15
Miles

INTRODUCTION

NEW YORK CLIPPER SHIP *CHALLENGE*, N. CURRIER, 1850.

*T*HE UNITED STATES' RELATIONSHIP WITH CHINA IS COMPLEX AND critically important to America's future. Every day Americans are inundated with news that describes, dissects, and analyzes the many facets of this historic relationship. For the most part the coverage is unsettling and tinged with no small trace of alarmism. Americans are clearly worried about China's rise, and much of that worry focuses on economic and trade issues. The concerns are many: Does China own too much of America's debt? Is the gaping trade deficit with China sustainable? Do China's currency policies give its products an unfair advantage in the marketplace? Underlying these and a host of other concerns is a nagging question—will China, now the second-largest economy in the world after the United States, someday be number one? Or, to put it more bluntly, does China's rise inevitably mean America's downfall, and will the twenty-first century become the Chinese century?

I have asked the same questions, but as a historian my primary interest is what America's relationship with China was like in the past. That is why every time I heard or read news stories about America and China, it occurred to me that—given the intense focus on the evolving ties between these two countries—it might be revealing to explore the origins of their relationship. Therein lay the genesis of this book, whose goal is to tell the story of how America and China first met, and what their relationship was like in the beginning. As it turns out, the story revolves mostly around trade, for that was the primary medium through which America and China came to know each other.

Determining where to begin this story was simple, because America's first direct encounter with China came on the heels of the American Revolution, when the American ship the *Empress of China* sailed to Canton (Guangzhou). Figuring out the appropriate place to conclude the story, however, proved problematic, since the China trade, as it has been colloquially called, continues to this day, and there is no historical marker that clearly signifies "Here is the end of the beginning." But as the narrative wended its way through the course of Sino-American history, there appeared a transition that proved to be a good point at which to bring my story to a close, and that was in the late 1860s, when the China trade lost much of the drama and tragedy that had characterized it in earlier years, and its very nature shifted with the rise of steamship travel and the completion of the transcontinental railroad.

My first intimation that the China trade would be an intriguing topic came while I was working on my last book, *Fur, Fortune, and Empire: The Epic History of the Fur Trade in America*. Part of that history revolves around the colorful and lucrative trade that sprang up in the late 1700s, in which American merchants sent sea otter pelts to China to exchange for a variety of goods. This piqued my interest, and in researching this work I discovered that the sea otter trade was only part of a much larger tale of how the American-Chinese nexus developed.

In the first eighty or so years of the new Republic's history, American ships sailed around the Cape of Good Hope and Cape Horn on their way to China, the mysterious so-called Middle Kingdom, with cargoes of silver, ginseng, furs, sandalwood, bêche-de-mer (sea cucumbers), cotton fabrics, and many other items, which were traded for a variety of goods, including silks, porcelain, furniture, and most importantly, hundreds of thousands of tons of tea—the "brew of the immortals." The China trade was critical to the growth and success of the new nation. It bolstered America's emerging economy, enabling Boston, New York, Philadelphia, Salem, Providence, and other ports to thrive after the ravages of the war. In doing so it helped create the nation's first millionaires, instilled confidence in Americans in their ability to compete on the world's stage, and spurred an explosion in shipbuilding that led to the construction of the ultimate sailing vessels—the graceful and exceedingly fast clipper ships. The trade also helped the United States expand into the Pacific Northwest, and it laid the foundation for a lasting artistic legacy that remains in evidence in museums and homes throughout the country.

THIS BOOK EXPLORES a time many years ago when the desire for trade and profit first brought together two disparate cultures that often failed to fully understand or appreciate each other, leaving many Americans and Chinese alternately frustrated and furious. It also tells a tale of unfulfilled commercial expectations and large trade deficits, one based on keen competition, exploitation, and war. In their search for merchantable items, American adventurers laid waste to sea otter and seal populations, devastated the forests on Pacific islands, and engaged in the opium trade. Worse still was America's trafficking in Chinese coolies, who were forced to work as virtual slaves picking sugar and other crops in Latin America, and collecting guano (bird waste) on the Chincha Islands off Peru.

Hardly a mere concatenation of dramatic events, however, the story possesses a wide-ranging cast of compelling characters. These include not only the Founding Fathers and dynastic emperors of top-down history, but also the seamen, merchants, and native peoples who were swept up in its currents. To this list must be added a motley assortment of explorers, opportunists, castaways, murderers—and women who liked to break the rules—all of whom bring the China trade vividly to life.

WHEN
AMERICA
FIRST MET
CHINA

One

"THE ADVENTUROUS PURSUITS OF COMMERCE"

GEORGE WASHINGTON'S ENTRY INTO NEW YORK ON
THE DAY THE BRITISH EVACUATED THE CITY, NOVEMBER 25, 1783,
CURRIER & IVES, 1857.

Soon AFTER THE TREATY OF PARIS WAS SIGNED ON SEPTEMBER 3, 1783, officially ending the American Revolution, the former colonies were hit by one of the worst winters in recent memory. From Maine to Virginia the temperature plummeted in mid-November, and for the remainder of the year the region was battered by a string of powerful storms, some dumping nearly two feet of snow. Ice, at first appearing as a thin glaze at the edges of harbors and riverbanks, spread, swallowing open water at a quickening pace. Two brief but intense thaws in January melted the snow and set ice floes in motion, but at the end of the month winter clamped down again and there was nothing John Green could do except wait. As captain of the *Empress of China*, Green had wanted to sail out of New York in early February, but ice in the East River and the harbor beyond barred his way. The situation worsened as the mercury dipped below zero for days on end. Finally the temperature rebounded, causing the ice to retreat, and on Sunday, February 22, as the sun rose in the brilliant blue sky and gentle winds rippled the surface of water, it was time to get under way. The *Empress of China* cleared the wharf, and Green and his forty-two-man crew began their groundbreaking voyage, thus launching America's trade with China.[1]

At the same time another ship, the *Edward*, also headed down the East River, bound for London with the "Public dispatches of Congress, for the respective courts, containing the definitive articles of peace."[2] The coincidental sailing of these two ships provides a historical juxtaposition that could have been conjured by a novelist. While the *Edward* was delivering what could arguably be called the birth certificate of the United States, proclaiming the arrival of the newest nation, the *Empress of China* was making a very important statement of its own, announcing to the world that this new nation was ready to compete in the international arena. The symbolism didn't end there. Even the date of departure provided its own dramatic flourish, for February 22 was George Washington's fifty-second birthday. Although that, too, was just a coincidence, it was particularly fitting that the infant nation's first foray to the Far East should have commenced on the birthday of the man who had done more to found the United States than any other person. Washington couldn't have asked for a better omen than the departure of these two ships, which embodied the hope for America's future.

The *Empress of China's* voyage was borne on the twin pillars of necessity and opportunity. With the signing of the Treaty of Paris, one trial had ended and another had begun. America had broken free of the constrictive political and economic bonds of Great Britain, and the Americans who had fought so long and hard for this day basked in the warm afterglow of freedom and possibility. They were subjects no more. A toast raised in Charleston, South Carolina, on July 4, 1783, after the preliminary articles of peace had been ratified by the Continental Congress, captured the jubilant mood of the country: "To this glorious day, by which we secured, among the powers of the earth, the separate and equal station, to which the laws of nature and of nature's God entitle us."[3] At the same time, however, this freedom came at a terrible cost. The nation was mired in an economic depression, much of its commerce hobbled, its central government in disarray, and the states were squabbling with one another over their powers and responsibilities. Given all this, it was not uncommon for Americans to wonder how their country would make its way in the world.

Many enterprising merchants, who had profited handsomely during the war and still had ships and resources at their disposal, believed that the answer lay overseas, but with whom would they trade? The Revolution had severed the formal union between the colonies and Great Britain, and cast asunder the long-standing mercantile connections between the two. The British government, viewing the United States as a potentially dangerous competitor, cut off virtually all American trade with the British West Indies, which had been one of the main arteries of colonial commerce prior to the Revolution. At the same time it was becoming clear that America was going to face trade barriers from other European nations intent on protecting their own commercial interests. Confronted with this increasingly hostile landscape, the United States needed not only to establish improved trading relationships with European powers but also develop new ties with other countries in order to ensure its economic future.[4] To that end China presented a tantalizing opportunity.

In the decades leading up to the Revolution, Americans had

obtained the Chinese goods they desired—including porcelain, silk, tea, and a rough, sturdy cotton fabric called nankeen—from British merchants or from smugglers who brought the goods to America's shores. One thing that the Americans couldn't do, however, was trade directly with China. The only entity in the British Empire allowed to do so was the monopolistic British East India Company, which had been established in 1600. Since America was no longer part of the empire, its merchants were now free to go to China. Leading the way was Robert Morris.

BORN IN LIVERPOOL in 1734, Morris remained in England until the age of thirteen, when he came to America to join his father, a tobacco merchant who had settled Oxford, Maryland, on the eastern shore of Chesapeake Bay. An industrious boy with an inquisitive mind, Morris quickly outgrew the narrow confines of Oxford, and two

ROBERT MORRIS, BY CHARLES WILLSON PEALE, FROM LIFE, 1782.

years after he arrived his father sent him to Philadelphia, already a cosmopolitan metropolis of twenty thousand people, the largest British city on the continent. After a brief tenure as a librarian, Morris began clerking at the shipping firm of Charles Willing. Morris swiftly rose through the ranks and became fast friends with Willing's eldest son, Thomas, who also worked at the firm and was being groomed to lead it one day.[5]

When Mr. Willing died in 1754, Thomas took over the firm, and installed Morris as his trusted lieutenant, soon elevating him to partner in the firm of Willing, Morris & Company. Willing, whose friends called him "Old Square Toes" on account of his serious demeanor and conservative nature, chose wisely in selecting Morris. Together they built Willing, Morris & Company into one of the premier merchant houses in America. By the early 1770s Morris had married, started his own family, and was firmly ensconced at the pinnacle of Philadelphia society.[6]

During the Revolution, Morris pursued two paths, one public and the other private. As a delegate to the Continental Congress, he favored negotiating with Britain, and would not sign the Declaration of Independence until August 2, 1776. In so doing he affirmed his unreserved support for the cause, purportedly declaring, "I am not one of those politicians that run testy when my own plans are not adopted. I think it is the duty of a good citizen to follow when he cannot lead."[7] When the Continental Congress needed someone to curtail government spending, reduce public debt, coordinate foreign loans, and breathe life into America's woefully underfunded war effort, it tapped Morris. As a member of Congress and as superintendent of finance, Morris established the first national bank and did the fiscal equivalent of spinning straw into gold. Time and again Morris drew upon his financial acumen, his connections, his negotiating talent, and his own fortune to pull together money and materials, the twin fuels without which the war could not be waged. At Valley Forge and Yorktown, when George Washington needed infusions of cash and supplies to keep his troops from literally walking off the job and bringing the war effort to a grinding halt, Morris spearheaded the effort to provide these essential items.[8]

Morris also served as the agent of the marine, to develop what he called "our infant and unfortunate navy."[9] It was a sensible choice. Morris had the requisite background, having been heavily involved in maritime trade before the war through his fleet of merchantmen, and he applied his financial skills to get the bankrupt navy on an even keel.

In and out of government, Morris, "the Financier of the Revolution," also attended to his private business, for however ardent a patriot he was, he was equally committed to making money. Morris expanded his trading empire, outfitting privateers to plunder British shipping. Although many regarded Morris as a profiteer as a result of his wartime business activities, the latter "elevated him to a position where he was acknowledged as the most prominent merchant in America."[10]

As the Revolution wound to a close, Morris began withdrawing from public service and turned more of his attention to his business affairs. One of the investment prospects foremost on his mind was the China trade. In 1780 two of Morris's business associates, the New Yorker William Duer and the French consul in Philadelphia, John Holker, tried to entice him to fund a trading voyage to China, but Morris declined, arguing that the resources necessary to mount such an expedition were not available. The next year Holker approached Morris again, with the same result.[11] But by mid-1783, as peace finally hove into view, Morris was nearly ready. All he needed was the spark provided by John Ledyard.

BORN IN GROTON, CONNECTICUT, in 1751, Ledyard had compiled a rather undistinguished résumé by the outbreak of the Revolution, having been expelled from Dartmouth College, followed by stints as a divinity student and as a seaman transporting mules, molasses, flour, and sugar between Africa, Europe, the West Indies, and Connecticut.

PAINTING OF
JOHN LEDYARD
BY JOSEPH SWAN,
1991.

Perhaps his most notable achievement was carving a canoe out of the trunk of a pine tree and paddling it 140 miles on the Connecticut River, from Hanover, New Hampshire to his parents' home in Hartford, Connecticut, becoming the first known white person to traverse that stretch of water. In March 1775 Ledyard sailed to England, where he was impressed into or volunteered for the British army, and then within a few weeks managed to get transferred to the navy. Ledyard found his life as a marine based dockside in Plymouth dull and enervating. He was a restless wanderer who needed adventure, which he found on July 5, 1776, when he signed on as a corporal on HMS *Resolution*, one of two ships that the famed British explorer James Cook was leading to the Pacific Ocean in an attempt to find the fabled Northwest Passage to the Orient.[12]

The passage was never found, but one discovery had a major impact on subsequent events. It began innocently enough in March

1778, when Cook's ships reached the Pacific Northwest coast and anchored in Nootka Sound on the west side of present-day Vancouver Island. The local Indians paddled out to the ships in their canoes, and, according to Cook, "a trade commenced betwixt us and them, which was carried on with the strictest honesty on both sides. The articles which they offered to sale were skins of various animals, such as bears, wolves, foxes, deer, raccoons, polecats, martens; and, in particular, . . . sea otters."[13] Cook's men snapped up the furs to make new clothes to replace theirs, which were in tatters after nearly two years at sea, giving the Indians "knives, chisels, pieces of iron and tin, nails, looking-glasses, and buttons." In the coming months Cook's crew would accumulate fifteen hundred pelts in all.[14]

Although Cook's men had acquired the pelts for strictly utilitarian purposes, when they arrived at the port of Canton, China, in late 1779, they realized they had a veritable fortune on their hands. The Chinese, who treasured furs for their warmth and beauty, were willing to pay exorbitant prices. Of all the pelts the men had, the most valuable were the sea otters', for good reason. The sea otter (*Enhydra lutris*) is enveloped in a sensationally lustrous and soft fur coat that

SEA OTTER, BY JOHN WOODHOUSE AUDUBON, 1845–47.

is the densest of any mammal, with as many as one million hairs per square inch. One nineteenth-century American merchant declared that it gave him "more pleasure to look at a splendid sea-otter skin, than to examine half the pictures that are stuck up for exhibition, and puffed up by pretended connoisseurs. . . . Excepting a beautiful woman and a lovely infant," the sea otter's pelt was, he maintained, the most beautiful natural object in the world.[15] Particularly fine skins commanded as much as $120 apiece in Canton, and even worn-out pelts garnered a good price. Such huge sums had a galvanizing effect on the men, precipitating in them an almost uncontrollable urge to return immediately to the Pacific Northwest to gather more furs. In fact a near mutiny ensued, but order was maintained, and the ships returned to London in early 1780.[16]

Ledyard didn't forget those wondrous transactions in Canton, and when, at the age of thirty-two, he returned to America in 1782, he wrote a book about his adventures with Captain Cook, including the riches of the northwestern fur trade. "The skins," Ledyard wrote, "which did not cost the purchaser six pence sterling sold in China for 100 dollars. Neither did we purchase a quarter part of the beaver and other fur skins we might have done, and most certainly should have done had we known of meeting the opportunity of disposing of them to such an astonishing profit."[17] Ledyard predicted that his book, published in June 1783, would be "essentially useful to America in general but particularly to the northern states by opening a most valuable trade across the North Pacific Ocean to China & the East Indies" ("East Indies" was a catchall phrase used at the time that typically included China, India, Japan, and the rest of the Far East).[18] Before his book was published Ledyard was already looking for investors to back his fur-trading plan. Rebuffed in New York City, he ventured to Philadelphia and was granted a meeting with Morris in early June 1783. There he found a receptive audience, for Ledyard's plan suggested immense profits, and Morris was finally ready for a China voyage. After his second meeting with Morris, Ledyard wrote to one of his cousins with the joyous news:

I have been so often the sport of fortune, that I durst hardly credit the present dawn of bright prospects. But it is a fact, that the Honorable Robert Morris is disposed to give me a ship to go to the North Pacific Ocean. . . . What a noble hold he instantly took of the enterprise! I have been two days, at his request, drawing up a minute detail of a plan, and an estimate of the outfits, which I shall present him with tomorrow. . . . I take the lead of the greatest commercial enterprise, that has ever been embarked on in this country; and one of the first moment, as it respects the trade of America.[19]

Morris partnered with Daniel Parker & Company of New York, including Holker and other merchants. The goal was to send three ships around Cape Horn, with one heading for China while the other two would sail to the Pacific Northwest for furs, then to Canton. As Parker and Ledyard looked for ships, Morris and Parker worked on financing the scheme and landing a group of Boston investors.

That summer Parker purchased a splendid ship nearing completion in Boston, designed by the "celebrated" John Peck, whom many regard as America's first naval architect. Christened *Empress of China*, at just over one hundred feet long, twenty-eight feet wide, and 360 tons burden, the copper-bottomed, black-hulled vessel was graceful, with clean lines, yet sturdy and strong. It was patterned after the *Bellisarius*, an American privateer that had been captured by the British during the Revolution and was found to be the fastest ship in the Royal Navy.[20]

The public first heard of the planned expedition in late August, when the *Salem Gazette* published an exciting bit of news:

We hear that a ship is fitting out at Boston for an intended voyage to CHINA; that her cargo out, in money and goods, will amount to £150,000; and that she will sail the ensuing fall. Many eminent merchants, in different parts of the continent, are said to be interested in this first adventure from the New

World to the Old. We have, at an earlier period than the most sanguine Whig could have expected, or even hoped, or than the most inveterate Tory feared, very pleasing prospects of a very extensive commerce with the most distant parts of the globe.[21]

Convinced that they should be thinking bigger, Morris and Parker pursued an even more extravagant design, involving not three ships but a small flotilla of half a dozen, with three heading west via Cape Horn, while the others sailed east, around the Cape of Good Hope and across the Indian Ocean to China. No sooner had this new plan been hatched than it began to fall apart. Parker and Ledyard had difficulty lining up additional ships. Skittish Boston investors failed to buy in, forcing Parker's group and Morris to split the cost. And Morris, still enmeshed in efforts to get the nation's finances in order, could not give the China project his full attention, while his partners resorted to bickering and maneuvering against one another.

In late November, however, Morris remained confident enough about the prospects for the enterprise to write to John Jay, his friend and one of the signers of the Treaty of Paris, with promising news: "I am sending some ships to China to encourage others in the adventurous pursuits of commerce." But even this was too optimistic. By early December, as the hard winter enveloped the coast in snow and ice, the China fleet had been reduced to one. Only the *Empress of China* would be sailing, and it would not be heading west. Morris and Parker couldn't afford more ships, nor were they willing to stake their entire bet on Ledyard's untested scheme, but rather decided to follow the safer eastern course taken by European merchants who had already successfully made their way to China.[22]

Ledyard was furious. "The flame of enterprise that I excited in America," he confided bitterly to one of his cousins, "terminated in a flash, that equally bespoke the inebriety of head & pusillanimity of heart of my patrons."[23] Rather than give up, however, Ledyard sailed for Europe looking for investors who shared his vision and were willing to see it through.

———

LACKING LEDYARD'S NORTHWESTERN FURS, the *Empress of China* would have a cargo of roughly thirty-two tons of lead, fifty tons of cordage, five hundred yards of woolen cloth, twelve casks of spirits (wine, brandy, and rum), a box of furs (mainly beaver), $20,000 in Spanish silver coins (specie), and nearly thirty tons of ginseng. Together, ship and cargo represented an enormous investment of $120,000, of which the silver and the ginseng were the most valuable.[24]

The world's economy at this time literally ran on silver, and more specifically Spanish pieces of eight, the "first truly global currency."* Since the 1500s the mines in Mexico and South America had produced a genuine flood of the precious metal—more than 3 billion ounces,

SPANISH AMERICAN DOLLARS, OR PIECES OF EIGHT,
FROM 1791 AND 1807, MINTED IN MEXICO CITY.

the vast majority of the world's supply—which was transformed into coinage that greased mercantile transactions from West to East. There was no doubt that the silver coins on the *Empress of China*, referred

* They were called pieces of eight because each was equal to eight *reales*; the *real*, or "*royal*," being a smaller-denomination Spanish coin.

to as "Spanish Dollars" by the Americans, would be most welcome in Canton.[25] The same could be said for ginseng.

For thousands of years the Chinese had used the thick, fleshy roots of *Panax ginseng*, found in the forests of northern China, as an energy booster, an aphrodisiac, and a curative for an impressive array of maladies, including pleurisy, poor vision, dizziness, and vomiting. No wonder, then, that Carl Linnaeus named the genus *Panax*, which is Greek for "cure-all"; thus, the word "panacea." To the Chinese ginseng truly was "the dose for immortality."[26]

Prior to the early 1700s only *Panax ginseng* had been used in China. In 1717, however, the Jesuit priest Joseph-François Lafitau discovered another, less potent though still highly desirable species of ginseng growing in Canada—*Panax quinquefolius*. Soon the French were feverishly digging up Canadian ginseng and sending it to Canton. Not long thereafter *Panax quinquefolius* was found growing in the mountains and forests of New England, New York, and farther south, and the Americans began selling ginseng to the British East India Company for the China trade.

Both the French and the Americans relied primarily on Indians to gather ginseng, because they were relatively cheap labor and were very familiar with the root, having long used it for medicinal purposes. This arrangement alarmed the conservative American theologian Jonathan Edwards. Writing to a friend in 1752, Edwards noted that the recent discovery of ginseng in the woods of New England and New York had "much prejudiced the cause of religion among the Indians," because they were spending so much time digging for ginseng that they were not coming to church. Even worse in Edward's eyes was the Indians' using their wages to buy rum, "wherewith they have intoxicated themselves."[27]

Regardless of the dangers of ginseng to the mortal souls and physical well-being of the Indians, they, and many non-Indians as well, continued to scour America's forests for the valuable root. And now with the *Empress of China*'s hold to fill, it was time for the Americans to do the buying. In late August 1783 Parker hired a Philadelphia ginseng supplier, who in turn enlisted Doctor Robert Johnston to purchase ginseng in the small towns, outposts, and Indian lands of Virginia and Pennsylvania. Johnston, who would go on to become the surgeon aboard the *Empress of China*, spent more than three months in his peripatetic search for the prized root. When he wasn't traveling through the wilderness to procure ginseng—made scarce as a result of decades of collecting—he was shuttling to Philadelphia and New York to beg for the scarcest commodity of all, money with which to pay his far-flung suppliers. These obstacles notwithstanding, Johnston succeeded in gathering roughly thirty tons of ginseng. Between mid-November and mid-December this impressive haul was sent on a small armada of ships to New York, where it was sorted for quality, stored in 242 casks, and loaded onto the *Empress of China*.[28]

AS IMPORTANT AS THE SHIP'S cargo was its captain, on whose back rested the fate of the voyage. John Green, forty-seven, cut an imposing figure at six feet four inches tall and nearly three hundred pounds. With admirable concern for prospective pallbearers, Green had directed in his will that his coffin be "carried to the grave by eight laboring men of the neighborhood."[29] Arriving in Philadelphia from Ireland as a teenager, Green had worked for Willing, Morris & Company as a shipmaster. During the war Green commanded privateers in which Morris had an interest, and also saw action as a captain in the Continental navy. But his luck ran out in the late summer of 1781, when his ship, *Lion*, was captured by the British frigate *La Prudente*, after a fourteenth-hour chase off the Brittany coast. Green spent thirty days' detention on a British man-of-war, and then the next nine months at the notorious Mill Prison, in Plymouth, England, where he passed much of the time building ship models, caring for his fellow prisoners, and waging a letter-writing campaign for his and their freedom. Finally, in late June 1782, with peace negotiations under way, the British Admiralty approved a prisoner release, which sent Green along with 215 other Americans back to Philadelphia. Upon Green's return one of the local newspapers lauded his selflessness during incarceration. "In every apparent respect, where the honor or credit of our republic were concerned . . . he always demeaned himself in such a manner as justly entitles him to the good-will and thanks of his country."[30]

Just as critical as the captain were the supercargoes, the men responsible for overseeing business activities, including the trading that would take place in China. The senior supercargo on the *Empress of China* was Samuel Shaw, a twenty-nine-year-old Bostonian, who had distinguished himself during the Revolution in a variety of army posts, including aide-de-camp to Major General Henry Knox, the former bookseller who would go on to become America's first secretary of war. At the war's end Knox heaped praise upon his aide, noting that he "has, in every instance, evinced himself an intelligent, active, and gallant officer, and as such he has peculiarly endeared himself to his numerous acquaintances," sentiments that were echoed by Washington as well. The junior supercargo was Thomas Randall, another Bostonian and a close friend of Shaw's, who served with him in the army and after a short time as a prisoner of war became a successful Philadelphia merchant.[31]

These three men—Green, Shaw, and Randall—along with Johnston and another officer on the *Empress of China*, as well as Parker and Morris, shared a connection that extended beyond the ship. They were all members of the Society of the Cincinnati (Morris only honor-

SAMUEL SHAW.

ary), a group conceived by Knox and founded in May 1783 by officers of the Continental army. The society promoted continuing friendship and the cause of union among the states, and it assisted the widows and children of its deceased members. In honor of France's support during the war, French officers were also welcome to join. The society was named after Lucius Quinctius Cincinnatus, the Roman farmer turned soldier who heeded the call of his countrymen to become dictator and then led them to victory in two wars, only to return to his farm after the victories rather than retain the mantle of absolute power that his grateful followers had gladly bestowed. Fittingly Washington, the society's first president general, was widely hailed as the "Cincinnatus of the West," for his selfless behavior at the end of the American Revolution, when he refused the urgings of some to become king. Having been united in the fight for independence during the war, the Cincinnati men of the *Empress of China* now made common cause for their country on the battlefield of international commerce.[32]

WHILE THE BACKERS of the *Empress of China* were developing their plans, gathering a cargo, and filling out the ship's complement, other American merchants were also eagerly looking to the Far East—Morris and Parker weren't the only ones who sensed opportunity. Salem men were known to be interested in trade with China; and in late 1783, Col. Isaac Sears, a Boston merchant, sent a ship in that direction. Earlier in the year one of Sears's European contacts claimed that five tons of American ginseng would sell in the Swedish port of Gothenburg for eight dollars per pound, as long as it arrived by February 20, 1784, to be transshipped to Canton on Swedish ships. Sears proceeded to purchase the ginseng, but it proved to be a race against time. In order to get the ginseng to Gothenburg on schedule, Sears estimated that he would need to ship it out on his fifty-ton sloop, the *Harriet*, by the middle of December. Sears failed to make that deadline, so he literally changed course.

According to the story most often told in history books, when the

Harriet sailed in late December, Sears told its captain, a Mr. Hallet, to go to Canton, but the sloop never made it that far. In Cape Town, near the southern tip of Africa, the *Harriet* caught the attention of officers of the British East India Company, who realized that Hallet's designs ran counter to Britain's economic interests in China. To eliminate the threat they bought Hallet off, offering him two pounds of Chinese tea for each pound of ginseng. The deal struck, Hallet headed home with a healthy profit.

As dramatic as the story may be, it is in fact apocryphal. While it is possible that the British officers *thought* they had stymied the competition by their quick dealing, that wasn't the case. Sears meant to send the *Harriet* only as far as Cape Town, not China. He knew that Cape Town was a popular stopping-off point for ships engaged in the China trade, and he hoped that Hallet would find a buyer there. Thus, although the voyage of the *Harriet* is interesting, it was not the first ship from the United States to attempt to go to China.

The *Harriet*'s return to the United States in July 1784 gave Americans a tangible example of just how radically the world had changed, and it offered a glimpse of a brighter commercial future. One patriotic citizen crowed that the *Harriet*'s arrival "must fill with sensible pleasure the breast of every American, and cause their hearts to expand with gratitude to the Supreme Ruler of the universe, by whose beneficence our commerce is freed from those shackles it used to be cramped with, and bids fair to extend to every part of the globe, without passing through the medium of England, that rotten island." Even more tangible was the tea in the *Harriet*'s hold, which Bostonians eagerly purchased.[33]

BY EARLY FEBRUARY 1784 the *Empress of China*, still in port when the *Harriet* sailed from Boston, was ready to go, with cargo loaded, clearance papers signed, and the officers and crew standing by. Tucked away in Green's cabin was a most interesting document, thought essential to the trip's success. Since the voyage was so utterly novel, the owners were not sure how their ship would be received in China. So they figured it was wise to arm Green with an official introduction from the government of the United States, in case the legitimacy of the ship and its purpose were questioned. The sea letter provided by the Continental Congress contained a comically long and rather obsequious salutation, designed to be of use wherever the ship alighted, in or outside of China. It began, "Most serene, serene, most puissant, puissant, high, illustrious, noble, honorable, venerable, wise, and prudent Emperors, Kings, Republics, Princes, Dukes, Earls, Barons, Lords, Burgo-Masters, Counsellors, as also Judges, Officers, Justiciaries and Regents of all the good cities and places, whether ecclesiastical or secular, who shall see these patents or hear them read." The letter went on to clarify that the *Empress of China* "belongs to" the citizens of the United States, and to ask that those who welcome Green may do so "with goodness and treat him in a becoming manner," while allowing him to "transact his business where and in what manner he shall judge proper."[34]

When the deep freeze finally broke on February 22, the *Empress of China* sailed down the East River past the Grand Battery and Fort George at the tip of Manhattan, where a throng of people onshore let out three cheers. Green ordered his men to fire a thirteen-gun salute to represent the thirteen states, to which the fort responded with cannon blasts of its own. As Green gazed upon the exhilarating scene, he couldn't miss the American flag fluttering in the breeze over the fort. So much had changed in such a short time. A mere three months earlier British forces had occupied New York City, and it was the Union Jack, not the Stars and Stripes, that flew over the fort. The British finally left in the early afternoon of November 25, 1783, later christened Evacuation Day, but before departing they heaped one more insult upon their former colonists.

No sooner had the British embarked than American troops, led by Knox and accompanied by jubilant New Yorkers, paraded into Fort George to prepare for the triumphant arrival of General Washington and the official reclaiming of the city. The crowd's excitement turned into anger when they saw the Union Jack on the flagpole, and their anger became rage when they realized that the British had nailed their flag in place and greased the pole. After a few men tried unsuccessfully to scale the pole to remove the offending symbol, a call went out to go to gather saws, wood, and nails. Cleats were affixed to the pole, and a young sailor started to climb, but before he got too far, a ladder arrived, which he used to reach the top, tear down the British flag, and replace it with America's colors, resulting in shouts of joy and a thirteen-gun salute.[35]

As the *Empress of China* passed within view of the fort, the British and their disdain were gone. "If we may judge from the countenances of the spectators," the *New York Packet and the American Advertiser* observed, "all hearts seemed glad, contemplating the new source of riches that may arise to this city, from a trade to the East-Indies; and all joined their wishes for the success of the *Empress of China*."[36] Another paper added, "The Captain and crew . . . were all happy and cheerful, in good health and high spirits; and with a becoming decency, elated on being considered the first instruments, in the hands of Providence, who have undertaken to extend the commerce of the United States of America to that distant and to us unexplored country."[37]

Philip Freneau, known as the "Poet of the American Revolution," wrote a heartfelt and patriotic piece to honor the occasion, of which a few stanzas will suffice:

With clearance from Bellona* won
She spreads her wings to meet the Sun,
Those golden regions to explore
Where George forbade to sail before.
. . .
To countries placed in burning climes
And islands of remotest times

* Bellona is the Roman goddess of war.

She now her eager course explores,
And soon shall greet Chinesian shores.

From thence their fragrant teas to bring
Without the leave of Britain's king;
And Porcelain ware, enchased in gold,
The product of that finer mould.

. . .

Great pile proceed!—and o'er the brine
May every prosperous gale be thine,
'Till freighted deep with Asia's stores,
You reach again your native shores.[38]

Duly feted on its departure, the *Empress of China* crossed the Atlantic, stopping first at Cape Verde, and then sailed around the tip of Africa and across the Indian Ocean, arriving on July 18 at the Sunda Strait, between Java and Sumatra. The only real excitement up to that point occurred less than two weeks after leaving New York, when a ferocious week-long Atlantic gale pummeled the ship, once generating a huge wave that broke over the stern and stove in a cabin window, and another time causing the ship to roll so hard that Captain Green careened against a deck railing, bruising his arm and head. Other than that, according to the purser, John Swift, thus far it had been an exceedingly boring trip. "We have had no agreeable passage," he wrote to his father. "It has been one dreary waste of sky & water, without a pleasing sight to cheer us. I am heartily tired of so long a voyage, more especially as we are not yet at our journey's end by about sixteen hundred miles." Swift's grumblings notwithstanding, the *Empress of China* was having a "textbook" trip, with Green relying on Samuel Dunn's recently published *A New Directory for the East-Indies* for maps and sailing directions.[39] Now, at the Sunda Strait, poised to cross the Java and South China Seas, Captain Green's situation grew far more interesting and potentially dangerous, fraught with navigational challenges and the ever-present threat of well-armed pirates, who patrolled the shipping lanes and attacked merchant ships with ruthless efficiency. At that moment, however, a friend appeared.

On the day the *Empress of China* arrived at the strait, two French ships, the *Triton* and the *Fabius*, lay at anchor in one of the bays. Captain d'Ordelin of the *Triton* and a few of his officers visited the *Empress of China* to welcome the Americans and invite them to dinner the next evening. Onboard the *Triton*, as the brandy flowed, there was talk about the Revolution, and how the Americans and their French allies had triumphed over the mighty British lion. Adding to the bonhomie was d'Ordelin's news that the day before he left Paris, Lafayette had been granted the Order of the Society of the Cincinnati, and that the French people were "much pleased with the honor done to their nation by the institution." Better than the warm feelings was d'Ordelin's offer to escort the *Empress of China* to their mutual destination. The French captain had been to China eleven times before, and therefore knew the way and which hazards to avoid. And since the *Triton* carried sixteen light cannon and 184 men its presence would force pirates to think twice before attacking.[40]

At sunrise on July 22 the *Empress of China* and the *Triton* got under way; and a little more than a month later they entered the broad Pearl River (Zhujiang) estuary in China. The representatives of the newest country in the world were about to come face-to-face with those of one of the oldest. Americans were finally entering the Middle Kingdom.

Two

THE MIDDLE KINGDOM

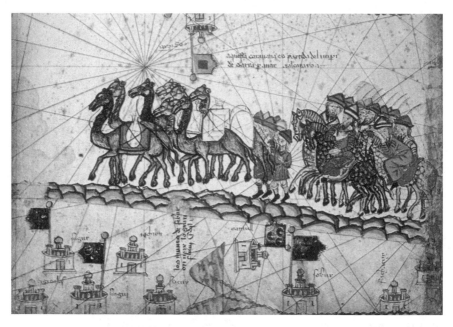

DETAIL FROM THE CATALAN ATLAS (1375) SHOWING MARCO POLO, WITH
HIS FATHER, UNCLE, AND OTHERS TRAVELING THE SILK ROAD.

*A*DAM SMITH, THE BRITISH POLITICAL ECONOMIST AND KEEN
observer of human nature, said that people have an elemental
"propensity to truck, barter, and exchange one thing for another."[1]
Exactly when that impulse inaugurated China's trade with Europe
is unknown, and probably unknowable. But at least two thousand

years before the *Empress of China* arrived in China, that trade had begun. As the Americans would soon learn, the rules of the Chinese marketplace, forged over the millennia, were different from any other country's.

Probably the first Chinese product to be traded to Europe was silk. As early as the fourth century BCE, Aristotle mentioned a woman on the Greek island of Cos who wove silk into diaphanous garments. Soon thereafter the Romans developed a love-hate relationship with this gossamer fabric, which they called "woven wind," worth its weight in gold. While rich and powerful Romans adorned themselves in sheer, colorful silk attire, others decried the use of so immodest a material. Seneca (4 BCE–65 CE) lamented seeing "silken garments, if they can be called garments, which cannot afford any protection either for the body or for shame: on taking which a woman will scarce with a clear conscience deny, that she is naked. These are sent for at an enormous price . . . in order that our matrons may display their persons to the public no less than to adulterers in their chamber!" Pliny the Elder (23–79 CE) not only worried about silk's impact on womanly virtues, but also how men who wore silk were degrading their manliness—much better for them to wear wool or leather rather than flimsy, effeminate silk![2]

The marketplace ignored the critics, however, and Chinese silk flowed into Greece and Rome via multiple land routes extending into the heart of Asia, some more than six thousand miles long, which became known collectively as the Silk Road. It was the trade of middlemen. Arabs, Persians, Turks, and others journeyed east and west in camel caravans along this shifting thoroughfare of commerce, bartering along the way, and bringing back silk, which was sold in Middle Eastern bazaars and then transported throughout the Mediterranean. There was also a maritime version of the Silk Road, which hopscotched, port to port, from China to India to the Persian Gulf and the Red Sea, then overland to its final destination.

The Greeks and Romans had no real understanding of China, and instead referred broadly to the Far East as Serica, the "land of silk,"

DYEING AND WINDING SILK IN CHINA, BY THOMAS ALLOM, 1843.

and to its inhabitants as Seres, "silk people." This ignorance extended to the origin of silk itself. Here Pliny again, claimed that silk was a type of "wool" that grew on the leaves of trees. After "steeping" the fuzzy leaves "in water," laborers would simply "comb off" the "white down."[3] As is usually the case, the real story is far more fascinating.

SILK COMES FROM *Bombyx mori*, a moth native to northern China. The larva, or caterpillar, of the moth, commonly called a silkworm, feasts upon the leaves of mulberry trees, and then spins a cocoon from a single strand of silk that can be up to a mile long. Within a week or two the pupa, or chrysalis, within goes through a metamorphosis, transforming itself into a small, off-white moth that escapes its silken womb by exuding an enzyme-rich solution that pierces a hole in the fibers, through which the moth wriggles out. The key to obtaining high-quality silk was keeping the cocoon intact. If the moth emerged from the cocoon, the continuity of the silk strand was broken, rendering the silk unusable. To avoid this the cocoons were plunged into boiling water, simultaneously killing the moth inside and dissolving the glue that bound the strand together. Once the end of the strand was found, the cocoon was unraveled, and strands from multiple cocoons were intertwined and reeled onto spools to be used as thread.[4]

According to legend, sometime around 2600 BCE, Lei Zu (Lei Tsu), the wife of the mythical Yellow Emperor of China, accidentally discovered the mystery of silk. Enthralled by the caterpillars in her garden munching incessantly on mulberry leaves, Lei Zu became transfixed when the caterpillars spun their cocoons and then burst forth as moths a few weeks later. While she inspected one of the cocoons, it fell from her hands into a cup of hot tea. She poked the sodden mass, and it began to unravel. Then she pulled a strand from the liquid, gazing with wonder at the silken fiber dangling from her fingers. Soon Lei Zu taught others to raise silkworms and process cocoons (sericulture), as well as how to weave silk, earning her the title "Goddess of Silkworms." It appears, however, that Lei Zu's discovery was not a first. Dyed silk and spinning tools dating from before 3000 BCE have been discovered: so too has an ivory cup from around 4900 BCE whose carved images appear to be silkworms, hinting at the possibility of even more ancient sericulture.[5]

However sericulture began, it soon became one of China's most assiduously practiced art forms, replete with an exceptionally long list of dictums on the proper procedures to be followed. Lengthy treatises on the subject included a range of practical, straightforward advice about tending to the eggs, rearing the silkworms, and handling the cocoons. But other directions were a bit more unusual: The building, or nursery, in which the silkworms were raised had to be kept "exempt from all noise" and the "clamor of men," for silkworms "love repose, and fear loud cries . . . [and] are disturbed by crying or weeping." And only people who were "perfectly clean" were permitted in the nursery, and therefore women who had slept with a man within the past thirty days or ones who were going through menstruation were barred from entering. The mysteries of sericulture were also jealously guarded as state secrets, and any person caught sharing this information with foreigners, or transporting silkworm eggs or silkworms out of China, would be executed.[6]

The specter of death served as an excellent deterrent for many years, but eventually the secret got out. Risking their lives to take silkworms and mulberry tree seeds or saplings with them, Chinese emigrants had settled in Korea by around 1000 BCE, launching that country's sericulture industry. By the third century CE the Japanese had begun producing silk, obtaining the necessary materials and skills either from Chinese transplants or as one of the spoils of war after invading Korea. Next, Justinian the Great, the Roman emperor from 527 to 565 CE, entered the silk business as a result of state-sponsored espionage. During his reign the demand for silk was particularly strong among the upper classes. There was a problem, though, with supply. Justinian's sworn enemies, the Persians, controlled the flow of silk from east to west; thus, when Rome and Persia were at war, that flow was cut off, and during times of peace the Persians gouged the Romans on price. So when two Nestorian monks who had been missionaries in China offered to travel there, steal silkworms, and provide a means of cutting out the Persian middlemen, Justinian threw his financial support behind the venture and sent the monks on their way. The mission succeeded, and when the monks returned to Constantinople (modern Istanbul) in 555, they knelt before Justinian, opened the tops of their hollow walking staffs, and showed him the precious silkworms concealed within. The monks also shared their knowledge of sericulture; and with that, as well as the leaves of indigenous mulberry trees, Rome launched its own silk industry. Subsequently sericulture spread, and by the late Middle Ages "woven wind" was being produced in India, Egypt, Syria, Persia, Italy, Spain, France, Portugal, and England. Although this expanded production cut into silk imports from China, it did not eliminate them, for Chinese silks were still the best in the world.[7]

While Europeans coveted silk the most, it was hardly the only Chinese product they desired. From the earliest days of the Silk

COVERED TUREEN AND STAND WITH VIEW OF CANTON,
CIRCA 1780.

Road through the beginning of the fifteenth century, Europeans also acquired other items from China, including spices, bronze, pearls, gold, rubies, jade carvings, and rhubarb, which was used as a laxative. During the latter part of this period, Chinese ceramics traveled the Silk Road, the most prized of which were made of porcelain, a Chinese invention. The first step in creating porcelain was combining white clay called kaolin with finely ground petuntse, a granitic rock known as "China stone," and then adding water. Next the resulting mixture was molded into the desired forms, and then fired at extremely high temperatures to produce exquisitely hard, heat-resistant, translucent, and waterproof ceramics. The addition of colored glazes and graceful decorations transformed porcelain, widely known as "china," into some of the most dazzling human-made objects ever created.[8]

AS MUCH AS EUROPEANS focused on the goods China provided, they were also fascinated by Chinese culture, or what they learned of it from the growing tide of Christian missionaries, traders, and adventurers traveling to and from that distant empire. The most famous of these travelers was the Venetian explorer and trader Marco Polo, who (along with his father, Niccolò, and uncle Maffeo) spent

seventeen years as an agent in the court of Kublai Khan, the grand-
son of Genghis Khan, and the Mongol ruler of China during the late
thirteenth century. Marco returned from China in 1295, enlisted
in Venice's war with Genoa, and after being captured spent nearly
a year in jail, where he met the romance writer Rustichello of Pisa.
Rustichello knew a good story when he heard one, and after listening
to Polo wax eloquent about his time with the great Kublai, the two of
them teamed up to write an account of Polo's experiences, titled *The
Travels of Marco Polo*.

Largely a paean to Kublai Khan, *Travels*—published around
1300—begins by telling readers that the "lord of lords . . . is the most
powerful man in people, and in lands, and in treasure, that ever was in
the world or that now is, from the time of Adam our first father till this
moment." It goes on to paint a picture of astonishing magnificence,
which mainly focuses on China. There are vibrant descriptions
of ornate and massive palaces, beautiful arched bridges, dramatic
victories over enemies, grand canals, lavish feasts and festivals, and
luxurious silks. When speaking of the Chinese city of Hangzhou
(Hangchow), which he called the "city of Heaven," Polo claimed that
it was "the greatest city which may be found in the world, where [there
are] so many pleasures . . . that one fancies himself to be in paradise."[9]

Polo's contemporaries viewed many of his stories as fantastical,
and the book came to be called "Il Milione," for the number of lies
it supposedly contained. The appellation is not without some merit:
Polo and Rustichello had as much flair for drama as for history, and
they added imaginary elements and flourishes to their tale that were
designed to titillate and thrill rather than document and inform. Still,
most of Polo's story was true. Even if only half of what he claimed
had been accurate, Europeans would have had plenty of reasons to
be mightily taken by the Chinese. At the time of Polo's travels China
was arguably the most advanced civilization on earth—the source
of many of the world's most significant inventions, not least among
them gunpowder, paper, and the compass, as well as silk thread and
porcelain. In the arts and literature, too, the Chinese surpassed all

others. "Their betters as craftsmen in every art practiced by man," wrote a Franciscan friar who visited China in the mid-thirteenth century, "are not to be found in the whole world." The Chinese were far ahead of the Europeans in publishing, producing numerous tomes on history, politics, science, and religion, as well as works of poetry and fiction.[10]

WHILE EUROPEANS THUS had cause to be impressed with Chinese civilization, the Chinese held a dim view of the Europeans, as well as all other foreigners. The Chinese believed, and had for more than a thousand years, that they were the most special people on earth. The emperor was thought to be the "Son of Heaven," who ruled under a heavenly mandate. With such divinely inspired leadership, it is not surprising that China considered itself the Middle Kingdom or the Celestial Empire, positioned between heaven above and all the rest of the world below. As a result the Chinese looked down on foreigners as uncivilized barbarians, a perspective that was reinforced when the Chinese compared themselves with their closest neighbors, whose cultural attainments often paled in comparison to China's. That didn't mean, however, that the Chinese eschewed contact with foreigners; in fact they welcomed and encouraged it. But that contact had to take place within the larger context of Chinese exceptionalism. In other words the barbarians had to know their place, which was well beneath that of the Chinese.[11]

China viewed itself as a beacon for humanity, and it expected all other countries to accept willingly its elevated position as the Middle Kingdom. After all, the Chinese thought, once the barbarians gazed upon China's brilliance, how could they come to any conclusion other than that China was indeed on a loftier plane? To show that they accorded China such status, foreigners were expected to send envoys to offer tribute to the emperor in the form of gifts, and further demonstrate their subservience by kowtowing before the Son of Heaven; the kowtow being the act of kneeling three times, each time touching one's forehead to the ground three times—the so-called three kneel-ings and nine prostrations. Once such due deference was received, the envoys were showered with precious gifts and their countries officially designated as tributary nations, thereby becoming, in effect, vassals of the Chinese empire—the newest additions to the "all-embracing sinocentric cosmos." With this transformation came the biggest prize of all—the right to trade with China. But if the foreigners did not offer adequate tribute, or if they caused problems within the empire, their trading privileges could be revoked.[12]

The most impressive Chinese tribute missions took place in the early fifteenth century, during the Ming Dynasty, with the voyages of Zheng He (Cheng Ho), the great eunuch admiral. Under orders from the emperor, Zheng He commanded seven heavily armed treasure fleets between 1405 and 1433, which visited more than thirty coun-tries spread throughout the South China Sea and the Indian Ocean, from Java and Sumatra all the way to the Red Sea and the east coast of Africa. These expeditions were enormous undertakings, most including hundreds of ships and tens of thousands of men. Some of the ships were more than 400 feet long and 180 feet wide, far larger and grander than anything that Western nations had put to sea. The treasure fleets were the most spectacular maritime ventures the world had ever seen, securing China's place as the foremost naval force of the day.

Although the treasure fleets engaged in some military actions, their primary purpose was to "display the splendor and the power of the new Ming Dynasty" and to add to China's roster of tributary nations. The expeditions accomplished both goals, but after the last one, in 1433, the emperor halted any further maritime exploration. One reason for the change in policy was cost. Building and equip-ping the treasure fleets was rapidly depleting the imperial treasury of money that many believed could be better spent on bolstering China's defenses, and on domestic projects intended to improve the quality of life at home. Another key factor was that the Confucian bureaucrats who had gained the upper hand in the royal court "disliked foreign contacts and influences on principle," and argued convincingly against any further attempts to reach out to barbarians.[13]

What might have happened had the emperor redoubled his efforts, and sent treasure fleets farther afield, into the Atlantic or the Pacific Ocean beyond the South China Sea, will never be known. Perhaps historians would be writing about the great age of Chinese exploration and discovery, rather than the exploits of the Europeans who would soon begin circling the globe. Instead China chose to focus on itself, still supremely confident in the belief that it was the Middle Kingdom. But just when China was turning inward, Europe was beginning to focus increased attention on the Far East. That meant only one thing: Soon more barbarians would be knocking on China's door.

AS EUROPE EMERGED from the Middle Ages, its major lifeline to the Far East had been almost completely severed. The disintegration of the Mongol Empire in the late 1300s, the fall of Constantinople to the invading Ottomans in 1453, and the subsequent spread of the Ottoman Empire into the lands bordering the eastern Mediterranean seriously interrupted the flow of goods along the Silk Road. Although such goods still came west, the cost of purchasing them grew exorbitant. Thus it was becoming increasingly clear to many Europeans that if they wanted Far Eastern goods, especially at reasonable prices, they would have to go get them. Instead of relying on tenuous routes through other countries, which could be summarily cut off by changing political fortunes, the Europeans sought to establish all-water routes to the Far East, ones that they could more easily control.[14]

Over the next two centuries many European powers beat a maritime path to the Far East, and what they wanted most of all were the exotic spices of the Orient, most of which had been staples of the Euro-Asian trade since its inception, and were used to make food taste better. Spain was the first to attempt to find an all-water route to the Far East, sending Christopher Columbus on his voyage of discovery in 1492. However convinced Columbus was that he had actually made it to the "Indies," and achieved his goal, of course, he hadn't. That laurel would go to the Portuguese explorer, Vasco da Gama, who rounded the southern tip of Africa in 1497, and sailed into the Indian Ocean, arriving on the west coast of India, a major crossroads of the Far Eastern spice trade. In subsequent years other expeditions extended Portugal's reach to the Malay Peninsula and the fabled Spice Islands (the Moluccas in modern-day Indonesia).

Although Spain would not be first to the Far East, it did not want to be last, so when a disaffected Portuguese nobleman named Ferdinand Magellan came to the Spanish court with a proposal to sail west and then around the southern tip of South America to the Spice Islands, Spain's king agreed to sponsor him. Magellan made it to the Philippines in 1521, where natives killed him, but his men journeyed on, trading in the Spice Islands before limping back to Spain, with only one of the original five ships having survived this groundbreaking venture—the first circumnavigation of the world. The next Europeans to arrive in the Far East were the Dutch, touching at Java at the end of the sixteenth century, to be followed only a few years later by the English, who also traded in Java as well as the Spice Islands.

Like plants in search of water, the Europeans spread throughout the Far East, gaining footholds wherever spices could be found. Although spices were their primary goal, a close second were the treasures of China. In the beginning Europeans acquired Chinese goods by trading for them at the many ports where they were already trading for spices. This was easy to do because the entire Far East was one vast emporium, with thousands of ships and smaller craft traveling north and south, east and west, finding buyers for their wares, and bringing the riches of other countries back to their home markets. China actively participated in this vibrant trading network, thus Chinese goods could be found throughout the region.[15]

But the Europeans were not satisfied with this indirect China trade; they wanted to trade directly with the Middle Kingdom, and that was easier said than done. The Chinese were extremely wary of Europeans. Unlike many of the barbarians China had dealt with in the past, who were by and large respectful, peaceful, and interested only in trade, the new European barbarians were often violent, unpredictable, and at times seemed as intent on gaining Christian converts as they were on bartering for goods. Of the unscrupulous behavior of the Portuguese, for example, the historian Charles Patrick Fitzgerald observed, "Trade was only the weaker alternative to a plundering foray. When the enemy was weak or unprepared the Portuguese plundered his ships and cities, massacred the 'heathen' and seized the harbors as bases. When he was strong or ready for battle they traded—always ready to assume the more congenial role of marauders if the opportunity presented itself." And when the Europeans weren't threatening or killing Asians, they were beating up one another. In their all-consuming desire to obtain Far Eastern goods, and to stymie their enemies, they regularly resorted to piracy and even murder.[16]

Initially resisting European efforts to open direct trade, the Chinese relented slowly over time, in the face of the Europeans' exceptional persistence—in large part because they wanted the silver that the Europeans would be pumping into China's economy, since the Chinese used silver to pay taxes, which in turn funded the government and the military. But China was less interested in obtaining tribute from the Europeans than it was in ensuring that they behaved themselves and stayed as far away as possible from the capital, Peking (Beijing). Therefore, although a few European countries sent official tribute missions to the emperor, the relations between the Europeans and the Chinese typically focused solely on trade. Nevertheless, in the emperor's eyes, all European countries were tributary nations, whether or not they sent tribute missions to Peking.

The Portuguese were the first to gain direct trading rights, renting the peninsula of Macao (Aomen), on China's southern coast, from the Chinese in the mid-1500s, and carrying on trade there as well as farther inland at Canton, which had long been a center of international trade between China and other Asian countries. Part of the reason that the Chinese let the Portuguese establish themselves despite their deserved reputation for violent behavior was the latter's promise to

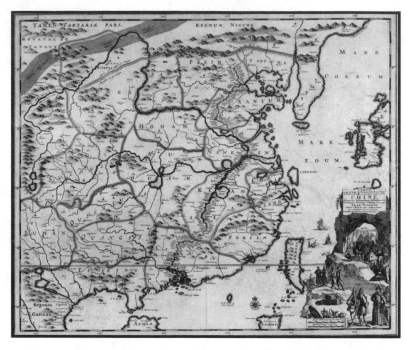

DUTCH MAP OF CHINA, BY JOHANNES NIEUHOF, LATE 1600S.

drive off the pirates who had been terrorizing the region. By the late 1600s the English and the Dutch had also made inroads, trading at the cities of Zhoushan (Chusan), Xiamen (Amoy), and on the island of Taiwan (formerly called Formosa by Westerners). Then, in the early 1700s, foreign trade became increasingly concentrated at Canton, catering not only to the Portuguese, the Dutch, and the English, but also the French, Danes, Prussians, Austrians, and Swedes. Around this time the Chinese began referring to the foreigners in their midst as *fan qui*, or "foreign devils," and to distinguish among them the Chinese used unique "devil" appellations, calling, for example, the English the "Red-haired devils," and the Portuguese the "Western ocean devils."[17]

A NUMBER OF FEATURES worked in Canton's favor. Of all the major Chinese cities it was the closest to Europe. As a result it had been trading with foreigners longer than any other, and its procedures were the easiest to follow and understand. Located on a large river, the Pearl, with many tributaries, Canton had good access to supplies, raw materials, and trading goods coming from the hinterlands. And its large population of craftsmen provided the skills necessary to repair ships, construct buildings, and generally service the needs of commerce.

Finally, in 1757 the emperor confined foreign traders to Canton, where they operated according to the rules of the so-called Canton System (this did not include the Russians and the Japanese, who came under different trading arrangements). The emperor's decision was practical, since virtually all foreigners were already using Canton, but the decision also had a political justification. After roughly two hundred years of dealing directly with the often arrogant and dangerous Europeans, the Chinese did not trust them to behave with civility. By limiting all transactions to Canton, Chinese authorities could maintain stricter control over the foreigners, thereby helping to ensure peace and tranquillity in the Celestial Empire. And China's concerns about Europeans ran deeper than an immediate fear of unruly traders, to what might happen to China itself if foreign intrusions were not kept in check. As early as 1717 Emperor Kangxi (K'ang-hsi, r. 1661–1722) prophetically warned, "There is cause for apprehension, lest in centuries or millenniums to come, China may be endangered by collision with the various barbarians of the west, who come hither from beyond the seas."[18]

Under the Canton System the foreigners' commercial dance began when their ship anchored in the Macao Roads, a relatively shallow part of the Pearl River estuary located to the east of Macao. The first order of business was for the ship's captain to visit the customhouse on Macao, called the chophouse, where he announced his arrival, met with local officials, and received a chop, or stamped permit, to begin the next leg of the journey. A pilot provided by the chophouse now guided the ship forty miles north to another customhouse, located at the Bogue or Boca Tigris (tiger's mouth), the gateway to the Pearl

River, which was guarded on either side by multiple forts. Inspectors took notes on the size of the crew, the number of armaments, and other information about the ship, all of which was sent on to Canton.

With a new river pilot on board, the ship sailed to Whampoa (Huangpu), a long narrow island located in the middle of the Pearl River, roughly twelve miles below Canton. Rice fields and orange groves flanked Whampoa's customhouse and its small village of a few thousand inhabitants, but the most noticeable feature of the island was its striking nine-story brick pagoda, which served as a navigational guide for vessels ascending the river. Foreign ships anchored off Whampoa and were placed under the care and protection of the Cohong, the imperially appointed merchant guild that oversaw trading. The Cohong comprised a maximum of thirteen hong merchants, but typically there were fewer than ten. Each ship was paired with a hong merchant, who in turn was responsible for the foreigners while they were in Canton.

The hong merchant had to ensure that the foreigners acted properly, for if they didn't, it was the merchant who had to answer to the local governor for misbehavior, and cover any debts incurred. In addition to paying customs fees, purchasing most or all of the ship's cargo, and supplying goods in return, the hong merchant was responsible for hiring a linguist, who would help the foreigners communicate with Chinese officials. The linguists rarely lived up to their title, however, since precious few of them knew any European languages, but rather communicated in pidgin English—"pidgin" being how the Chinese said the English word "business"—a very rough and often slightly comical amalgamation of mispronounced English, Portuguese, and other words, which could sound like gibberish to the uninitiated. One solution to overcoming the communication barrier—namely teaching the foreigners Cantonese—was not an attractive option, for any Chinese person caught doing so would be put to death. Nevertheless some foreigners did learn the local dialects from Chinese willing to risk their lives, and some Chinese became similarly skilled in foreign languages, so that communication, especially higher-level official communication, could be carried on in a manner that was reasonably intelligible to all sides.

The hong merchant also hired the compradors, or stewards, who performed many services, including maintaining the quarters where the foreigners stayed in Canton. One of the comprador's most important jobs was engaging the services of a shroff, or money handler. Most of the Canton trading economy ran on silver, and since there was no central treasury or banking system, the merchants employed shroffs to weigh and assay the silver used in business transactions. Each shroff had an individual mark, or chop, which he would impress into the coin attesting to its purity and value. Silver coins that passed through this process were called chopped dollars, and the greater the circulation of the coins, the more chops they received, sometimes to the point that the dollars were literally chopped into pieces. Over time many small pieces of silver would collect in between or underneath the floor tiles of the shroff's store, and sometimes the shroff would sell an enterprising individual the right to rip up the floor and keep any silver he found, which could add up to a considerable sum.

Shortly after the ship anchored at Whampoa, the hong merchant invited his superior—the hoppo, or customs official—to visit. The grandly dressed hoppo, retinue in tow, arrived with considerable pomp aboard a fine boat bedecked with silk streamers. Once onboard, and after lengthy and often obsequious welcoming speeches and toasts from both sides, the hoppo assessed port fees, a process that was referred to as "cumshaw and measurement." The cumshaw (literally "gold sand") was a present, usually payable in silver, which the foreigners gave for the "privilege of entering the port." The measurement was "equivalent to tonnage duties," and would be calculated by the hoppo's assistants using silk ribbons to measure the length and width of the ship. Foreigners were also subject to other fees, such as paying for pilotage, and then there was the additional cumshaw that had to be doled out, since everyone who provided any sort of assistance to the foreigners expected and usually received a present in return. The most interesting transaction came after the measurement ceremony ended, when the hoppo asked the supercargo to see the "sing-songs" (mechanical devices such as wind-up clocks) or other curiosities onboard. Once these were arrayed before him, the hoppo picked the nicest ones, and asked the hong merchant to buy them on his behalf. The hong merchant then sold the items to the hoppo at a fraction of what they were worth, as a thank-you for the hoppo's services. The hoppo, in turn, gave some of these items to his superiors in gratitude for having been appointed the customs official.

Now the final stage of the journey commenced. While the ships, officers, and crew waited off Whampoa—where they passed the time repairing their ships, entertaining one another, and occasionally visiting some of the local islands in the river—the supercargoes continued to Canton, taken there by boats loaded with the goods the foreigners wanted to trade. After landing at Jackass Point in Canton, the supercargoes were escorted to their factory, which served as a place of business and living quarters during the trading season, from October to March (the term "factory" being used because the foreign traders were also called "factors"). Located within a walled enclosure just twelve acres in size, and bordered on one side by the Pearl River, the foreign factories—rented to foreigners by the hong merchants—were really a city within a city, separate and apart. At the end of the trading season purchased goods were loaded on boats, and sent to Whampoa, where the goods were transferred onto the ships. Before departing Canton, foreigners paid respects to their hong merchant, exchanged more cumshaw, and received the "Grand Chop," an elaborately inscribed two-color document, stamped with the hoppo's seal, that served as an exit permit.[19]

To ensure that the foreigners knew what was expected of them while in China, and behaved themselves accordingly, the emperor issued the "Eight Regulations," a detailed list of do's and don'ts. Among them, "all vessels of war" were admonished to stay out of the Pearl River and remain at sea while the merchant ships conducted business, and then sail away once that business was completed. Trading ships were not allowed to "loiter about outside the river," and "rove about the bays" selling goods to "rascally natives" engaged in smuggling. No "women, guns, spears, nor arms of any kind" were to be brought to the factories. Foreigners were not permitted to row about the river "on their own boats for 'pleasure,'" but they could leave the factory area and visit select places in Canton, including the Buddhist temple and the flower gardens, but only on three days per month, and never in "droves of over ten at one time." Such visits had to conclude before nightfall, and foreigners were not "allowed to pass the night 'out,' or collect together to carouse." Although not one of the Eight Regulations, another imperial stipulation limited the amount of time foreigners spent in Canton. During the trading season the foreigners were welcome to live in their factories, but once the season was over they had to leave immediately, either heading for home on a return voyage, or staying behind in Macao until the next trading season. In keeping with the not-illogical reasoning behind the imperial point of view, it was felt that restricting the barbarians' presence in Canton would lessen the locals' exposure to potentially troublesome influences.[20]

By the time the Canton System was instituted, China had been trading with Europe, both directly and through middlemen, for roughly two thousand years. During that time the quantity and nature of the goods traded often shifted to reflect the vagaries of supply and demand. Occasionally new goods entered the stream of commerce, and of all those that did, the most consequential were opium and tea. In time they would shake the very foundations of American, British, Chinese, and, indeed, world history.

THE WORD "OPIUM" is derived from the Greek *opion*, or "poppy juice." The opium poppy (*Papaver somniferum*) produces a seed capsule, which, when gently incised just before it ripens, emits a thick, milky latex that is the raw opium. Unlike the seeds within the capsule, which are harmless, opium contains alkaloids, including morphine, whose punch makes it such a powerful drug (morphine, in turn, can be synthesized into an even more dangerous drug, heroin). The seed capsules are cut multiple times over a week or two, and the resulting opium is collected, dried, and then molded into bricks or balls for transport and sale. Opium manufacture is labor-intensive, with one estimate claiming that it takes roughly eighteen thousand capsules, or about an acre's worth of poppies, to produce twenty pounds of the drug.[21]

Nobody knows exactly where or when the first opium poppies grew, but the oldest fossilized remains of this plant were found in Switzerland at sites that date back as early as the fourth millennium BCE. It is possible that poppies originated there, but there are those who contend that its origins are farther to the east, and perhaps even deeper in the recesses of time. Regardless of where and when they first appeared, by 1000 BCE, opium poppies were found throughout much of Europe, Northern Africa, and the Middle East, and opium, either eaten or dissolved in alcohol, was being used as a curative for a wide range of illnesses and conditions, including headaches, asthma, and melancholy. Homer in his epic poem the *Odyssey* claimed that opium "quiets all pains and quarrels," and his fellow Greeks also employed the drug as a tranquilizer and as a means of attaining higher spiritual states. From these beginnings the plant and the drug spread eastward.[22]

When opium was first introduced into China remains a bit of a mystery. There are a few references to it as early as the third century CE, but not until about the seventh or eighth century did the record become clearer. By then Arabs had already begun trading opium with the Chinese, and the Chinese were growing poppies and harvesting the drug. For many centuries thereafter, opium's reach was rather limited, it being used exclusively by the elite as a medicine and an aphrodisiac, for it was thought to "aid masculinity, strengthen the sperm and regain vigor," and more generally to enhance "the art of alchemists, sex and court ladies." Up to this point, opium was eaten or drunk in solution—only after the Europeans arrived did the Chinese start smoking the drug.[23]

Europeans, who had themselves discovered the addictive pleasure of smoking tobacco only in the early 1500s, introduced it into
China later that century. When the Dutch began adding a pinch of
opium to their tobacco to give it a jolt, the Chinese followed suit.
Then, in the late 1600s, the Chinese enlarged their smoking reper-
toire by cutting out the tobacco entirely and smoking the opium on
its own. Before the opium could be smoked, the balls or bricks of
the drug had to be further refined through a multistep process that
involved soaking them in water, cutting them up, boiling and stirring the pieces, decanting the solution through a filter, boiling and
stirring the solution again to eliminate most of the water, and then
cooling the resulting thick syrupy mixture and letting it cure for a
few months. In this way "three pounds of raw opium yielded about
two pounds of smokable opium."[24]

The process of smoking opium was nothing like that of smoking tobacco. The opium pipe, usually made of bamboo or wood,

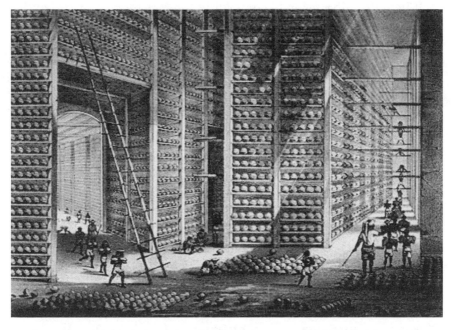

OPIUM BALLS IN INDIA BEING STACKED AND DRIED BEFORE BEING PACKED
IN BOXES AND SENT TO CALCUTTA, EN ROUTE TO CHINA, CIRCA 1850.

approached two feet long and was about an inch to an inch and a half wide. A small ceramic bowl, roughly the shape of a doorknob, was attached to a hole in the pipe via a hollow metal fitting. The bottom of the bowl had a small opening that connected to the fitting, and the top of the bowl had another opening a little larger than a pinhole. The opium smoker placed a very small drop of the viscous drug on the end of a needle-like rod called a dipper, roasted the drop over a flame, then transferred it to the hole in the top of the bowl. Next the smoker, either sitting up or lying comfortably on his side, placed the stem of the pipe in his mouth while holding the bowl over the flame. As soon as the opium began to sputter and smoke, the smoker inhaled and exhaled repeatedly for about thirty seconds, until the opium itself burned away.

As the smoke bathed the lungs and the drug entered the system, a whole range of sensations washed over the body. Duncan McPherson, a British doctor who smoked opium in the mid-1800s, offered the following insights on the experience.

> The pulse vibrates, it becomes fuller and firmer, . . . the temperature of the skin is elevated, and it becomes suffused with a blush; . . . a glow of warmth, and sensations similar to those which often attend highly pleasurable and agreeable feelings, overspreads the body; . . . The perceptions become more vivid, the imagination more prolific with ideas. . . . Under its operation every task seems easy and every labor light. The spirits are renovated, and melancholy is dissipated.[25]

Opium didn't affect all users the same way, however, and smokers might also experience other sensations, including a deep sense of calm, sleepiness, as well as dizziness, nausea, and intense hunger.

When ingested orally, opium is only moderately habit forming; however, when it is smoked it becomes a more addictive narcotic. For many the occasional or regular high sufficed, but for a few, opium smoking could become an addiction with potentially disastrous results. "At first," wrote an early nineteenth-century Chinese scholar, the opium smokers "merely strive to follow the fashion of the day; but, in the sequel, the poison takes effect, the habit becomes fixed, and the sleeping smokers are like corpses, lean and haggard as demons."[26] To this McPherson would add, "The unhappy individual who makes himself a slave to the drug, shuns society, and is indifferent to all around him."[27]

Through the early 1700s China never imported more than two hundred chests of opium per year, with each chest containing between 130 and 160 pounds of the drug. Virtually all of that opium, which was supplied mainly by Portuguese and Dutch traders, came from India, for although the Chinese produced opium, they greatly preferred the Indian variety, and their own output was limited. Even at these low import levels, the Chinese government grew concerned about the ill effects of the drug. A report sent to Emperor Yongzheng (Yung-cheng, r. 1723–35) in the 1720s noted that "shameless rascals lure the sons of good families into [the habit of opium smoking] for their own profit . . . youngsters become corrupted by smoking it until their lives collapse, their families' livelihood vanishes, and nothing is left but trouble." Disturbed by this trend, the emperor issued an

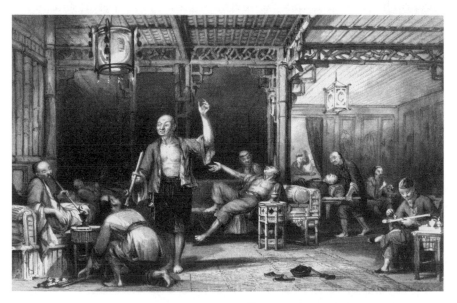

CHINESE OPIUM SMOKERS, BY THOMAS ALLOM, 1843.

edict in 1729 banning the selling of opium, and the operation of opium dens or houses where people gathered to smoke the drug. The punishment for opium traffickers was one month in a *cangue*—a large wooden board with a hole in it that was placed snugly around the neck, and attached by chains to the hands, which were often similarly encumbered by a smaller board with two holes. Those caught operating opium dens faced being beaten, kicked out of their houses, or arrested and possibly sentenced to execution. The edict exempted opium used for medicinal purposes and didn't ban imports of the drug, which climbed to one thousand chests by 1767.[28]

WHILE THE INFLUENCE of opium on the China trade was just beginning to be felt in the mid-eighteenth century, tea had already become a major force. The origins of tea, like those of opium, are problematic. There is no debating that the tea bush (*Camelia sinensis*) first evolved somewhere in the eastern Himalayas or farther to the southeast, but the actual location is anyone's guess. Equally unclear are attempts to determine who first discovered that tea leaves could be brewed. One legend claims that it was the mythical Chinese emperor, Shennong (Shen Nung), and that he did so during an expedition in southern China, around 2700 BCE. When his retinue stopped to rest, one of his men boiled water to purify it before drinking. A gust of wind sent leaves from a nearby tea bush fluttering into the pot, where they began to steep. Shennong drank the slightly bitter brew and enjoyed the taste and the curious combination of calm and energy it provided. Then he gathered tea leaves so that he could share this exciting find with his people. Though we will never know who had the first cup of tea, there is no doubt that it was the Chinese who first cultivated tea, raised tea drinking to an art form, and introduced it to the world.[29]

The earliest reliable references to tea in Chinese literature appear in the third or fourth century CE when the practice of cultivating tea rather than just harvesting it from the wild began spreading throughout the land. Over the next few hundred years, tea transitioned from being a drink used mainly for medicinal purposes, touted as a great cure for constipation and headaches, to one consumed for both health and pleasure. The first book on tea, the *Ch'a Ching*, or *The Classic of Tea*, was written in the late 700s by Lu Yu, the Chinese "Tea Sage." In it Lu Yu, who had been abandoned at birth and raised in a monastery where he first learned the mysteries of tea, offered intricate details about the growing, brewing, and serving of this pleasing beverage, whose "liquor," he said, was "like the sweetest dew of heaven." The diligent and respectful consumer was expected to have on hand twenty-four very specific items—the equipage of tea—in order to prepare and present a perfect and harmonious cup. These ran from a stove "made of brass or iron" and a "roller" to grind the tea, to ceramic bowls of the right shape, color, and size. The reader was coached on selecting the proper source of water—the best coming from "mountain streams"—and was warned "never [to] take tea made from water that falls in cascades, gushes from springs, rushes in a torrent or that eddies and surges as if nature were rinsing

TEA PLANT.

its mouth," for too much of this would cause illness in the throat. "Moderation is the very essence of tea," Lu Yu counseled. "Tea does not lend itself to extravagance."[30]

At the same time that Lu Yu was extolling the mysteries of tea, Chinese poets waxed lyrical about the marvelous drink, which was called "the froth of the liquid jade." In one of the most memorable passages, Lu Tong (Lu Tung) intoned:

> *The first cup moistens my lips and throat;*
> *The second cup breaks my loneliness;*
> *The third cup searches my barren entrails but to find therein*
>   *some thousand volumes of odd ideographs*
> *The fourth cup raises a slight perspiration—all the wrongs of*
>   *life pass out through my pores;*
> *At the fifth cup I am purified;*
> *The sixth cup calls me to the realms of the immortals.*
> *The seventh cup—ah, but I could take no more! I only feel the*
>   *breath of the cool wind that raises in my sleeves.*
> *Where is Elysium? Let me ride on this sweet breeze and waft*
>   *away thither.*[31]

A less ethereal and more practical contemporary observation concluded, "Tea is better than wine, for it leadeth not to intoxication, neither does it cause a man to say foolish things, and repent thereof in his sober moments. It is better than water, for it does not carry disease, neither does it act like a poison, as does water when the wells contain foul and rotten matter." If the importance of tea within China needed any more confirmation, one need only consider that when Lu Yu and Lu Tong were rhapsodizing about tea, the imperial government was busy slapping taxes on its sale. So central did tea become in Chinese society that during the Song (Sung) Dynasty (960–1297) it was anointed as one of the seven necessities of life, along with rice, firewood, oil, salt, vinegar, and soy sauce.[32]

Although the Chinese jealously guarded their tea crops, Buddhist monks by the ninth century managed to transport tea seeds from China to Korea and Japan, where cultivation of the plant also took hold. To the rest of the medieval world, though, the spread of tea came through trade rather than through cultivation. Often formed into dense bricks and used as money, tea became an article of commerce to the north, the south, and west, from Siberia to Tibet, and along the Silk Road all the way to the Middle East, where the earliest mentions of this soothing beverage appeared in the mid-800s.

The Portuguese certainly knew of tea in the early 1500s, and had no doubt tasted it in one of the many Far Eastern ports they visited, but it was not until 1559 that the first European account of tea appeared in print, written by the Venetian author Giambattista Ramusio, who had heard of the beguiling drink from Persian travelers. Fifty-one years later, in 1610, the Dutch became the first to import tea to Europe, and from that point forward tea drinking radiated throughout Western society, but nowhere did it have a greater impact than in England.[33]

BY THE 1650s tea from Dutch suppliers was being sold in London, and in 1660 Thomas Garraway, the proprietor of the city's premier coffeehouse, issued a lavish broadside aimed at enticing patrons to come in and purchase a cup of the exotic brew. "The said [tea] leaf is of such known virtues," proclaimed Garraway, "that those very nations so famous for antiquity, knowledge and wisdom, do frequently sell it among themselves for twice its weight in silver." Among the virtues enumerated were the following, guaranteed to excite desire or at least arouse curiosity in even the most dispassionate of people.

> It maketh the body active and lusty. . . .
> It taketh away the difficulty of breathing . . . [and] cleareth the sight.
> It removeth lassitude, and cleanseth and purifieth . . . a hot liver. . . .

It overcometh superfluous sleep, and prevents sleepiness in general . . .

It is good for colds, dropsies, and scurvys.[34]

The nuptials of King Charles II in 1662 raised the prominence of tea in English society, especially among women, when his Portuguese bride, Princess Catherine of Braganza, a tea drinker herself, brought in her dowry a small supply of the splendid leaves. Soon thereafter the British East India Company began importing tea, and by the turn of the century the tea-drinking habit had captivated the upper classes, who could afford the relatively high price of this Eastern luxury. Both sexes shared tea at home, while men also took theirs alongside other precious imports, such as coffee and chocolate, at London's coffeehouses, where talk of politics, business, and social concerns filled the air.[35]

Tea drinking received an additional boost from physicians who recommended consuming the beverage to ensure a healthy constitution. In 1679 Dr. Cornelis Decker of Holland urged everyone to drink at least eight to ten cups daily, "augmenting the dose to whatever the stomach can hold." As a measure of his sincerity, Decker—nicknamed "Doctor Good Tea" on behalf of his ardent advocacy—noted that he consumed as many as two hundred cups a day. In light of rumors that Dutch tea merchants had paid him off, there was reason to question the good doctor's advice, but Decker was hardly the only doctor singing tea's praises. Not everyone, however, was enamored with the purported "virtues" of tea, and some people railed against the concoction and its supposed deleterious effects. Many years before Decker weighed in with his pronouncement, a German doctor, Simon Pauli, argued, "As to the virtues they attribute to it [tea], it may be admitted that it does possess them in the Orient, but it loses them in our climate, where it becomes, on the contrary, very dangerous to use. It hastens the death of those who drink it, especially if they have passed the age of forty years."[36]

The naysayers were ignored, and tea drinking at the end of the seventeenth century gained adherents at a tremendous pace. During the early eighteenth century the tea habit in England moved beyond the home and the coffeehouses to the pleasantly situated "Tea Gardens," and the newly conceived teahouses, the first of which was established by Thomas Twining, who opened the "Golden Lyon" in London in 1717. Whereas the coffeehouses were a man's domain, the tea gardens and teahouses catered to both sexes, further cementing tea's grip on society. Within a little more than a century of tea's introduction, British imports from China had risen from hundreds of pounds per year to roughly nine million pounds in 1770. That was only the official tally, to which had to be added the millions of pounds of tea that were smuggled into England, mainly by the Dutch, to avoid the onerous taxes the government levied on the tea imported legally by the British East India Company.[37]

This great volume of tea flooding into Britain forced down prices, delivering the brew to rich and poor alike. Samuel Johnson, the British lexicographer and critic, painted a self-portrait in 1757 that could have applied with equal facility to millions of his fellow citizens. He described himself as "a hardened and shameless tea drinker who has for twenty years diluted his meals with only the infusion of this fascinating plant, whose kettle has scarcely time to cool, who with tea amuses the evening, with tea solaces the midnight, and with tea welcomes the morning." Britain had, indeed, become a veritable "nation of tea drinkers."[38]

THE PRIME TEA-GROWING AREAS in China were in the middle to the southern half of the country, with the provinces just to the north and south of the Yangtze River producing the finest crops. Rather than on sprawling tea plantations, the tea was grown on innumerable small family farms, each a few acres in size. The tea bushes, which were repeatedly pruned back so that at maturity they stood only about waist high to facilitate picking, were planted in rows about four feet apart, in rich, well-drained soil on hillsides generally facing east to benefit from the rays of the rising sun. Each row was, in turn, separated from the rows above and below it by four feet, giving the landscape a pleasing linear symmetry of green ribbons undulating over the rolling terrain. Three times per year—from early spring through late summer—on dry days, entire families headed for the hills to bring in the harvest. Young and old alike plucked leaves from the bushes one by one, and collected them in bamboo baskets, gathering as much as fifteen pounds of leaves per day.

As quickly as possible the leaves would be taken back to the family's cottages for processing, which, broadly speaking, involved some variation of drying the leaves in the sun, roasting or steaming them in iron pans or bamboo baskets over fires, rolling the leaves by hand, and sometimes repeating part of all of the steps—this manipulation was intended to remove excess moisture while retaining the components that gave tea its unique flavor. Next the leaves were taken to local towns and sold to dealers acting on behalf of the hong merchants. Placed in crates, the leaves were tamped down by barefooted men, and then the crates were transported by river and canal to the hong merchants' warehouses in and around Canton. Sorted by type and quality, the leaves were once again tamped into crates before being sold to foreigners.

There were two main categories of tea in China, green and black, distinguished by the method of processing. Each of these broad categories was divided into varieties, based on a range of factors including the age and size of the leaves when picked, the condition of the soil, and the blend of leaves in the final product. Green tea comprised the bulk of the earliest tea shipments to England. But there was a problem with this choice. Green tea, so called because the leaves retained their chlorophyll, was unfermented and not completely dry, and easily spoiled, a troubling characteristic for a commodity that had to be shipped halfway around the world. Black tea, in contrast, was fermented, very dry, and could be stored for long periods without spoiling. Over time, because of concerns about spoilage as well as changing tastes, England began drinking less green tea and more black, which soon made up the majority of the imports. The best and most expensive black tea was pekoe, followed by souchong, congo, and finally bohea, the lowest grade and cheapest kind, which might contain not only leaves but stems, as well as the sweepings from the ground where the tea was processed. A similar scale for green teas ran from the highly prized bing tea to hyson to singlo.

One problem that plagued the drinkers of both green and black teas was adulteration. In China and England unscrupulous merchants added all sorts of unpleasant substances to tea to make it go farther—and, unfortunately for the consumer, taste worse. The name for these adulterants was "smouch," and they included the leaves of other plants and used tea leaves to add bulk; Prussian blue, turmeric, and various vegetable dyes to make the tea's color more appealing; and gypsum and iron filings to make the mixture heavier, thereby increasing profits since the tea was sold by weight. One recipe for smouch called for ash leaves to be dried, baked, stomped into small pieces, gathered, sifted, soaked in a solution of sheep's dung and ferrous sulfate, then finally dried again before being mixed with real tea leaves.[39]

It wasn't only the volume and the types of tea that changed over time but also the way in which tea was consumed and served. The Chinese didn't add anything to their tea, thereby allowing the essence and flavor of the brew to shine through. They drank their tea in handleless ceramic cups or bowls, which could be cradled without fear of burning, because the tea was served warm, not scalding. The Europeans, in contrast, tinkered with their tea, adding sugar and milk to sweeten it, cut its bitterness, and give it a creamier consistency. This, in turn, led to other changes. Since sugar dissolves best in hot liquid, Europeans served their tea hot, and in the process created a market for cups with handles, or teacups as they came to be called. To heap the sugar into the teacups, the teaspoon was born. Ceramic saucers beneath the cups were added to the ensemble to have a convenient place to rest the teaspoon after use, and also to protect the gleaming wood of the "tea table" from being scratched by the teacup or stained by errant drips of tea. The saucer served another purpose as well, allowing those of a less refined nature the option of pouring hot tea into the saucer to let it cool, then slurping it up—a procedure that gave rise to the phrase "a dish of tea." A final alteration to the ceremony of tea concerned the teapot. Although Europeans didn't invent the teapot—the Chinese had at least a thousand years earlier— they tended to make them much larger, more rotund, and out of silver as well as ceramics.

As the consumption of tea rose in Europe, so too did the demands for ceramic ware, silver, and sugar. Millions of pieces of Chinese porcelain arrived in Europe each year. Silversmiths worked longer hours to supply the tea-crazed public with teaspoons and teapots, while sugar plantations in the Caribbean and elsewhere expanded to keep the tea sweet. That sweetness, however, came at a terrible cost, for sugar is a labor-intensive crop, and most of that labor in the seventeenth and eighteenth centuries came from African slaves.

Increased tea consumption in Europe led to a fundamental change in the nature of the goods transported out of China. No longer were silk and porcelain the primary objects. Part of this could be attributed to competition. Since the Nestorian monks had spirited silkworms out of China in the sixth century, Western silk production had expanded and improved. And with advances in European ceramics, including the making of porcelain at the Meissen factory in Germany in the early 1700s, Chinese porcelain was not the only option for the tea drinker in search of equipage, or the connoisseur looking for an objet d'art. But the real reason that the glow had begun to fade on Chinese silk and porcelain was that tea had become the most desired Chinese commodity, the one that addicted Europeans sought more than any other. Thus every year the holds of European ships coming from Canton were filled with ever greater quantities of tea, and "porcelain, once packed in tea to prevent breakage, was now carried largely as 'kintledge,' or ballast to stabilize sailing ships too lightly laden with dried leaf."[40]

———

WHILE MUCH OF EUROPE rushed to the Far East and battled for its share of the China trade, Britain's American colonies watched from afar. Although the Americans were not direct participants in the trade and sent no ships to Canton, they were vitally interested in China. As part of the international trading network, and more particularly as a part of the British Empire, the colonies had been greatly affected by Chinese goods, some of which had become integral parts of America's cultural landscape. That connection to China enhanced the quality of colonial life, but even more importantly, it helped set the stage not only for revolution, but also for America's first commercial venture to the Middle Kingdom.

Three

CHINA DREAMS

BOSTON TEA PARTY, DECEMBER 16, 1773, N. CURRIER, 1846.
DESPITE WHAT THE PICTURE SHOWS, THE ACTUAL EVENT TOOK PLACE
AT NIGHT, AND THE CROWDS WERE SILENT.

*A*NYONE WHO HAS READ WASHINGTON IRVING'S "THE LEGEND OF
Sleepy Hollow" will recall that Ichabod Crane visits the mansion
of Baltus Van Tassel, a prosperous farmer of Dutch descent, whose
daughter Crane hopes to woo. The year is 1790, and the mansion is
located in Sleepy Hollow, a small, secluded glen in Tarrytown, New
York, nestled along the eastern bank of the Hudson River. Upon
entering the mansion's parlor, Crane witnesses "the ample charms of

a genuine Dutch country tea-table, in the sumptuous time of autumn." There are "platters of cakes of various and almost indescribable kinds," as well as delicious pies, smoked beef, preserved plums, and boiled shad, "together with bowls of milk and cream, all mingled higgledy-piggledy . . . with the motherly teapot sending up its clouds of vapor from the midst—Heaven bless the mark!"

A similar though less elaborate scene would not have been out of place in the mid-1600s, when New York was still the Dutch colony of New Netherland. This is because Sleepy Hollow had been preserved, as it were, in a sort of cultural amber, and the customs of its inhabitants differed little from their Dutch ancestors'. In fact it was the colonists of New Netherland who first drank tea in America. And since they drank Chinese tea supplied from Holland, the Dutch colony is where America's infatuation with things Chinese began.[1]

Thus when England took over New Netherland in 1664, transforming it into the colony of New York, the English inherited a community of tea drinkers. From that point forward the consumption of tea spread throughout the American colonies in much the same way as it had throughout England. Coffeehouses and tea gardens patterned after the British model sprang up in many cities, and thousands of newspaper advertisements trumpeted the availability of high-quality imported tea at local shops. Initially a habit of the well-to-do, tea drinking filtered down to the rest of society as tea imports increased and prices fell. "Tea, coffee, and chocolate," wrote a clergyman from Delaware in 1759, "are so general as to be found in the most remote cabins, if not for daily use yet for visitors, mixed with muscovado or raw sugar."[2]

Travelers were often amazed at how besotted the colonists had become with tea. While in Boston in 1740, the Englishman Joseph Bennett observed, "The ladies here visit, drink tea, and indulge every little piece of gentility to the height of the mode, and neglect the affairs of their families with as good a grace as the finest ladies in London."[3] The great demand for tastier tea in New York City led local officials to build special "tea-water pumps" to draw sweet springwater from deep underground. Discriminating New Yorkers, in turn, used that water instead of the foul liquid that issued from other city wells to brew their tea to perfection. By the early 1770s most colonists had become fervent tea drinkers. Estimates of colonial consumption of tea at this time range from 5.7 to 6.5 million pounds per year. Assuming that a pound of tea makes two hundred cups, that means that Americans drank between 1.1 and 1.3 billion cups of tea each year, or roughly 1.4 to 1.6 cups per person per day.[4]

TEA WAS BUT ONE of the Chinese goods that flowed into the colonies. Along with it came great quantities of Chinese silk, lacquerware, tea tables, and, most of all, porcelain china. As the historian Caroline Frank has shown, the colonies were literally awash in Chinese artifacts. For example, when Capt. Andrew Cratey of the small fishing town of Marblehead, Massachusetts, died in 1695, he left behind a dozen lacquered chairs as well as a few pieces of china. Thirty-five

HAND MODELING AND MOLDING OF PORCELAIN VASES AND FIGURES,
CIRCA 1825.

years later a fellow Marbleheader, Nathaniel Norden, bequeathed to his heirs twenty-three small, Chinese porcelain statues. These were not isolated cases but were repeated over and over again up and down the coast.[5]

As the colonial economy expanded during the mid-1700s, purchases of Chinese goods kept pace with increases in wealth. Even those who couldn't afford to emulate their more affluent peers were often swept up in the tide of consumerism, a problem illuminated by a concerned New Yorker, who wrote in 1734, "I am credibly informed, that tea and china ware cost the province yearly near the sum of ten thousand pounds; and people that are least able to go to the expense, must have their tea though their families want bread. Nay, I am told [they] often pawn their rings and plate to gratify themselves in that piece of extravagance." What had begun as a trickle of Chinese goods entering the colonies in the mid-1600s had become an absolute torrent on the eve of the Revolution. And if Americans couldn't get the real thing, imitation Chinese goods were available. Starting in the seventeenth century, artisans in Europe had begun creating a wide selection of chinoiserie, decorative and functional objects patterned after Chinese motifs, which ranged from bowls and vases to tapestries and wallpaper.[6]

Evincing a sense of cultural inferiority they had somehow internalized, many colonists—especially the wealthy—eagerly followed the trendsetters in London so as to imitate refined society in the mother country. George Washington, for example, ordered his first set of Chinese porcelain in 1755, telling his London agent to "choose [pieces] agreeable to the present taste, and send things good of their kind"; later he amended his request, adding, "Pray let them be neat and fashionable or send none."[7] And in subsequent years Washington and his wife, Martha, filled their Mount Vernon manor with numerous pieces of chinaware. But there was more than mimicry at work, and Americans' love for things Chinese was only partially a reflection of English tastes. Many countries beyond England's shores jockeyed for the riches of China, and the American colonies, although part of the British Empire, were also influenced by the wider world. The colonists' desire for Chinese goods resulted from many forces—the budding development of a uniquely American identity and aesthetic, as well as a growing fascination with the exotic not least among them.

IN THEORY, ALL THE CHINESE goods entering the colonies were supposed to have come via England, and more specifically, through the British East India Company, which had the monopoly on Far Eastern trade within the British Empire. Had that not been enough of a restriction on the flow of Chinese imports, the British Navigation Acts, first enacted in the mid-1600s, essentially required that the Americans trade directly with England alone. But the commercial net that England placed around the colonies turned out to be exceptionally porous.

In the late 1600s dozens of ships leaving from American shores traveled beyond the Cape of Good Hope, into the Indian Ocean and the Red Sea, and brought back riches from the Far East, including numerous items of Chinese origin. The men on these heavily armed ships were labeled pirates or privateers, depending on one's perspective, and certainly most of their treasure came from plundering the ships of other countries rather than from peaceful trade. Many of them set forth with the encouragement—or at least the complicity—of colonial governors, appointed by the Crown. In return the governors often received payment in the form of Far Eastern booty.

Whether or not their actions were sanctioned by the Crown's colonial representatives, the men on these ships were flouting the British East India Company's monopoly as well as the Navigation Acts, and the London authorities frowned darkly on their activities. So the Crown fought back, using its navy, the courts, new antipiracy laws, and a few high-profile executions of offenders to eliminate this scourge to English interests on the high seas. By the early 1700s, that goal had been achieved.[8]

Much more damaging to England's control of the Far Eastern trade than pirates or privateers was smuggling. The thousands of miles of American coastline acted like an irresistible magnet for smugglers, who brought tea into the colonies without having to pay any duties. Most of the smuggled tea came from the Dutch, a fact that was particularly galling to the British, who had passed the Navigation Acts in large part to keep the Dutch, as well as other European merchants, out of America. Britain's special disdain for the Dutch made perfect sense. For much of the seventeenth century the English and the Dutch were on a military and commercial collision course, sometimes resulting in war. Ever since the two nations had first ventured to the Far East they had been engaged in a vicious, at times deadly, battle to monopolize as much of the region's trade as possible. Thus the last thing England wanted was to allow their despised competitors to benefit from access to lucrative American markets.

Two of the main American smugglers were none other than Robert Morris and his partner Thomas Willing. They and their peers would run ships down to one of the islands in the Dutch West Indies, purchase tea, and then head back home. The volume of the illicit tea trade was not inconsiderable. In 1757 a Philadelphia merchant estimated that during the two previous years, only about 10 percent of all the tea consumed in the city was imported legally from England, with the rest being smuggled in. Although exact numbers, for obvious reasons, are hard to find, the amount of smuggled tea entering the colonies by the early 1770s might have been as much as 75–95 percent of the total consumed.[9]

DESPITE ALL THE TRADE in Chinese goods, illegal and otherwise, the average American colonist knew almost nothing about China itself—an imperial, exotic empire that remained shrouded in myth. Educated Americans, perhaps, knew more, but even if they did, their understanding was broad, not deep. After all, no more than a handful of colonists, maybe as few as a half dozen, had ever set foot in China, and they were men who had crewed on English ships and therefore were not in the best position to comment on Chinese society. As far as we know, none of them committed any of their thoughts, however limited, to paper. Still, American colonists who wanted to learn about China could turn to a number of European books, which generally painted a very favorable image of the Middle Kingdom.

First among these was Marco Polo's book of travels, a well-known classic, which couldn't help but amaze its readers. Another was Jean-Baptiste Du Halde's *General History of China*, published in 1735. Du Halde, a Jesuit priest, never visited China, but he compiled his four-volume work based on reports written by Jesuit missionaries who had worked in the country. A very popular book—both Thomas Jefferson and Benjamin Franklin owned a copy—"the *General History* held up China's government, law, and philosophy as models for emulation." Du Halde claimed that China was "the most remarkable of all Countries yet known," and "the largest and most beautiful Kingdom" in the world. If these books didn't persuade the reader that China was indeed an astonishing place, there was always Voltaire. Although the French philosopher argued that Europe was much more advanced than China in the sciences, he was nonetheless an unabashed sinophile who greatly admired Chinese morality, agriculture, political economy, and arts. In his *Philosophical Dictionary*, published in 1764, Voltaire declared, "The Chinese, for four thousand years, when we were unable even to read, knew everything essentially useful of which we boast at the present day."[10]

Counterbalancing these positive images were some that were far less glowing. Europeans had tried to breach the walls of China for centuries before establishing a stable beachhead at Canton. During that time, they had been frustrated, rebuffed, and, in their eyes at least, treated poorly (leaving aside for the moment the fact that in many cases, it was the Europeans who acted poorly toward the Chinese). This treatment, plus the Chinese belief in their own superiority to other nations, angered many Europeans who thought themselves at least equal to the Chinese, and didn't appreciate being referred to as foreign devils or barbarians.

The negative view of China intensified after British commodore George Anson and his naval squadron returned from four years on the high seas spent attacking Spanish ships. When the battered and bloodied squadron sailed to Canton in desperate need of supplies, and with a silver-laden Spanish galleon in tow, its reception infuriated Anson. The commodore rebelled against the Chinese demand that he pay duties on his ships, pointing out that they were ships of war, not merchantmen. He was insulted when the local governor would not meet with him right away, but repeatedly put off the day with thin excuses. He was horrified when one of his officers was beaten and robbed while onshore. And he thought that the Chinese tried to cheat him at every turn, in one instance cramming dead ducks with gravel, thereby inflating the price of these provisions, which were sold by weight. All of this led Anson to conclude in his widely read account of the voyage, "that in artifice, falsehood, and an attachment to all kinds of lucre, many of the Chinese are difficult to be paralleled by any other people." At another point Anson added that China's "magistrates are corrupt, their people thievish, and their tribunals venal."[11]

Charles-Louis de Secondat, baron de La Brède et de Montesquieu, the eminent eighteenth-century French political philosopher, viewed the Chinese in a light similar to Anson's. Using many of the same Jesuit sources that Du Halde and Voltaire relied on, Montesquieu came to vastly different conclusions. He found the Chinese government less than admirable, its means of punishment excessive and cruel, and he labeled China "a despotic state, whose principle is fear."[12]

These differing perspectives notwithstanding, many Americans remained intrigued by positive aspects of Chinese culture—none more so than the learned members of the American Philosophical Society. In the inaugural volume of the society's transactions, published in 1771, Charles Thomson, one of the organization's secretaries, stated that he and his colleagues were dedicated to applying knowledge to practice, and that they therefore proposed "to confine their disquisitions, principally, to such subjects as tend to the improvement of their country, and advancement of its interest and prosperity." On this score, Thomson continued, China had a special role to play:

> Such of the plants of *China* as have been introduced here, seem to agree with our soil and climate, and to thrive in a degree equal to our warmest expectations; witness the rice, the whisk and the *Chinese* vetch. These may encourage us to try others. . . . Thus by introducing the produce of those countries, which lie on the east side of the old world, and particularly those of *China*, this country may be improved beyond what heretofore might have been expected. And could we be so fortunate as to introduce the industry of the *Chinese*, their arts of living and improvements in husbandry, as well as their native plants, *America* might in time become as populous as *China*, which is allowed to contain more inhabitants than any other country, of the same extent, in the world.[13]

Quite an arresting aspiration, given that at the time the population of China was fast approaching 300 million, while the American colonies had only recently passed 2 million. Yet such China dreams were perfectly in line with America's growing confidence and its steadfast belief that improvements in society were not only possible but also inevitable.

While the American Philosophical Society was keen on obtaining useful knowledge, other Americans viewed China principally as a commercial opportunity. In 1777, when he was aide-de-camp to Gen. George Washington, Alexander Hamilton took time to reflect upon the enticing suite of goods issuing forth from China. The future secretary of the treasury noted that these goods included "all those in Europe with the addition of many either in greater abundance than there or not produced there at all." On the list were traditional items, such as silk and tea, as well as "diamonds, pearl, gold, silver, copper, iron, sulphur, . . . potters earth (of which is made the porcelain), . . . cinnamon, peppers, indigo, . . . vermillion, . . . dragon's blood [a deep rcd rcsin], . . . ambergris and many other of the valuable drugs and gums."[14]

The closest America came to launching an independent trade with China was a threat made in a letter published in a London newspaper in 1770, authored by "The Colonist's Advocate," a pseudonym for either Benjamin Franklin or James Burgh, a British Whig with strong sympathies for America. The letter decried the Townshend Acts, which were passed in June 1767 and placed taxes on tea, glass, paper, lead, and paint imported into the colonies. It also raised the possibility of Americans doing the unthinkable:

> What will they [the British in favor of the Townshend Acts] say when they find, that Ships are actually fitted out from the Colonies (they cannot, I suppose hinder their fitting out ships) for all Parts of the World; for China, by Cape Horn; for instance, to sail under Prussian, or other Colors, with Cargoes of various Kinds, and so return loaded with Tea, and other East India Goods. . . . The whole Navy of England, if stationed ever so judiciously, cannot prevent smuggling on a Coast of 1500 Miles in Length. Such Steps as these will soon be taken by the Americans, if we obstinately go on with our unjust and oppressive measures against them.[15]

This was only bluster. It would take a revolution before America finally entered the China trade. And interestingly enough, the China trade itself played a key role in hastening the arrival of that day. To see how, one must consider tea, which truly became the brew of revolution.

ALMOST EVERY AMERICAN schoolchild is familiar with the story of the Boston Tea Party: how, on the evening of December 16, 1773, colonists disguised as Indians boarded the *Dartmouth*, the *Eleanor*, and the *Beaver*, which contained a total of 342 chests of British East India

Company tea, smashed the chests, and dumped the tea—roughly ninety thousand pounds—into Boston Harbor. The question that many scholars have asked about this event is why tea had become such a lightning rod for American anger, and why the controversy over it helped spark the American Revolution. The short answer is that it had everything to do with the monopoly power of the British East India Company, and the ubiquitous nature of tea in American society.[16]

When the Townshend Acts were passed in June 1767, America exploded with rage. Customs officials intent on collecting the new taxes were often attacked, and when the British sent troops to the colonies to enforce the acts and keep the peace, their presence only served to inflame the colonists more. The colonists, furious over this case of taxation without representation, fought back by boycotting the British goods, with one of the most widespread boycotts focusing on tea. Americans vowed to stop drinking it until the acts were repealed. Newspapers ran articles imploring people to abstain, and instead drink locally grown substitutes such as Hyperion tea, made from raspberry leaves, or Labrador tea, which was made from a small evergreen plant in the heath family that grows on the edge of northern swamps and lakes. Although the boycotts were neither universal nor particularly well enforced, they along with other colonial protests were effective enough to force Parliament to reconsider its approach to the unruly Americans, and repeal the Townshend Acts in March 1770. But the repeal of the acts was not complete: The threepence-per-pound duty on tea remained in force, so that Parliament could show the colonies that it still had the right to govern them as it saw fit. While Parliament was willing to admit the defeat of the acts, it was not willing to concede its power to tax the colonists.

The next few years were relatively calm ones in the colonies. The boycotts faded away and people returned to drinking tea, happy to jettison the substitutes, all of which were by comparison rather difficult to swallow. The vast majority of the tea entering the colonies still was smuggled in, and for that, of course, no duty was paid. But at the same time Americans were annually importing nearly three hundred thousand pounds of tea from the British East India Company, which included the Townshend duty, yet there were few complaints about this added charge. Then, in May 1773, Parliament passed the Tea Act, and America erupted anew.[17]

The Tea Act was basically a government bailout of the British East India Company. Arguably the largest corporation in the world, the British East India Company was a colossus that not only had the monopoly on the China trade but also controlled a significant chunk of India as a result of conquest. The company was almost a country unto itself, having been granted the power to "acquire territory, coin money, command fortresses and troops, form alliances, make war and peace, and exercise both civil and criminal jurisdiction."[18] As Edmund Burke, the renowned British statesman and philosopher, remarked, "The East India Company did not seem to be merely a Company formed for the extension of the British commerce, but in reality of the whole power and sovereignty of [the United Kingdom] sent into the East."[19] And the taxes the company paid had for a long time constituted

EAST INDIA HOUSE, BY JOSEPH C. STADLER, 1817.

a significant percentage of the British budget. Despite all this, the East India Company was in economic freefall by the early 1770s. It had been hobbled by a number of factors, including decreasing revenues from India, unwarranted hikes in dividend payments, plunges in the value of the company's stock, and a depression in Britain's financial market. Yet another critical factor was tea. Although about 90 percent of the British East India Company's profits came from the sale of tea, those profits had been plummeting for years, pushing the company's ledgers further into the red and leaving it with twenty million pounds of tea sitting in its warehouses, with no buyers in sight. The company's tea crisis was partly the result of fallout from the Townshend Acts, but mostly due to the fact that smugglers, who had long been the tea suppliers of choice, were literally taking money that otherwise would have gone into the East India Company's coffers.

With all these problems to contend with, the British East India Company appealed to Parliament for help, and the Tea Act was its response. The act's goal was to financially resuscitate the insolvent Company by allowing it to sell its surplus tea to the colonies at greatly reduced prices. To accomplish this Parliament agreed to waive British export taxes on the tea, and also allow the East India Company to sell the tea directly to the colonists, without the services of American merchants who traditionally brokered the transaction. To Parliament it appeared to be a winning policy. The British East India Company would have an outlet for its warehoused tea, and the colonists would be able to purchase that tea for half the price paid by consumers in Britain. Because the price of tea would be so low, the smugglers would have a more difficult time competing with the British East India Company, further strengthening its position. Of course, the threepence Townshend tax on tea would still apply, but even so, the tea would be incredibly cheap.

Parliament, however, made a major miscalculation. The colonies rebelled against the act, with the Boston Tea Party serving as the most dramatic symbol of defiance. Although few Americans had complained about the retention of the threepence duty on tea after the repeal of the Townshend Acts, the Tea Act reignited the debate over taxation without representation, and an increasing number of colonists began to worry that if the tea tax stood, it would quickly be followed by taxes on other goods. American merchants who imported British tea legally and American smugglers alike were also upset because the Tea Act threatened to put them out of business or at least significantly cut their profits.[20]

The fury engendered by the Tea Act was broader and deeper than just concerns about taxation and lost profits. To some Americans the Tea Act was far more sinister. They saw it as the opening salvo in a long-term strategy of the British East India Company to monopolize not only the trade in tea, but in other foreign commodities as well, in effect transforming the colonies into a cog in the company's commercial empire. This was particularly unnerving for those Americans who believed, somewhat irrationally, that since the British East India Company had behaved ruthlessly in gaining control over portions of India, the colonies were next in line for such treatment. "A Mechanic," writing in a broadside dated December 4, 1773, warned his fellow citizens of the extreme dangers of continuing to buy and drink British tea:

> The East India Company, if once they get footing in this (once) happy country, will leave no stone unturned to become your masters. They are an opulent body, and money or credit is not wanting amongst them. They have a designing, depraved, and despotic ministry to assist and support them. They themselves are well versed in TYRANNY, PLUNDER, OPPRESSION, and BLOODSHED. Whole provinces laboring under the distresses of oppression, slavery, famine, and the sword, are familiar to them. Thus they have enriched themselves—thus they are become the most powerful trading Company in the universe.[21]

Another colonist claimed that "the importation and use" of British tea would lead to the "ruin of government, its trade—and what is infinitely more valuable, its liberty," and therefore tea should be treated as if it were "THE PLAGUE."[22] According to the historian James R. Fichter, "For patriots, tea signified monopoly as much as anything else—the monopoly of the East India Company, which engrossed all of British trade with Asia. And to them monopoly . . . was a tool of a dangerous state."[23]

SATIRICAL BRITISH CARTOON OF AMERICAN WOMEN
FROM EDENTON, NORTH CAROLINA, PLEDGING TO BOYCOTT
ENGLISH TEA, BY PHILLIP DAWE, 1775.

In response to the implementation of the Tea Act, Americans "vowed," as the historian T. H. Breen has observed, "to teach [the British government] that their love of liberty exceeded their love of tea." Calls went out to refrain from drinking tea to show one's patriotism, and Americans eagerly and earnestly responded. Some abstained entirely, others turned to substitutes, and still others burned their tea in public bonfires to show their contempt for British actions. Those Americans who did not have enough intestinal fortitude to give up tea on their own were often shamed into doing so by their peers who equated tea drinking with treason, and who were willing to use humiliation as motivation.

A large part of the reason why the Tea Act caused such uproar was the nature of the product it sought to manipulate. Tea was a commodity with which the vast majority of Americans could easily identify, since so many of them had been drinking it for years. It "had become," Breen notes, "the master symbol of the new consumer economy," which had grown so vigorously in the colonies during the decades leading up to the Revolution. And because it was such a powerful, universally appreciated symbol, the rebellion against British tea and the East India Company became a shared experience, and a patriotic cause around which Americans could rally.[24]

THE EMOTIONALLY CHARGED battles over tea, however, had an impact that lingered beyond the war. Many Americans, embittered by these events, gave up tea for good, and turned to coffee instead, leading to a dramatic rise in its consumption. Nevertheless there was still quite a large number of tea drinkers left in the newly formed United States. It was because of them that the *Empress of China* found itself at the threshold of the Middle Kingdom in the waning days of the summer of 1784.

Four

THE "NEW PEOPLE"

PORCELAIN PUNCH BOWL DEPICTING SWEDISH SHIP,
BROUGHT BACK FROM CANTON ON THE *EMPRESS OF CHINA* BY
THE SHIP'S CARPENTER, JOHN MORGAN.

*I*N THE FACE OF LIGHT RAIN, "FRESH BREEZES AND A TUMBLING swell," the *Empress of China*, accompanied by the French ship the *Triton*, sailed up the Pearl River estuary on August 23, 1784, and into China's realm. Six months after leaving New York, having traversed about eighteen thousand miles of ocean, the Americans had triumphantly arrived. After the *Empress of China* anchored in the Macao Roads, Captain Green ordered a seven-gun salute, which was returned by the fort on Macao, just three miles away. Then Samuel Shaw, the ship's supercargo, and John Swift, its purser, unfurled the Stars and Stripes and hoisted it aloft. This was the first time the American flag had flown in this part of the world, and it was a thrilling sight for all the men onboard. But Shaw took only a few moments to relax and reflect on their achievement. Captain Green had succeeded in getting the *Empress of China* to its destination. Now it was Shaw's turn to take the helm of this venture.[1]

The next day Shaw and others from the ship visited the Portuguese outpost of Macao, paying their respects at the governor's residence, stopping by the customhouse to get a chop, and dining with the French and Swedish consuls. Although Macao had, as Anson observed some forty years earlier, "fallen from its ancient splendor," it was still a striking place. About three miles long, and from a half to one mile wide, Macao had a population of around twenty thousand, about four thousand of whom were Portuguese and their African slaves, with most of the rest being Chinese, along with a smattering of other Europeans. Sandwiched between a harbor on one side and a stunning crescent-shaped beach—Praya Grande—on the other, Macao was a

PRAYA GRANDE, MACAO, BY THOMAS ALLOM, 1843.

WHAMPOA ANCHORAGE, BY YOUQUA, CIRCA 1845.

sliver of Europe in the Orient. Its narrow, winding streets were lined with impressive buildings of stone and brick, including a few Catholic churches and the mansions where foreign merchants lived when they weren't in Canton.[2]

With a pilot onboard, the *Empress of China* left Macao on August 26 and arrived at Whampoa two days later. Most of the thirty-five foreign ships that would trade at Canton that year were already anchored in this relatively narrow and congested stretch of the river. When Green saluted them with thirteen guns, they all responded with resounding salvos of their own, which echoed across the water and the hills beyond. The French, the Danes, the Dutch, and the British sent welcoming parties, and later that day Shaw, Green, and Randall returned the visits. "The behavior of the gentlemen on board the respective ships," Shaw commented, "was perfectly polite and agreeable. On board the English it was impossible to avoid speaking of the late war. They allowed it to have been a great mistake on the part of their nation,—were happy it was over,—glad to see us in this part of the world,—hoped all prejudices would be laid aside,—and added, that, let England and America be united, they might bid defiance to all the world."[3]

Shaw and Randall left Whampoa for Canton on August 30. It is striking indeed that Shaw, the only person onboard who kept a journal while in China, failed to record a single thought about the sights and sounds that greeted the Americans as they traveled from Macao to Canton. In this completely alien land, Shaw must have been amazed by the landscape unfolding around him, but perhaps he was too sober to give voice to his wonder. Fortunately others were not so reticent. A Frenchman who had covered the same ground twenty years earlier began his narrative on the approach to the mouth of the Pearl River. The first thing that arrested his attention was the "forest of masts, and soon after an innumerable multitude of boats, which covered the surface of the water." Thousands of fishermen, plying their ancient trade, were trolling the depths for the ocean's bounty. The river itself was also choked with boats, "its banks lined with ships at anchor; [and] a prodigious number of small craft . . . continually gliding along in every direction, some with sails, others with oars, vanishing often suddenly from the sight, as they enter the numberless canals dug with amazing labor, across extensive plains, which they water and fertilize." Beyond the river's edge farmers toiled in "immense fields, covered with all the glory of the harvest," and "stately villages" could be seen in the distance. Mountains, "cut into terraces, . . . shaped into amphitheatres," and carpeted with the lush, green growth of summer, formed "the background of this noble landscape." Arriving at Canton, the traveler was greeted by a new and no less dramatic scene. "The noise, the motion, the crowd augments," as both the water and the land were "covered with multitudes" of people, perhaps as many as a million.[4]

The number of Chinese vessels on the river in the vicinity of Canton ran into the tens of thousands, and ranged in size from five-hundred-ton junks, with fierce eyes painted on their bows, to small sampans used for fishing or ferrying supplies. Ornate flower boats, where prostitutes offered themselves to wealthy Chinese customers, competed for space with much plainer houseboats, on which extended families lived and worked in cramped quarters. Canton might really

ON THE PEARL RIVER AT CANTON, 1837.

have been two cities, one terrestrial and the other aquatic, both humming with ceaseless activity.

The Americans, being from a "new country," didn't yet have a factory in Canton. So once again their fast friends, the French, lent a helping hand, housing the Americans until September 6, when their own factory, a formerly empty building, was ready. Constructed of granite or brick in an imposing European style, the factories were located about three hundred feet from the river on the edge of a partially stone-paved courtyard called the Square, and each one had a flagpole out front to identify the nationality of the occupants within. The factories were quite large, two or three stories high, with bedrooms, parlors, offices, a dining room, and a veranda above, and a kitchen, servants' quarters, and storage areas below. Behind the factories ran a broad avenue called Thirteen Factory Street, which was connected to the Square by three much narrower streets or alleys, ranging from just three to fifteen feet wide. Along these crowded and noisy thoroughfares vendors and peddlers hawked their wares from shops and carts, offering a fantastic choice of objects for sale, from silks and China sets to carved ivory and ornamental wood-and-lacquer boxes. A profusion of brightly colored and curiously translated signs vied for the attention of passersby. Establishments called "Collective Justice," "Peace and Quiet," and "Perfect Concord" enticed customers with catchy, and often quirky slogans such as "Rich customers are perpetually welcome," and "Here are sold superior goods, in whose prices there is no change." A common water tub was labeled "the bucket of superlative peace," and a chest "the box of great tranquility."

Foreigners, including crewmen, who were occasionally shuttled up to Canton from Whampoa, passed the time wandering these streets and buying presents to bring home. They also witnessed the incredibly varied Chinese diet. Alongside the chickens and exotic fruits and vegetables were rats, cats, and dogs for sale, the sight of which amused and alarmed the foreigners, who often wondered if there was anything the Chinese wouldn't eat. The sailors would be sure to make a special visit to Hong Lane—or as it was more appropriately called by the foreigners, Hog Lane—where all types of local liquor could be had for a price, and it was not uncommon to witness brawls or see men sprawled on the street, sleeping off the effects of some potent

CHINESE JUNK ON THE PEARL RIVER, 1833.

brew—perhaps a few too many drafts of *samshoo*, a popular Chinese wine made from fermented rice. Shaw later said that what transpired on Hog Lane "surpasses *fable*: it is the residence and resort of pick-pockets and knaves of all nations, and always in an uproar with hogs, dogs, &c."[5]

SHAW AND RANDALL were invited to dine at other factories on a few occasions, and they reciprocated in kind. They also attended concerts at the Dutch factory, and accompanied other Europeans on trips across the river to eat at the palatial estates owned by the hong merchants. Nevertheless, Shaw's opinion of social life in Canton was rather bleak. "The gentlemen of the respective factories" kept to themselves, he noted, except for occasional gatherings, and even then the men were "very ceremonious and reserved." Shaw did not envy the Europeans. "Considering the length of time they reside in this country," he said, "the restrictions to which they must submit, the great distance they are at from their connections, the want of society, and of almost every amusement, it must be allowed that they dearly earn their money."

The Chinese had never heard of the United States, and were not quite sure what to make of the Americans, at first thinking that they were Englishmen, since they looked similar and spoke the same language. Once the Chinese were disabused of that notion, however, they dubbed the Americans the "New People" (in later years the Chinese would call the Americans the "Flowery-Flag Devils," because the stars in a field of blue on the American flag looked to the Chinese like flowers). The more the Chinese learned of the Americans, the more intrigued they became. According to Shaw, when he showed the Chinese a map, and "conveyed to them an idea of the extent of our country, with its present and increasing population, they were not a little pleased at the prospect of so considerable a market for the productions of their own empire."

FROM SEPTEMBER THROUGH mid-December, as fall gave way to the relatively warm and humid winter for which subtropical Canton was known, Shaw and Randall, with the assistance of their hong merchant, traded for Chinese goods. Alternately impressed and disgusted with the process, Shaw thought that the Canton system was "perhaps as simple as any [commerce] in the known world." As for honesty, however, it depended on whom you were talking about. "The knavery of the Chinese, particularly those of the trading class, has become proverbial," Shaw contended:

> There is, however, no general rule without exceptions; and though it is allowed that the small dealers, almost universally, are rogues, and require to be narrowly watched, it must at the same time be admitted that the merchants of the Cohong are as respectable a set of men as are commonly found in other parts of the world. It was with them, principally, that we transacted our business. They are intelligent, exact accountants, punctual to their engagements, and, though not the worse for being well looked after, value themselves much upon maintaining a fair character. The concurrent testimony of all the Europeans justifies this remark.[6]

It is important, however, to place Shaw's comments in context. "Knavery" or unscrupulous behavior in the merchant class, was not something exclusive to China, and at another point in his narrative Shaw admitted that it occurred elsewhere in the world. If some of the Chinese merchants were in fact any worse than their foreign counterparts, it was only a difference in degree, not kind.

No sooner had Shaw and Randall begun trading than they learned a painful lesson in supply and demand. Prices for goods were not static. Increasing supply inevitably drove prices down, ginseng in this case being the unfortunate example. The *Empress of China* had arrived with the single largest shipment of ginseng Canton had ever seen. But the Europeans had also brought an enormous amount of the prized root, leading purser Swift to claim, "This year ten times as much arrived as ever did before." By the time Shaw and Randall sold their ginseng, the price had already fallen precipitously, since many of the Europeans had already sold theirs.[7]

Despite the disappointing sale of ginseng, Shaw's disgust with "small dealers," and his belief that "every servant in the factories . . . [was] a spy," the trading went well, with only two issues. The first came early on, after the hoppo finished measuring the *Empress of China* to assess port duties. According to convention, the hoppo asked the foreigners to see the sing-songs or gifts. This posed a problem, since there were none onboard. Shaw apologized, saying that the Americans were "from a new country, for the first time, and did not know that it was customary to bring such things." The hoppo accepted this explanation but warned them not to make the same mistake on future visits. Despite this lapse in etiquette, the hoppo followed through with another tradition—that of sending foreign ships a present from the emperor, to let them know that the Son of Heaven wished them well. Hours after the hoppo departed the *Empress of China*, Green accepted delivery of "two bulls, eight bags of flour, and seven jars of country wine."[8]

A FAR MORE SERIOUS problem than the absence of sing-songs arose on November 24, just as a dinner party on the *Lady Hughes*, a British ship anchored at Whampoa, was coming to an end. To salute the guests on their departure, live cannons were fired. One of the blasts inadvertently hit a boat that was "lying alongside" the *Lady Hughes*, injuring three of the Chinese onboard, one of whom died the next day. The Chinese officials demanded that the gunner who fired the shot be turned over, but the British reported that he had "absconded" and couldn't be found. The head of the British factory also informed the Chinese that the British East India Company had no authority over the *Lady Hughes*, since it was a "country ship," licensed by the company but owned by private British traders who shuttled between India and Canton. If the Chinese wanted answers, they should speak with George Smith, the supercargo of the *Lady Hughes*.

Three days after the incident Smith received a message saying that his hong merchant wanted to see him on business. Smith left the factory area only to discover that the message was a ruse when sword-wielding soldiers took him into custody. Immediately thereafter all trading was halted, the streets around the factories were blocked and filled with soldiers, and the Chinese merchants, linguists, and compradors evacuated the area. Although the hoppo had forbidden communication between Canton and Whampoa, the supercargoes managed to get word to their ships in Whampoa to send boats with armed men to Canton in order to protect the factories. Four to five hundred men responded and headed upriver.

The "Canton War," as Shaw dubbed it, had thus begun. The Chinese fired on the approaching force, wounding two men, but all the boats arrived safely. At about the same time the region's governor sent a message to the foreigners, saying that whether the deaths were by "accident or design," the gunner needed to be produced and tried according to Chinese law, and that as soon as the gunner stepped forward, Smith would be released. The governor added that the foreigners must comply, and that he would array his forces to keep them from leaving. "Reflect therefore, & see what is your force and your ability," the governor concluded. "If you dare in our country to disobey & infringe our laws, consider well that you may not repent when it is too late."

The British, Danish, French, Dutch, and American supercargoes formally protested the taking of Smith, who was clearly innocent, having been in Canton the day of the event. They also defended their sending for armed boats, claiming that it was necessary to protect themselves and their property. The governor responded on the evening of the twenty-eighth, asking the supercargoes of all the countries except Britain to attend a meeting, at which time he told them his quarrel was with the British and not with them. The governor repeated his desire that the gunner be turned over, and also assured the supercargoes that if he was found innocent he would be let go. Although the foreigners had violated Chinese law by bringing armed boats into Canton, the governor said he would excuse this infraction as long as the boats left, which they all did but for the Americans who decided to stay and support the British cause. With that, trade between the Chinese and all the non-British Europeans resumed.

As the armed European boats were departing, Smith wrote a letter to Mr. Williams, the captain of the *Lady Hughes*, asking him to send the gunner to Canton, which was done on November 30. As soon as the gunner was handed over, Smith was released, and on December 6 the embargo on trade with the British and the Americans was lifted. The next day the *Lady Hughes* left for India. A little more than a month later, the emperor found the gunner guilty, and he was strangled to death.[9]

TO THE BRITISH what happened was a clear miscarriage of justice. They felt that the gunner was not guilty of a crime. He had not meant to kill anyone, the deaths were accidental or unintentional, and it was unfair to require "blood for blood" under such extenuating circumstances. Leniency, not a charade of a trial, was what was called for. Holding the British collectively responsible for the gunner's act, and taking Smith hostage, was viewed as equally unjust. More ominously the British perceived this event as part of a larger pattern. Four years earlier a French sailor and a Portuguese sailor on a British ship anchored in Whampoa got into a fight, leaving the latter dead. Although the British claimed that the Frenchman acted in self-defense, the Chinese demanded that the sailor be turned over and come before a Chinese tribunal. This was done, and a day later the sailor, having been found guilty of murder, was strangled at a location near the factories. In British eyes, therefore, the two cases meant that should another accidental death occur in the future, they would be faced with one of two unpalatable choices: handing over an innocent man to be killed, which would dishonor Britain, or getting out of the Canton trade altogether.[10]

Shaw's perspective was in line with that of the British. Writing after the gunner had been turned over but before he had been strangled, Shaw concluded that this "troublesome affair, which commenced in confusion, [and] was carried on without order . . . [had] terminated disgracefully. Had that spirit of union among the Europeans taken place which the rights of humanity demanded, and could private interest have been for a moment sacrificed to the general good, the conclusion of the matter must have been honorable, and probably some additional privileges [regarding the handling of such cases] would have been obtained."[11]

The Chinese, in contrast, viewed the situation quite differently. According to the historian Li Chen, who has dug deeply into both the British and the Chinese records, there is "little evidence for the traditional belief that the *Lady Hughes* case best demonstrated the corruption, arbitrariness, and/or inhumanity of Chinese law and justice." Chen raises many valid questions, among them that, although it might have been an "accidental homicide," it could still have been the result of criminal negligence, and therefore liability would have applied. The Chinese boat was clearly alongside the *Lady Hughes*, within the line of sight for the gunner, and the gunner should not have fired live rounds, since Chinese law forbade the possession or use of firearms in its territory. Furthermore the delays in turning over the gunner were seen as an obstruction of Chinese justice, and given past misbehavior of British and other foreigners on Chinese soil, it was important for the emperor not to be seen as incapable of protecting his own people and enforcing the law.[12]

Determining who was right or wrong in this situation, or who acted properly, is well beyond the scope of this book. What is critical, though, is how this situation affected the course of history. It was the British view of events that became the standard interpretation in the

West. In Britain in particular, the *Lady Hughes* incident remained an open wound that would fester and dramatically affect future relations not only between China and Britain, but also between China and the United States.

ITS TRADING DONE, the *Empress of China* set sail for America on December 28, 1784, just a few months before John Adams would become the first U.S. ambassador to Britain. In the ship's hold were the fruits of Shaw's and Randall's efforts in Canton: seven hundred chests of bohea tea, one hundred chests of hyson tea, twenty thousand pairs of nankeen trousers, and a large amount of porcelain. The return voyage was uneventful, the only exception being the death of the ship's carpenter, John Morgan, who had begun the trip in poor health and expired just after crossing the equator in the Atlantic. At noon on May 11, 1785, after a fifteen-month absence, and having sailed, according to the ship's log, a total of 32,458 miles, the *Empress of China* anchored in New York's East River and once again saluted the city with thirteen guns.[13]

Soon after docking, Shaw, justifiably proud of the *Empress of China*'s accomplishment, submitted a report to John Jay, the minister for foreign affairs, intended "for the information of the fathers of the country." Shaw recounted the strict trading protocols of the Canton System, said that his Chinese and European hosts had treated him and his men well, and concluded with a hopeful thought: "To every lover of his country, as well as those more immediately concerned in its commerce, it must be a pleasing reflection, that a communication is thus happily opened between us and the eastern extremity of the globe." Jay responded by telling Shaw that the members of Congress felt "a peculiar satisfaction in the successful issue of this first effort of the citizens of America to establish a direct trade with China, which does so much honor to its undertakers and conductors."[14] One of those members, the Virginian William Grayson, shared his sense of

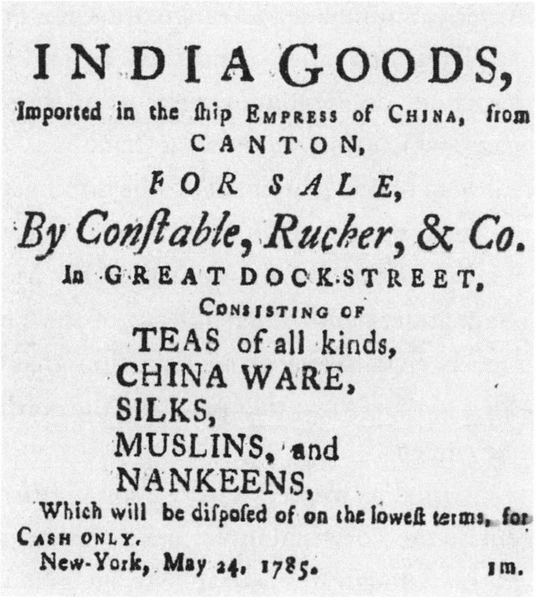

INDIA GOODS,

Imported in the ſhip EMPRESS of CHINA, from
CANTON,

FOR SALE,

By Conſtable, Rucker, & Co.

In GREAT DOCK-STREET,

CONSISTING OF

TEAS of all kinds,
CHINA WARE,
SILKS,
MUSLINS, and
NANKEENS,

Which will be diſpoſed of on the loweſt terms, for
CASH ONLY.

New-York, May 24, 1785.   1 m.

NEWSPAPER
ADVERTISEMENT
ANNOUNCING THE
SALE OF ITEMS
FROM THE *EMPRESS*
OF *CHINA*.

"satisfaction" with James Madison (then a member of the Virginia House of Delegates), writing in late May 1785:

> I imagine you have heard of the arrival of an American vessel at this place in four months from Canton in China, laden with the commodities of that country. It seems our countrymen were treated with as much respect as the subjects of any nation, i. e., the whole are looked upon by the Chinese as Barbarians, and they have too much Asiatic hauteur to descend to any discrimination [Grayson used the term more in the sense of "loftiness" that that of outright arrogance]. Most of the American merchants here are of the opinion that this commerce can be carried on, on better terms from America than Europe, and that we may be able not only to supply our own wants but to smuggle a very considerable quantity to the West Indies. I could heartily wish to see the merchants of our state engage in the business.[15]

Thomas Jefferson, America's minister to France, took the opportunity of the *Empress of China*'s return to send the French foreign minister, Charles Gravier, comte de Vergennes, a report on the ship's momentous maiden voyage, which also served as a thank-you to the French for their kind treatment of the Americans: "The circumstance which induces Congress to direct this communication," noted Jefferson, "is the very friendly conduct of the consul of his Majesty at Macao, and of the commanders and other officers of the French vessels, in those seas. It has been with singular satisfaction, that Congress have seen these added to the many other proofs of the cordiality of this nation towards our citizens."[16]

The *Empress of China* earned its backers $30,727, for a return of a little more than 25 percent on their original investment—not nearly as much as they had hoped, but enough to make the voyage a financial success.[17] Newspapers announced the ship's return, and its cargo radiated outward from New York City to be sold in stores up and down the coast. One paper reported that since the ship "brought such articles as we generally import from Europe, a correspondent observes that it presages a future happy period of our being able to dispense with the burdensome and unnecessary traffic which heretofore we have carried on with Europe, to the great prejudice of our rising empire, and future happy prospects of solid greatness: And that whether or not the ship's cargo be productive of those advantages to the owners, which their merits for the undertaking deserve, he conceives it will promote the welfare of the United States in general, by inspiring their citizens with emulation to equal, if not exceed, their mercantile rivals." Just above this pronouncement, as if to highlight the significant break with the past symbolized by the *Empress of China*, there was a notice of a new book just published in London, titled, *"The Prospect of a Reunion Between Great Britain and America*, by an American Officer."[18] But such a reunion was not to be. America was getting back on its feet after the Revolution, and heading in new and profitable directions—the *Empress of China*'s voyage was proof of that.

Less than a month after the *Empress of China* docked, a British gentleman residing in New York City wrote a letter to a friend back home, reflecting on the venture. "Among the many novelties which daily flow from the copious sources of fortune, none more singular . . . has presented itself here, than the arrival of the ship the *Empress of China*," which had succeeded in bringing back the "golden fleece" in the form of Chinese goods. "This voyage . . . is an immense thing, and opens a vast resource to the United States." But at the same time the correspondent realized that this success posed a serious threat to the European, and in particular the British, trade with China. "It strikes me as an event that should open the eyes of my native country to the real situation of this rising empire . . . as the great rival to Europe. . . . It has now opened the gates of the East, and the first beams of their morning have promised a splendid meridian to their commercial day."[19]

This gentleman's prescient musings eloquently captured the hope embodied in the *Empress of China*'s triumphant voyage. He wasn't the only one who saw in the ship's return the prospect for the dawning of a new "commercial day," in which America would bid fair to compete with Britain, and all of Europe, for the riches of the East. As word of the *Empress of China*'s successful trip spread, a growing number of American merchants headed out to get their piece of the proverbial China pie.

Five

CHINA RUSH

ATTACK AND MASSACRE OF THE CREW OF THE *TONQUIN*,
OFF VANCOUVER ISLAND, SUMMER 1811.

*T*HE UNITED STATES WAS WELL POSITIONED TO CAPITALIZE ON
the China trade. From its inception as a loose collection of colonies,
America had been wedded to the sea. The new nation's survival and
growth depended as much on the ocean as they did on the land. Its
shipyards had built thousands of the finest vessels afloat. Its villages,
towns, and cities had raised an army of men who were at home on
the waves, and were eager to venture wherever profits could be made.

Americans were, James Fenimore Cooper observed, "a people more maritime in their habits and pursuits, compared with their numbers, than any that exist, or who have ever gone before them." And as Alexis-Charles-Henri Clérel de Tocqueville noted, the "Declaration of Independence broke the commercial restrictions which united them [Americans] to England, and gave a fresh and powerful stimulus to their maritime genius."[1]

An ardent patriot, confident that China was destined to play a critical role in America's future, proclaimed in the summer of 1785:

> But one branch of commerce is left us, for which we owe no gratitude to the European powers. Thank God, the intrigues of a Christian court do not influence the wise decrees of the eastern world. Our pretentions there are equal: nor is it in their power to prevent us sharing the most profitable trade, whenever we have the ability and spirit to build and fit out proper ships for the purpose. . . . Believe me, my fellow citizens, you want ships only; which if directed by men of information and business, will soon render profit to yourselves and honor to your country.

A few months later, John Adams added his voice to the chorus of people urging Americans to take advantage of this brilliant new opportunity. "There is no better advice to be given to the merchants of the United States," Adams wrote to John Jay, "than to push their commerce to the East Indies as fast and as far as it will go."[2] The merchants, however, didn't need any prodding: The *Empress of China*'s success was incentive enough.

The ship's success purportedly impelled a southerner to proclaim, "every little village on every little creek with a sloop that could hold five Yankees was now planning to embark upon the Far Eastern trade."[3] This was hyperbole, of course, for a voyage to China was a major logistical and financial undertaking that only a relatively small number of merchants and ports were capable of pulling off. Nevertheless, between 1784, when the *Empress of China* blazed the trail, and the end of the War of 1812, in 1814, nearly three hundred American ships made a total of 618 voyages to Canton, and if the ships engaged in smuggling—not reflected in the official records—were added, the tally would be higher still. The number of American ships at Canton fluctuated dramatically from year to year, from a low of zero (in 1785) to a high of forty-five. Of course most sailed from the nation's most cosmopolitan cities—Boston, New York, and Philadelphia—but there were also many entries representing smaller harbors along the Eastern Seaboard, including such established whaling ports as Nantucket and New Bedford, and growing commercial centers from Massachusetts to South Carolina. The ships' names reflected pride in the new nation, admiration for its Founding Fathers, the love that mariners felt for their womenfolk, and the nature of the trade itself, with the shipping lists showing the likes of *True American, President Adams, Nancy* and *Grace*, and *Canton* and *Tea Plant*.[4]

This steep rise in the number of ships heading to China reflected a far larger trend, as the United States began to establish itself as a major maritime power. "The growth of American shipping, from 1789 to 1807, is without parallel in the history of the commercial world," declared the late nineteenth-century economist Henry Carter Adams. In that eighteen-year period "American tonnage, engaged in foreign trade . . . increased six and eight-tenths times."[5] The activity in the port of Boston one day in late October 1791 offers a snapshot of the vitality of America's expanding maritime presence. On the twenty-fourth of that month more than seventy vessels sailed from Boston "for all parts of the world," including the *Margaret*, commanded by James Magee, "bound on a voyage of observation and enterprise [read furs] to the Northwest coast of this continent."[6]

The China trade came to reflect America's fledgling commercial aspirations as clearly as any endeavor. Early on, some argued that the only way for the new nation to compete successfully in the China trade was for the government to step in and take a significant role, perhaps even going so far as to establish a monopoly, a turn of events that would have been cruelly ironic since one of the forces that led America to revolution was its hatred of the monopolistic British East India Company. "I must confess it is my opinion," Thomas Randall—the onetime junior supercargo on the *Empress of China*, and now a merchant in New York—wrote to Alexander Hamilton, the secretary of the treasury, in 1791, "that the trade to Canton will never flourish, [unless] in the hands of a well-regulated Company, which will not easily be performed without the protection of government—for individuals have neither influence, nor consequence enough with the Chinese to withstand the rivalship of established companies."[7] But Randall and other like-minded individuals were wrong. The enterprising men who developed America's China trade were cut from the same cloth as the Americans who had, during the colonial era, taken whaling and the fur trade to such great heights. They were men of means who on their own or with investors at their back planned the voyages, manned the ships, took the risks, and shared in the spoils.

Still, Americans engaged in the China trade didn't eschew government assistance. Indeed, they eagerly sought and accepted it, beginning in the late 1780s and early 1790s, when many states and the federal government increased duties on Chinese goods imported on foreign ships, kept duties on American importers low, and allowed American tea traders to delay paying taxes on their imports for up to two years—a suite of measures that afforded domestic merchants a great advantage over their competitors. Nonetheless this kind of government protectionism was a far cry from monopoly or government-sponsored companies. It was America's China merchants, and not the government, who were most responsible for their own success. This squared well with the young nation's evolving self-image, echoing the broadly free-market philosophy propounded by Adam Smith in *The Wealth of Nations*, published in 1776. Although Smith was at the time one of Britain's most celebrated thinkers, it was the Americans, not the British, who most warmly adopted Smith's notions, and the China trade provides a case in point. While the British East India Company's monopolistic operations were firmly rooted in the past,

America's China merchants were among the vanguard who put Smith's philosophy of relatively uninhibited and highly competitive trade into action, and with impressive results.[8]

AMONG THE MERCHANTS who took the lead in the China trade were John Jacob Astor of New York, Stephen Girard of Philadelphia, and Elias Hasket Derby of Salem. Astor, the son of a butcher from Walldorf, Germany, immigrated to New York City in 1784, hoping to make a living selling musical instruments made by his brother in London. He achieved that goal but quickly got swept up in the lucrative fur trade, and caught China fever in the late 1790s, when he began offering his customers Chinese silks and teas in addition to exquisite

JOHN JACOB
ASTOR.

pelts. Astor purchased these Chinese goods from merchants who had sent their own ships to Canton. That worked well enough, but Astor, never a fan of middlemen, possessed a better idea. In 1800 he took on partners and sent the *Severn* to China to trade directly on his account. Astor later purchased the *Severn* outright, and added other ships to his China fleet, including the *Magdalen*, named after his eldest daughter; the *Sylph*; the *Fox*; the *Enterprise*; and the *Beaver*, a particularly appropriate name for an Astor vessel since so much of his fortune rested firmly on the back of this wonderful rodent with its lustrous fur. Astor's success in his Far Eastern endeavors would earn him the title "Prince of the China Trade."

But Astor's success in this arena was not complete. One of his only failures was also closely tied to the China trade. In 1807 he hatched a plan to establish a string of fur-trading outposts snaking their way up the Missouri River, over the Continental Divide, then on to the Pacific Ocean via the Columbia River. The most critical post would be at the mouth of the Columbia, giving his fur-trading empire a western anchor, and also serving as a portal for sending furs to Canton. To realize this dream Astor sent large, well-financed expeditions by sea and land to the Pacific Northwest, whose travails provide some of the most compelling and tragic tales in the history of American exploration. In the end, however, the expeditions were for naught. Although Astor's men built a rudimentary outpost dubbed Astoria at the Columbia's mouth in the spring of 1811, it had only a fitful existence and was summarily taken over by the British Northwest Fur Trading Company at the end of the War of 1812. Nevertheless the fact that Astor invested so much of his time and fortune in this effort offers further proof of the importance of the China trade at this point in American history.[9]

Stephen Girard, like Astor, was an immigrant, having come from France to New York in 1774, and then moving two years later to Philadelphia, the city he would call home the rest of his life. Girard, blind in one eye, had little formal education. He had begun his life at sea at the age of fourteen, sailing on French merchant ships, arriving in Philadelphia just a month before the signing of the Declaration of Independence. But his interest was trade, not revolution, and soon he was in the employ of none other than Thomas Randall, who sent him as the master on trading ships to the West Indies. For much of the war Girard engaged in the West Indian trade and privateering. After the war he continued in the West Indian trade until the late 1780s when he began investing in China-bound ships. Then, in the mid to late 1790s he went from investor to owner, building six ships, including four named after French philosophers he admired—*Voltaire*, *Rousseau*, *Montesquieu*, and *Helvetius*—which made many successful voyages to Canton, and were later joined by other Girard ships in the China trade.[10]

Unlike Astor and Girard, Elias Hasket Derby was American from the start, born and raised in Salem, Massachusetts. His father, Richard Derby, handed over a small fleet of merchant ships to his son just about the time that the first shots of the Revolution rang out on

ELIAS HASKET DERBY, BY JAMES FROTHINGHAM, EARLY NINETEENTH CENTURY.

the Lexington town green. Elias used these ships as the nucleus of a privateering fleet, and during the war he owned or invested in more than twenty-five armed ships prowling the ocean for British prizes. In 1780 Derby commissioned a brand new three-hundred-ton privateer, christening it the *Grand Turk*. Ready for battle, with gunports capable of handling twenty-eight cannons, the *Grand Turk* worked wonders. In a little less than two years, it captured sixteen British ships, including one, the *Pompey*, whose value was equal to that of the *Grand Turk*.

The war behind him, Derby focused on business. Most of the *Grand Turk's* gunports were sealed, and its decks refitted to handle cargo. After two quick West Indian trading voyages, the *Grand Turk* headed in a new direction. Intrigued by the reports of the *Harriet's* successful tea-trading venture to the Cape of Good Hope, Derby decided to do the same with the *Grand Turk*. When the ship anchored at Cape Town's spectacular harbor on the edge of Table Bay in February 1785, however, its captain, Jonathan Ingersoll, was stymied. British ships were not allowed to "break bulk" on their trips back to England, but finally Ingersoll managed to salvage his trip when he found a British captain willing to sell him bohea tea from his "private venture," the portion of the cargo allowed to the officers as a way to make money on the side. Ingersoll sold most of that tea in the Caribbean, getting in return a load of rum and sugar, which he took to Salem.

This taste of the Far Eastern trade led Derby to send the *Grand Turk* out again, in December 1785, this time to the Isle of France (Mauritius), in the Indian Ocean, where he hoped that Capt. Ebenezer West would be able to barter for China goods. The voyage, however, became much more noteworthy in the annals of Salem's history because West, finding the trade at the Isle of France rather dull, pushed on to Canton, reaching Whampoa in September 1786. To his surprise, he discovered that his was the third American ship to arrive, as the *Empress of China*, on its second China voyage, and the *Hope* out of New York, were already there. Not long after, two more American ships hove into view: *Experiment*, a sloop from New York, and the *Canton* from Philadelphia. It had been barely two years since the *Empress of China* inaugurated America's China trade, and now there was a small flotilla of American ships anchored within sight of Whampoa's impressive pagoda.

When the *Grand Turk* returned to Salem, on May 22, 1787, its hold contained more than five hundred chests of tea, seventy-five boxes of china, and an assortment of finely woven handkerchiefs and muslin cloth. A throng of Salem's citizens greeted the *Grand Turk*, the first Salem ship, and the first ship from New England, to visit China. The public auction that followed was an exciting affair, drawing prospective bidders from miles around, the most illustrious being a slightly stooped but still trim and dignified John Hancock, the recently elected governor of Massachusetts and former president of the Continental Congress (and first signer of the Declaration of Independence), accompanied by his wife, Dorothy, who came by carriage from Boston. Derby doubled his investment selling the *Grand Turk*'s cargo, and in subsequent years sent many more ships to China, India, and other East Indian locations, all of which added to his considerable fortune, and helped earn him the moniker "King Derby." Derby's great success, as well as the maritime exploits of his fellow merchants in Salem, turned this formerly somewhat sleepy New England town, made infamous by the gruesome witch trials of 1692, into one of America's leading ports in the early 1800s, and the country's richest city on a per capita basis. The China trade was only part of the reason for this transformation, but a critical one nonetheless.[11]

Astor's, Girard's, and Derby's China trading and other business activities made them among the wealthiest people in the United States, with Derby becoming the country's first millionaire, Astor its first multimillionaire, and Girard nearly equaling Astor's fortune. On a list of history's 75 richest people of all time, compiled in 2008, these three financial titans stack up quite well. Astor ranks eighteenth, Girard twentieth, and Derby seventy-second, their wealth in current dollars tallying 115 billion, 99.5 billion, and 31.4 billion respectively.[12]

Surprisingly, one person not on the list of highly successful China merchants during these early years is Robert Morris. Although Morris followed up on the *Empress of China* by sponsoring another successful voyage to China a few years later with the *Alliance*, after that he left the China trade and was swept up in the land speculation craze gripping the nation, purchasing millions of acres along the frontier. While some of these investments proved wise, most did not. Sales faltered, debts mounted, and creditors called in their loans, as Morris watched his world slowly slip away. The denouement came on February 16, 1798, when he was arrested at his unfinished mansion in Philadelphia, and taken two blocks away to debtor's prison. The night before the arrest, Morris wrote to his business partner, "My money is gone, my furniture is to be sold, I am to go to prison and my family starve. Good night." Morris's wife, Mary, grief stricken and furious at the same time, lunged at the men who were taking her husband away, and had to be restrained from doing them harm. Morris stayed in prison for three and a half years, and soon after his release in 1801, the bankruptcy commission expunged his remaining debts, leaving him, as he said, "a free citizen of the United States without one cent that I can call my own." Four years later the man who had done so much for his country, and who had initiated America's China trade, died at the age of seventy-one, ending one of the most brilliant and tragic lives in American history.[13]

MERCHANTS BENEFITED THE most from the China trade, but they weren't the only ones who were enriched. During the Revolution, much of America's merchant fleet was destroyed by the British navy, which tenaciously targeted American ships at sea and in port. That meant that new ships had to be built for the burgeoning China trade, bringing shipyards back to life and employing thousands of men in various trades. Those ships had to be outfitted, employing thousands more, and they had to be manned, which created a high demand for officers and crew. Each time a ship returned, its owners had to pay customs fees to the government, and when the ships' cargoes were sold in shops they created another source of revenue. Thus in myriad ways the impacts of the China trade were felt far and wide. The money funneled into shipbuilding, outfitting, and manning the ships, paying the taxes, and selling the goods cascaded through the economy and made it stronger. The emerging China trade placed the United States on a firmer footing to defend its rights upon the seas by serving as a nursery for seamen who could be called upon by the merchant marine and naval forces to help grow and defend the country. Even the fortunes made by the merchants had an enormous effect on the evolution of the young nation, when they were reinvested in other critical industries and were used to support philanthropic and civic causes, the most noteworthy instance of which was when Girard and Astor used their vast wealth to purchase U.S. Treasury bonds, essentially loaning the government millions of dollars it desperately needed to finance the War of 1812.[14]

ONE THING THAT virtually all American ships engaged in the China trade had in common was their relatively small size. Whereas the vessels the Europeans sent to Canton, called East Indiamen, were quite large, with British ships averaging twelve hundred tons, their American counterparts, befitting their scrappy upstart origins, were almost all less than five hundred tons, and many were below two hundred, making them Lilliputians among giants. Some of the smaller American vessels that went to China were embarrassingly mistaken for tenders of much larger ships. The *Experiment*, in fact, which sailed from New York in December 1785, was a mere fifty-nine feet long, and just eighty-five tons. Soon after it returned to New York in April 1787, the *Worcester Magazine* reported with some satisfaction:

> It was matter of surprise to the natives and Europeans in those seas to see so small a vessel arrive from a clime so remote from China; and must have given them an exalted conception of the enterprising spirit of the citizens of these United States.—The

successful and safe return of . . . [the *Experiment*] has taught us, that fancy often times paints danger in much higher colors than is found really to exist, and that by maintaining a spirit of enterprise, diligence, and activity, we are enabled to surmount difficulties, which on a cursory view, are deemed fraught with dangers.[15]

One of the few American ships in these early years that approached the size of the European ships fared poorly, not because of its size but rather due to poor planning. Soon after returning to China in 1786, Shaw hatched a plan with Randall to build a magnificent ship for the China trade, and they sent orders back to the States to begin construction. The end result was the *Massachusetts*, which at 820 tons was the largest American merchant ship built up to that point. Launched in September 1789, and then moved from the shipyard in Braintree to Boston, the *Massachusetts* "excited a considerable sensation in the commercial part of the community," recalled Amasa Delano, its second officer (a distant relative of President Franklin Delano Roosevelt). "Parties of people in every rank of society frequently came on board of her to gratify their curiosity and express their admiration."

The ship's departure was curiously delayed due to Moll Pitcher, a fortuneteller of considerable fame from Lynn, Massachusetts, who predicted that all the men who shipped out on the *Massachusetts* would be lost at sea. As a result panic-stricken crewmembers, always prone to believe in rumors and portents, kept leaving, and it wasn't until the third entire crew was signed on that the men stayed put. "It seems strange," Delano observed, "that a class of men, who are continually exposed to storms hardships, and dangers, should be so powerfully affected by the traditions which are handed down from generation to generation concerning omens, charms, predictions, and the agency of invisible spirits."

By this time Shaw had returned to Boston and was ready to head out again onboard his new ship, which left for Canton on March 28,

1790, a departure attended by a large crowd, some of whom had come from a great distance to wish the massive ship and its crew well. The officers and crew, in turn, did their best to head out in fine fashion, but while weighing anchor and getting under way with all the sails set, the hook used to hoist and secure the anchor failed to hold. The anchor promptly sank back to the bottom, halting the ship's progress and giving the men onboard "not a little mortification." The anchor was soon recovered, and the *Massachusetts* fired a salute to the crowd on the wharf and then sailed out of Boston Harbor.

Shaw had planned to stop in the Dutch outpost of Batavia (modern-day Jakarta) to sell his cargo for silver coins, then head to Canton to buy Chinese goods. At Batavia, however, the Dutch governor forbade Shaw from selling anything. Gravely disappointed, Shaw and his fully loaded ship left for Canton, where his disappointment quickly turned into despair.

According to Delano, the *Massachusetts* "was loaded principally with green masts and spars, taken on board in winter directly out of water, with ice and mud on them." Once the lower hold was filled with this cargo, the lower deck hatches were sealed shut and not opened until the ship reached China. That turned out to have been a huge blunder. When the cargo hold was opened at Whampoa, Delano continued:

> The air was then found to be so corrupt that a lighted candle was put out by it nearly as soon as by water. . . . We had between four and five hundred barrels of beef in the lower hold placed in the broken stowage. When fresh air was admitted so that the men could live under the hatches, the beef was found almost boiled, the hoops were rotted and fallen off, and the inside of the ship was covered with a blue mould more than half an inch thick.

The cargo was mostly ruined, and what wasn't found no buyers in Canton. Fortunately for Shaw and Randall, who was in Canton when

Shaw arrived, the Dutch, who had just had one of their behemoth East Indiamen dismasted in a typhoon, were looking to buy a new ship, and they thought the *Massachusetts* a beauty. So Shaw and Randall duly sold it to the Dutch for sixty-five thousand dollars. Given that the *Massachusetts* cost roughly forty thousand dollars to build, and that Shaw and Randall had to pay five thousand dollars in port fees before handing it over to the Dutch, this deal, while profitable, was much less than what they could have expected to earn had things gone according to plan. The men of the *Massachusetts* disbanded and went in many directions, some staying in China—as did Shaw and Delano—while others sailed back home on American ships or became crewmen on Dutch or English ships.[16]

THE *MASSACHUSETTS* DEBACLE notwithstanding, America's China fleet began to flood the states with exotic goods. The dining rooms, parlors, and bedrooms of well-appointed houses contained porcelain, furniture, silk, paintings, wallpaper, and curiosities from the Middle

PART OF THE TEA SERVICE BROUGHT BACK FROM CHINA BY
REUBEN JOY OF NANTUCKET, CIRCA 1800. THE DECORATION ON
THIS TEA SET IS DERIVED FROM THE EAGLE DESIGN ON
THE MASSACHUSETTS COPPER CENT, FIRST MINTED IN 1787.

Kingdom. By one estimate as much as one-tenth to one-fifth of all the items in many early nineteenth-century homes in Boston and Salem came from China. And these objects were often spectacular. According to the art historian H. A. Crosby Forbes: "The artisan community of Canton, with its porcelain and enamel painters, its painters of oils and watercolors, its weavers and embroiderers, its silversmiths and other metal workers, its carvers, gilders, and cabinet makers, produced more goods of consistently high quality and good taste, in greater variety over a longer period of time, than any other artisan community the world has ever known." Tea imports also soared, with Americans consuming an average of 2.5 million pounds of tea annually during the 1790s, a number that shot up nearly 50 percent in the next decade.[17]

The most intriguing Chinese imports were the reproductions. For a small fee Chinese painters in Canton would copy any image that the foreigners provided (they would also create unique paintings of Chinese scenes). Many famous American paintings, engravings, and prints were thus duplicated and brought back to the United States, and among the more popular were representations of Lady Liberty, John Paul Jones, the landing of the Pilgrims, and the Battle of Lexington. The most popular subject, however, was George Washington, and the most desirable image of the great man was the one by Gilbert Stuart, called "the Athenaeum" portrait, of which there were multiple versions (it is also the model for the engraving of Washington that appears on the one-dollar bill). When Chinese copies of this portrait began to arrive in America, Stuart was infuriated. The people who had purchased one of the originals from him had signed an agreement stating that they would not allow it to be copied, yet here was proof that the agreements were being flouted. One customer in particular, a captain John E. Swords of Philadelphia, was a major offender, purportedly placing orders in Canton for one hundred copies of the portrait to be done as reverse paintings on glass. Stuart sued Swords in court, and the judge ordered the captain to stop. How many copies of Stuart's Washington portrait ultimately made their way to the United

States is unknown, but however many there were, they were joined by many other Chinese paintings that hung on the walls of some of America's finest homes.[18]

AMERICA'S CHINA TRADE benefited greatly from turmoil in Europe. The outbreak of the French Revolution in 1789, and the subsequent rise of Napoleon Bonaparte, mired Europe in what have been collectively labeled the "French wars," which lasted (with only one minor interruption) from 1792 until 1815.[19] With all the major European nations engulfed in years of vicious fighting, the oceans too became a battlefield, making it nearly impossible for many of the antagonists to import goods on their own ships. This created an opportunity for the United States to fill the void. "From the state of European warfare," observed a representative of the British East India Company, "the Americans, being a neutral nation, have derived great advantages; they have had access to countries from whence the English were shut out, where they disposed of considerable quantities of the commodities of India and China,"[20] A little more blunt and understandably gloating about America's fortuitous situation, Boston's *Columbia Centinel* crowed in May 1795, "The wars of Europe . . . rain riches upon us; and it is as much as we can do to find the dishes to catch the golden shower." Consequently, during the "French wars" a significant percentage of what the United States imported from China was promptly exported to European ports.[21]

The key to sustaining the China trade was ensuring that American ships carried goods that the Chinese desired. Silver was always welcome in Canton, but since coinage or specie was a limited commodity in the early years of the Republic, merchants often had difficulty gathering enough of the precious currency for their ships. The market for ginseng, although considerable, was not boundless, and when too much arrived in Canton, the price plummeted, making it an unsteady anchor for a vibrant trade. Thus, from the outset, American merchants were forced to confront the same question that other countries had faced for centuries: What else does China want? The Americans answered this question in large part by adding sealskins, sea otter furs, and sandalwood to their cargoes.

AMERICA'S FORAY INTO the sealskin trade began with an educated guess. William Rotch, a member of a famed Nantucket whaling family, was in London in 1785 when he read Captain Cook's recently published journals. The description of sea otter furs selling in Canton for tremendous prices got Rotch thinking about the seals his family's ships had encountered in pursuit of whales during earlier voyages to the Falkland Islands. Perhaps sealskins too would command a good price. Rotch's brother, Francis, took up the idea and sent the *United States* to the Falklands in 1786, where Capt. Benjamin Hussey gathered thirteen thousand sealskins, as well as ninety tons of whale oil. Before leaving the islands Hussey was approached by Nathaniel Portlock, a British captain who was en route to the Pacific Northwest to

FUR SEALS IN ALASKA.

SEALERS CLUBBING SEALS ON BEAUCHENE ISLAND, THE
SOUTHERNMOST OF THE FALKLAND ISLANDS.

trade for sea otter pelts. Portlock had been on one of Cook's ships, so he knew of the incredible demand for furs in China. Thinking that "there was a great probability" that the sealskins would sell well in Canton, Portlock offered to buy them from Hussey, but Hussey declined, stating that he intended to take the skins to China himself. Hussey never made it that far. The skins were sold in New York for fifty cents apiece, and were ultimately delivered to Canton onboard the New York ship *Eleanora*, captained by Simon Metcalfe, where they sold for ten times that amount.[22]

The Americans, however, weren't the first to bring sealskins to China. Decades before the *Eleanora* sailed up the Pearl River, the Russians had engaged in this trade. But the Americans were particularly good at sealing, as well as very determined. Over the next few decades they dominated the trade, as scores if not hundreds of ships left ports in the eastern United States and spanned the world in search of their quarry. And not just any seals, but fur seals, the generic name applied to a number of species to distinguish them from the so-called hair seals, including sea lions, whose pelts were not so plush and therefore less desirable.

The ships traveled to islands where fur seals congregated, and then the killing began. What happened after the crewmen went ashore depended on whether sealers had ever been to the island before. As James Fenimore Cooper relates in his classic *The Sea Lions; or, The Lost Sealers*, if it was a newly discovered "sealing-island," the seals would not yet be fearful of humans. Thus "a man might walk in their midst without giving the smallest alarm." All the men would have to do to kill the seals, therefore, is approach and hit them over the head with a wooden club. "It would be," Cooper observed, "like picking up dollars on a sea-beach."[23]

If sealers had already visited the island, however, then the men used a different strategy. First they positioned themselves between the seals and the water. Sensing danger, the seals would huddle together, barking wildly, as the men advanced. Some crews would then rush in, wooden clubs at the ready, giving the seals a blow to the head. Other crews would form a lane with men on either side, then drive the seals through this bloody gauntlet, clubbing them as they fled toward the water. Although seals were usually easily killed, there were a few instances in which they fought back, sometimes biting their attackers or knocking them off rock ledges to their deaths.

The dead seals were skinned, any blubber, meat, and sinew being scraped off with a so-called beaming knife. Although this was a laborious process, one veteran sealer claimed that he knew a man who could skin an almost unbelievable sixty fur seals in an hour. Next the skin was rinsed in saltwater before being stretched on wooden pegs and left to dry. The now-rigid skins were stacked in a pile for a few days, during which time they would "sweat," requiring them occasionally to be separated to air them out. After that the skins were stored on the islands or stowed in the ship's hold, where they could keep for years.[24]

As the killing crews swarmed the islands in search of the lumbering and largely defenseless prey, the mother ship anchored nearby or left the men behind to hunt until it returned to pick them up along with their precious cargo. Those who remained lived in caves or built huts. To pass the time when they weren't sealing they drank, gambled, told tall tales, gardened, and occasionally even read books. The wait could be months or years, and if the ship was wrecked it didn't return at all, leaving the men stranded until another ship arrived with a sympathetic captain who was willing to transport them off the island.

A few sealers became nearly permanent fixtures on the islands. Some were deserters and others had been kicked off their ships. These "alone men," or "lopers," as they came to be known, often found island life to their liking. To get by they would kill seals and sell the skins to visiting ships. William Moulton, who had become an alone man on Más Afuera (Alejandro Selkirk), off the coast of Chile, after quarreling with the captain of the New London ship *Onico*, built himself a hut and developed his own style of dealing with the outside world. "I resolved," he wrote in his journal, "to avoid insolent and ill-bred contradictions, and dogmatical abruptness from sailor officers, by a well-timed civility, and by evading any particular intimacy." Another alone man on the same island, known as "Hermit Bill," chose to live in a cave, and seemed to subsist on rum and bread, given him in exchange for skins. One visitor said that Hermit Bill was happier than he ever had been because "there is no larboard watch, no reefing topsails, nobody to quarrel with, and he sleeps when he pleases and works when he pleases."[25]

On trips averaging two to three years' duration, sealers scoured islands in the Pacific, the South Atlantic, and the Indian Ocean. While many ships pursued only seals, a significant number were dual-use operations that hunted for whales as well. This was an understandable and efficient combination, since many whalemen routinely chased their quarry in regions where fur seals were plentiful, and the added value of those pelts could be the difference between the success and failure of a voyage, especially when the whaling was poor and the hold contained but a small amount of oil and baleen.

The scope of carnage was almost beyond belief. American ships brought 2.5 million sealskins to Canton between 1792 and 1812, according to one estimate, and others claim that the number was considerably higher. The skins sold for anywhere from thirty-five cents to five dollars apiece. High-quality skins were used to make capes, belts, mittens, and caps, whereas poor-quality skins were shorn and the hides tanned into leather, while the loose fur was made into felt. The profits were often considerable, as was the case for the *Betsey*, a ninety-ton sealing ship, which sailed from New York to the South Pacific in 1797 and returned twenty-three months later with $120,467 worth of China goods. After deducting the cost of the venture, the owners cleared $53,118. "The depots of peltry" the Americans found on their sealing journeys gave "them in return," wrote a French observer in the late eighteenth century, "both teas of which habit has made a want to which perhaps they owe their liberty," as well as the luxuries of the Orient.[26]

The most valuable peltry of all, however, was the one that enveloped the sea otter. Plusher, softer, thicker than any other fur traded at the time, the sea otter's pelt was what the Chinese wanted most. It was

A 1799 ENGRAVING
OF A CHINESE FURRIER
HAWKING HIS WARES
IN CANTON, CHINA.

the eagerness of the Chinese to pay handsomely to satisfy that desire that led American sailors to aggressively pursue the sea otter trade.

NOT LONG AFTER the *Empress of China* left for Canton, John Ledyard departed America for Europe hoping to find backers to fund a voyage to the Pacific Northwest. Ledyard still harbored deep resentment over his treatment in his homeland, and after hearing that the Russians and the British were sending ships to the Pacific Northwest to trade for sea otters, Ledyard vented to a relative: "You see the business deserves the attention I have endeavored, and am still striving to give it; and had Morris not shrunk behind a trifling obstruction, I should have been happy, and America would this moment be triumphantly displaying her flag in the most remote and beneficial regions of commerce. I am tired of my vexations." But Ledyard had no more luck abroad than he did in the United States. A French-sponsored expedition fell through, as did one supported by the Revolutionary War hero John Paul Jones, then living in Paris. With this final rejection, Ledyard wrote to his cousin Isaac, "Upon the whole I may venture to say that my enterprise with Paul Jones is no more—that I shall inter this hobby at Paris."[27]

As it turned out, Ledyard was just a little ahead of his time. In 1787 a group of Boston merchants who were familiar with Ledyard's book as well as Cook's journals decided to enter the sea otter trade with China. They pooled their resources to outfit the *Columbia Rediviva* and the *Lady Washington*, and sent them to the Pacific Northwest for furs. The *Columbia*, as it came to be called, returned; the *Lady Washington* didn't. Although the *Columbia*, captained by Robert Gray, barely made a profit, it did become the first American ship to visit the Pacific Northwest and Hawaii, as well as the first to circumnavigate the globe. When the *Columbia* arrived back in Boston in 1790 it inaugurated what the author David Lavender called "the famous three-cornered trade of the Yankees: Massachusetts gimcracks to the Northwest; Northwestern furs to Canton; and Chinese goods on around the world to Boston."[28]

The Russians, the British, the Spaniards, and the Japanese preceded the Americans in the sea otter trade. But many of the American ships that followed in the *Columbia*'s wake profited handsomely, and the sea otter trade with the local Indians blossomed to the point that by the early 1800s it was, in the words of the historian Mary Malloy, "an American specialty, almost an American monopoly." Of all the American ports that pursued that trade, none sent more ships than Boston, which nearly cornered the market. That is why, observed William Sturgis, one of America's leading sea otter traders, "the Indians [of the Pacific Northwest] had the impression that Boston was our whole country. Had any one spoken to them of *American* ships, or *American* people, he would not have been understood. We were only known as *Boston* ships, and *Boston* people."[29]

The northwest coast was not the only place where Americans sought sea otters. About a decade after the *Columbia* tapped the region's furs, American ships began arriving off the coast of Alta California, part of New Spain. Disregarding Spanish warnings not to trade along the coast, the Americans obtained pelts from local Indians, becoming the first of their countrymen to set foot on land that would one day become the state of California. In 1803 another wrinkle was added to this branch of the trade, when Americans teamed with Russian fur traders to launch a new business. The Russians in Alaska had long viciously abused the natives of the Aleutian and Kodiak islands, as well as the Cook Inlet area, forcing them to hunt for sea otters. Now the Russians sent hundreds of these natives on American ships to Southern California, and the pelts they gathered were divided between the Americans and Russians, and sold in China. This lucrative partnership lasted about ten years.

The Alaskan natives pursued sea otters off the coast of California in one- to three-person, skin-covered kayaks called *baidarkas,* which were twelve to twenty-one feet long, and less than two feet wide. In this highly maneuverable, shallow-draft watercraft, the natives could stealthily approach sea otters sleeping among fronds of kelp floating at the surface, and hurl a bone- or shell-tipped spear into the animals'

ALEUTIAN IN *BAIDARKA*, OFF ST. PAUL,
PRIBILOF ISLANDS, ALASKA.

flanks, or even club them to death. If the otters were awake, the hunters would form a broad circle around the spot where the otter was
last seen, and wait for it to resurface. As soon as it did, one of the
baidarkas would rush forward, while the other hunters yelled, the
goal being to force the sea otter to dive before it could catch a good
breath. The circle would grow ever smaller as the procedure was
repeated until the increasingly tired otter was so close that that one of
the men was able to kill it. On occasion the natives also used nets to
snare the otters, and guns to shoot them.[30]

Hundreds of thousands of sea otter skins were funneled from
the Pacific Northwest and California to Canton. But the astounding
sums that Cook's men had obtained for their sea otter pelts were not
sustained, because as more pelts entered the market, prices dropped.
The pelts remained quite valuable, however, selling mostly in the
range of twenty to thirty dollars apiece, fueling profits that often
exceeded 300 percent of the cost of the voyage, and once rose as high

as 2,200 percent. "The lucrative traffic in which the rich furs of north-western America were exchanged for the dollars of Canton," observed a nineteenth-century writer, "may be compared to the collection of stream gold, yielding an unalloyed gem with the exertion of very little labor or skill, as long as the deposit lasts."[31]

American sea otter traders made a point of stopping in Hawaii on their journeys across the Pacific to rest, gather supplies, hire natives to work on the ships, and enjoy the seductive charms of island life, not the least of which were the sexual favors freely offered by native women. There on this beautiful chain of islands, a paradise, really, sitting like iridescent jewels in the midst of the vast Pacific, the Americans found something else that they could trade with the Chinese—sandalwood.[32]

THERE ARE MANY SPECIES of the sandalwood tree (*Santalum* spp.), which can be found along an arc from the islands of the South Pacific to India. At first glance there is nothing to indicate why these trees were commercially desirable. They are not particularly large, usually topping out at around thirty feet, and the small fruits they produce are generally not pleasing to the palate. But some species of sandalwood have a secret within: Their heartwood and roots contain a fragrant oil that makes the fine grained, yellowish brown wood prized in China, where it was, and still is, carved into exquisite, aromatic furniture, and used to make sweet-smelling incense that is burned in houses of worship.

Long before the Americans arrived in Canton, the Chinese used sandalwood from India and Malaysia. Although Hawaiian sandalwood—called *iliahi* by the natives, and used to make a stringed instrument called the *ukeke*, and ground into a powdery perfume for clothes—is of lesser quality, it smelled good enough to entice the Chinese. It is not clear who was the first American to bring Hawaiian sandalwood to China, but the trade began in the early 1790s, and by the eve of the War of 1812 as many as a dozen sea otter traders a year

FLOWERS (AND IN ONE CASE, LEAVES AND FRUITS) OF
THREE SPECIES OF SANDALWOOD.

were stopping at the Hawaiian Islands to top off their cargo with a load of the freshly cut wood. A little more than ten years after the Americans initiated the Hawaiian trade, they added to their supply chain by obtaining sandalwood in the Fiji Islands.

Oliver Slater first alerted the Western world to Fiji's sandalwood groves. Around 1800 he was a crewman on the American schooner *Argo*, which was on its way to an English penal colony in Australia when it foundered on a reef about eleven miles from the Fijian island of Lakeba. Slater lived for two years in Fiji before a ship from Australia picked him up. But no sooner was he onboard than the crew mutinied and headed for China. While in Fiji, Slater made note of the sandalwood trees, and once in Canton, and then later when he went to Australia, he told others about his discovery. Soon ships from

America, Australia, and England sailed to Fiji—dubbed the Sandalwood Islands—to get their cut of the fragrant bounty.

In Hawaii and Fiji, as well as other locales where the sandalwood trade spread, including Tonga, the Society Islands, and Samoa, American success depended on the natives. The islands' kings or chiefs controlled the forests, and the Americans had to gain their consent before obtaining the wood, making the first order of business establishing a relationship with the rulers. This was done by exchanging gifts and reaching agreements that laid out how much and under what conditions the sandalwood could be cut. Sperm whale teeth were the most coveted item, which the traders obtained by bartering with American whalemen who ranged throughout the Pacific in search of the mighty leviathans of the deep. The massive teeth, some weighing more than two pounds, were considered sacred and used in dowries and to cement alliances; it was also thought that the teeth made the wearer invincible in battle. Almost as much in demand as the real thing were imitation sperm whale teeth fashioned from elephant tusks. Trinkets such as cloth, mirrors, axes, glass bottles, and nails were also highly valued.

Some relationships were forged in a very personal manner. A Mr. Brown, the first mate on the *Hope* out of New York, lived for a while on Vanua Levu in 1807, and learned the language well enough to converse without the assistance of an interpreter. The local chief grew so enamored of his curious and agreeable guest that he adopted him as a son, and the friendship that arose between the two helped the *Hope*'s captain broker a deal for sandalwood. Upon leaving the island, Brown vowed that he would return on another ship, and he did, in December 1808, on the *Tonquin*, also out of New York. When the king boarded the *Tonquin*, a heartfelt reunion ensued, recorded by Edmund Fanning, the ship's captain. "The King instantly encircled [Brown] in his arms, as if a child, when one minute passed, and another, and yet another—His Majesty seemingly too much absorbed by his feelings to be willing to slack up his embrace—with the continued expressions, 'My son! my son!' The large, pearly drops rolled down his cheeks, and he was, to all appearance, quite overjoyed, and affectionately unmanned in again meeting with his adopted son! This scene seemed, apparently, not only to petrify our officers and men, as they gazed on it, but also the natives, fixing them, like statues, on the deck."

Once the gifts were exchanged and the agreements signed, the Americans relied on the natives to do the work. A large gang of the king's choosing marched up the mountainside, along with men from the ship to supervise the operations. The largest trees were selected, then cut with a crosscut saw rather than an ax, to avoid creating chips, which were no more than wasted wood. According to one American sandalwood trader, cutting down the tree was "a highly favorite part of the work, and was frequently severely disputed for between the natives, owing to the exquisite and delightful music to them, in the ringing of the saw." After the tree was felled, the top lopped off, the limbs trimmed, and the roots dug out, the wood was shaved down until only the oil-saturated heartwood remained. Though it took many days of grueling work before enough of a load was gathered to transport down the mountain to the waiting ship, the returns were usually quite impressive. For example, in 1812 the captain of the *Hunter*, out of Boston, bought a few hundred tons of Fijian sandalwood for eight hundred dollars, which sold for eighty thousand dollars in Canton—a profit that led a newspaper in Newburyport, Massachusetts, to declare, "This is making money with a witness!" But all the work could be for naught unless the correct trees were cut. One of the earliest American cargoes of sandalwood from Hawaii was all of the wrong species, with little of the precious oil that the Chinese demanded, and accordingly it garnered a pittance in Canton.[33]

THE FUR SEAL, SEA OTTER, AND SANDALWOOD trades resulted in what the twentieth-century ecologist Garrett Hardin called "the tragedy of the commons." In each case strong demand, limited supply, greed, and a lack of regulation inevitably left a path of destruction as those shared natural resources—the "commons"—were decimated by individuals acting in their own self-interest, while disregarding the long-term implications of their actions. Rookery after rookery of fur seals was ravaged, as scores of ships were filled with thousands, often tens of thousands of skins, year after year. By the early 1800s the sealers themselves began reporting that their prey were becoming scarce, and in some areas had completely disappeared. It was the same story for sea otters, whose numbers weren't large to begin with. As for sandalwood, the verdant hillsides of Hawaii and Fiji were quickly transformed into an ecological wasteland, denuded of much of their forests and littered with mangled branches and stumps. The fur seal, sea otter, and sandalwood trades would persist for many more years, as traders tried to wring as much profit from nature as possible, but the trajectory was clear.[34]

There was yet another natural resource that America's China traders relied on to round out their cargoes, one that didn't suffer from the inevitability of the tragedy of the commons. In the fields of Turkey poppies were cultivated, and from their oozing seed capsules came opium that the Americans took to Canton. Here, too, the Americans were not the first in the trade. They were following a path blazed most energetically by the British.

THROUGHOUT MUCH OF the eighteenth century the British East India Company had very few ways of paying for the growing quantities of tea necessary to slake the thirst of the British population, as well as the much smaller amounts of silk, porcelain, and other Chinese goods that Britons demanded. The primary British imports that the Chinese wanted were woolens, cotton fabrics, lead, and tin, but in amounts that covered only a small fraction of the company's purchases in Canton. Into the breach, therefore, flowed an enormous river of silver, what the Chinese valued most. This drain of silver strained the company's financial reserves and created an expanding and, to the British government, worrying trade deficit between Britain and

China, especially since it was often difficult to gather enough silver to meet demand due to contractions in international supplies. One solution to this problem was getting the Chinese more interested in accepting British manufactures in place of silver. That in part is why the British government sent Lord George Macartney to China in 1792, as the head of a massive trade mission to the emperor Qianlong (Ch'ien-lung, r. 1736–96).[35]*

The mission failed abysmally, and one of the main messages the emperor sent back to King George III was, basically: You've got nothing we want. "I set no value on objects strange or ingenious," the emperor solemnly intoned,

> and have no use for your country's manufactures. . . . Our Celestial Empire possesses all things in prolific abundance and lacks no product within its own borders. There was therefore no need to import the manufactures of outside barbarians in exchange for our own produce. But as the tea, silk and porcelain which the Celestial Empire produces are absolute necessities to European nations and to yourselves, we have permitted, as a signal mark of favor, that foreign *hongs* should be established at Canton, so that your wants might be supplied and your country thus participate in our beneficence.[36]

Although China was a highly advanced country, with a diversified economy, the emperor's arrogant claim of China's self-sufficiency was not true. The Chinese, for example, imported many staple products, such as rice, pepper, wood, and copper, from countries in Southeast Asia, as well as other goods from around the world.[37] The problem for Britain, however, was that China indeed needed very few of the products the British could provide, making it difficult to replace silver

---

* Generating interest in British products was only one of the mission's goals. Others included establishing a British diplomatic presence in Peking, and opening more Chinese ports to British merchants.

as the import of choice. But there was something else in addition to silver that the Chinese desired, and that was opium, which proved to be the perfect commodity for the British East India Company. "For nearly three centuries," wrote the anthropologist Marshall Sahlins, "China was the tomb of European silver—from which none ever returned."[38] Opium, however, provided the company with the key to opening the tomb and possibly reversing the flow of the precious metal. Since the Chinese paid for the drug with silver, the more opium the company sold, the more silver it earned. And if sales of the drug generated a greater amount of silver than was required to purchase Chinese goods, then the British could ship the surplus silver back home. In other words, selling enough opium to the Chinese would enable the company, and therefore Britain, to stanch the stream of silver into China, and better balance its books.

Obtaining opium was not a problem since by the late 1700s the British East India Company monopolized the production and sale of it in northeastern India (Bengal), one of the most productive opium-growing regions on the subcontinent. The opium trade, however, was not without obstacles. Although the imperial edict of 1729 didn't ban the importation of opium, the British viewed it as a de facto prohibition, in large part because many Chinese officials viewed it that way, as did most of the hong merchants with whom the British dealt. In fact, in private communications at the time, company officials made it clear that they believed that if a British ship were even caught carrying the drug, the ship and its cargo would be seized on orders of the emperor. Therefore, in the company's estimation, to engage in the opium trade was to deal in contraband, which it was hesitant to do, for fear of possibly upsetting the emperor and threatening the all-important tea trade. Nevertheless the company wanted to profit from the increasingly lucrative opium trade. So, according to the historian Michael Greenberg, the company "perfected the technique of growing opium in India and disowning it in China" as a way of appearing to wash its hands of the opium trade without actually doing so.[39] Rather than send the opium to China in company ships, the company sold its opium at auctions in Calcutta (modern Kolkata) to so-called country traders, who were mainly private British merchants licensed by the company to traffic opium between India and China. Company officials claimed it was the private country traders, not the company, who were responsible for all the Indian opium making its way to China. That the company was licensing the traders, profiting from the auctions, and that the auctions wouldn't exist but for the trade, was beside the point.

Once the country traders reached Chinese waters they could not simply bring the illicit opium to Canton to sell; instead it had to be smuggled in. The traders sailed to anchorages off Macao and Whampoa, where their ships would be met by smugglers who paid cash for the opium, which was then lowered down onto their boats and taken

OPIUM BALLS IN THE DRYING ROOM OF AN OPIUM FACTORY IN INDIA, CIRCA 1850.

to the mainland for distribution and sale. Smuggling was widespread, and a big part of the reason why it worked so well was that a significant number of Chinese officials—who often smoked opium themselves—were complicit, bribery becoming endemic to the system. Those bribes came not only from smugglers, but also from the traders themselves, who referred to the payoffs as "tea money."

This system did not solve the company's cash flow problem, because most of the silver resulting from the sales of opium in Canton went to the country traders (some of it did come back to the company when the traders purchased opium at the auctions). So the company devised a simple mechanism for getting more of the traders' silver into its own hands. In exchange for the silver the company's treasury office in Canton gave the traders banknotes or bills redeemable for cash in Calcutta or London. Thus, the traders got paid, and the company got the silver it so desperately needed to pay for Chinese goods. And business was good: By 1800 more than three thousand chests of British opium were imported into China.* Since opium was such a high-value item, selling for nearly six hundred Spanish dollars per chest that year, it generated large quantities of silver—but not yet enough to cover the company's purchases in Canton.[40]

The escalating imports of opium greatly disturbed Emperor Qianlong and his son and successor, Emperor Jiaqing (Chia-ch'ing, r. 1796–1820), since increased opium consumption led to more addiction, which degraded the physical and moral character of the people. Emperor Jiaqing fought back, issuing edicts banning the importation of opium: "The pernicious effects arising from the use of opium were formerly confined to" a couple of provinces, he proclaimed in 1799, "but have spread in the course of time through the other

---

* There are no truly "accurate" numbers for the amount of opium imported into China, especially during the early years of the China trade. The same goes for the price per chest of opium. This is in part because the trade was, after all, a smuggling trade, which worked against responsible bookkeeping and in favor of secrecy. Also, the numbers are often drawn from different sources that used varied methods of collecting data.

provinces of the empire." As a result addiction intensified, worrying the emperor, who claimed that addicts stayed up all night and spent that time "in the gratification of impure and sensual desires, whereby their respective duties and occupations are neglected." Furthermore he maintained that opium use created hunger pangs, forcing addicts to spend more on food. Since many of them didn't have enough money to satisfy their hunger, they would "in the course of a few years [become] wholly dilapidated and wasted away." The "infirm and weak [would] perish gradually from want and hunger, while the strong and vigorous [would] become thieves and robbers, the ultimate ruin of all being thus equally certain and inevitable." Thus it was, the emperor concluded, "that foreigners by the means of a vile and excrementitious [sic] substance, derive from this empire the most solid profits and advantages, but that our countrymen should blindly pursue this destructive and ensnaring vice, even till death . . . is indeed a fact, odious and deplorable in the highest degree." To stop the flow of opium, which the Chinese called "foreign mud," the edict forbade foreigners from bringing opium into China, warned smugglers that they would be discovered and punished, and put officials on notice that if they took any bribes to allow opium to enter the Middle Kingdom, they too would be held to account.[41]

Words are not actions, and the edict had virtually no effect because it was not enforced—the smuggling continued much as it had before. There was one significant change, however. As the demand for opium increased, and the supplies remained fairly steady, the price of the drug rose. Between 1805 and 1809, while the number of opium chests imported hovered around four thousand, the price per chest stayed for the most part above one thousand Spanish dollars. It was during this period—in 1806, to be exact, according to one source—that, for the first time, the amount of silver generated by opium sales, added to the bartering power of other goods that the company traded, exceeded the cost of Chinese goods purchased. Now Britain no longer had to send silver to China. Instead silver was flowing in the other direction, creating the first-ever trade deficit for the Middle Kingdom, which would only grow in subsequent years. The tomb had finally opened.[42]

Given its financial ambitions, the company cared little about Chinese prohibitions or the damage opium might be causing the Chinese people; instead it focused solely on the bottom line: As long as the silver kept flowing out, the British were happy to keep sending opium in. The governing rationale was, as the historian John K. Fairbank observed, that "the Chinese would have to look out for themselves; and if they would persist in buying and smuggling opium, that was their problem, not the foreigners'"—a convenient yet morally bankrupt position that the Americans also adopted.[43]

When Shaw went to Canton on the *Empress of China*, he made note of the opium trade, and later told some American merchants that there was a "good market" for the drug in China, and that it could be "smuggled with the utmost security," earning the seller a "handsome profit."[44] In the near term, few if any Americans pursued this avenue for profits. Although there is some evidence that at least one American ship brought opium to China as early as 1788, consistent American involvement in the trade didn't begin until 1804, when Philadelphia merchants started trafficking in the drug. The opium they shipped to Canton, however, did not come from India but from Turkey, purchased at the port of Smyrna (modern Izmir), on the Aegean Sea. The Turkish opium was not as highly esteemed in China as the Indian, but it was good enough to sell, and was often mixed with the Indian drug to make it go further. Before long, merchants from other American cities, including Baltimore, Boston, and Salem, entered the nineteenth-century drug trade. The Americans had no qualms about dealing in opium, viewing it just as they would any other business proposition. "I am very much in favor of investing heavily in opium," Girard wrote early in 1805. "While the war [the French wars] lasts, opium will support a good price in China." Like the British, the Americans coordinated their efforts with smugglers, and used the silver received to purchase goods. The Americans, however, were relatively minor players in this branch of the trade. While each year the British sent thousands of chests of opium, earning millions of dollars, the Americans sent at most a few hundred, realizing annual sales on the order of one to two hundred thousand dollars.[45]

THE AMERICAN TRADE in fur seal skins, sea otter pelts, sandalwood, and opium, although profitable, did not generate enough income to come close to covering the costs of Chinese goods purchased in Canton. Even after other items that Americans brought to China to trade—including ginseng, cotton, shark fins, and bird's nest (the last two used to make soup)—were added, it still was not enough to pay the bills. To close the gap the Americans, as the British had done, relied on specie. Hence, during the first three decades of America's China trade, silver coins paid for roughly 65 to 70 percent of America's imports from Canton. And virtually all those coins were Spanish dollars, which continued to be legal tender in the United States until 1857. Thus it was that from the very start of the United States' commercial relationship with China, there was a hefty trade deficit. In other words, America imported a far greater value of goods from China than it exported in return.[46]

The route ships took to Canton varied considerably. Many sailed straight for China with only silver or goods onboard, but more took a circuitous route, heading to various locales (in the tradition of true Yankee peddlers), turning over their cargo multiple times in the hope of arriving with a mix of items that would excite the interest of the hong merchants. Some sailed to the Pacific Northwest or islands in the Pacific or the Atlantic to gather furs and sandalwood, others went to ports in South America and Europe, to exchange goods for silver, while still others visited Caribbean, Middle Eastern, African, and Asian ports to barter. An excellent example of the roving nature of the trade is provided by the *General Washington*, a ship owned by John Brown, the Providence merchant, that sailed in 1787, loaded with a motley cargo—everything from anchors, cannon shot, and bar iron; ginseng, tar, and spermaceti candles; to Jamaica spirits, sailcloth, and

New England rum—valued at fifty-seven thousand dollars. On the way to China the ship stopped in Madeira, where it sold most of its cargo for wine, and then went on to Pondicherry, in India, where the wine was traded for cotton. That cotton, in turn, was exchanged in Canton for one hundred thousand dollars' worth of Chinese goods. The ultimate profits for the *General Washington* were twenty thousand dollars—a return of 30 percent.[47]

NO MATTER WHAT American ships brought to Canton or how they got there, a China voyage was fraught with many dangers. The first obstacle was getting there at all. More than a few ships were lost at sea and never heard from again, succumbing to the wrath of a mighty tempest or some other terrible calamity. Others foundered on unseen reefs or sandbars, a problem exacerbated by the fact that for many of the places the traders went there were no maps to guide them. There were also many violent and often deadly human encounters along the way, the best known of which was the case of the *Tonquin*, one of Astor's ships, which got into trouble trading with Indians in Clayoquot Sound on the coast of Vancouver Island in the summer of 1811.

The *Tonquin*'s imperious captain, Jonathan Thorn, took umbrage at the price a local chief demanded for his furs, and instead of bargaining or simply saying no, Thorn slapped the chief across the face with a rolled-up sea otter pelt. That precipitated a series of actions in which the Indians killed all the men onboard, save for six. One, an Indian interpreter, took refuge with the local tribesmen, while four others took to one of the ship's boats, attempting to escape, but were tracked down and killed. The last man, who had been mortally wounded in the Indian attack, crawled to the hold of the ship, where he lit the nine tons of gunpowder, blowing up the ship and the two hundred Indians who had climbed aboard to claim their prize.[48]

A little more than two decades before the *Tonquin* blew up, a tragic series of events of almost operatic proportions played out in Hawaii. After delivering Francis Rotch's cargo of sealskins to Canton in 1788,

Capt. Simon Metcalfe sailed the *Eleanora* to the Pacific Northwest to gather more furs, and on his way back to Canton stopped at the Hawaiian island of Maui, anchoring off Honuaula in late February 1790. One night two natives from Olowalu, a village to the west of Honuaula, stole one of the *Eleanora*'s boats. A crewman asleep in the boat was killed before he could cry out. On the beach the natives pried the boat apart, taking all the iron nails, then returned home.

The next morning Metcalfe and his men stormed ashore, killing a native and capturing two others, one of whom identified the real thieves. Metcalfe sailed to Olowalu and offered a handsome reward for information on the crewman and the boat. The natives delivered a few of the sailor's bones, and Metcalfe, appearing to be in a forgiving mood, told them the reward would be theirs, and then invited them to the ship to trade. When a considerable number of canoes had arrived, Metcalfe ordered them to the starboard side of the ship, and as soon as the expectant crowd of natives assembled there, his men fired the cannon, which had been filled with nails and musket balls for maximum damage. The thunderous blasts killed one hundred natives instantly, and wounded many more. "The natives dragged for their bodies with fish-hooks," said one account, "and collected the mangled masses upon the beach, where, to use their own expression, 'their brains flowed out of their broken skulls.' "

Satisfied, Metcalfe sailed for the big island of Hawaii, anchoring in Kealakekua Bay, where Captain Cook had been killed. While Metcalfe's men gathered a load of sandalwood, his eighteen-year-old son Thomas sailed the *Fair American*, a twenty-six-ton tender, into Kawaihae Bay, about forty-five miles to the northeast. Neither Metcalfe knew that the other was there, because they had been separated in a storm after leaving Canton together in the fall of 1788.

Thomas couldn't have chosen a worse place to stop: A few weeks earlier, the elder Metcalfe had flogged the local chief, Kameeiamoku, for some minor transgression, so the chief was very angry. He and his retinue boarded the *Fair American*, bearing presents, and suddenly attacked the six Americans. Kameeiamoku grabbed Thomas Metcalfe and threw him into the water, where others beat him to death with canoe paddles. Four of the crew were slain, the fifth was taken captive, and the ship was run aground and looted.

Word of the massacre soon arrived at Kealakekua Bay, where the mighty chief Kamehameha, fearing the response of the elder Metcalfe, forbade anyone from leaving the island. Unfortunately John Young, the *Eleanora*'s boatswain, was onshore at the time and couldn't get back to the ship. Metcalfe fired the ship's guns intermittently to summon the boatswain, but after two days he gave up. Metcalfe sailed for Canton, unaware that his son had been killed, or that his own actions had played a role in his death.[49]

In addition to these two rather dramatic examples, there were scores, if not hundreds, of other outbreaks of hostilities involving the China trade during the late 1700s and early 1800s, many of which occurred in Fiji, where battles over the control of the increasingly scarce sandalwood led to bloodshed, resulting not only from clashes between natives and traders, but also among the natives themselves.

Perhaps the most violent place that the China trade was pursued was in the Pacific Northwest, where Indians routinely stole from visiting ships. As the historian James R. Gibson notes, the Indians viewed "the vessels in their waters" as "drift liable to salvage, and they regarded the Euroamericans' cutting of wood and drawing of water on their shores as theft of their property, as well as trespass on their territory."[50] While the Americans sometimes overlooked Indian thievery, they also often responded swiftly and without mercy, as was the case with the *Jefferson* in 1794. In retaliation for the theft of a canoe and rope, crewmen swooped into an Indian village in Clayoquot Sound on the west coast of Vancouver Island, retrieved the items, then killed a couple of Indians, injured more, destroyed houses, and stole a few canoes.

There were other flashpoints as well. When Americans thought that the Indians' prices were too high, some traders set their own prices by holding Indians hostage until their peers paid a ransom, in furs. When the trades seemed to go off without a hitch, problems arose later if the Indians discovered that the Americans had cheated them by placing rope at the bottom of a barrel of gunpowder or watering down a cask of rum or molasses. Indians were also known to cheat the traders by stretching the tails of river otter skins to pass them off as sea otter skins, or by dyeing the skins to achieve the same end.

Given these various transgressions it is no wonder that tensions along the coast were perpetually high, and altercations common. Violence inevitably bred more violence, a point eloquently made by John Jewitt, an English crewman on a fur trader out of Boston, who spent more than two years (1803–5) as a captive after his ship was attacked by Indians and most of its crew slaughtered. "I have no doubt," wrote Jewitt,

> that many of the melancholy disasters [along the Pacific Northwest coast] have principally arisen from the imprudent conduct of some of the captains and crews of the ships employed in this trade, in exasperating [the natives] by insulting, plundering, and even killing them on slight grounds. This, as nothing is more sacred with a savage than their principle of revenge, and no people are more impatient under insult, induces them to wreak their vengeance upon the first vessel or boat's crew that offers, making the innocent too frequently suffer for the wrongs of the guilty.[51]

While both the Americans and the native peoples often acted badly, at times horrifically so, the Americans behaved worse. According to William Sturgis, perhaps the most socially conscious and culturally sensitive of America's China traders, the Indians of the Pacific Northwest were often the "victims of injustice, cruelty, and oppression, and of a policy that seems to recognize *power* as the sole standard of *right*." Another time Sturgis added that the Indians were "more 'sinned against' than 'sinning.'"[52] The same could be said of the Hawaiians and Fijians who were drawn into the orbit of the China trade.

Even when American traders made it safely to China, the danger was not over. Pirates patrolling the South China Sea and the mouth of the Pearl River—as many as seventy thousand of them, manning eight hundred vessels—were an ever-present threat, as the close call of the *Atahualpa* makes clear. Arriving from Boston with three hundred thousand dollars of silver coin on board, it had anchored in the Macao Roads in late August 1809, when one of the passengers alerted Captain Sturgis to the rapid approach of sixteen Chinese junks. Thinking that they might be fishermen, Sturgis ordered a blast across their bows to see whether they changed course. They didn't, and Sturgis prepared to fight.

He was lucky he had the option of fighting at all. The ship's owner, apparently oblivious to the risks of a China venture, had forbidden Sturgis to arm the ship. But Sturgis, a seasoned hand at the China trade, had secretly stowed four cannons onboard. Before firing, though, Sturgis had a barrel of gunpowder brought up from below and placed at his side. Then he lit a cigar and told the men that rather than let the pirates take the ship he would blow it up. With that the battle commenced.

As the ship made a run for the safety of Macao, Sturgis's men fired at their pursuers, who lobbed fireball grenades at the *Atahualpa*, and let out blood-chilling yells. The pirates took high losses, but kept coming. Only when the *Atahualpa* got close to Macao, and the fort trained its cannons on the pirates, did they back down. The pirate leader, Apootsae, was later captured by the Chinese authorities and put to death using the torture of a "thousand cuts."[53]

THE DAMAGE THAT the Americans caused to native peoples went well beyond direct physical violence. Traders spread venereal diseases as well as other illnesses like measles and tuberculosis, which tore through the local populations that had no immunity to these invisible foreign invaders. The introduction of alcohol compromised the natives' health, and generated other problems associated with inebriation.[54] And although there were many instances in which traders shot natives, the guns that the natives acquired often caused more trouble, Fiji being a case in point.

Some American captains, like Edmund Fanning, refused to supply arms to the Fijians, or "children of nature," as he called them, fearing that they would be "the cause of much bloodshed and massacre." Fanning's humanitarian perspective, however, was not shared by all traders, many of whom acquiesced when pressed by local chiefs for guns, the human consequences be damned.[55] The chiefs used the guns in intense internecine warfare to maintain control over the valuable sandalwood forests. While most of these guns were obtained through trade, the Fijians got their first guns from a shipwreck. Capt. Hill Corey of Providence, Rhode Island, was after sandalwood in 1808, when his brig *Eliza* struck a reef off the Fijian island of Narai. Corey and the rest of the men made it to shore, with most of them ultimately leaving Fiji on other trading ships. But Charles Savage stayed behind.

Savage, an appropriately named brutish Swede with a hot temper, was not part of the *Eliza*'s crew but had been picked up on Tonga, where he too had been involved in a shipwreck of an Australian ship out of Port Jackson (Sydney). After the *Eliza* foundered, Savage hatched a plan. He persuaded the chief on the island of Mbau to salvage the ship's guns and ammunition. Next Savage gathered a small fighting force, culled from the ranks of Fiji's beachcombers—the term applied to an odd assortment of shipwrecked sailors, deserters, escapees from Australian penal colonies, and others who lived on the islands. Some beachcombers were innocuous wanderers, accepted and treated well by the Fijians. Others, however, were inveterate troublemakers, like the ones whom Savage recruited.

The firepower salvaged from the *Eliza* transformed Savage, backed by his motley band, into a power broker. He offered his services to the Mbauian chief, who, with Savage's arsenal and men at his side, proceeded to slaughter his way to becoming the supreme power in Fiji. For five years Savage maintained his bloody perch, before being destroyed by his own predisposition to violence. Taking sides in a dispute over sandalwood, Savage was caught off guard by his foes, who disarmed him and held his head under water until he drowned. Then they dismembered his body, roasted and consumed the pieces, and whittled his bones into needles that were used to repair the sails of canoes.[56]

The tragedies that befell the natives due to their involvement in the China trade should be weighed against the positive things that occurred. In exchange for the goods they provided, the natives received many things that they valued, such as beads, cloth, whale's teeth, metal tools, and even Chinese pottery. Still, the trade took far more than it gave. The spread of violence, guns, disease, and alcohol, along with the devastation of their land and their natural resources, was an incalculable price for the natives to pay.

IN ADDITION TO LEAVING behind a wake of damaged cultures and resources, America's early China traders, in at least one case, solved a mystery. In April 1807 the Nantucket captain Mayhew Folger, a well-seasoned sailor and uncle to the famed nineteenth-century Quaker abolitionist Lucretia Mott, left Boston on a sealing cruise onboard the *Topaz*. Since many of the traditional sealing locations had already been stripped, Folger set out to find new islands. Sailing widely through the South Atlantic, and into the South Pacific, he accumulated a paltry six hundred skins. Early in 1808 Folger decided to visit Pitcairn Island, about thirteen hundred miles southeast of Tahiti, to get fresh water and find a few seals.

The British captain Philip Carteret had been the first European to discover Pitcairn in July 1767, but no one had reported seeing it since. Folger arrived off the island on February 6, and saw a plume of smoke rising into the air, which greatly surprised him since Carteret had said that Pitcairn was uninhabited. As Folger approached the shore in whaleboats, three men paddling a canoe came into view. Before they got too close, one of the men yelled to Folger in English, asking him who he was and where he came from. When Folger supplied the information, the man responded, "You are an American; you come from America; where is America? Is it in Ireland?" Thus began one of the most fascinating and surprising conversations in the annals of maritime history, recounted here by Amasa Delano, who heard it firsthand from Folger himself.

Captain Folger thinking that he should soonest make himself intelligible to them by finding out their origin and country, as they spoke English, inquired, "Who are you?"

"We are Englishmen."

"Where were you born?"

"On that island which you see."

"How then are you Englishmen, if you were born on that island, which the English do not own, and never possessed?"

"We are Englishmen because our father was an Englishman."

"Who is your father?"

With a very interesting simplicity they answered, "Aleck."

"Who is Aleck?"

"Don't you know Aleck?"

"How should I know Aleck?"

"Well then, did you know Captain Bligh of the *Bounty*?"

Although Folger didn't know Bligh, he certainly knew of him, as did most of the Western world. In April 1789 Fletcher Christian led a successful mutiny onboard the *Bounty*, a British naval ship, casting Capt. William Bligh and eighteen crewmen afloat in a twenty-three-foot open boat, which Bligh masterfully navigated more than 3,600 miles to safety at Timor, in the Dutch East Indies, from which he and the other survivors were transported back to England. For nearly nineteen years people puzzled over the fate of the mutineers. Finally Folger had provided the answer—they had settled on Pitcairn Island. "Aleck" turned out to be Alexander Smith (alias "John Adams"), the last surviving mutineer, and when Folger visited the island he learned that it was home to thirty-five people, quite a few of whom were

Aleck's wives and children. After leaving Pitcairn, Folger reported his discovery, thereby providing the final chapter in the story of the mutiny on the *Bounty*.[57]

WARY OF ANY COMPETITION, the British closely watched America's growing China trade. At first they discounted the naïve Americans, assuming they would fail in their attempt to enter the trade in which the British Empire reigned supreme. As the number of American ships heading to Canton rose ever higher, Britain's dismissiveness turned into a growing alarm, alternating between hoping that the Americans would falter and bemoaning their success. Nobody exemplified this perspective better than Phineas Bond, an American by birth and Loyalist by choice, who became the British consul in Philadelphia after the Revolutionary War. Writing to Lord Carmarthen, the British secretary of state for foreign affairs, in May 1787, Bond noted, "The encouragement the Americans have met with in their trade to China has induced them to enter largely into this speculation." While Bond sympathized with this trend—later noting, "In the restricted state of the American trade it is natural for men of enterprise to engage in such speculations"—he feared where it might lead. Bond thought, rightly as it turned out, that "the number of ships already employed" in the trade would "overstock the American market," which would lead to their sending China goods to Europe. That would be a disaster, he argued, because such an American trade "might prove greatly detrimental to the Revenue and commerce of Great Britain."

Like many of his peers Bond was surprised by America's China surge. "It was at first thought, my lord," he wrote Carmarthen in July 1787, that "the delays of the voyage, the necessary expense of the outfit, [and] the difficulty of making suitable remittances to obtain the proper investments, would soon have discouraged this undertaking:—but if one may judge from the present rage, it should seem as if new sources of profit appeared, and that the means of investment were facilitated so as to secure the future extension of the trade." But there was still hope, he assured his lord, that Britain could turn back the tide. American merchants were "so weak" financially, Bond contended, that "if an early check or restraint can be thrown in their way, either by thwarting their credit, or by withholding the articles suitable to their commerce, I am convinced they would never rally." But no checks or restraints were forthcoming, and the Americans were far more solvent and resourceful than Bond assumed. Bond's plaintive missives to Carmarthen lost much of their stridency over time as it became clear that the Americans were in the China trade to stay, and there was nothing the British could do about it.[58]

If the British had only listened more closely to Edmund Burke they wouldn't have been surprised at all by America's rapid advance in the world of maritime commerce in general, and the China trade in particular. On the eve of the American Revolution, Burke urged his countrymen to reconcile their deep differences with the colonies and choose peace, not war. In his three-hour-long speech to Parliament, he noted that the "commerce of your Colonies is out of all proportion beyond the numbers of the people." Focusing particular attention on America's whaling industry, Burke said:

> Look at the manner in which the people of New England have of late carried on the Whale Fishery. Whilst we follow them among the tumbling mountains of ice, and behold them penetrating into the deepest frozen recesses of Hudson's Bay and Davis's Straits; whilst we are looking for them beneath the Arctic Circle, we hear that they have pierced into the opposite region of polar cold, that they are at the antipodes, and engaged under the frozen Serpent of the south. . . . No sea but what is vexed by their fisheries. No climate that is not witness to their toils.[59]

The spirit, drive, and determination that Burke so admired were not peculiar to the whaling industry. Rather they were part of the very nature of the American condition. Once the Revolution set the United

States on its own path, those traits helped Americans pursue the China trade with great success.

With that success came a marked change in the attitude of the British in Canton. When Shaw first arrived in China in 1784, the British were quite courteous and helpful, despite the recent war. A few years later, however, the situation had changed markedly. "I shall only observe," Shaw wrote from Canton to John Jay in December 1787, that our trade "is viewed with no small degree of jealousy by our late mother country," adding that the Englishmen and the Americans "can barely treat each other with civility." The cause of this shift was clear. "I think it is not difficult to account for the difference," Shaw wrote to Henry Knox, America's portly secretary of war, in 1786. "We were then [in 1784] a single ship, come upon them by surprise, and as they had no instructions respecting us, they, like sensible people, made us welcome. We are now [in 1786] five vessels. This competition alarms them . . . nationally, I believe they all wish us to the d——l."[60]

It wasn't only the British attitude towards the Americans that had soured. The bile flowed both ways. In 1799 Ebenezer Townsend, the supercargo of the sealing ship *Neptune*, noted at Macao, "There is a jealousy always between the English and Yankees here; there is much *hauteur* with the English and enough independence in the Yankee to despise it. As one of our ships was dropping down past an Englishman he hails in a Yankeefied manner, 'Where are you bound?' and was answered also Yankeefiedly, 'To Boston with a load of tea; don't you want to go and see Bunker Hill?' "[61]

WHILE THE BRITISH seethed, the Americans reveled in their profitable commerce with the Far East. Richard Henry Lee, one of the signers of the Declaration of Independence, and later a senator from Virginia, wrote to Samuel Adams a little more than a week after the *Empress of China*'s return, averring that its "successful voyage . . . is a proof of American enterprise, and will probably mortify, as much as it will injure our old oppressors, the British." The *Providence Gazette and*

Country Journal reprinted a dispatch from Dublin in August 1787 that must have made its readers smile with satisfaction and pride: "Notwithstanding the English papers continually set forth, with such avidity, the distressed situation of America, the general want of money, and the insufficiency of American credit, for the purposes of carrying on trade, &c, we however find, by the latest accounts from India . . . that the five" American ships are in China, "and in all likelihood would make very great returns." Nine years later William Bentley, the pastor of the East Church in Salem, recorded in his diary, "The trade to . . . the East Indies now extend[s] through all the great Towns of these States." And in 1807 an American writing home from London noted, "America is no longer viewed with indifference by this country, as regards her commerce—but is considered a powerful rival. . . . We have almost destroyed the East India and China trade of this country."[62]

Apparently this last commentator got a bit carried away. Although the United States was most certainly a "powerful rival" to the British, it was nowhere near to destroying Britain's grip on the China trade. While it is true that by the early 1790s America was second only to Britain in the number of ships in the trade, and that over the next two decades the Americans sometimes sent more ships to Canton than did the British East India Company, numbers alone are a poor measure of relative success. The company's ships were much larger than the American ships, and the volume of British business far outstripped that of the Americans. If the British country-trader ships are added to the tally, the disparity in business activity grows even wider. Take tea, for example, the most important and valuable of all Chinese goods. British exports of tea from Canton far exceeded those of America every single year, often by ten to one and in a few instances by twenty to one. The upstart Americans, evoking a mercantilistic brashness already on display in the Revolution, had taken a considerable bite out of Britain's trade with China, but the British lion was still very powerful, and far from destroyed.[63]

Britain had the lead, but America's China traders had plenty to celebrate during the 1790s and the early 1800s. Hundreds of ships plied the routes between America and China, most quite profitably, some spectacularly so. From 1805 to 1812—excluding one year in which the United States placed an embargo on foreign trade—the value of the China trade (imports and exports of goods) was roughly $5 million per year, or about 3 percent of the nation's total foreign trade, and in some years the duties paid on imports exceeded $1 million. This financial activity, and the related industries it supported, helped bolster the young and growing economy. As the historians Sydney and Marjorie Greenbie noted, the China trade "not only set the Atlantic coast states on their feet after the Revolution: it furnished capital which gave them their initial industrial impetus. It may not have been very great; but it takes only a little to prime a cold engine." And in Canton, America's prospects were clearly improving. Other countries that had traditionally engaged in the China trade, such as Denmark, Spain, Sweden, Prussia, and France, virtually disappeared from the scene by the early 1800s, altogether accounting for a couple of ships a year at most, and in some years none at all. As other nations' commerce in Canton dwindled, America's trade there thrived.[64]

FACTORIES IN CANTON, BY UNIDENTIFIED CHINESE ARTIST, CIRCA 1805.

Although America's rise was propelled by the French wars in Europe, which made U.S. vessels the neutral carriers of choice, America's China traders also benefited from other distinct advantages. Lacking the restrictions of monopoly, they had more flexibility in their operations and could easily seize business opportunities. Americans' maritime skills and the quality of their ships made for quick and efficient voyages. And in the art of trading, improvising, and deal making, they were particularly adept. As Adam Johann von Krusenstern, the admiral who led Russia's first circumnavigation of the globe (1803–6), observed:

> The spirit of commerce is, perhaps, no where greater than in America. Being skilful seamen, they man their ships with a smaller crew, in which respect it appears altogether impossible to excel them. Their vessels are, besides, so admirably constructed, that they sail better than many ships of war, and I have known the captains of some of them at Canton who have made the voyage from thence to America and back again in ten months. . . . The Americans avail themselves quickly of every advantage that is offered to them in trade.[65]

But no matter how freewheeling, skilled, or efficient, the Americans were not immune to outside forces. For many years there had been troubles at sea, and in 1808 those troubles severely damaged America's China trade.

THE AMERICANS AND the British had been playing a maritime cat-and-mouse game since the early 1790s. British warships, claiming that many American sailors were British subjects who had deserted the British navy, would stop American ships and take purported deserters by force, a process called impressment. In some instances the British claims were correct, but many times they were not, and in those situations rather than impressing British citizens, the British were essentially kidnapping Americans. This angered people in the States, and in the summer of 1807 that anger turned into fury.

In one of the most notorious events in early nineteenth-century American diplomatic history, the USS *Chesapeake* was leaving port at Norfolk, Virginia, on June 22, 1807, when Lt. John Meade of HMS *Leopard* boarded the *Chesapeake* and demanded that Capt. Samuel Barron call his crew to the main deck so that British deserters could be identified. Barron refused, and Meade returned to the *Leopard*, whereupon his men blasted the *Chesapeake* at close range, causing Barron to surrender. Meade took four members of the *Chesapeake*'s crew, only one of whom was actually a British deserter. The *Chesapeake* affair produced a jingoistic fervor like none other, becoming a rallying cry for those who wanted to declare war on Britain. Instead of war, however, President Jefferson decided to punish the British—as well as the French, who had also harassed American shipping—by implementing an embargo that prohibited American ships from sailing to foreign ports, and foreign vessels from obtaining cargo at American ports. The thought was that cutting off trade would cripple Britain's and France's economies, and force them to respect America's neutrality.[66]

America's maritime merchants, including the China traders, opposed the embargo. It was better, they believed, to suffer the relatively small financial losses resulting from the depredations of foreign forces than it was to shut down trade entirely and lose everything. The merchants' concerns were ignored, and the embargo went into effect on December 22, 1807. Although a few China merchants flouted the embargo and sent ships to China, most suspended operations, not wanting to run afoul of the law. John Jacob Astor, however, was able to evade the embargo because of a Chinese man named Punqua Wingchong.[67]

SAMUEL LATHAM MITCHELL, a senator from New York and a friend of Astor's, wrote to President Jefferson on July 12, 1808, introducing

Wingchong as a Chinese merchant who had come to New York about nine months earlier and wanted desperately to return to China so that he could attend to family affairs and prepare for the funeral of his ninety-year-old grandfather, whose death was imminent. Wingchong hoped to charter a ship for that purpose, which is why he needed the president's help. Only Jefferson could make an exception to the embargo.

Wingchong and his interpreter had come to Washington to meet with Jefferson, but by the time they arrived, Jefferson had already left for Monticello. Undeterred, Wingchong, who by this time was being referred to in newspaper accounts as not just a merchant but a higher-status "mandarin," wrote directly to the president, reiterating his desire to engage a ship for himself and the property that he had accumulated while in the States. A supportive letter from James Madison, Jefferson's secretary of state and another of Astor's friends, urging the president to grant Wingchong's request, strengthened his case.[68]

This was enough for Jefferson, who wrote to Albert Gallatin, the secretary of the treasury, on July 25:

> The departure of this individual with good dispositions, may be the means of making our nation known advantageously at the source of power in China, to which it is otherwise difficult to convey information. It may be of sensible advantage to our merchants in that country. I cannot, therefore, but consider that a chance of obtaining a permanent national good should overweigh the effect of a single case taken out of the great field of the embargo.

Jefferson ordered Gallatin to make the arrangements necessary for one "Punqua Wingchong, the Chinese Mandarin," to sail from New York, and he included with his letter a "blank passport for the vessel" to facilitate that goal.[69]

But suspicions about Wingchong's authenticity were raised in late July, when it was learned that he was planning to take forty to fifty thousand dollars' worth of goods and specie with him, and those suspicions intensified in early August when it became known that the ship he had hired was Astor's *Beaver*. Other China merchants took notice, started their own investigations, and cried foul. On August 10 a group of Philadelphia merchants wrote to Gallatin, declaring that Wingchong was a fraud, and that he was part of an elaborate ruse by Astor to get a voyage to China in spite of the embargo. Some of them said they knew Wingchong to be nothing more than a "petty shopkeeper in Canton," while others noted that they had never heard of him, and that fact alone was enough to discredit his claim, for if he was an important mandarin, they would surely have made his acquaintance in China. New York merchants chimed in as well, calling Wingchong "a Chinaman picked up in a park" or "an Indian dressed up in silk and adorned with a peacock fan."[70]

The press in New York relished the erupting scandal. "The public attention is particularly invited to a transaction of a most extraordinary complexion," wrote an anonymous contributor to the *New-York Commercial Advertiser* on August 13, in an article titled, "The Ship *Beaver* and the Mandarin." After noting the ostensible purpose of the trip, and the exception granted by the president, it continued:

> It is, however, well known that the person for whom the permission has been obtained, is no Mandarin; is not even a licensed or security merchant. . . . It is also believed, that the owner of the ship, would not accept all the property of all the Chinese in this country as a compensation for the voyage, and it is known that he had offered to contract for bringing home goods on freight. Whatever may have been the motives of the President in granting the permission, it is therefore, certain, that the object of the owner of the ship is to make a China voyage, at a time when other merchants are restrained by the embargo.[71]

The same day the *New-York Gazette & Advertiser* issued a satirical "Notice to Mandarins," offering between twenty and fifty thousand dollars to "a Mandarin, who, during the present embargo, will obtain permission from the President of the United States for a ship . . . to proceed from New York to Canton and back to New York." The notice said that whether the applicant is "a native of Asia, or America, is immaterial, provide he is a *genuine Mandarin*." The mandarin also had to "have an aged father," and "if more than one Mandarin should apply (as is very probable) the one whose father is oldest will . . . be preferred." Higher still would the applicant rise in the eyes of his prospective employer if he could gain permission from the president to transport silver coin to Canton.[72]

Astor entered the fray by putting his accuser on the spot. In a letter to the editor of the *Commercial Advertiser*, published on August 15, he asked the person who wrote the article on the thirteenth to provide his name so that Astor could send him a "statement of facts relative to the transaction in question," which would make it clear that nothing unseemly had transpired. "He shall be convinced," asserted Astor, "that the Government has not been surprised by misrepresentations in granting permission, and that the reputation of those concerned cannot be in the slightest degree affected."[73] What Astor's "statement of facts" would have contained will never be known because his letter didn't get a response, his accuser preferring to remain shrouded in shadows.

Despite the pleas of numerous China merchants and journalists to look into the matter further before letting the *Beaver* go, the Jefferson administration did nothing. It is not clear if the president, still at Monticello, knew of the brewing controversy. As late as August 15 he wrote to Gallatin still believing that Wingchong's voyage home would likely "bring lasting advantage to our merchants and commerce with that country." Gallatin, on the other hand, had considerable doubts about the true nature of the enterprise, surmising that "there is some speculation at bottom," but whether his friendship with Astor or some other calculation took precedence, he let the matter drop.[74]

The *Beaver* left New York on August 17. Two days later the *Portland Gazette and Maine Advertiser* noted the departure, caustically observing that "the only proof adduced to convince Mr. Jefferson that this man was not an imposter, was his resemblance to figures on *China teapots!*—Was our good President deceived?—or did the ship *Beaver* belong to some good democrat?—Be that as it may, the president's palace is said to have been completely besieged by *Chinese Mandarins*, since the *Beaver* got away."[75]

Deceived or not, Jefferson soon had cause to question his decision. He received an anonymous letter on August 23 that laid out the case against Wingchong and Astor. Jefferson said he "had no means of judging" the merit of the writer's claims, since all the earlier communications he had received presented Wingchong's identity and aims as "settled fact." If, however, the ship was still in port, Jefferson asked that it be detained to ascertain the truth. But it was too late, of course: The ship had gone. When the *Beaver* returned from Canton nearly a year later, on June 1, 1809, it had onboard a great variety of teas and silks, and nankeen fabric, which resulted in a profit of more than two hundred thousand dollars, giving Astor a reason to smile.

The true identity of Punqua Wingchong, as well as the veracity of his story, remains a mystery. That he was a man from China there is little doubt. There are records of him and his servant visiting Nantucket in 1807, being brought from Canton onboard the ship *Favorite*. One of his hosts on the island described him as a "merchant . . . [who was] the color of our native whites."[76] And Wingchong returned to the island two more times after the War of 1812. As for the rest of the story, there are strong reasons to question it. Not only would a Chinese mandarin who had the ability to gather some fifty thousand dollars' worth of specie and goods during his sojourn in America probably have made more of a splash during his stay—because he was a rare visitor from China, and a very wealthy one at that—but one also wonders how he came to learn of his grandfather's impending death, and why he would have left China in the first place, if his grandfather was so close to the grave (or at least old enough to start preparing for that eventuality). Also the fact that the *Beaver*'s trip ended up being so lucrative for Astor and other merchants with whom he made deals before the ship's departure leads one to think that perhaps Astor found Wingchong to be a very convenient foundation upon which to build a wily and duplicitous scheme.[77]

THE EMBARGO WAS a colossal failure. Rather than injure Britain and France, it sent America reeling. Within a year of the act's passage, American exports dropped from $108 million to $22 million, and the China trade declined along with the rest of the economy.[78] The year prior to the embargo, 1807, was one of the best for America's China traders, with forty-four ships arriving in China and bringing back about 6.5 million pounds of tea. The following year, when the full force of the embargo bore down, those numbers sank to fifteen ships and barely 1 million pounds of tea, and most of those ships had left the States before the Embargo Act took effect, and therefore hadn't broken the law.

On March 1, 1809, just a few days before he left the White House, Jefferson repealed the embargo. The China trade quickly revived, and that year arrivals in Canton again rose to forty-four and the imports of tea to the United States hit nearly 10 million pounds.[79] The rejoicing didn't last long, however. By 1811 the United States was on the verge of another debilitating war with Britain, and after it was declared, on June 1, 1812, the China trade was imperiled yet again.

While merchants were free to send their ships to Canton, any who did so assumed great risks. The wide-ranging British navy, still the finest in the world, looked upon American merchant ships as fair game, and particularly soft targets at that. Nevertheless, during the two and a half years of the conflict, dozens of ships left American ports for Canton, their fears of capture overcome by the powerful lure of profits.

Some of these intrepid and perhaps foolhardy Americans were caught in the British snare, and taken as prizes, as the China seas became a battleground. But American privateers in the region fought back, taking British prizes of their own. All the while the Chinese looked on with growing horror at the war being played out on their doorstep, and they grew quite angry when combatants violated China's neutrality by bringing their prizes to Whampoa. China halted such transgressions by threatening to close down trade, and then implored the British and the Americans to take their fight somewhere else. "If the English and Americans have petty quarrels," observed one Chinese official, "let them go to their own country and settle them."[80]

The American ships that left their home ports after war was declared voluntarily assumed the risk, but there were also those who left before and, as a result, sailed into unanticipated troubles. Of the latter the most interesting voyage was that of Stephen Girard's *Montesquieu*, which arrived in Canton in February 1812 and then headed back to Philadelphia toward the end of the year, with its captain, Robert Wilson, unaware that the war had begun. In late

STEPHEN GIRARD'S SHIP *MONTESQUIEU*, OFF MACAO,
BY UNIDENTIFIED CHINESE ARTIST, 1812.

March 1813, off Cape Henlopen at the mouth of Delaware Bay, Wilson saw a schooner approaching, no bigger than one of his ship's small boats. As it pulled alongside Wilson was shocked to discover that the schooner—crammed with thirty "miserable starving men and boys," armed with ten small carronades and guns—was His Majesty's ship *Paz*, which had come to take the *Montesquieu* as a prize of war. Wilson didn't resist, and he and his crew were sent ashore, whereupon the negotiations began. By this time Sir John Beresford, commander of HMS *Poictiers*, had arrived, and he set the ransom price for the *Montesquieu* at $180,000 "Spanish milled dollars." The *Montesquieu*'s cargo was valued at only $165,000, but Girard willingly paid the ransom, and he had the last laugh. Because of war shortages, prices were high, and Girard sold the ship's cargo for nearly $500,000.[81]

DURING THE WAR OF 1812 a number of ships successfully ran the gauntlet between America and China, but overall the trade took a significant beating. Imports fell precipitously, and the amount of tea coming into the United States dwindled to about 1.5 million pounds per year. The end of the war, however, marked by the signing of the Treaty of Ghent on December 24, 1814, ushered in a new phase in the China trade.

Six

THE GOLDEN GHETTO

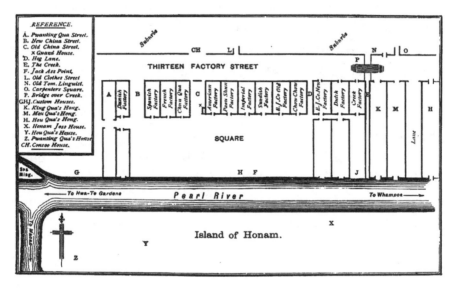

REFERENCE.
A. *Pwanting Qua Street.*
B. *New China Street.*
C. *Old China Street.*
x *Guard House.*
D. *Hog Lane.*
E. *The Creek.*
F. *Jack Ass Point.*
L. *Old Clothes Street.*
N. *Old Tom. Linguist.*
O. *Carpenters Square.*
P. *Bridge over Creek.*
G.H.J.*Custom Houses.*
K. *King Qua's Hong.*
M. *Mau Qua's Hong.*
H. *Hou Qua's Hong.*
X. *Honam Joss House.*
Y. *Hou Qua's House.*
Z. *Pwanting Qua's House*
CH. *Consoo House.*

THIRTEEN FACTORY STREET

SQUARE

Pearl River

Island of Honam.

To Hwa-Te Gardens

To Whampoa

MAP OF THE FOREIGN FACTORIES IN CANTON.

THE RETURN OF PEACE UNLEASHED AN AVALANCHE OF COMMER-
cial activity, as American merchants, full of confidence and optimism,
turned their full attention once again to the business of making money.
From 1816 up until 1839, the China trade averaged roughly $7 million
per year, or about 4 percent of foreign trade. Throughout this entire
period there were many ups and downs, and business failures and
successes as the United States experienced panics and prosperity.
And for all that time America still had a trade deficit with China. But
overall the China trade was not only a significant source of wealth

for merchants, fueling some of America's largest fortunes, but also an important revenue stream for the government, which collected duties on imports. While the raw numbers reflect the respectable volume of the China trade through the late 1830s, they say nothing about the experiences of the people involved. That is a story of both—and at once—change and continuity.[1]

The twenty-five years after the War of 1812 witnessed a major consolidation in the China trade. Large firms with many ships and greater capital at their disposal displaced many of the smaller independent traders who had been so active in the prewar years. Astor and Girard, two of the heavyweights in the China trade, remained major players until the mid-1820s, when increasing friction with the Chinese over opium, and the lure of brighter business prospects stateside, led them to abandon China altogether.

The number of ships in Canton each year ranged from a low of eighteen to a high of fifty-nine, with the bulk sailing from New York, Boston, Providence, Philadelphia, and Salem. On their return,

MERCHANT SHIPS AT SOUTH STREET, ALONG THE EAST RIVER
IN NEW YORK CITY, BY WILLIAM I. BENNETT, 1828.

however, an increasing number of ships were offloading in New York, which had surpassed Philadelphia as the largest city in America, and had become the premier center for the sale and distribution of tea. Although the ships in the trade were getting bigger to handle more goods, the crews were getting smaller, as voyages became more routine and efficient.² The composition of the cargoes also changed over time, as some of the traditional exports, in particular sealskins, sandalwood, and sea otter pelts, became scarcer.

BY THE END OF THE second decade of the nineteenth century, fur seals had been driven to commercial extinction in many places, forcing sealers to seek new killing grounds. The men of Stonington, Connecticut, took the lead in this endeavor and soon discovered an untapped population near the bottom of the world. Rumors emanating from South America had been swirling for years about islands beyond the tip of the continent, "where seals which had never been disturbed by man were as tame as kittens, and more plenty than at any other place on earth."³ To Stonington's intrepid merchants and ship's captains, leaders in the sealing industry, this shadowy tale was as flowers to the bee, and finally in 1819, a group of Stonington men sent forth the *Hersilia*, captained by James P. Sheffield, to search for this sealskin El Dorado.

At the Falklands, Sheffield spoke to a Briton who had seen the mysterious islands, and with that information he sailed the *Hersilia* about four hundred miles beyond Cape Horn to the South Shetland Islands. The rumors proved abundantly true, and Sheffield soon loaded a cornucopia of nearly ten thousand skins. When he returned to Stonington, the town's sealers were ecstatic, and in short order nine more local ships were following the *Hersilia*'s lead. Wanting to keep the spoils for themselves, Stonington's merchants tried to convince the outside world that these ships were heading out on nothing more than whaling voyages. But nobody was deceived, the result being that the 1820–21 sealing season in the South Shetlands was a very busy one, with thirty American vessels on hand, not only from Stonington, but also from Nantucket, New York, New Bedford, Salem, New Haven, and Fairhaven—and they were joined by ships from Britain and Russia.[4]

During this intense season one of the Stonington ships, the sloop *Hero*, captained by twenty-year-old Nathaniel B. Palmer, searched for other islands brimming with seals. After sailing his diminutive vessel—just forty-seven feet long and only forty-four tons—a few hundred miles south, Palmer and his five-man crew sighted a mountainous landscape covered in snow and ice. What Palmer didn't know was that he was gazing upon the continent of Antarctica. Frequent thick fogs forced him to turn back, and soon he had quite a shock. On the morning of February 6, 1821, while the *Hero* was shrouded in fog so dense that all the crew could do was drift slowly and hope to avoid knocking into anything, Palmer rang the ship's bell, and heard what sounded like a bell in the distance reply. Thinking that he must be mistaken, Palmer resumed his watch, but a half hour later when he rang the ship's bell twice, the tolls were answered yet again. "I could not credit my ears," Palmer later recalled. "I thought I was dreaming, [because] save for the screeching of the penguins, the albatrosses, the pigeons and the Mother Cary chickens [Wilson's petrels], I was sure no living object was within leagues of the sloop."

As the fog lifted, Palmer and his men found themselves bobbing in between two Russian warships, sent by the czar on a worldwide voyage of scientific exploration. The commanding officer of the Russian expedition, Adm. Fabian Gottlieb Benjamin von Bellingshausen, was even more shocked than Palmer. He couldn't believe that a ship so small could have come all the way from America, and ventured into such treacherous waters. Before meeting up with the *Hero*, Bellingshausen had thought he was the first explorer to reach this area, but according to one account of his conversation with Palmer, the admiral said, "We must surrender the palm of enterprise to you Americans, and content ourselves with following in your train." Bellingshausen then apparently promised to name this new land Palmer's Land on Russian charts, in honor of the Stonington sealing captain. Despite Bellingshausen's magnanimous gesture, there is still disagreement over whether Palmer was the first person to sight Palmer's Land, and therefore deserves credit for discovering Antarctica.[5] Nevertheless the gutsy voyage of the *Hero* provides yet another example of the maritime skills that had catapulted America to the front rank of merchant nations roaming the seven seas in the "adventurous pursuits of commerce."

Despite Palmer's failure to find other seal-strewn islands, the 1820–21 season was a robust economic success. The South Shetlands provided more than enough bounty to fill the ships' holds, and the next year many of the sealers came back for more. In those two seasons of rapacious slaughter, 320,000 seals were skinned. There would be no third season, however. The South Shetland Islands had been added to the long list of locales devastated by men who had no reason to moderate their killing, and in fact had every incentive to kill as many seals as fast as they could. Reflecting on the situation a few years later, the British seal hunter James Weddell expressed a sense of stewardship that was as insightful as it was rare for the times:

> This valuable animal, the fur seal, might, by a law similar to that which restrains the fishermen in the size of the mesh of their nets, have been spared to render annually 100,000 fur seals for many years to come. This would have followed from not killing the mothers until the young were able to take the water, and even then only those which appeared to be old, together with a proportion of the males, thereby diminishing their total number, but in slow progression. . . . [A] system of extermination was practiced, however, at the South Shetlands; for whenever a seal reached the beach, of whatever denomination, he was immediately killed and his skin taken, and by this means, . . . the seals became nearly extinct.[6]

The American fur seal trade to China continued throughout the balance of the 1820s, but there were no more mother lodes like the South Shetlands to be had. By the mid 1830s the number of fur seal skins brought to Canton on American ships dwindled to near zero.[7] There simply weren't enough fur seals left to make their pursuit profitable.

The sandalwood trade followed a similar trajectory, and Fiji was the first to succumb. Even before the War of 1812 Fiji had been largely shorn of this fragrant tree, but the trade there managed to stagger on until 1816 when there was almost nothing left to cut down. About the same time a new source of sandalwood appeared thousands of miles to the northeast in the middle of the South Pacific, on the Marquesas Islands, the spectacular remains of ancient volcanic eruptions. During the War of 1812, Capt. David Porter of the USS *Essex* took shelter at the Marquesas, bringing with him a number of armed British whaleships he had captured along with their crews. Porter's prisoners noticed that the steep, jagged mountainsides were covered in sandalwood. When one of the whaleships escaped to Sydney, word spread, and Australians, Americans, and others rushed to the Marquesas to participate in the next sandalwood frenzy, which was fueled by the Marquesans' infatuation with sperm whale teeth. "No jewel, however valuable, is half so much esteemed in Europe or America, as is a whale's tooth here," Porter later commented. "I have seen them by fits laugh and cry for joy, at the possession of one of these darling treasures. . . . A ship of three hundred tons burthen, may be loaded with sandalwood at this island, at the price of ten whales' teeth of a large size."[8] With so many whalemen prowling the South Pacific, the sandalwood traders had little difficulty satisfying the Marquesans' demands for teeth, and in three years the islands were stripped nearly bare of the sweet-smelling wood.

It was on the lush Hawaiian Islands, however, that the sandalwood trade prospered most.[9] After the war King Kamehameha I—who unified the islands into the Kingdom of Hawaii, and is also known as Kamehameha the Great—used the islands' sizable sandalwood

KAMEHAMEHA I,
KING OF HAWAII.

reserves as his private bank, making whatever withdrawals were necessary to purchase ships to build his infant navy. The Americans encouraged Kamehameha's proclivities, and happily imported beat-up old vessels to exchange for thousands of tons of valuable wood, which were taken to Canton, where the Chinese referred to Hawaii as *Tan Heung Shan*, the Sandalwood Mountains. In addition to trading vessels for sandalwood, Americans also purchased wood from Kamehameha, or took loads of it to China on consignment, returning a percentage of the profits to the king.

Kamehameha's subjects worked so hard cutting sandalwood that their health deteriorated and they neglected their own crops and families. According to the Hawaiian historian Samuel M. Kamakau, "Slavery replaced freedom to the people. Natives were treated like cattle. Up and down the treacherous mountain trails they toiled, . . . sandalwood strapped to their sweating shoulders. Men and women actually became deformed due to the tremendous weight of the logs on their backs. The forced laborers in the sandalwood forests had no time to farm—food grew scarce and famine came."[10] Concerned about this debilitating trend, as well as the rapid diminution of the islands' sandalwood, Kamehameha restricted the amount of time people could spend cutting trees, and he also protected saplings from being cut. But when Kamehameha's son Liholiho (Kamehameha II) took over in 1819, the situation worsened. Less conscientious and more profligate than his father, Liholiho allowed individual chiefs to trade sandalwood, and soon they and the king were cutting trees with reckless abandon to buy rum, guns, champagne, silks, furniture, and more vessels. All the while the people of Hawaii continued to suffer.

One of Liholiho's more unusual purchases was the eighty-three-foot-long *Cleopatra's Barge*, the first oceangoing yacht built in America. Originally owned by George Crowninshield, Jr., the scion of a prominent Salem merchant family, and launched from that town in October 1816, it was patterned after Europe's royal yachts and decked out like a palace, with velvet-covered sofas, finely painted chairs, chandeliers, and sideboards full of exquisite glass and porcelain. After a triumphal tour of the Mediterranean, and Crowninshield's death, *Cleopatra's Barge* was stripped of most of its contents and then served as a trading vessel for a few years before being sold to the company of Bryant and Sturgis, who promptly sent it to Hawaii to entice the king to purchase it with a huge load of sandalwood.

Soon after *Cleopatra's Barge* arrived in Lahaina in early November 1820, Liholiho and his minions boarded it to take a look around. The king fell in love, buying the ship within a week's time on credit for five hundred tons of sandalwood, and renaming her *Haaheo o Hawaii*, or the *Pride of Hawaii*. In subsequent years Liholiho took the *Pride* on numerous alcohol-fueled jaunts around his island empire, often abusing his forlorn subjects wherever he landed. He was so enamored of the ship that Charles Bullard, one of the agents for Bryant and Sturgis, claimed that "if you want to know how Religion stands at the Islands I can tell you—All sects are tolerated but the King worships the Barge."[11]

The ship's end came during a cruise on April 5, 1824, when it was dashed against Kauai's rugged shore and was wrecked. All onboard, save for the captain, were purportedly drunk. Liholiho didn't witness the destruction of his prize possession. He was in England at the time to meet King George IV. The British monarch dreaded the thought of entertaining the Hawaiian ruler, and referred to Liholiho and his wife as a "pair of damned cannibals." George needn't have worried. The meeting never happened, since Liholiho and his wife, exposed to the insalubrious air of London, contracted measles and died two months after arriving.[12]

On account of their extravagant purchases Liholiho and the chiefs under him were soon buying what they couldn't pay for and racking up enormous debts, which went unpaid for many years until the Hawaiian government finally settled the accounts. Far more damaging than the debt, however, was what greed had done to ravage the islands. Hawaii's sandalwood forests were virtually destroyed by the late 1820s. No longer did American traders go to Hawaii for the scented wood, because there wasn't enough to fill a ship. Even when a small amount of Hawaiian sandalwood made it to Canton in subsequent years, it was of such puny size and poor quality that it sold for very little.

As with fur seals and sandalwood, so too with sea otters. By the early 1820s the American sea otter trade was in its death throes. Instead of sending nearly eighteen thousand pelts to Canton annually, the Americans were shipping barely a fifth of that amount. A decade later that had dwindled to just three hundred, leading a prominent American sea otter merchant to inform one of his captains in 1832: "I shall not make any outfit this season, the trade appears fairly run out." The sea otter had been hunted nearly to extinction, not only in the Pacific Northwest but all along the coast, from California to Alaska. Not a prolific breeder to begin with, the sea otter didn't stand a chance against human avarice.[13]

NO SUCH FATE awaited the opium trade, however, which only increased from earlier years, revealing that the human capacity for self-destruction would play itself out against a much longer timetable. As a result, instead of a few hundred chests of opium, American traders regularly brought upwards of five hundred chests to China, and at times above fifteen hundred, mostly from Turkey but also from

India. Although Americans rarely accounted for more than about 10 percent of the opium trade to China, it remained a powerful income stream, generating as much as $1 million in annual sales, thereby reducing the need for Americans to bring money to Canton to pay for Chinese goods. However, because reliable information on the scope of American opium imports from India is lacking, and since there are indications that that branch of the trade was significant, it is likely that America's participation in the opium trade was even more extensive and lucrative. Most American China-trade firms trafficked in opium, one noteworthy exception being New York's Olyphant & Company, which opposed the trade on religious and moral grounds. As a result of this principled stance, other American traders derisively referred to the rooms that Olyphant & Company occupied in the Canton factory as "Zion's Corner."[14]

The system for smuggling opium into China changed in the early 1820s in response to stepped-up Chinese efforts to curtail the drug trade. Two incidents involving Americans were major reasons for the clampdown. In the first, Chinese pirates attacked the Baltimore ship *Wabash* in May 1817, killing several of the men onboard and stealing ten thousand dollars of specie and about thirty-five chests of opium. Alarmed by this attack, especially the loss of life, Chinese authorities quickly apprehended the pirates, five of whom were put to death— one by having his body neatly chopped into twenty-four pieces, with the rest being decapitated. The silver was promptly returned to the Americans, but the discovery of opium in the cargo elicited a firestorm of reproach, and generated the first official scolding of the Americans on the subject of the drug trade. The hong merchants, at the direction of the viceroy, or governor of the province of Canton, instructed the American consul "to write a letter immediately back to your country and tell . . . your honorable country's president" that opium importation into Canton was prohibited "by an order received from the Son of Heaven," and that if another American ship was caught with the drug, the responsible hong merchant would be investigated, the ship prosecuted, and its departure impeded.[15]

This situation greatly embarrassed the hong merchant who had secured the *Wabash*. It also cost him three hundred thousand dollars in fines, "squeezed" out of him by higher-level officials. All the hong merchants—equally guilty of involvement in the drug trade—subsequently agreed that they would not secure any more foreign ships unless the captains of those ships signed a bond promising to forswear opium smuggling. Bonds were signed, and some drug trafficking was hindered as a result, but opium, like molasses from a jug, still flowed into China because, as the historian Jacques M. Downs observed, "The hapless Hong merchants were never strong enough to resist the opposition of their Western trading partners," who didn't want the smuggling to end.[16]

The second opium incident involving the Americans had harsher repercussions.[17] The *Emily* (out of Baltimore) arrived at Whampoa in May 1821, and proceeded to sell its cargo of opium without any interference from local officials. By September much of the opium was gone, but then one afternoon an event took place that sent shockwaves through the Canton trading community. Francis Terranova, a crewman on the *Emily*, was bartering for fruit with a Chinese woman on a sampan that had pulled up alongside the ship. What happened next depends on the source of the story. Some accounts claim that Terranova, angered by the woman's demands, threw an "olive jar" or a piece of pottery, which struck her in the head, causing her to fall into the water and drown. Other accounts say that the jar was accidentally dropped or make no mention of a projectile, rather claiming that the woman lost her balance while using a pole to maneuver the sampan. Whatever happened, the woman's husband accused Terranova of murder, and the severity of the ensuing drama revealed that Chinese anger had been pent up for far too long: It was in fact a response to an era of transgression, not merely the drowning of a woman.

Benjamin Chew Wilcocks, the American consul in Canton at the time, was immediately informed of the incident. His hope was to resolve the dispute quickly and quietly before government officials got involved by paying off the family—such bribes being a common technique used by foreigners to avoid trouble. Wilcocks had two good reasons for wanting the matter resolved in this manner. The Daoguang emperor (Tao-kuang, r. 1821–50) was intent on halting the opium trade, and if the Terranova incident became public, he might use it as an example of what happened to foreigners caught selling the drug. Secondly, and in more personal terms, Wilcocks was heavily involved in the trade, and therefore had a vested interest in keeping the incident under wraps.

With the backing of the hong merchants, Wilcocks urged the *Emily*'s captain, William S. Cowpland, to pay the husband, even offering a personal line of credit up to fifteen thousand dollars that the captain could tap. But Cowpland believed that the death was an accident, and that Terranova was innocent. Instead of paying hush money, Cowpland wanted a trial.

Local government officials soon got wind of the affair and they demanded that Terranova be turned over at once. The Americans responded by establishing a fifteen-member committee to negotiate on the sailor's behalf. Initially the committee wouldn't budge, fearing that Terranova would not get a fair trial. Finally, however, they relented, since the only alternative was having the Chinese stop all American trade.

The trial that ensued onboard the *Emily* was not so much a judicial process as a fait accompli, at least in the eyes of the foreigners who witnessed it. The Chinese magistrate listened to the clearly cowed Chinese witnesses lay out the case against Terranova, but when the Americans tried to provide evidence that proved their case—including that the star witnesses for the government had changed their story, and could not have possibly seen what transpired from their vantage point—the magistrate could barely contain his rage. He had already made up his mind that Terranova was guilty, and didn't want to hear anything that contradicted his version of the events. Compounding the situation for the Americans was the court-appointed linguist's lack of facility with the English language, meaning that the Americans could neither get their points accurately translated nor fully understand what the Chinese were saying. According to one contemporary account, the exasperated magistrate finally said that "he had himself seen the woman and the jar; he believed the man guilty; if he had judged wrongfully, it was heaven's business, and in a passion rose from his chair to conclude the trial." The outcry of the Americans, who still wanted their witnesses to be heard, caused the magistrate to sit down again, but as soon as an American sailor stepped forward and began to offer testimony, the magistrate stormed off the ship. "Thus concluded" what was in American eyes a "mockery of justice."[18]

Refusing to turn over Terranova, the Americans made it clear that they wouldn't put up a fight if Chinese officials took him away. In a statement given to the head of the hong merchants, the Americans said that although they thought the "case prejudiced," since Terranova had been "condemned" without being heard, they were "bound to submit" to Chinese laws while in Chinese waters, even though they believed they were "unjust."[19] Rather than take Terranova, however, the viceroy halted all trading with the Americans.

For three weeks the standoff continued. The Chinese didn't want to take Terranova for fear of a violent reaction from the Americans, even though the Americans reiterated that they would not stand in the way. When the members of the Cohong promised that once in Chinese hands, Terranova would receive another, fairer trial, and that the Americans would be able to attend, the impasse ended. Chinese soldiers took Terranova into custody on October 23. The promised trial took place a few days later, but without any Americans on hand. The Chinese claimed that Terranova confessed to the crime, and therefore was found guilty, tied to a wooden cross, and strangled on the twenty-seventh. The following day the authorities delivered Terranova's body to the Americans, who transported it to the foreigners' cemetery at Whampoa, where it was given a proper burial. The next day the embargo was lifted, and the Chinese resumed trade with the Americans.

Soon thereafter, the viceroy sent the hong merchants an edict that made it clear that he thought justice had been served: "Rightly did Heaven send down punishment, and cause Francis Terranova to commit a crime for which he was strangled." The viceroy noted that China allowed tea, rhubarb, and other goods to be exported—without which, he claimed, the foreigners would die. (The Chinese had long harbored the belief that without the laxative powers of rhubarb, Westerners' bowels would be blocked, leading to death. Tea was also viewed as necessary for Westerners' survival.) "Those persons who are annually kept alive thereby," the viceroy continued, "are more than ten thousand times ten thousand. How substantial a favor is this! Yet these foreigners feel no gratitude; nor wish to render a recompense; but smuggle in prohibited opium, which flows and poisons the land."[20]

The British condemned the Americans' capitulation. "As for the Americans," noted a report by British East India Company officials, "who have thus barbarously abandoned a man serving under their flag to the sanguinary laws of this Empire without an endeavor to obtain common justice for him, their conduct deserves to be held in eternal execration by every moral, honorable, and feeling mind."[21] This excoriation notwithstanding, the British did not behave any better when confronted with a similar situation in the *Lady Hughes* affair, where they abandoned one of their sailors, whom they deemed innocent, to Chinese authorities who also later strangled him. As with the Terranova incident, the continuation of trade took precedence over everything else.

BUT THE OPIUM TRADE, at least, would not continue as it always had. The situations with the *Wabash* and the *Emily*, combined with the arrest of a Chinese smuggler who identified those who were most involved in trafficking drugs, led to a renewed and more effective crackdown on the opium trade at Whampoa. Rather than abandon the trade, the foreign dealers improvised, moving their operations to

Lintin (Nei Lingding), a small mountainous island, just three miles long, located in the Pearl River estuary about twenty miles northeast of Macao.

Lintin's main peak rises two thousand feet from the sea's surface and can be seen for many miles. The British were the first to employ this new site, in 1822, and the Americans relocated the following year. The opium traders now sailed to Lintin and offloaded the drug to permanently anchored "depot" ships, which transferred the opium on an as-needed basis to smugglers whose heavily armed boats arrived by day and by night. These boats, with colorfully appropriate names like "fast crabs," "smug boats," or "scrambling dragons," were powered by as many as fifty oarsmen whose combined strokes propelled the long, narrow vessels at speeds up to fourteen miles an hour to Canton or to other spots onshore. There the opium would be offloaded for distribution. Whereas under the old system, smugglers paid for the opium on the spot, now the cash changed hands at the factories. Another technique used by foreigners to get opium into China was to sail up the coast, stop at towns and cities along the way, and sell the drug to local merchants, thereby taking the smuggler middlemen out of the equation and boosting profits. Even though Chinese officials were well aware of these new arrangements, they rarely tried to intervene because many of them were still corrupt, taking bribes for looking the other way. On those few occasions when the local authorities put on a show of clamping down on smuggling by sending out armed patrols to enforce the law, the patrols were usually no match for their swift, wily, and aggressive adversaries. Nor was the relatively weak Chinese navy an effective deterrent.[22]

Beyond opium, and dwindling stocks of sealskins, sea otter pelts, and sandalwood, American merchants regularly sent many other goods to China, including ginseng, lead, mercury, cotton, beef, rum, and iron. An array of exotic items, most obtained in the South Pacific, also made their way onto American ships, among them bird's nests, tortoiseshell, and mother-of-pearl. But the most unusual and storied of all was one with the exotic name "bêche-de-mer."[23]

BÊCHE-DE-MER, ALSO CALLED "trepang" or "sea cucumber," is a member of the phylum Echinodermata, along with starfish, sea urchins, and sand dollars. It is much softer and more gelatinous than its prickly relatives, resembling a waterborne slug—a likeness that led Charles Darwin to call it "slimy [and] disgusting," which is much too harsh a description of this curious creature. Most species of sea cucumber are cylindrical and anywhere from an inch to a foot long. Scavengers par excellence, eating any organic material that lies in their path, they are especially populous in the shallow waters surrounding the islands of the South Pacific. And that is how they became ensnared in the American China trade.[24]

The Chinese had long used dried bêche-de-mer to flavor soup, particularly relishing the jellylike texture it lent to other ingredients, as well as its ability to meld their flavors. Equally treasured was the animal's alleged power to rejuvenate the body and enhance sexual prowess, traits that caused the Chinese to refer to bêche-de-mer as *hai-*

ONE OF MANY SPECIES OF BÊCHE-DE-MER.

shên, or "sea ginseng."[25] The American trade in bêche-de-mer grew up alongside the sandalwood trade, but before the War of 1812 it was not pursued with much avidity. As sandalwood grew increasingly scarce, however, the Americans focused more attention on sea cucumbers—or rather on the island natives, particularly in Fiji, Hawaii, and the Marquesas, who were willing to harvest the succulent sea slugs.

Once the ship's captain had struck a deal with the locals, the hunt

DRIED BÊCHE-DE-MER.

began. The natives usually drifted over a reef in their canoes and dived in, descending two to five meters to the bottom, where the most valuable species lived. (Less valuable species of bêche-de-mer were obtained by wading through the shallows and plucking the animals from the sand.) They would also head out at night when the creatures were most active, using torchlight or the moon's glare to sight their slow-moving targets. The search for bêche-de-mer was called "fishing for a musket," since guns were one of the most coveted trade items, and the natives would contract to bring in so much bêche-de-mer for each musket tendered. In the late 1820s the going rate per musket was sixteen hogsheads, or roughly one thousand pounds of bêche-de-mer. Even a single iron chisel was enough to purchase one native's labor for an entire day.[26]

Getting the sea cucumbers out of the water was the easy part compared with what came next. If the sea cucumbers were left to bake in the sun, they quickly turned into a worthless stringy mass; therefore it was essential that they be covered as soon as they were hauled into the canoe. After a promising batch was collected, they were taken ashore for processing. First the sea cucumbers were drained of excess water by letting them sit in square enclosures made of coconut logs set into the sand. Next the animals were slit open and the guts squeezed out; then the outer bodies were pitched into an iron kettle and boiled for three-quarters of an hour before being transferred to the drying hut, where they were placed on racks suspended over a slow-burning fire for three to four days. The finished product, a shriveled blackish or brownish mass about one-sixth the weight of the original animal, was then stowed in bags for the trip to Canton.

Gathering and processing bêche-de-mer was extremely labor intensive. Hundreds and sometimes thousands of natives were involved, and huge amounts of firewood were needed to keep the operation going, exacerbating the deforestation that resulted from the clear-cutting of sandalwood. The bêche-de-mer trade reached its greatest heights during the 1820s and 1830s, with men from Salem in the vanguard, and profits were considerable. Salem captain John H. Eagleston once paid the equivalent of $3,500 for eighty tons of bêche-de-mer, which sold in Canton for $27,000.

NATIVES DIVING FOR BÊCHE-DE-MER.

———

THE BÊCHE-DE-MER TRADE was marred by many violent encounters between the traders and the natives, the best known of which involved the *Glide*.[27] Joseph Peabody, Salem's most prosperous merchant after the War of 1812, was an old hand at the China trade by the late 1820s, when he sent the *Glide*, captained by Henry Archer, to Fiji. James Oliver, a member of the crew, later wrote that he and his fellows "were mostly young men, some of whom were entering, for the first time, on a sailor's life, exchanging the comforts of home for the rough berth and coarse fare of the forecastle, and the courtesies of friends for submission to the authority of the quarter-deck." Soon after the *Glide* arrived in Fiji, late in 1829, it was sailing through uncharted waters when it struck a large coral head "with a tremendous crash." As water rushed into the breached hull, the men manned the pumps, barely able to keep up with the torrent, while "the darkness of a starless night" settled on the crippled ship. A few days later the *Glide* made it to Vanua Levu, the second-largest island in Fiji, where it encountered another Salem ship, the *Quill*, already at work processing bêche-de-mer. With the men from both ships pitching in, the *Glide* was hove down, patched up, and made seaworthy again in twelve days.

In the following weeks thousands of natives gathered bêche-de-mer for the two Salem ships, and then the *Glide* left for Manila to sell its cargo to Chinese traders, before returning to Fiji by way of Hawaii. On the way back, off one of the Cook Islands, Archer spied a large group of natives paddling out to the ship. Eager to obtain grass for the goats he had bought in Hawaii, Archer waited for the natives to arrive. But—well aware of the South Pacific's history of violence, and wary of the size of the approaching contingent—Archer had his men grab their guns and load the cannons with grapeshot. Fifty or sixty natives were soon alongside the ship, speaking and gesticulating wildly. "Their whole aspect was truly terrific," Oliver later recalled.

Archer let them clamber up the side and stand on the gunwale, but he kept them off the main deck.

While Archer bent over to grab items to trade, one of the natives hurled a spear at him so quickly that none of the crew had time to warn the captain. If Archer hadn't turned his head at that moment, the spear would have pierced his neck. Instead it miraculously only grazed his skin. Before the natives could attack, Archer commanded "Fire!" Shots rang out, and a half dozen natives "fell back with a death shriek into the sea." Others were wounded with boarding spikes and cutlasses. Archer ordered the ship to get under way, and the *Glide*'s motion, combined with the crew's continued attack, drove off the natives. "Had the captain's order been a moment delayed," Oliver believed, "the savages must have gained an ascendancy over us, and the fate of the *Glide* and of her crew been sealed, and never, probably, known."

Back in Fiji, off Ovalau Island, Archer traded for bêche-de-mer, tortoiseshell, and small amounts of sandalwood. One day a group of natives visited the ship with fruit, seemingly intent on trade. But the crew's suspicions were raised when the natives began counting the number of men on board and whispering to one another. Archer was informed of this troubling behavior, but before he arrived on deck the second officer saw the natives in the canoes handing weapons up to their fellows on the gunwales. The men aloft, witnessing the same, hurried down and shot their muskets over the natives' heads, causing them to leap from the ship into the water so fast that they left many of their spears and clubs behind.

A few days later the *Glide*'s voyage of misfortune continued when a ferocious storm lashed the ship and parted two anchor cables, leaving only one anchor operational. As the storm died down, a powerful aftercurrent pushed the *Glide*, its remaining anchor dragging along the bottom, into a reef from which it only became disengaged a few hours later after a providential wind billowed the sails. The next day Archer visited the site where another China trader from Salem, the brig

Fawn, had recently been wrecked, and the men recovered its anchors and cables. Back at Ovalau eight heavily armed crewmen went ashore to cut timber for new anchor stocks. Seven of them tramped into the forest, while one, a boy, remained with the boat.

Twenty natives suddenly appeared on the beach, some armed and others bearing fruit. Since the men in the woods were "too busy to trade," the natives went down to the water and began taunting the boy, then started taking things from the boat. The boy's screams alerted the other sailors, who quickly ran down the beach only to be confronted by the natives running toward them. The crewmen raised their muskets and retreated toward the boat, parrying the clubs and spears flying through the air. Five of the men made it to the boat; two didn't.

One of the unfortunates fired his weapon and "was instantly attacked." Bleeding profusely from the head, he broke through to the water and swam feebly toward the boat, which in the commotion had been shoved into the surf, but the natives dragged him back to the beach and finished him off. The other crewman, who had rushed out of the woods last, used the butt end of his musket to beat back the natives but was nonetheless clubbed to death. When the boat returned to the *Glide* with only six men, and the rest of the crew learned of the calamity, "unbidden tears fell from the eyes of all on board." The two men killed were Joshua Derby and Enoch Knight, both of Salem. (This proved to be a doubly tragic time for the Knight family, because a few months later natives in Sumatra murdered Enoch's brother Charles, the first officer of the Salem ship *Friendship*, which was there trading for pepper.)

Seeking revenge, the crew of the *Glide* prepared for battle, and rowed two boats to the beach. A brief firefight ensued, killing a local chief and wounding others. While the rest of the natives scattered, the men of the *Glide* destroyed several canoes and then returned to the ship.

In the coming months other skirmishes would leave more natives dead. But by March 20, 1831, it looked as if the *Glide*'s troubles were at an end. The ship was ready to leave Fiji with a valuable cargo of bêche-de-mer. That evening the men were in good spirits as they gathered upon the forecastle singing songs, including "Home, Sweet Home." The next evening, however, twenty-two months after leaving Salem with such great expectations, and now longing to see their friends and families again, the crew of the *Glide* faced a hurricane of terrifying force. The anchors retrieved from the much smaller *Fawn* were not big enough, and as the tempest mounted, the ship dragged its anchors ten miles until it foundered on a reef.

Thus abruptly ended the voyage of the *Glide*, "one of the stateliest ships that ever sailed from Salem." Most of the crew survived and were picked up by other American ships. For many of the *Glide*'s men it would be years before they returned to the United States. James Oliver's homecoming took place in the summer of 1833: Having traveled in different ships first to Hawaii, then to Brazil, he found passage on the *Lucy Ann* (out of Boston), and finally caught his first glimpse of the American coast on July 4, just off Cape Cod. The next day the ship pulled into Boston, and within an hour of docking, Oliver caught a coach to Salem, where he was reunited with his happily startled and overjoyed mother.

ALTHOUGH AMERICAN MERCHANTS were profiting from the China trade, paying for Chinese goods remained a challenge. Through 1825 specie and bullion accounted for 75 percent or more of the purchases made in Canton, which frustrated merchants because silver was scarce, and using it tied up precious capital. This currency drain diminished dramatically in the late 1820s with the use of another financial instrument—the bill on London. American merchants would obtain a credit or advance from a British bank and then take that paper "bill" to Canton, where it was negotiable. The Americans could sell the bill to British opium dealers for silver and use the silver to purchase goods, or they could give the bill to the hong merchants in exchange for goods. The Americans then sold the goods in the United States or other ports and used the proceeds to pay off the advance, plus interest. The opium dealers got paid when they cashed the bills in London, while the hong merchants used the bills to purchase British goods, and the merchant with whom they dealt took the bills to London for payment. Alternately the American merchants could sell American goods in London, take the proceeds in the form of a bill, and then use it to buy goods in Canton. Bills on London eliminated the need to gather and then transport silver halfway around the world. And unlike silver, they were not targeted by pirates, making them a more secure form of currency to transport on the high seas. Despite the convenience and safety, however, using bills entailed considerable risk. Exchange rates could fluctuate, affecting the cost of a bill, and obtaining one or paying it off was contingent upon the merchant's ability to sell a large quantity of goods for a decent price, which was not always guaranteed.[28]

One alternative to sending China a never-ending stream of silver or bills on London was sending more American goods. American merchants were eager to do this, but the Chinese were not terribly interested in American goods, just as they eschewed the temptations of most British goods. Americans, however, were making some inroads: As the American manufacturing sector, specifically the domestic textile industry, expanded, fewer Chinese nankeens were imported, and more American cotton fabrics were sent to Canton. Still, China remained a vast market that America had only limited success in tapping, which frustrated America's China merchants as well as American farmers and manufacturers, echoing a theme that has persisted into the twenty-first century. After all, if the more than 300 million Chinese became eager consumers of American goods, the merchants would profit enormously by selling those goods in China, and American farmers and manufacturers would profit right along with them. Even a small shift in consumption could have a tremendous impact: As a British cotton manufacturer observed, "If

BOLTS OF SILK SENT IN THE EARLY 1800S TO MRS. EDWARD
CARRINGTON, OF PROVIDENCE, RHODE ISLAND, IN THE ORIGINAL BOX.
("WASHING" IS THE NAME OF THE SALEM SEA CAPTAIN WHO BROUGHT
THE SILK BACK FROM CHINA.)

we could add but one inch to the shirt of every Chinese, we could
keep the mills of Manchester running forever." The Americans had
similar dreams.[29]

In exchange for the specie, bills on London, and goods that Americans brought to Canton, they received equally diverse items in return.
Tea and silk continued to be the major imports. Cinnamon, sugar,
coffee, and rattan and rush matting were also prominent in the cargoes, joined by a range of smaller-volume articles, including furniture,
glassware, candy, shoes, and exotic plants. As for Chinese porcelain,
it was relegated to relatively minor status in the face of stepped-up
competition from highly skilled European ceramics manufacturers.[30]

THERE WAS, HOWEVER, also an entirely new type of import from
China—the Chinese knockoff. By the early 1830s the Carnes brothers

of New York City, Francis and Nathaniel, had grown rich importing goods from France, such as perfumes, porcelain, fans, and silk. That's when they came up with a novel idea: Why not have Chinese crafts-men replicate French goods for a fraction of the cost? After all, since the Chinese had shown great facility copying Western paintings and artistic styles, why couldn't they do the same for other items? And how about making cheaper versions of popular European foods and drugs as well? So the Carneses sent European samples to Canton, and the results were spectacular. In this way a new era was born.

Americans, especially the slowly emerging middle class, who had discretionary income and a hankering for the exotic, were ready to buy. Faux-French silk scarves and feather fans, along with delicious sauces, sweetmeats, syrups, rose oil, and other impressive imitations, flooded into French-crazed New York, where they were sold for authentic prices. This was excellent news for the Carneses, since the knockoffs were ridiculously cheap compared to the real things. The Chinese even managed to find a pulpy wood that when pickled and packaged just right could pass for the much more expensive rhubarb. Although a few children reportedly died from eating too much of this product, it sold quite well. Finally the Carneses' greed got the better of them. They imported so many fakes that the market became saturated and prices tumbled, forcing the brothers to shut down their Canton operation.[31]

WHILE AMERICAN SHIPS sailed back and forth to Canton, the rhythm of life for the Americans in China shifted as well. The Canton system of trading, with all of its peculiarities, remained intact, but a new player emerged. After the War of 1812 the dominant American trading firms largely jettisoned supercargoes in favor of company agents who resided in China year round; and many of them stayed in Canton for the duration, since the regulation requiring all foreigners to repair to Macao at the end of each trading season was no longer enforced. Agents were better able to develop strong working relationships with the hong merchants, track market trends, and strike deals when terms were most beneficial. Being an agent was a plum job, and all the men who were fortunate enough to gain that position had one major goal in mind—to earn a competency, which was enough money to enable them to return to the States independently wealthy. Not all agents achieved this goal but many did, such as John Perkins Cushing, who left Canton in 1828 with a fortune estimated to be nearly $750,000.[32] It was this potential to amass great wealth that caused John Fairbank to call the small area that housed the Canton factories the "Golden Ghetto."[33]

Some agents earned their competency not in Canton, but by working the opium trade at Lintin Island, the route chosen by Robert Bennet Forbes. Going by the name of Ben, Forbes didn't think he had any "real proclivities for the sea," but the vicissitudes of nineteenth-century adventure proved otherwise.[34] Born in 1804 in Jamaica Plain on the outskirts of Boston, Forbes made his first crossing of the Atlantic at the age of six, in the company of his mother and brother. A few years later, during the War of 1812, he and his family were onboard the small schooner *Orders in Council*, sailing under an American letter of marque from Bordeaux to Boston, when it was attacked by British cruisers. It managed to beat them off during a harrowing fight but was then promptly recaptured by a British frigate and taken to Corunna, Spain. There the Forbeses gained passage on the *Caroline*, an American brig bound again for Boston, but soon after leaving port the British frigate *Pomone* captured it and towed it back to Spain. The seemingly star-crossed Forbes family soon escaped on a fishing boat to nearby Lisbon, and embarked on the *Leda* (out of Baltimore), which arrived in Newport in late August 1813. It was quite a maritime adventure for a boy who had yet to turn ten.

Although Ben's father, Ralph Bennet Forbes, was a failure in business, Ben's uncles James and Thomas Handasyd Perkins had become commercial magnates, and with their support Ben was launched into the China trade in 1817, at the age of thirteen, as a cabin boy on their ship the *Canton Packet*. "With a capital consisting of a Testament, a

CAPT. ROBERT
BENNET FORBES,
BY LAMQUA,
CIRCA 1845.

'Bowditch,"* a quadrant, a chest of sea clothes, and a mother's bless-
ing," Forbes later recalled, "I left the paternal mansion full of hope
and good resolutions." Undeterred by his father's example, he rose
quickly through the ranks, and became a shipmaster at the age of
twenty. By 1827, he reckoned, "during the ten years of my sea-going
life, I had not been on shore more than six months, and much of that
time had been spent at Canton,—very little at home."

Tragedy, however, struck on August 9, 1829, when Forbes's older
brother Thomas, who was in charge of the Perkins & Co. house in

---

* A "Bowditch" is shorthand for *The New American Practical Navigator*, by
Nathaniel Bowditch of Salem, Massachusetts. First published in 1802, it revolu-
tionized seafaring by setting forth accurate nautical and navigational information
by which mariners could safely travel the world's oceans. Bowditch's *Navigator*
has been updated over the years, and more than a million copies have been sold. It
is now published by the U.S. National Geospatial-Intelligence Agency and is still
widely used by mariners today.

Canton, drowned when his bark was caught in a hurricane off Macao. Forbes was urged to go to Canton to become an agent as his older brother had been, but he had other plans. "I had looked forward to the command of the Lintin station-ship as the summit of my ambition." That was, he thought, "the only business that I can engage in that would suit my health, interests, and happiness, and leave me at liberty to return and enjoy a moderate competency with them most dear to me."[35]

With the help of his uncle Thomas, he purchased the *Lintin* in May 1830, and sailed it to Lintin Island, where it became the opium depot and supply ship not only for Perkins & Co., but also Russell & Co., and J. P. Sturgis, two other American firms. Although Forbes found this stationary life stultifying, he earned a princely sum of money, reportedly more than thirty thousand dollars in commissions in a single year. With much more than a "moderate competency" in hand, he sold the *Lintin* in spring 1832 and returned home to share the spoils with his family. By 1834, he later recalled, "I had become gray, and imagined myself approaching old age. I had attained the summit of my ambition. I was what was then thought to be comfortably off in worldly goods; I had retired from the sea professionally, and had become a merchant."

AN AMERICAN AGENT'S most prized asset was his relationship with the hong merchant. The most revered of all hong merchants with whom the Americans dealt was Wu Ping-Chien (Wu Bingjian), known to foreigners as Howqua—the "qua" being an honorific like "mister," and "How" an attempt at his first name. A slight man, with a friendly mien and a warm and inviting manner, Howqua was universally regarded as honest and shrewd—in short, someone who could be trusted. That trust was critical, since there were no written contracts between the hong merchants and the agents. In Canton a man's word was his bond, and Howqua's word inspired confidence.

Stories of Howqua's generosity were legendary, but one in particu

HOWQUA,
BY LAMQUA,
EARLY 1800S.

lar stands out. The Philadelphian Benjamin Chew Wilcocks, so tall that the Chinese called him the "high devil," had amassed a fortune by the early 1820s importing Turkish opium. He had nonetheless lost it all through irresponsible and lavish expenditures, whose exact nature remains not clear—although it is known that he had a penchant for things known to attract gentlemen of means, among them fine food and wine, exotic women, and expensive art. He vowed to rebuild his fortune, and his friend Howqua was eager to help out, making available a line of credit. After a few years Wilcocks was no closer to solvency; in fact he was in debt for $72,000 to Howqua. Even so the beneficent merchant graciously accepted a promissory note from Wilcocks for that amount, and tucked it away in his strongbox. For years Howqua was very patient and never raised the issue, until one day he asked Wilcocks why he didn't return to America. Wilcocks said he desperately wanted to, but first he had to pay off his debt.

1. *Silkworms at different stages of development.*

2. *Branch, leaves, blossom of a tea plant (*Camelia sinensis)*, unidentified Japanese artist, circa 1878.*

3. *This painting (1790–1800) by an unidentified Chinese artist shows the steps involved in the production of tea, from cultivation to packaging the tea for shipping.*

4. *Poppy (*Papaver somniferum*), by Daniel Wagner (1828–30).*

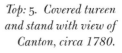

Top: 5. *Covered tureen and stand with view of Canton, circa 1780.*

Above:
6. *Chinese porcelain teapot, circa 1755, purchased by George Washington from London in 1757, as part of a complete set of china.*

7. *Paul Revere holding a silver teapot, by John Singleton Copley, 1768.*

8. *Robert Morris,*
by Charles Willson
Peale, from life,
1782.

9. *American ginseng*
and whippoorwill,
by Mark Catesby, 1748.

10. *A painted paper and mother-of-pearl*
fan, made in China and presented to
Samuel Shaw in 1784. The ship at the
far left is the Empress of China, *at*
Whampoa. This is the only image of
the ship known to exist.

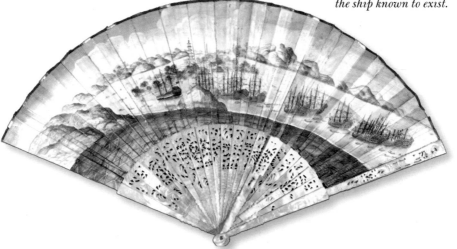

11. *Rosewood bookcase by unidentified Chinese artist (before 1795), brought to America in 1796 by Andreas Everardus van Braam Houckgeest.*

12. *Hand-painted wallpaper depicting the cultivation of rice, made in China, circa 1784, and brought back on the* Empress of China *for Robert Morris.*

13. *Copy of Gilbert Stuart's portrait of Washington, attributed to the Chinese artist Foeiqua. Reverse painting on glass, date unknown.*

14. *John Jacob Astor, by John Wesley Jarvis, 1825.*

15. *Stephen Girard,
by Bass Otis,
1832.*

16. *Elias Hasket Derby,
by James Frothingham,
early nineteenth century.*

17. Cleopatra's Barge, *by George Ropes, 1818.*

18. *View of the Praya Grande, Macao, by unidentified Chinese artist, circa 1830.*

19. *Whampoa anchorage, by Youqua, circa 1845.*

20. *Canton, with factories in the foreground, by unidentified Chinese artist, circa 1800.*

21. *Factories in Canton, by unidentified Chinese artist, circa 1805.*

22. *View of the foreign factories, Canton, with American factory
in the center, by Lamqua, circa 1835.*

23. *Capt. Robert Bennet Forbes,*
by Lamqua, circa 1845.

24. *Howqua, by*
Lamqua, early 1800s.

25. *View of workers loading tea crates onto a sampan at Canton, by Tingqua, 1855.*
The Spark, *in the background, brought to Canton by Robert Bennet Forbes,*
was the first American paddle-wheel steamer to work the coastal waters of China.

26. *Tea warehouse in Canton (1820–40), by unidentified Chinese artist.*

27. *Hand modeling and molding of porcelain vases and figures, circa 1825.*

28. *View of the foreign factories at Canton during the fire of 1822, unidentified Chinese artist, 1822.*

29. *Harriet Low, by George Chinnery, 1833.*

30. *Dr. Peter Parker with his student Kwan Ato, operating on a patient at the Ophthalmic Hospital in Canton.*

31. *Nathan Dunn, by George Chinnery, 1830.*

32. *The Daoguang emperor (r. 1821–50).*

33. *Clipper ship* Stag Hound, *by James E. Buttersworth, 1855.*

34. *Sailing card advertisement for the clipper ship* Comet, *which was built in New York City in 1851 and made runs to California and China.*

35. *Tea caddy,
unidentified
Chinese
craftsman,
circa 1850.*

36. *View of the
American
garden at the
Canton factory,
unidentified
Chinese artist,
1844–45.*

37. *The 360-foot, 3,800-ton steamship* China, *launched by the Pacific Mail Steamship
Company in 1867, took passengers and freight from San Francisco to Yokohama and
Hong Kong, and brought back tea, rice, silk, and other Asian goods, as well as many
thousands of Japanese and Chinese immigrants. Lithograph by Endicott & Company,
New York, circa 1867.*

Howqua inquired if the debt was the only thing keeping Wilcocks in Canton, and if it were to disappear, would he have the financial means necessary to reestablish himself back home. Wilcocks answered both questions affirmatively, whereupon Howqua told one of his assistants to retrieve the promissory note. "You and I are No. 1, 'olo flen,'" Howqua reportedly said, "you belong honest man, only got no chance," his pidgin English anticipating the grammar of Charlie Chan a century later. With that Howqua ripped the note into small pieces and threw them in a wastebasket. He then told the astonished Wilcocks that the debt was no more. Thus assured that he was free to leave, the stunned American did just that.[36]

While Howqua was good to the Americans, the Canton trade smiled equally upon him. In the mid-1830s his fortune was estimated to be $26 million, a figure that would have made him, if not the richest man in the world, then certainly very close to the top of the list. Howqua didn't let his money sit idle. As early as 1828 he began invest-

ONE OF HOWQUA'S TEA CRATES, CONTAINING HYSON SKIN TEA.
("HOWQUA" WAS SPELLED BOTH WITH A *U* AND *W*.)

ing in the United States, relying on his trusted American contacts to act as his agents and select promising opportunities.[37]

THE AMERICAN COMMUNITY in Canton was rather small, with as few as a dozen traders right after the War of 1812, but had increased to three times that amount two decades later. They were part of a larger, remarkably diverse, and cosmopolitan population that could daily be found just beyond the factories' walls. Of course the Chinese were in the majority, with one American reporting that the open area in front of the factories was "the rendezvous of multitudes of the natives, who assemble daily to transact business, gratify curiosity, or murder time."[38] As for the foreigners, in addition to the British, who made up the largest contingent, there were other Europeans, including the French, Dutch, and Portuguese. But the most exotic foreigners of all were the non-European merchants and traders, who hailed from India, Armenia, the Philippines, the Middle East, and other areas—all attired in the traditional costumes of their homeland.[39] To the Chinese all these foreigners appeared just as striking.

Many of the Americans would fondly recall their time at the factories. "The business transacted within their walls was incalculable," wrote William C. Hunter, who spent the better part of two decades in Canton as an agent. He especially enjoyed "the social good feeling and unbounded hospitality" that always existed between the Americans and the hong merchants. Other Americans were not so enamored of a Canton posting, viewing it as one that mixed equal measures of boredom and misery. Among the chief complaints was the torrid heat of the summers, the grueling hours of work during the trading season, and the longing for home. Perhaps the most persistent complaint of all was the ban on women.[40]

The Chinese went to great pains to enforce the regulation that forbade foreign women from entering Canton. The rationale for this exclusion was simple: "If we permit your women to land and live in our country," a Baltimorean visiting Canton was told in 1827,

VIEW OF THE FOREIGN FACTORIES, CANTON, WITH AMERICAN FACTORY
IN THE CENTER, BY LAMQUA, CIRCA 1835.

you will soon establish your homes amongst us; and, by the
natural growth of your families and your contented condition,
you will in course of time, form a permanent colony. But if we
forbid your wives, your sisters and your daughters to reside in,
or, even to visit, the "Flowery Land," we may be confident that
after you have been successful in trade, you will depart for your
native country and make room for another race of dissatisfied
bachelors![41]

It is doubtful that many Americans were interested in living in China
permanently, but there was no persuading the Chinese of that. So
the Americans remained single while in Canton, a situation that
transformed them into "half wild mans," according to one Chinese
observer. If American agents wanted female companionship they
could go to Macao, where their wives or mistresses might be waiting for them, or they could enlist the services of prostitutes, whose
presence was hard to miss. As a China merchant commented, "There

are a lot of bastard children kicking around Macao."[42] There was one time, however, when American women entered Canton, with Harriet Low leading the way.

ON MAY 29, 1829, Low accompanied her uncle William Henry Low, a partner in Russell & Co., on a trip to China, serving as a companion to her sickly aunt Abigail. Only twenty years old, Harriet had striking good looks and a vivacious personality. Over a period of four years in China she recorded her thoughts in journals and letters, her writing serving as an important cultural commentary on the time.[43]

Creating a verbal tableau perhaps typical for a pre-Victorian woman abroad, she used the word "romantic" repeatedly to describe her surroundings: Macao viewed from the water, for example, looked "beautiful, with some most romantic spots." As one of only two single women in the small community of Westerners, Low relished her unique position, which afforded her plenty of opportunity to socialize at the dances, dinners, teas, and performances that regularly took place: "There are twenty times as many gentlemen, only a little sprinkling of ladies. I have no rivals, as there is but one other spinster in the place." Nevertheless some of her suitors brought her to such exasperation that she exclaimed in her journal, "Oh dear, what animals* men are! They are certainly incomprehensible."

Low was amused by all the boats in the harbor that had "a large eye painted on each side of the bow." When she asked some Chinese why that was done, they looked at her with some puzzlement, asking in response how it was supposed to see without an eye. Low also witnessed foot binding, the ancient Chinese practice in which the feet of women were bound from an early age, the goal of which was to make the feet no longer than three to four inches, creating the prized and—to the Chinese—sexually appealing "golden lotuses" or "golden lilies."[44]

* She was using the word in the sense of "creatures" rather than making a comment about their attitude toward women.

HARRIET LOW,
BY GEORGE
CHINNERY, 1833.

Foot binding began with girls as young as five, and although it was first practiced by the elite, it later filtered down to the lower classes. The four small toes were broken, tucked underneath the foot, and bound in position, with the large one remaining free. The entire foot was then bound, with every effort being made to pull the toes and the heel as close together as possible. After that, the feet were crammed into tight-fitting shoes. Every few days the bandages were taken off, the feet cleaned, and the bandages reapplied, and whenever possible the old shoes were exchanged for ones that were tighter still. Through this gradual process, the arches were broken and the feet transformed into objects that looked more like the hooves of a small animal than anything human. Foot binding was excruciatingly painful. The victim's often bloody, pus-covered feet ached all the time, and infections, gangrene, peeling skin, and ulceration were common, sometimes resulting in complications that led to death.

It is not clear how foot binding came about, but it is thought that it arose in the Song Dynasty, when female dancers with tightly bound and pointed feet, who performed on carved, gilded lotus blossoms, became an object of male erotic desire, and the ruling men, in turn, forced women to emulate that shape by distorting their own bodies. Foot binding was also a way in which the male-dominated Chinese society kept women in their places, as subordinate, inferior members of society, by literally hobbling them and making it more difficult for them to get around, and therefore less likely that they would stray far from home.[45]

It was during a walk down to the Praya Grande that Low first saw evidence of foot binding. "On our way . . . we saw two of their women with small feet. I was perfectly astonished, although I had heard so much of them; but I never believed it, and always supposed I must be deceived. These women's feet were about the size of our little Char-

SILK SLIPPERS DESIGNED FOR WOMEN WHO HAD HAD
THEIR FEET BOUND, CREATING THE SO-CALLED
GOLDEN LOTUSES OR GOLDEN LILIES.

ley's [a boy of three]. Only think of a full-grown and rather fat person having such feet! . . . Both women carried little canes."

Low had a free spirit, and at one point, after hearing one of her uncle's acquaintances talk about all the exotic places he had visited, she railed against the societal restrictions on the freedom of movement borne by her sex. "I could not help audibly wishing," she exclaimed, "that I was a man, that I could take up my bundle and go where I pleased." Not only could she not travel the world without male chaperones, she was not even allowed to walk the streets of Macao unaccompanied. As for her urgent desire to go to Canton, that was forbidden with or without a man in tow. When she asked one of the hong merchants why ladies couldn't visit the factories, he told her that Canton was too small, and that the men there would all ogle her. But this did not satisfy Low. She knew that women attached to men with the British East India Company had been allowed to reside in Canton for quite a while, one supposedly doing so by claiming that her husband was sick and needed to be taken care of—a blatant lie, according to Low. If the British could have women, why not the Americans?

With the reluctant acquiescence of her uncle, Low and her aunt disguised themselves as boys, and departed Macao for Canton in early November 1830, onboard an American merchant boat. On a brief stop at Lintin Island, she counted fifteen opium ships, or "outlaws," as she called them. Approaching Canton near midnight, she observed the moon rise "in splendor, so that we had a fine view of the pagodas . . . and the endless variety of boats. . . . Everything was still and quiet, thousands and thousands at rest in a small space. . . . The tea-boats are immense, and ranged along in such order that they form complete streets upon the water." Wearing long cloaks, and clutching their caps tight to their heads, the two women quickly walked to the American factory door and entered, their secret still safe.

Within a few days, however, Chinese officials discovered the ruse—although how is not known, since key pages of Low's journal are missing. Soon thereafter they ordered Mr. Low to "immediately remove his family to Macao," or all trade with Russell & Company would be stopped. The threat worked, but it was a few more weeks until Low and her aunt finally left, and on their last day in Canton, they took a final evening stroll. They walked in front of the factories without much notice, but on the side streets they "were discovered to be Fanquis [foreign devils]." The Chinese lit fires so that they could gaze upon the two women. By the time they reached the door of the factory, a considerable crowd had gathered. "They were all perfectly civil," Low recalled, "and made no noise, but only showed a little curiosity."

Back in Macao, Low wrote to her sister, "I long to know what you think of our trip to Canton. I daresay you will think we were wrong to attempt it, thereby breaking the laws of even the Chinese; but I assure you there is no comparison to be drawn between the Chinese and any other nation in the world. They will not allow any innovation upon 'old custom,' and will ding those words into your ears forever if it is not for their interest to violate it, when it is quite a different thing."

Low left Macao in mid-November 1833, and after a sojourn in Cape Town and London, she returned to Salem in the late summer of 1834. "Four years' residence there [Macao] cools one's love of it, and I for one give up all the pleasures and comforts it does possess without a sigh. I shall often think of it, and with much pleasure; time, like the grave, will bury many of the thousand annoyances I had there, and I trust it was not all time spent in vain."

DESPITE ALL THE REAL and perceived hardships of life in Canton, the posting had many advantages. The factory buildings were impressively spacious and well appointed, and there were plenty of servants to attend to one's every need, making the normal burdens of daily life very light indeed. The food, although not typical American fare, was plentiful and often quite tasty. Ennui could be minimized in many ways. There were occasional outings into Canton proper, and lavish meals hosted by the hong merchants across the river. The foreign population in Canton provided the Americans with many opportunities for socializing. Dinner parties and even dances were held in which men took one another as willing albeit awkward partners. Some of the factories housed lending libraries with hundreds of volumes, and clubs were formed to discuss the books people were reading. For those with less literary inclinations, there were always the few English-language newspapers published in Canton, including the *Canton Register*, the *Canton Press*, and the *Chinese Repository*. These publications kept people up to date on what was happening, and helped to create a common point of reference to use in speaking or debating with one another.

In addition to fraternizing with agents and the hong merchants, the Americans often socialized with the small number of Western missionaries who were attempting—with little success—to establish a beachhead for Christianity in the Celestial Empire. The most famous of these was Peter Parker, a Yale University graduate (as so many of the missionaries were) in both divinity and medicine who came to Canton in October 1834 as a Protestant medical missionary. At his ordination and appointment ceremony, Parker laid out the task before

HONG MERCHANT'S HOUSE NEAR CANTON,
BY THOMAS ALLOM, 1843.

DR. PETER PARKER WITH HIS STUDENT KWAN ATO, OPERATING ON A PATIENT AT THE OPHTHALMIC HOSPITAL IN CANTON.

him. China "has mind, she has wealth, she has civilization, she has hundreds of millions of immortal souls! The work is great; our faith in God must be proportionate; our efforts also." In subsequent years Parker no doubt "saved" a few of those souls, but his real and lasting achievement lay in the work he did at the Ophthalmic Hospital that he opened in Canton in November 1835. He treated thousands of Chinese patients, many of whose lives were much improved by his expert and tender care. Parker's selflessness, devotion, and good works made him far and away the most revered foreigner in China at the time. According to one of the American agents, he was "looked up to by the Chinese as little short of a deity."[46]

The area around the factories provided exotic forms of entertainment for the Americans, including fortune-tellers, acrobats, sword swallowers, and snake charmers. It wasn't only performers who kept the Americans amused. Even a simple shopping excursion through the streets surrounding the factories could be an enjoyable diversion. As one American in Canton noted, "The daily lounge through such cool and picturesque streets is as entertaining as a museum."[47]

One of the most pleasurable activities in Canton was boat racing. Although the Eight Regulations prohibited foreigners from boating on the Pearl River, they did so despite the protestations of the Chinese. Racing was taken quite seriously, with country and individual pride on the line. Teams representing the various factories had uniforms, and there were cash and trophy prizes, and weekly awards banquets. By the time the Canton Regatta Club was established in 1837, the racers not only rowed but also used sailboats that were handcrafted for speed by ships' carpenters.[48]

PERHAPS NO SINGLE event disrupted the pleasant, orderly flow of Canton life more than the great fire of 1822.[49] In the early evening

VIEW OF THE FOREIGN FACTORIES AT CANTON DURING THE FIRE OF 1822,
UNIDENTIFIED CHINESE ARTIST, 1822.

of Friday, November 1, a fire flared in a merchant's shop in Canton about a mile away from the factory walls and soon spread to adjoining buildings. An alarm bell rang out, and hand-pulled fire trucks belonging to the British factory and the hong merchants rushed to the scene. When they arrived all was in disarray, with people fleeing from the flames screaming and clutching their belongings. There being no coordinated response, and very little water to supply the trucks, the fire quickly engulfed ever-larger swaths of the city. Foreign merchants urged local officials to knock down buildings beyond the fire's perimeter to halt its advance, but those calls were ignored. At nine o'clock people gathered on one of the verandas of the British factory to watch the conflagration and debate the likelihood of its reaching them. Just in case, the call went out to Whampoa for crews of the trading ships to make haste to Canton to assist in an evacuation if need be.

After midnight the residents at the factories began gathering important papers and valuables, including the trading goods stored in local warehouses, and moving them onto the boats assembling at the river's edge. By eight o'clock on Saturday morning the factories were ablaze. All day long the foreigners, assisted by many Chinese, fought against the wind-driven flames, but by nightfall the battle was lost. Dawn on Sunday revealed a scene of utter carnage and devastation. The Golden Ghetto, as well as a considerable part of Canton, had been transformed into a charred and smoldering wasteland. Some compared the conflagration to the Great Fire of London in 1666, which had destroyed so much of that city. In Canton thousands of buildings lay in ruins, some fifty thousand people were made homeless, and perhaps as many as one hundred lost their lives. "Twenty-seven persons were trampled to death at one spot," according to one account, "in consequence of a scramble for dollars, which fell to the ground when a robber cut the bag on a man's back, which contained the coins."[50] Although the foreigners and the hong merchants were able to save much, their losses were considerable. The factories and warehouses were gone, and with them tens of thousands of chests of tea and an untold quantity of silk. The fire cost the British an estimated $4 million, while American losses were pegged at one hundred thousand dollars. A proclamation regarding the fire, issued by a high-ranking government official, noted, "The flowery gaiety and glory of Canton was all at once consumed, like the gaudy insect that makes into the burning flame."[51]

But foreign trade was too valuable to be laid low for long. From the ashes the factories were quickly rebuilt, but this time without a wall surrounding them, so that interactions between the foreigners and the Chinese were greater than before, a change that some traders thought was for the worse. "The want of the enclosure," wrote an American, "has rendered [the Square] . . . a positive nuisance, for beside containing a Chinese market, which in itself is disgustingly offensive, it is the rendezvous of all the idle men and boys of the neighborhood, and the theatre of action of conjurors, quack-doctors, barbers, thieves, and vagabonds of every description." Rounding out the scene was the great pile of burned rubble and rubbish collected after the fire, which remained off to one side of the Square and became a de facto garbage heap for the neighborhood, added to on a daily basis.[52] Such annoyances notwithstanding, the familiar rhythms of Canton life soon returned, and the Golden Ghetto once again lived up to its name.

A LESS DRAMATIC but still significant event in the commercial life of Canton took place in 1833, when the British Parliament voted to strip the British East India Company of its monopoly in the China trade. It was a development that was a long time in coming, and one in which the Americans played a not-insignificant role. Ever since the United States had been created, Americans had been cutting into the British East India Company's profits in China, in large part because they were more efficient, bold, and resilient than the lumbering, bloated bureaucratic monopoly against which they were competing. Even before the American Revolution, British merchants had complained to Parliament that the company's monopoly status in China should be revoked so that there could be free and fair competition in the Middle Kingdom. It wasn't only the merchants who were complaining, however. Many British citizens had long chafed at what they perceived to be the unnecessarily high prices charged by the company, which were thought to be a direct consequence of monopoly.

In 1807 George Nugent Temple Grenville, the chancellor of the exchequer, gave voice to the frustration felt by so many of his fellow Britons: "The China trade has always been the object of competition among all the commercial powers of Europe, and the question is how shall we, as a nation, be best able to maintain our interest in it against that competition." Grenville mocked the supposed benefits of maintaining the "magnificent and aristocratic commerce of our [East India] Company" by pointing out that the Americans had managed quite well to ramp up their trade with China without the "benefit" of a monopoly. He argued that breaking the company's monopoly, and allowing other British merchants "the freedom" to trade and compete with one another, would allow the British people to purchase Chinese goods "at a reasonable price, instead of being wholly at the mercy of a monopoly for their supply; a monopoly which makes them pay, in the price of a favorite article, for so much of the extravagance, waste, and unskillful management of the joint stock company." One of Grenville's contemporaries was equally acerbic, but more succinct: "Of the utter failure of the monopoly projects we have too many examples. Of the success of free trade we have one great one in the [East] Indian commerce of the Americans."[53]

The British East India Company was attacked for its trade monopoly in both China and India, and for many of the same reasons. Parliament decided to act in 1813, when the East India Company's charter came up for renewal. But those who had been clamoring for change received only half of what they sought. While Parliament voted to end the company's monopoly in India, the one in China was retained. Nevertheless there was much rejoicing in Britain. A commentator in a London newspaper enthusiastically noted, "The largest fortunes which have been accumulated in America, have been by merchants trading with India. Our enterprising merchants will now have their turn."[54]

Over the next twenty years the pressure to end the company's monopoly in China intensified for many reasons, not least of which was American competition. Although the value of Britain's overall trade with China—which was a combination of the company's business and the extremely lucrative opium trafficking done by the British private traders—dwarfed America's, sometimes by as much as 6 to 1, the value of the company's trade alone was a different story. During the 1818 season Americans' trade totals eclipsed the company's for the first time, causing great consternation in Britain, where people were warily monitoring America's success. And although in subsequent years the value of America's trade trailed the company's, it was not far behind. All the more infuriating to the British was that some of the Americans' profits came from beating the company at what should have been its own game. Americans often bought British goods in London, then sold them in Canton for less than the company could—a fact that British merchants used to illustrate how uncompetitive the company had become. The calls for reform were finally answered in 1833 with the dissolution of the company's monopoly in China, effective the following year. With that an era came to an end.[55]

THUS FAR THE CHINA TRADE had yet to make much of an impression on America's domestic politics. There was one exception, however, involving the ultimate disposition of the Oregon Territory in the Pacific Northwest, a huge swath of land that ran from the top of California, or the forty-second parallel, all the way up to the southern tip of Alaska at latitude 54°40', and from the coast inland to the Rocky Mountains. Starting in 1818, and for nearly three decades thereafter, the United States and Great Britain waged a war of diplomacy over which country would gain control of this valuable parcel. The conclusion of this diplomatic tug-of-war came only in 1846, when the United States and Great Britain signed the Oregon Treaty, which set the border between the two countries at the forty-ninth parallel, and provided Britain Vancouver Island, part of which fell below the line. The land the United States gained in this transaction later became the states of Oregon and Washington, as well as most of Idaho and parts of Montana and Wyoming, which in the end turned out to be a geographic windfall to the burgeoning nation.

The China trade played two important roles in the diplomatic process that resulted in the territory being divided in this manner. The first had to do with the dispute over which country owned the land. To strengthen its case that it had rights to the southern half of the Oregon Territory—the land below the forty-ninth parallel—by virtue of discovery and occupation, the United States pointed to the exploits of Robert Gray, Meriwether Lewis and William Clark, and John Jacob Astor, all of whom were directly or indirectly associated with the China trade. In May 1792 Robert Gray, on his second trip as captain of the *Columbia* in search of sea otter pelts to bring to China, "discovered" the mythical Great River of the West, now known as the Columbia, claiming the river and the lands surrounding it for the United States. A little more than ten years later President Thomas Jefferson sent Lewis and Clark and their Corps of Discovery on a mission of exploration beyond the Mississippi River, which took them up the Missouri over the Continental Divide to the mouth of the Columbia and back again. One of the main goals of this journey was to scope out western lands as a place to expand the fur trade, with the capture of the great value of the fur trade in the Pacific Northwest of particular interest. When Lewis returned he told Jefferson that he viewed the "passage across the continent as affording immense advantages to the fur trade," and argued that all the furs gathered in the areas that he and Clark traveled through could be transported to the mouth of the Columbia for shipment to China, faster than the British could get their furs to market (the furs Lewis was talking about were mainly beaver, which, along with sea otter, seal, and the pelts of other animals, also found an excellent market in Canton). A few years after Lewis and Clark's return, Astor launched the expeditions that would result in the establishment of Astoria, his ill-fated fur-trading outpost at the mouth of the Columbia, which was supposed to serve as a conduit for sending furs to Canton.[56]

The China trade also affected the ultimate division of the Oregon Territory when politicians encouraged the United States to fight for its fair share of the land because of the role it could play in expanding trade with the Middle Kingdom. The most ardent advocate of this position was Representative John Floyd of Virginia. During a congressional debate in 1822 over whether the United States should occupy the land around the mouth of the Columbia River, Floyd emphasized the China trade as a powerful reason for doing so. Settling the Columbia and "connecting the trade of that river and coast with the Missouri and the Mississippi," Floyd argued, "is to open a mine of wealth to the shipping interests and the western country, surpassing the hopes even of avarice itself." America's furs, he believed, would enable the United States to purchase Chinese goods at a great profit, "without carrying one dollar out of the country."[57] Similar arguments were made in subsequent years, and they were amplified by other voices outside of the halls of Congress, such as that of Hall Jackson Kelley, a New Englander who spent much of his life fervently and publicly promoting the settlement of the Oregon Territory. Such settlement, he wrote in 1829, would stimulate "the spirit of American enterprise" and help bind America and the Far East closer together by opening "new channels" of trade, which would in turn "conduct the full tide of a golden traffic into the reservoir of our national finance."[58]

Although many other factors contributed to the boundary resolution embodied in the Oregon Treaty—chief among them the reality that by the early 1840s thousands of Americans had already settled in the Pacific Northwest, creating tangible facts on the ground that encouraged Britain to settle the border dispute—there is no denying that the fur-trade-related claims to the land, and the arguments about enhancing the prospects for the China trade, also played a critical role.[59]

———

FROM THE SAILING of the *Empress of China* through the late 1830s, the American China trade flooded the United States with goods that became woven into the fabric of American life. But the trade was not only a commercial proposition. Along with the goods came knowledge. In a little over five decades of trading with China, Americans had been given a hint of what life was like in the Middle Kingdom. Though only a shadow of reality, it was all they had to go on as they tried to satisfy their curiosity about this far-off and mysterious land.

Seven

CHINA THROUGH AMERICAN EYES

AFONG MOY, THE "CHINESE LADY."

*T*HE REVEREND EZRA STILES, THE PRESIDENT OF YALE UNIVERSITY, delivered a sermon on May 8, 1783, in Hartford, Connecticut, in honor of recently elected state officials. The Revolutionary War was over, and the final peace was in sight, so Stiles took the opportunity to expound on what lay ahead for his new country. "This great American

Revolution, this recent political phenomenon of a new sovereignty arising among the sovereign powers of the earth," Stiles declared, "will be attended to and contemplated by all nations. Navigation will carry the American flag around the globe itself, and display the thirteen stripes and new constellation at Bengal and Canton, on the Indus and Ganges, on the Whang-ho [Yellow river] and the Yang-tse-kiang [Yangtze (Chang Jiang)], and with commerce will import the wisdom and literature of the East. . . . [T]here shall be a universal traveling to and fro, and knowledge shall be increased."[1] With regard to Canton, and China more generally, Stiles was both correct and overoptimistic. The American flag did travel the globe and alight at Canton with impressive regularity over the next fifty or so years, but it was the commerce of China that increased most rapidly. As for the increase in knowledge about China, that was in much shorter supply.

During the early years of the China trade Americans' perceptions of China came partly from imports—the porcelain, paintings, silks, fans, and decorated furniture, which offered overly idealized depictions of China, including exotically beautiful landscapes with waterfalls, majestic trees, verdant mountains, architecturally spectacular buildings, and people—the poor peasants intentionally excluded—going about their daily activities. Such scenes were the basis for imagining what China was like. It was largely through their "interactions" with such Chinese objects, argues the historian John Rogers Haddad, that "ordinary Americans . . . developed an unrealistic construction of China as a pastoral oriental dreamland: the fantastical kingdom of Cathay."[2] But such objects were not the only available source of information. As an increasing number of Americans visited China, they developed their own more detailed images of life in the Middle Kingdom, which filtered back to the States in the form of books, articles, speeches, and casual conversations.

In constructing these images, however, the Americans faced a severe handicap. Ever since the emperor instituted the Canton system in the mid-eighteenth century, foreign traders were restricted to the thin strip of land where the factories were located, along with select locations in Canton proper, which they could visit briefly a few times per month. This was hardly a propitious vantage point from which to learn about a country as large and diverse as China. Nevertheless Americans reported what they saw and, in so doing, found a very receptive audience back home. An indication of the depth of American curiosity about China can be gleaned from the comments of a merchant who noted in 1830, "Few return [to America] from a visit to the 'Celestial Empire' without evincing considerable annoyance at the multitude of questions (many of them inconceivably absurd) with which they are afflicted by their acquaintances."[3]

Many of the descriptions of China were quite positive, focusing among other things on its beauty, agricultural productivity, the great inventions of its people, the wisdom of Confucianism, and the skill of its craftsmen. No account was more glowing than Amasa Delano's rousing conclusion in 1817 that "China is one of the most fertile and beautiful countries on the globe. It affords the fruits and vegetables of almost all climates; abounds with most of the manufactures are useful to mankind; is favored with the greatest conveniences by water transportation of any country; and finally, is the first for greatness, riches, and grandeur, of any country ever known." One subject on which most observers agreed was the honesty and professionalism of the hong merchants with whom the Americans dealt, who were by and large extolled as responsible businessmen who tried their best to navigate the rocky shoals of Chinese commerce, albeit not always successfully. Howqua was held in the highest regard. His probity and friendship were cherished in Boston, New York, and other ports where the China trade flourished, making him arguably the best-known Chinese person in the United States.[4]

For all those Americans who viewed China in a positive light, there were many, if not more, whose opinions were far less charitable. "Prejudiced originally in favor of the Chinese," wrote an American merchant, "and very much influenced by the missionary travels, I was, as may be imagined, infinitely mortified to find on my arrival, that instead of exceeding the expectations which I had indulged, they fell considerably below the standard which I had formed of their moral and physical character."[5] As the historian John Kuo Wei Tchen observed, "The closer Americans got to real Chinese, dispelling their imagined 'Orient,' the more their respect for and emulation of Chinese civilization diminished."[6]

Since trade was the primary medium of contact, it is not surprising that the trade itself was at times a target of disdain. According to Tchen, "Americans believed that the creed of life, liberty, and happiness justified demands for 'free' trade, and having overcome British controls, they decried China's regulations of its trade and ports as 'despotism.'"[7] Some Americans thought that China's government was corrupt. "Notwithstanding the encomiums which are generally bestowed on the excellence of the Chinese government," noted Samuel Shaw, "it may, perhaps, be questioned, whether there is a more oppressive one to be found in any civilized nation upon earth."[8]

Condemnation of the government was often intensified by a negative view of the Chinese legal system. The *Emily* affair, in which Francis Terranova was ultimately convicted and strangled, greatly offended Americans' sense of justice. In their eyes not only was the death accidental, but the trial itself was a sham. As further proof that Chinese justice was unfair, the Americans pointed to the British and their experience with the *Lady Hughes*. The sentences handed down for violations of the law—including strangulation, decapitation, and scalding with hot oil—were also criticized. "China has been long celebrated for the cruelty of the punishments inflicted by her laws," wrote one American trader. "The variety and ingenuity of them are certainly little creditable to a people which boasts of so high a degree of civilization, and many of them are unequalled among the most barbarous nations."[9]

The military prowess of the Chinese was also lambasted: It was widely believed that against the modern weaponry and armed forces of the West, China wouldn't stand a chance. A Philadelphian who resided in Canton claimed that the Chinese "are literally a flock of sheep, in comparison with Europeans, and their armies of millions would be as easily routed and slaughtered."[10]

Some viewed the Chinese people themselves with contempt. "Of all uncouth figures that strut their little hour upon the stage of life," wrote an American visitor to Canton in 1832, "a China-man is surely the most grotesque animal. . . . the most unprepossessing figure ever beheld—the most awkward looking biped in the universe."[11] Other Americans called the Chinese "vindictive, lascivious, and roguish," "vile," "depraved," and "cowardly." The strongest criticism was reserved for the small-time traders or peddlers, who were seen as being "ruffians," ready to cheat the foreigners at every turn.[12] As one American merchant counseled, "The only good rule for the government of a man's conduct is to believe every Chinese a scoundrel, till you are convinced of his integrity."[13] Chinese cuisine was often ridiculed, especially the consumption of rats, dogs, and cats, as well as other items that would never appear on American menus. The practices of female infanticide and foot binding also came in for biting commentary, provoking claims that China oppressed women (Americans at the time were apparently incapable of understanding how they, too, subjugated women).[14]

Those who spent time in China frequently mentioned yet another unflattering piece of the culture—poverty (an aspect of life hardly unique to the country). "Multitudes of beggars are seen all about," Peter Parker observed soon after arriving in Canton.[15] Missionaries like Parker were alarmed not only by the widespread poverty but also the difficulty of gaining converts to Christianity, a failure they attributed in part to the alleged pagan nature of the Chinese. The more the missionaries ran into resistance, the greater their frustrations became. They often railed against Chinese idol worship, gambling, prostitution, opium smoking, and the despotic government, which they believed placed roadblocks in the way of their proselytizing.[16]

To a considerable extent the unflattering impressions of the Chinese that many Americans developed were a function of their limited perspective. Regarding the American community in Canton, Jacques Downs wrote: "Their enforced isolation, their daily association with the lowest classes of Chinese, the sumptuous existence at the factories, and the nearby spectacle of poverty and Chinese justice [that is, public executions] made for a series of cultural contrasts which created a very jaundiced view of the people and culture of China."[17]

STATESIDE, AMERICANS HAD virtually no opportunity to meet Chinese people and therefore create their own sense of what they might be like. With the exception of Punqua Wingchong, none of the handful of Chinese who made it to America on merchant ships left an indelible impression, and the residue of his visit was hardly ennobling to the people he represented. The five Chinese boys who came to America between 1818 and 1825 to attend the Foreign Mission School in Cornwall, Connecticut, were there less to inform Americans about China than, as one newspaper put it, to receive "a Christian education, hoping that on their return home, they may be useful in Christianizing the Chinese, the most populous heathen nation on the globe."[18] The only other Chinese who came to the States were not ambassadors for their culture but objects of entertainment, or "edifying curiosities" viewed more as freaks than respected members of another society.[19]

ONE SUCH EXAMPLE has become a mainstay of American lore in the nineteenth century. As the story goes, Abel Coffin, the captain of the *Sachem*, had quite a surprise for his wife, Susan, upon his return from a trading voyage to the Far East. "I have two Chinese boys 17 years old, grown together," he wrote her in 1829. "They enjoy extraordinary health. I hope these will prove profitable as a curiosity."[20] The two boys, called Chang and Eng, were conjoined at the abdomen, near the umbilical cord, by a span of flesh about five inches long and eight inches in circumference. They shared a liver and their blood supply, but other than that had everything else in duplicate. They were born

CHANG AND ENG,
THE "SIAMESE
TWINS," BY
JOHN M. ELLIOT,
1839.

and raised in Thailand, near Bangkok; however, their fisherman father was Chinese, their mother was reputed to be three-quarters Chinese, and their peers in Thailand referred to them as the Chinese Twins. Coffin and his partner, Robert Hunter, a British trader, didn't abduct Chang and Eng but rather persuaded their mother to part with them for two and a half years in exchange for five hundred dollars.

When the boys arrived in Boston, on August 16, 1829, they created a sensation. The *Boston Patriot* averred, "We have seen and examined this strange freak of nature. It is one of the greatest living curiosities we ever saw."[21] Doctors called in to do their own investigation duly reported that Chang and Eng's condition was real, thereby putting to rest rumors that the boys were part of a hoax. Soon thereafter Coffin's hope for profitability proved true. Within two weeks he had rented a tent capable of holding thousands of people, and launched a massive publicity campaign, replete with posters plastered citywide, to entice people to come see "The Siamese Double Boys." And come they did in droves, each paying fifty cents a head.[22] "All the town goes to see the Siamese twins," reported the *Boston Galaxy*, "and people are set to wondering, as well they may be, at this fantastical trick which nature has taken into her head to play for the special purpose of confounding the wits of us poor mortals."[23]

For nearly three years, under Coffin's management, the celebrated Siamese Twins toured the United States, England, Scotland, and Ireland, being presented at numerous venues where they often donned Chinese costumes, performed simple acrobatics, and sold autographed lithographs of themselves as souvenirs. In June 1832, however, when they turned twenty-one, they broke from Coffin, believing that they had fulfilled all their obligations to him—they were, they told him, "their own men." Over the next seven years they managed themselves, touring extensively throughout America, and also appearing in France, Belgium, Holland, and Cuba. One contemporary chronicler called them the "eighth wonder of the world."[24]

In 1839 the brothers settled in North Carolina, became naturalized citizens, purchased slaves to manage their estate, married two sisters, and produced twenty-one children between them, surnamed Bunker. Although they wanted to retire from performing, financial concerns forced them back into that life in 1849, and for many years thereafter they continued to tour to pay the bills, at one time performing in P. T. Barnum's shows. Finally, in January 17, 1874, they died within a few hours of each other, with Chang expiring first. Eng's last words were "May the Lord have mercy upon my soul." The conjoined twins were sixty-three years old.[25]

FIVE YEARS AFTER Chang and Eng came to America, the first known Chinese woman arrived onboard the *Washington*, which docked in New York City on October 17, 1834. The Carnes brothers, who had already grown rich selling Chinese knockoffs of French designs, owned the *Washington*, and now hoped to add to the allure of their "product line" by employing this Chinese woman to bring a so-called slice of China to America. Various papers referred to her as "Julia Foochee ching-chang king," or "Miss Ching-Chang-foo"—beginning a trend of making a farce of Chinese names—and claimed that her father was an important man in Canton, but history has not left a record of who she really was. The Carnes brothers soon had the young lady change her name to Afong Moy, and her career, such as it was, as the exotic "Chinese Lady" was launched.[26]

Out of an exhibition space at 8 Park Place, the Carnes showed Ms. Moy to all who would pay fifty cents, seemingly the going rate for viewing Chinese "curiosities." Legions of New Yorkers put down their money, and when they walked through the door they entered a parlor replete with lacquered furniture, Chinese silks, paper lanterns, paintings, and porcelain vases, where Ms. Moy, adorned in Chinese costume, would sip tea, hobble around every now and then on her "golden lilies," and answer questions from visitors through the intermediary of her Chinese servant and interpreter, a Mr. Atung, who had purportedly accompanied her from China. The *New York Gazette* reported that Ms. Moy "possesses a pleasing countenance, is 19 years of age, four feet ten inches in height, and her feet, including her shoes, are but four inches in length, having worn iron shoes for the first ten years of her life, according to the custom of the country."[27] Her tiny feet elicited the most attention in the press, and were the subject of the most impassioned reactions, with one reporter decrying her deformity and the culture that promoted it, stating that it was a "cruel process to which she has been subjected," and that it showed that Chinese women live in "vassalage to the lords of the other sex."[28]

Ms. Moy had an extended run in New York, followed by travels throughout the country, always drawing big crowds, much as Chang and Eng had done. "In many ways," as the historian Krystyn R. Moon notes, "Afong Moy's act . . . reemphasized what Americans saw as the differences between themselves and the Chinese, and by extension, the latter's inferiority." Ms. Moy purportedly left America for home in 1837, but she appeared again in New York and Boston about ten years later, performing native songs, and using her newfound facility for English to lecture audiences on Chinese customs. Soon after, the "Chinese Lady" faded from view, possibly heading to Europe for other engagements.[29]

CHANG AND ENG, along with Afong Moy, offered but the slightest—and hugely distorted—glimpses of China, little more than gross caricatures. Other reflections came from collections of Chinese objects and artifacts brought to the United States. The first of these belonged to Andreas Everardus van Braam Houckgeest, an American citizen of Dutch descent who worked for the Dutch East India Company in Canton during the 1790s. A heavy-set man with a large, round, inviting face, Houckgeest accompanied the Dutch ambassador on a mission to Peking in honor of the sixtieth year of the emperor Qianlong's reign. During the long and oft-interrupted trip Houckgeest marveled at his surroundings, sketching many of the fascinating scenes along the way.

The mission arrived in the capital city in January 1795 and spent forty days, during which Houckgeest became not only the first American to visit Peking, but also the first to be presented to the emperor in the imperial court. Houckgeest made quite an impression, performing the kowtow, and in the process having his hat tumble off his head, which caused the emperor to laugh. In that moment and the brief lighthearted exchange that followed, Houckgeest thought he had formed a special bond with the aged emperor. "I afterwards finished my salute of honor," Houckgeest later wrote, "and when I rose to retire, the Emperor, having his eyes still turned towards me, kept looking at me with a countenance expressive of the greatest kindness. Thus did I receive a mark of the highest predilection, and such as it is even said no envoy ever obtained before."[30]

The mission returned to Canton in May 1795, whereupon Houckgeest employed two Chinese artists to take his numerous sketches and render them into finely colored drawings and paintings. This was not the first time he had employed these artists. Before his trip to Peking he had hired the men "to travel at his expense throughout the whole of China, in order that they might collect views of every thing curious and picturesque which that country contains." The result of their efforts was monumental, nearly eighteen hundred images of the Celestial Empire. Houckgeest's goal was to create a collection that captured the essence of China. To that end he compiled the images into thirty-eight volumes covering a wide range of topics, including history, mythology, arts and trades, manners and customs, and two entire volumes containing views and monuments of Canton. To these volumes Houckgeest added many maps, charts, and plans, as well as a "number of other curious things," one of the most spectacular of which was a vase made of "rock crystal, supported by the trunk of a tree, and embellished with a garland of flowers."

Houckgeest arrived in Philadelphia in April 1796, bought a 430-acre farm near Bristol, Pennsylvania, and began building a grandiose house. During construction he rented a space in Philadelphia to exhibit some of his collection, and there a relatively small number of visitors—mainly the city's elite—were entertained by their host's animated tales of China, and by the presence of the five Chinese servants he had brought back from Canton. As one of the visitors remarked, it was "impossible to avoid fancying ourselves in China, while surrounded at once by living Chinese, and by representations of their manners, their usages, their monuments, and their arts."[31]

Upon completion of his fifteen-room mansion, Houckgeest called it China's Retreat, a most appropriate name since the money that paid for it came from the China trade. Atop the building sat a small pagoda bedecked with silver bells, and inside, his collection transformed the house into a Chinese museum, but one that only a select few invited guests ever saw, including George Washington and the Marquis de Lafayette on a visit from France. After about a year, however,

Houckgeest's lavish lifestyle ruined him. Overextended, he ended up in debtor's prison for a short while, then left for London, where his prized collection was sold by Christie's auction house in 1799. Two years later Houckgeest died in Amsterdam, all but forgotten.[32]

AT THE SAME TIME that Christie's was selling the remains of Houckgeest's treasures, another collection of Chinese art and curiosities was just getting started in Salem, Massachusetts. In fact Salem's East India Marine Society was established in August 1799 by a select group of sea captains and supercargoes who had the distinction of having sailed beyond either the Cape of Good Hope or Cape Horn. One of the provisions of the society's charter called for establishing "a cabinet of natural and artificial curiosities," which had been brought back by members on their travels beyond the capes. The museum that resulted—the ancestor of the modern Peabody Essex Museum in Salem, which is the oldest continuously operating museum in the country—contained an enormous variety of objects from the Pacific Northwest, the islands of the Pacific, and the Far East, those from China being just part of the whole. A girl who visited the museum in the 1830s later recalled the wonderful effect its exhibits had on her inquisitive mind:

> It was an experience for an imaginative child to step from the prosaic streets of a New England town into that atmosphere redolent with the perfumes from the east. . . . From the moment I set my foot in that beautiful old hall, and greeted and was greeted by the solemn group of Orientals [including a Chinese mandarin in costume] . . . until the hour of closing came . . . [the time was] full of enchantment, and I think I came as near fairyland as one can in this workaday world.[33]

It was a failed businessman from Philadelphia named Nathan Dunn, however, who outstripped his contemporaries' efforts to educate Americans about the Middle Kingdom. He wanted to bring China to the States in a way that left people in awe, thereby serving as a counterbalance to the widespread derogatory portraits of the country. Propelled by his desire to get out from under a pile of debt he had accumulated, Dunn journeyed to Canton in 1818. The particulars of Dunn's fall are unclear, but he had seen other men make their fortunes in the China trade, and he decided it was his turn to try. He did spectacularly well, returning to Philadelphia in 1832 a wealthy man. Eager to present himself in a new light, he invited all his former creditors to a sumptuous dinner, and under each of their plates placed a check that covered his debts to them plus interest.[34] Money, however, was not all he had acquired. During his years in Canton he had assembled an extraordinary collection of Chinese objects, which came back with him as well.

Dunn's collecting strategy was both traditional and unique. He used his vast financial resources to purchase many items in Canton, but he also relied on strong personal ties with the Chinese to expand his collecting horizons beyond anything he could have achieved himself. His fervent opposition to the opium trade underscored his reputation as a highly respected foreigner, opening up wider avenues for adding to his growing collection of all things Chinese. According to a contemporary account, Dunn received "frequent presents . . . of valuable curiosities, and articles of interest, from the natives," as tokens of "their thankfulness for the virtue that induced him to abstain from [engaging in the opium trade, and] assisting in the ruin of thousands of their countrymen."[35] Dunn's actions greatly elevated him in the eyes of local, regional, and national government officials, all the way up to the emperor. With their support Dunn was able to hire Chinese agents to do what he, as a "foreign devil," couldn't—scour the empire for items to add to his collection.[36]

Dunn's goal was to display his collection in public. His wish was granted in late December 1838, when he opened an exhibit titled "Ten Thousand Chinese Things" on the first floor of the newly opened Philadelphia Museum, which had been largely funded by a major donation from Dunn himself. The hall was a little over 160 feet long, and 70 feet wide, with high ceilings supported by twenty-two ornate wooden columns. Upon entering the space, one was—according to the accompanying catalog—"transported to a new world. It is China in miniature. The view is imposing in the highest degree."[37] One visitor claimed that Dunn had created "a panoramic pageant of Oriental life and art, which places the whole nation within the reach of the remotest inquiring inhabitant of our union."[38]

While this was hyperbole, the exhibit was exceptionally comprehensive, if not a bit overwhelming. In fifty-three cases, plus numerous freestanding exhibits, Dunn's "Chinese Museum" employed fifty life-size clay figures and about twelve hundred objects to tell the story of China, which would have been a daunting task for an exhibit ten times as large. There were marble and copper Buddhas alongside detailed models of pagodas, bridges, houses, and many of the boats encountered on the watery thoroughfares of China. Three "literary gentlemen" in loose-fitting summer costumes could be seen with snuff bottles in hand, standing alongside delicately carved and highly polished wooden bookcases that gave mute testimony to Dunn's claim that the "Chinese are a reading people" who were producing grand works of literature during the eighth century, "when almost the whole of Europe was sunk in gross ignorance and barbarism." Skillfully rendered paintings helped visitors visualize the graceful architecture, verdant landscapes, and large cities of China, including Canton and Peking. There were portraits of well-armed warriors, stately mandarins, ladies at play, as well as the emperor and Howqua. The section on natural history presented a stuffed peacock, a Chinese fox, and a silver pheasant, while other areas showcased musical instruments, cooking pots, agricultural tools, and chopsticks in a sandalwood case. And along the edge of the hall, on the moldings surmounting the columns, Chinese maxims were inscribed, sharing the wisdom of the ages: "Those who respect themselves will be honorable," read one, "but he who thinks lightly of himself, will be held cheap by the world." Another declared, "Virtue is the surest road to longevity; but vice meets with an early doom."[39]

The exhibit was an enormous success, drawing one hundred thousand visitors during its three-year run, and selling fifty thousand copies of the museum catalog. It certainly helped to improve China's image in America. "Mr. Dunn, in the collection he has made and now offers to public examination," noted Enoch Wines, a Philadelphia minister, "has done more than any other man to rectify prevalent errors, and disseminate true information, concerning a nation, every way worthy to be studied by the philosopher who delights in the curious, by the economist who searches into the principles of national prosperity and stability, and by the Christian who desires the universal spread of that Gospel."[40]

EVEN AS DUNN'S EXHIBIT was presenting China as a society of the first rank, worthy of respect and admiration, it elicited some comments that were anything but laudatory. "Stopped in their progress, as the Chinese were," proclaimed an editor of the *Southern Literary Messenger*, "and without any likelihood of a change, . . . a collection like that of Mr. Dunn becomes of permanent value, for it exhibits not only the past and present of such a people, but their future also." This editor was merely reflecting a widespread belief in America and Europe that China was somehow stuck in the past—that while the Western world had galloped ahead during the late 1600s, 1700s, and early 1800s, making great strides in science, literature, the arts, and governance, China had remained stationary, advancing not at all.[41]

The true picture was anything but that. China had remained very much an illustrious and innovative civilization, even though by the early nineteenth century the ruling Qing (Ch'ing) Dynasty was showing serious signs of decay. What had changed, however, was the West's position and perspective, incredibly rapid advances enabling its countries finally to approach, and in many instances exceed, China

WESTERN GATE OF PEKING, BY THOMAS ALLOM, 1843.

on the various benchmarks by which we measure human progress. This was especially true with regard to scientific and technological achievements. So, to many in the West, it appeared that China was a case of arrested development.

WITH ONLY A FEW opium pipes on display, Dunn's exhibit barely touched upon opium smoking in China, but the catalog made clear just how central an issue this was. Dunn used the last 9 pages of the 120-page catalog to rail against the growing drug trade in China: "Opium is a poison, destructive alike of the health and morals of those who use it habitually, and, therefore, the traffic in it, under any circumstances, is nothing less than making merchandise of the bodies and souls of men."[42] Although most of his anger was directed against the British, the main suppliers of the drug, Dunn was also scornful of American merchants who sold opium to the Chinese. As visitors flocked to Dunn's Chinese Museum, and read his condemnation of the opium trade, events were transpiring in China that would bring the long-festering issue to a violent head.

Eight

THE OPIUM WAR

NATIVE BOATS IN INDIA CONVEYING OPIUM DOWN
THE GANGES TO CALCUTTA, 1850.

*E*ARLY IN THE MORNING OF SUNDAY, MARCH 10, 1839, WILLIAM
Hunter, an agent working for Russell & Company, joined a few other
Americans onboard a small schooner moored in front of the factories,
awaiting the arrival of Lin Zexu (Lin Tse-hsü). A little more than
two months before, after nineteen lengthy interviews, the emperor
had appointed Lin as high commissioner and charged him with the
responsibility of going to Canton to halt the opium trade. At fifty-five

COMMISSIONER LIN,
BY AN UNIDENTIFIED
CHINESE ARTIST,
1843.

years of age, Lin had shone as a student and risen through the government ranks, finally gaining the coveted post of governor-general of two key Chinese provinces, and earning along the way the nickname "Blue Sky," on account of his faultless and incorruptible nature. His reputation for honesty, hard work, and integrity, and his strong views on the evils of the opium trade, led the emperor to select him for the post. Lin began his journey to Canton on December 31, 1838, accompanied by an entourage of thirty men, and more than five thousand pounds of luggage. By river and overland, Lin's group slowly made its way south.

Hunter and his companions were not the only ones interested in Lin's arrival. The riverbanks on both sides were crowded with residents and soldiers "arrayed in bright new uniforms." Every patch of ground appeared taken, and people filled the doors and windows of all of the buildings hoping to catch a glimpse of the high commissioner. Not a single vessel was moving. All traffic had been cleared to make way for the procession. At eight thirty Lin's boat appeared in the distance, and as it approached they saw the man himself, sitting near the prow with high-ranking mandarins standing behind him. "He had a dignified air," Hunter recalled, with "rather a harsh or firm expression, [and he] was a large, corpulent man, with heavy black moustache and long beard." Other boats, loaded with government officials, followed Lin's, passing before the silent crowds. Nobody was quite sure what Lin would do after he got to work, but they all would soon find out.[1]

The high commissioner faced a monumental task. The Chinese government's efforts to halt the opium trade had been largely ineffective. Decades' worth of edicts prohibiting the trade—the one in 1799, and others that followed—had been ignored, and enforcement had been unsuccessful. "Foreign mud" continued to stream into China, and the problem was getting worse. The roughly eight thousand chests of opium imported in 1823 rose to twenty-four thousand in 1833, thirty thousand in 1835, and forty thousand in 1838.[2] Almost all this opium originated in India. Less than half, however, came from poppy fields controlled by the British East India Company. The rest came from the princely states of the Malwa region, in west-central-northern India, where opium production and sale were under the control of the Indians themselves (Malwa's entrance into the China-bound opium trade really only took off in the early 1820s). Even though the British didn't benefit directly from the sale of Malwa opium, they profited nonetheless when the Malwa merchants paid a duty to the British to convey their opium through British-controlled Bombay (modern Mumbai). And the British added to their profits by transporting much of the Malwa opium to Canton in their ships, getting a commission on its sale.[3]

This expanding drug trade was incredibly important to Britain. As a British writer observed in 1839, "From the opium trade the Honorable East India Company have for years derived an immense annual revenue; and through them the British Government and nation have also reaped, from the same trade, an incalculable amount of advantages, both political and financial." Profits from the sale of opium helped pay for the administration of Britain's sprawling domain in India, and taxes on Chinese goods bought with opium money, as well as taxes paid on the sale and shipment of opium, pumped roughly £6 million annually into the British treasury. Americans, too, were still getting rich from opium, transporting it from Turkey and India, but their share of the trade remained relatively small. Overall, however, opium was at the time arguably the most valuable commodity in the world.[4]

The exploding opium trade was a serious problem for China in both human and economic terms. As the volume of the drug entering the country rose, prices dropped; and as the prices dropped, producers in India stepped up production to maintain their profits. This self-reinforcing cycle not only quickly ratcheted up the amount of opium entering China, but it also meant that opium was getting cheaper all the time, enlarging the potential pool of users. The result being that

CHINESE MANDARIN WITH AN OPIUM PIPE, 1836.

opium smoking, once the domain of the elite, was increasingly filtering down to the lower classes. How many Chinese smoked opium, and how many of those were addicted is not clearly known; however, modern studies suggest that only a very small percentage of users became addicts. Parker believed that in Canton alone there were tens of thousands of addicts in the mid-1830s, and other estimates place the number of addicts nationwide at between 2 and 10 million. One of the groups that had the highest rates of addiction was government officials, the very people in charge of curtailing the opium trade and punishing offenders. Among the military, too, addiction was fairly widespread.[5]

To pay for the growing addiction, the Chinese were spending silver at a rapid rate. Indeed, for many years China had been sending much more of the precious metal out of the country than it was taking in. This was a problem, as the historian Jonathan Spence points out, because "a scarcity of silver meant that its price rose in relation to copper; since peasants used copper currency in their everyday transactions but still had to pay their taxes to the state in silver, a rise in the value of silver meant that peasants were in fact paying steadily higher taxes," which led to widespread unrest.[6] In 1838 the emperor had warned, "If steps be not speedily taken [to stanch this outflow of silver], and if we do not strenuously seek to recover ourselves, the useful wealth of China will all be poured into the fathomless abyss of transmarine regions. The evil consequences to the national resources and to the people's well-being will be great."[7]

Viewing these developments with increasing alarm, the Chinese government responded in predictable ways. More edicts were issued prohibiting the importation of opium. Enforcement actions were stepped up, the most dramatic of which was the government's burning of much of the smuggling fleet, not once but twice. Despite all this, and not surprisingly, given its proven ability to surmount all obstacles, the opium trade continued to flourish.[8]

The emperor Daoguang knew that something further had to be done to deal with this scourge. He asked his trusted advisers to offer potential solutions. From 1836 through 1838, recommendations flooded into Peking. They laid out four main ways in which the opium problem might be attacked: (1) guarding the maritime ports so no drugs could be brought in; (2) halting all foreign trade; (3) arresting and severely punishing opium dealers; or (4) legalizing and taxing the drug.[9]

THE FOREIGN TRADERS in Canton were well aware of what was transpiring in Peking. They translated the documents sent to the emperor, and actively discussed the possible outcomes of the deliberations. Some traders were happy to leave well enough alone, hoping that talk was the end of it and that nothing would change. "Up to this period," Hunter contended, the opium trade "had indeed been an easy and agreeable business for the foreign *exile* who shared in it at Canton. His sales were pleasantness and his remittances were peace. Transactions seemed to partake of the nature of the drug; they imparted a soothing frame of mind with three per cent commission on sales, one per cent on returns, and no bad debts!"[10] Other traders were favorably disposed toward legalization. To them opium was a commodity like any other, and since the Chinese seemed totally incapable of halting its spread, they should make it legal. But no matter what a trader thought about the emperor's deliberations, none—with the exception of those few who were opposed to the opium on principle—had any serious qualms about their role in the drug trade.

When the traders thought about the legal, ethical, or moral implications of opium trafficking, or its impact on the Chinese, they inoculated themselves against self-doubt by discounting the harm of the drug and painting the trade as a laudable enterprise, despite the fact that it violated Chinese law and hurt many people. One of the best expressions of this thinking comes from Robert Bennet Forbes, who had headed back to China in 1838 to recoup a fortune that had been dissipated during the Panic of 1837, a financial crisis in the United States that led to a prolonged depression. As the chief agent for Russell & Company, the biggest American dealer in opium, Forbes had a unique vantage point to comment on the trade. "As to the effect [of opium] on the people, there can be no doubt that it was demoralizing to a certain extent; not more so, probably, than the use of ardent spirits." He contended that as long as opium was sold in coastal waters, which he believed to be beyond China's jurisdiction, the transaction was not smuggling but a "legitimate business." For additional solace Forbes noted that he was just following the lead of the British East India Company, as well as the other American merchants that he had always "been accustomed to look up to as exponents of all that was honorable in trade,—the Perkins's, the Peabodys, the Russells, and the Lows."[11] In a letter to his beloved wife, Rose, Forbes tried to ease her mind, should she have any concerns about his activities, by telling her, "There has been no moral feeling of indignation connected with the business & if any thing were wanted to give it respectability in your eyes I would mention that I made my first fortune by the same."[12] Warren Delano II, who took over the reins at Russell & Company after Forbes, and who was also President Franklin Delano Roosevelt's grandfather, defended the opium trade just as heartily as his predecessor, insisting that it was "a fair, honorable and legitimate trade," no worse than the importation of liquor into the United States or any other country.[13]

This relatively cavalier attitude toward opium, held by both American and British traders, is easier to understand when one considers that in the United States and Britain the importation and use of opium were legal, and in both countries there were plenty of people who took various forms of the drug for medicinal and recreational purposes—the most common form being laudanum, a mixture of opium and alcohol. Among the most illustrious users, who often became addicts, were writers who employed the drug for everything from treating pain to unlocking the mysterious sparks of creativity. High on this list were Samuel Taylor Coleridge, Elizabeth Barrett Browning, and Thomas De Quincey, the author of the bestselling *Confessions of an English Opium Eater*, published in 1821. Thus the comparison of opium to alcohol—another legal yet often very harmful product—was hardly surprising. There is, however, a simpler and more persuasive explanation as to why the British and the Americans continued for so long to engage in the opium trade though they knew full well that they were flouting Chinese law and damaging many Chinese lives: As John Fairbank wisely pointed out, the "economic value [of the trade] for many decades outweighed its moral turpitude."[14]

FOR THE AMERICANS the economic imperative was paramount. After all, the main reason they had come to China was to earn a competency, their golden ticket back to the States. Never mind that in the lives they had left behind many of the traders were highly religious, upstanding members of their communities, who were active in philanthropic causes and were considered moral men by their contemporaries—in China they operated according to different rules. "China traders were," observed Downs, "rational, profit-maximizing entrepreneurs in Canton. They had come to seek a fortune; they would wrest it from China and go home to practice their ethics."[15]

If the British and American traders needed any additional reasons to pursue the opium trade without restraint, they could point to the fact that neither of their governments put any roadblocks in their way. The British government had repeatedly sanctioned the trade, preferring to place revenues above principles.[16] And as for the American government, although it was well aware that its citizens were participating in the trade, on the subject of whether they should be doing so it had said nothing at all. The only other government that could have stood in the way of the foreign traders was the Chinese, but its efforts to curtail the opium trade continued to be relatively ineffective. Indeed, the traders had nothing but contempt for such efforts, as Hunter's cynical analysis of the situation makes clear:

We were threatened and re-threatened with the "direst penalties if we continued to sell *foreign mud* to the people[.]" . . .

Truly, "forbearance could be no longer exercised," and we continued to sell the drug as usual. Our receiving ships at Lintin were no longer to loiter at that anchorage, but "forthwith to come into port or return to their respective countries." The heart of the ruler of all within the *Four Seas* was full of compassion. "Yet now, no more delay could be granted, and cruisers would be sent to open upon them irresistible broadsides;" and in spite of these terrors the ships never budged. . . . [E]verything worked smoothly and harmoniously by acting in direct opposition to what we were ordered to do. We pursued the evil tenor of our way with supreme indifference, took care of our business, pulled [rowed] boats, walked, dined well, and so the years rolled by as happily as possible.[17]

As the emperor carefully considered his options, it was becoming increasingly evident to the foreigners that the trade was not going to be legalized, because the Chinese redoubled their enforcement efforts with each passing year. Numerous opium smugglers and dealers were arrested, with one of the latter being tied to a wooden cross in Macao and strangled, then left hanging for two days as a warning to others who might disobey the law. The Chinese destroyed a floating hospital in Whampoa because they thought it was nothing more than a disguised opium depot. Nine foreigners selling opium, including one American, were ordered to leave China. Although the order was not carried out, the message was clear—the authorities were watching more closely than ever.

All this activity hindered the opium trade, but still it flourished. As a British missionary observed in early November 1838, "Even those deeply engaged in it stand amazed at the rapidly increasing demand, the intense eagerness with which it is sought, the risk and adventure willingly incurred by the native dealer to escape the punishment to which a breach of a law lays him open, and the bribery and corruption by which he defeats the end of justice."[18] About a month after these words were written, an event took place in Canton that brought the rising tensions over opium to the very doorsteps of the foreign factories.[19]

SHORTLY BEFORE NOON on December 12, a mandarin carried aloft in his sedan by servants, two jailers, and a few soldiers marched into the Square in front of the factories leading a prisoner with a chain about his neck. By the time the servants had erected a tent for the mandarin to sit under, and the jailers had pounded a wooden cross into the ground, a couple of the foreigners ascertained what was taking place. The prisoner, an opium dealer, was to be strangled. As with the opium dealer in Macao, this public execution was to be a tocsin, but this time the Cantonese officials wanted to transmit the message more forcefully, choosing this location in order to insult the foreigners and highlight their shameful involvement in the trade.

Word of the impending strangulation swept through the factories, and soon a crowd of seventy to eighty foreigners formed. Hunter, serving as spokesman, "protested against the square being turned into an execution ground." The mandarin responded that the Square was part of "His Celestial Majesty's Empire," and that the execution would proceed. Hunter, his anger rising, pointed out that the Square was leased to the foreigners, and they "would not permit its desecration by a public execution!" Hunter's exhortation had a galvanizing effect on a couple of British sailors who were up from Whampoa visiting the factories. They rushed forward, grabbed the cross, smashed it on the ground, and then used the shattered pieces of wood to rain blows upon the would-be executioners as well as nearby Chinese onlookers. The sailors then ripped down the tent and lunged at the mandarin, but the quick intervention of some of the foreign merchants averted the attack. Before the situation worsened, the mandarin and his retinue hastily departed with the prisoner, taking him just beyond the factories' walls, where the execution took place. As the sailors relished their triumph, one of them remarked, "I say, Bill, we don't get such a lark as this every day!"

A not-inconsiderable number of Chinese watched these events unfold, and once the mandarin had left, the foreigners assumed that everything would go back to normal; they would return to work, and the crowd would disperse. Instead the crowd grew larger and began closing in. Still, there was no sign of hostility; rather the Chinese seemed more curious than anything. When repeated calls by the foreigners to clear the Square were ignored, however, a few of the foreigners launched themselves into the crowd, wildly swinging sticks to beat it back. The Chinese responded by hurling stones and dirt at their attackers.

Word of the confrontation spread, and the crowd, which had now grown to eight thousand, according to one estimate, surged forward as the foreigners fled and hurriedly barricaded themselves in their factories, using barrels of coal and furniture to secure the entryways. The small contingent of soldiers and police on hand attempted to hold back the onslaught, but they were soon overwhelmed and then disappeared, leaving the foreigners on their own. The Chinese pelted the factories, shattering windows, and ripped fenceposts out of the ground, using them as battering rams to smash down the doors. The foreigners, fearing the worst, grabbed the few guns they had to defend themselves should the crowd break in.

Their best hope for rescue, the Americans believed, was to alert Howqua to their situation, in the hope that he would be able to get the authorities to intervene. Thus, late in the afternoon, Hunter and another American, Gideon Nye, made a break for Howqua's house, running along the roofs of the factories and through backstreets. Upon arriving, they found Howqua in a state of "some trepidation," having already received news of the disrupted execution and the growing crowd. He was, however, unaware of the ensuing melee, and when apprised of it, he immediately dispatched a messenger to Canton's chief magistrate asking for assistance. Finally, at half past six, the foreigners heard a most welcome sound, the gong announcing the arrival of the mandarins and their soldiers, whips at the ready. Pandemonium erupted as the crowd rushed from the Square, some people even jumping into the river. "Wide open flew the factory gates," Hunter recalled, "and in an instant their imprisoned occupants appeared with looks of relief indescribable." Amazingly, with the exception of a few Chinese who drowned, nobody else died, although many Chinese and a few foreigners were injured.

A few weeks after the riot the emperor made his decision. He wanted commissioner Lin to eliminate the opium trade. While giving Lin his orders, the emperor reportedly wept and said, "How, alas! can I die and go to the shades of my imperial father and ancestors until these direful evils are removed?"[20]

LIN WASTED NO TIME. Within days of arriving in Canton on March 10, 1839, he distributed letters warning local residents to abstain from smoking opium and to report those who did. He told them that smugglers, dealers, and users would be severely punished, and lest anyone think this was just another in a long line of ineffective crackdowns, Lin promised that "this time we are going on until the job is finished."[21]

Around March 16, Lin drafted a letter to twenty-one-year-old Queen Victoria, who was just shy of three years into her nearly sixty-four-year reign, the longest in British history. Lin urged her to open her eyes and her heart and help China halt the opium trade. He told her that the emperor had decided to crack down severely on opium dealers and smokers in order to "put a stop forever to the propagation of this vice." Treading lightly, Lin noted that "it appears that this poisonous article is manufactured by certain devilish persons in places subject to your rule." Then—mistakenly assuming that opium smoking was forbidden in Britain—Lin said this proved that the queen must be well aware of the drug's harmfulness. He told her that the best way to eliminate the opium trade was to stop producing the drug, and he implored her to use her power not only to halt the manufacture of opium in British dependencies but also to destroy what had already been produced by throwing it into the ocean. "So long as you do not take it [opium] yourselves, but continue to make it and tempt the people of China to buy it, you will be showing yourselves careful of your own lives, but careless of the lives of other people, indifferent in your greed for gain to the harm you do to others; such conduct is repugnant to human feeling and at variance with the Way of Heaven."

For unknown reasons, Lin didn't send this letter to the queen, but he did draft another, similar version later in the year, which he sent her via a British merchant ship. Although the ship arrived in London, the letter was either not delivered to the queen, or apparently not shown to her. Instead it was later published in the *Chinese Repository* and *The Times* of London, and although it had no impact on subsequent events, it provides a fascinating insight into Lin's thinking at the time.[22]

Next Lin turned his sights on the hong merchants and the foreigners. In an edict to the former he excoriated them for failing miserably to do their part in halting the opium trade. Decades earlier they had pledged to the emperor not to bond foreign ships carrying opium, and send them back whence they came. Nevertheless not a single merchant had ever failed to give his bond, nor was a ship ever turned away, although the merchants knew full well that most of them were transporting opium. "And even now, while the opium is pervading and filling with its poisonous influence the whole empire," Lin railed, the hong merchants "still continue indiscriminately to give such bonds, declaring that the ships that resort hither have brought none of it. Are they not indeed dreaming, and snoring in their dreams!"

For many years, Lin complained, the merchants and all those who worked for them had done everything in their power to facilitate the flow of opium into the country, including processing financial transactions and liaising with smugglers. "Can the hong merchants aver that they have heard and seen nothing of all this?" Lin was furious at the merchants for claiming that they bartered goods for goods, when they were actually overseeing a system in which "hundreds of millions" of dollars of Chinese silver had been used to purchase the opium, in contravention of Chinese law. "Truly I burn with shame for you," Lin told the merchants passionately, because they were "equally involved in the stench of" the trade, and all of them were in it purely to grow rich. Then Lin ordered the merchants to pass along to the foreigners another edict, ordering them to surrender all opium and sign a bond promising never again to import the drug. If the merchants failed to obtain these bonds within three days, Lin said, one or two of them would be executed.

The edict directed at the foreigners was no less damning. Lin painted them as ingrates. The Son of Heaven had allowed them to trade all these years, he said, and obtain tea and rhubarb, without which, he believed, they couldn't survive—"Favors never have been greater!" And the foreigners repaid these favors by bringing opium into China, all for the sake of profit, discounting basic decency and humanity, to say nothing of trampling on Chinese law. As for the opium, Lin told the foreigners to make sure that not even "the smallest atom [was] concealed or withheld." If the foreigners delivered the opium and signed the bonds, they could "continue to enjoy the advantages of commercial intercourse," but if they refused, severe punishment would ensue. Lin even threatened to bring to bear not only the "martial terrors and powerful energies of our naval and military forces" but also the anger of the people to put all the foreigners' "lives within . . . [his] powers."[23] Finally Lin forbade any foreigners from leaving Canton.

As dramatic as it was, the foreigners were not immediately swayed.[24] They decided to stall, telling Lin that they would respond when they had had a better chance to consider his demands (some of them didn't want to respond at all, thinking that Lin's demands were just a ruse to extort money). When Howqua and another hong merchant, Mowqua, pleaded with the foreigners at least to tender a token amount of opium to show good faith, they submitted a little more than one thousand chests, worth about half a million dollars. Lin, however, was not appeased, and he refused the offering. "This is merely a fraction of the opium," he thundered at the hong merchants standing before him. "There are tens of thousand of chests and I have demanded them all. Do you think my words are only air?"

Lin ordered one of the British agents, Lancelot Dent, to appear before him to answer for the foreigners' recalcitrance. When Dent refused, Howqua and Mowqua returned to the factories in an uncharacteristically humiliating state, with chains about their necks. Despondently they told Dent that this had happened because of him. "Last night when we had to report to His Excellency that you had not obeyed his order to come," they said, "he degraded us from our ranks and bound on us these chains which you now see. And he threatened us again that should you not go to him this morning, he would take the lives of two of our numbers. Howqua's son has already been thrown into prison, as has Gowqua, the third of our body."[25] Before this dangerous ballet played out, the negotiations took another turn, with Charles Elliot's arrival in Canton on March 24, 1839.

AFTER THE BRITISH EAST INDIA Company's monopoly was eliminated in 1833, Parliament appointed a chief superintendent of trade for Canton. The superintendent's purview was a bit murky, but in general he was to oversee British activities in China, and serve as a conduit between the traders and the Chinese government. Elliot, the current superintendent, was at Macao when Lin's edicts were handed down. Even before Elliot arrived in Canton, he had decided that all British subjects should immediately leave the factories and go to Macao, because he thought the situation had become too dangerous. Lin's threatening demands and his restriction of foreigners to Canton, combined with the growing concentration of Chinese troops and warships in the area, had contributed heavily to Elliot's decision. So too did a grisly event that had taken place almost a month earlier. On February 26 the Chinese succeeded where they had failed before. At five thirty, as the sun was beginning to set, when many of the foreigners were either taking a stroll along the river or rowing their boats, more than one hundred Chinese soldiers, accompanied by a few officers, marched quickly into the Square. Within ten minutes they had erected a wooden cross in front of the American factory, executed a

Chinese opium smuggler by strangulation, taken down the cross, and left. It happened so fast that the foreigners had no time to intervene. Later that evening all the foreigners, incensed by this affront, hauled down their countries' flags in protest.[26]

Given these developments, Elliot acted quickly upon arriving in Canton. He immediately wrote a rather pointed letter to the governor-general of Canton, demanding passports so that the evacuation could commence, but this only made matters worse. Convinced that if the British departed he would no longer be able to force them to comply with his edicts, Lin, who had read Elliot's demand, made the foreigners his prisoners. On the commissioner's orders some eight hundred Chinese who worked at the factories—the cooks, servants, compradors, and linguists—quickly and silently gathered up their belongings and left. The shops around the factories closed, and the exits from the factory area were blocked off by soldiers and hurriedly erected barricades of brick and wood. The Square filled with guards armed with pikes and rattan shields. A cordon of junks was drawn up along the river's edge to close off that avenue of escape. All trade in Canton came to a standstill. Elliot, shocked by this turn of events,

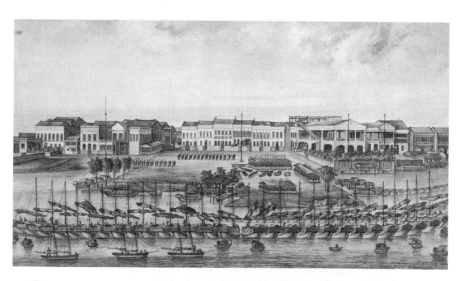

BLOCKADE OF THE FACTORIES DURING THE RUN-UP TO THE OPIUM WAR,
BY UNIDENTIFIED CHINESE ARTIST, 1839.

wrote to Lin again, this time in much more conciliatory tones, but the commissioner would not budge. When the foreigners turned over the opium, they would be free to resume trade or leave, but no sooner.

Faced with this stark new reality, Elliot blinked. Without consulting the British merchants, he agreed to turn over to Lin 20,283 chests of opium, worth as much as $10 million. This was the amount of the drug that was under the control of British subjects, and constituted the bulk of all of the foreign opium in the area at the time (about 1,500 of the 20,283 chests had been on American ships, but the Americans didn't own that opium; rather they had been transporting it on commission for British and Indian merchants). To gain the consent of his countrymen, Elliot assured them that the British government would cover their losses, although he was not authorized to make such a promise.

Over the next six weeks the chests were delivered to Lin in installments, while the foreigners remained prisoners. For some of this time they were completely on their own, forced to do all the numerous daily tasks usually performed by Chinese labor. Some took this as a terrible imposition. The American consul, Peter Snow, remarked, "Is this not too bad, . . . that a public official at my time of life, not owning a pound of opium, should be imprisoned, and compelled to do chamber-maid's work?"[27] Others did the best they could without complaining. The Americans even managed to make "light" of the situation "and laughed rather than groaned over the efforts to roast a capon, to boil an egg or a potato." The culinary results, however, were not always appetizing, and after one American managed to burn the toast to "death" and boil eggs until they had the "consistency of grape-shot," he was relieved of his kitchen duties and given the task of setting the tables and laying out linens.[28]

Since the foreigners' imprisonment had begun so quickly, and with no warning, they had no time to stock up on food. But while their rations dwindled a bit at the outset, they were never in danger of starving and in fact had plenty to eat. The Americans benefited from supplies secreted in by Howqua's servants, and the British, too, were not without their own sources of sustenance. As Forbes commented, the foreigners "suffered more during an imprisonment of several weeks, from absence of exercise, and from over-feeding, than from any actual want of the necessaries of life."[29]

For entertainment the men held foot races and cricket matches, and even took to hunting the numerous dogs and rats in the area, although it is not clear if they ever ate their targets. With each major installment of opium, Lin loosened his grip on the factories, sending back Chinese workers in dribs and drabs, and allowing food to be delivered. Then, on May 5, with most of the opium in hand, Lin lifted the blockade, and all the foreigners were permitted to leave, except for sixteen who were identified as the main drug traffickers, and who had to stay until the last of the opium was handed over on May 24.

Lin relished his triumph, and now it was time to get rid of the hated drug. Working feverishly about six miles above the entrance to the Pearl River, five hundred laborers at Lin's command excavated three wood- and stone-lined trenches, each 150 feet long, 75 feet wide, and 7 feet deep, and filled them with fresh water. On June 3 the trenches began receiving the nearly three million pounds of opium that had been collected. The opium balls were crushed and the pieces flung into the trenches, where they were mixed with lime and salt until they dissolved. The ends of the trenches were then opened, and the slurry flowed into the river. The laborers who prepared this noxious stew worked nearly naked so that they could be easily inspected at the end of their shifts to make sure none of the drug was being taken away. One reckless man who was caught stealing was beheaded on the spot.

Although Lin was happy to dispose of the opium, he was concerned that by polluting the ocean he would anger the spirit of the sea. So he wrote an "address" to the spirit, apologizing in advance for his actions. Then, a few days before the opium destruction commenced, while making a sacrifice to the spirit, Lin announced that he would "shortly be dissolving opium and draining it off into the great ocean," advising "the spirit to tell the creatures of the water to move away for a time, to avoid being contaminated."

It took nearly three weeks to complete the task, and during that time curious Chinese came in "throngs to witness the destruction of the opium." With the exception of two Americans the foreigners stayed away, but Lin believed they were watching. "The foreigners passing by in boats on their way up to Canton and down to Macao," Lin wrote the emperor, "all get a distant view of the proceedings, but do not dare show any disrespect, and indeed I should judge from their attitudes that they have the decency to feel heartily ashamed."[30]

LIN HAD THOUGHT that once the opium was handed over, the situation would settle down: The foreigners would sign the bonds promising not to import the drug and resume trading in Canton. The Americans took this course, signing the bonds with alacrity. For Russell & Company this came easily. Even before Lin arrived in Canton, the company, fearful of what Lin would do, and convinced that his actions would soon "render the opium business dangerous as well as disreputable," had already withdrawn from the trade entirely.[31] Now other American firms followed suit. Not only that, but some of those firms experienced a sudden metamorphosis in their stance on the trade. In a letter to the U.S. Congress, written shortly after Lin lifted the blockade, a number of American merchants in Canton claimed, "We have no wish to see a revival of the opium trade." Noting that opium had "been productive of much evil and of scarcely a single good to the Chinese," and that its introduction had "degraded the foreign character in the estimation of the better portion of the Chinese," they declared themselves "extremely desirous to see the importation and consumption of opium in China entirely at an end." The conviction behind this dramatic shift in opinion could perhaps be questioned, given past statements and actions, but be that as it may, it was the position that most of the American firms took at this time.[32]

The British, befitting their vaunted self-image, had an entirely different response to Lin's actions. They weren't ashamed over what had happened, they were furious about it. They refused to sign the bonds, and Elliot ordered all British traders out of Canton and all their ships out of Whampoa. The British repaired to Macao, and Elliot pleaded with the Americans to follow suit. "If your house goes," Forbes remembered Elliot saying, "all will go, and we shall soon bring these rascally Chinese to terms." Forbes replied that he "had not come to China for health or pleasure, and that I should remain at my post as long as I could sell a yard of goods or buy a pound of tea; that we Yankees had no Queen to guarantee our losses, &c." Surprised, Elliot asked Forbes if he "was willing to do business with a chain about [his] neck," and then warned him that "he would soon make Canton too hot for" the Americans. "The chain was *imaginary*," Forbes tartly responded, "the duty to constituents and the commission account were *real*." If the British "made Canton too warm," then Forbes said he would "go to Whampoa, retreating step by step, but buying and selling just as long as I found parties to operate with."[33]

Things were about to get very hot indeed, but not for the Americans.[34] Elliot thought the British could offload their goods at Macao and trade from there, but Lin forbade that. Elliot ordered British ships not to go to Canton, angering Lin. On July 7 British sailors rioted in Kowloon (Jiulong) across from the island of Hong Kong (Xianggang), leaving one Chinese man dead. Lin demanded that the "murderers" be turned over, but Elliot flatly refused, reflecting the policy of the British ever since the *Lady Hughes* affair not to hand over to the Chinese any British citizens accused of this crime. Instead Elliot held a trial onboard a British ship, finding five sailors guilty of rioting, not murder, sentencing them to prison terms and fines. Infuriated, Lin cut off all supplies to the British on Macao, ordered all Chinese working for the British to leave their employ, and sent menacing troops to camp on the peninsula leading to Macao, and occasionally to patrol the streets of the city. Toward the end of August, Elliot, fearing for the safety of British subjects in Macao, including women and children, evacuated them to British ships lying off Hong Kong. According to the *Chinese Repository*, "The little fleet" departing Macao, "consisting of small boats, schooners, and lorchas, crowded with passengers, presented an affecting spectacle as it moved slowly away from the harbor."[35]

Lin responded by issuing a proclamation encouraging the Chinese living along the coast and the outer islands to

> assemble yourselves together for consultation; purchase arms and weapons; join together the stoutest of your villagers; and thus be prepared to defend yourselves. If any of the said [British] foreigners be found going on shore to cause trouble, all and every of the people are permitted to fire upon them, to withstand and drive them back, or to make prisoners of them. They assuredly will never be able, few in number, to oppose the many. Even when they land to take water from the springs, stop their progress, and let them not have it in their power to drink.[36]

On the morning of September 4, 1839, Elliot sent a protest to the Chinese officers at Kowloon. "Here are several thousands of men of the English nation deprived of regular supplies of food," he wrote, "and assuredly if this state of things subsists, there will be frequent conflicts."[37] Elliot was correct. Later that day the British were able to purchase supplies in Kowloon, but when the locals tried to deliver the goods, Chinese war junks forced them to turn back. Elliot warned the local mandarins to deliver the provisions within half an hour or he would order the British warships that had recently arrived to sink the junks. When the half hour was up, the order was issued, and a fight ensued. The Chinese got the worst of it. As a British sailor observed, "The shrieking on board [the junks] was dreadful."[38] In subsequent days the food was permitted to get through.

Over the next couple of months the situation remained very tense. Lin was still demanding that the British sailors be turned over for trial, but Elliot would not do so. Lin pressed Elliot to have the British ships sign the bond, then relented, stating that the British could trade at the anchorage of Chuanbi (Chuenpee), located just outside the mouth of the Pearl River, without signing. But before this new arrangement could take effect, a British trading ship from Calcutta arrived, signed the bond, and proceeded to Canton, leaving Elliot enraged and the Chuanbi agreement in tatters. After all, Lin reasoned, if one British ship could agree to the bond, why not all of them? On October 25 Lin informed Elliot that if he didn't turn over the sailors, Lin would send war junks and fireboats to Hong Kong to destroy British ships and take the sailors by force.

Elliot responded by asking Capt. H. Smith of HMS *Volage* to take whatever steps he felt were necessary to keep any more British ships from heading up to Canton. To that end Smith ordered the *Volage*, along with HMS *Hyacinth*, to sail to Chuanbi to guard the entrance of the Pearl. Arriving on November 2, Smith and Elliot, who had accompanied him, were greeted by the sight of a formidable Chinese naval force collected nearby—Adm. Guan Tianpei's fleet of sixteen war junks and twelve fireboats. Smith had one of his men deliver to Guan a letter intended for Lin, which demanded that the commissioner withdraw his proclamation to destroy British ships, and let British citizens live on shore unmolested, with ready access to supplies. The next day Guan returned the letter unopened. At about the same time another British merchant ship, the *Royal Saxon*, arrived from Macao. It had also signed the bond and was trying to head to Canton. Smith stopped its progress with a cannon shot across the bow. Smith then sent another letter to Guan demanding that he back off, but instead of doing so he repositioned his fleet in a manner that posed an even greater menace to the British warships. At about noon Smith, with Elliot's consent, ordered his ships to fire.

The battle that followed was distinctly one-sided. The British warships sailed in among the Chinese fleet and unloaded a terrific cannonade, which could be faintly heard in Canton, thirty-two miles away. Four junks were sunk, one of which erupted into a fireball after its gunpowder magazine was hit. Other junks and fireboats were seriously damaged: fifteen Chinese were killed and many more injured. The British ships sustained relatively minor damage—mainly to the sails and rigging since the Chinese guns tended to overshoot their mark—and only a single sailor was hurt. After three-quarters of an hour the Chinese fleet, or what was left of it, retreated, and Smith stood down. Elliot called this battle "the most serious collision which has ever taken place between Her Majesty's forces and those of this empire, during our whole intercourse with this country."[39]

A FEW WEEKS AFTER the Battle of Chuanbi, Elliot told Lin that no more British ships would be allowed to enter the Pearl River. Lin responded by banning the British from trading in Canton "forever."[40] But this ban was more apparent than real. As soon as the British abandoned Canton earlier in the year they faced a problem. They had plenty of goods to trade but no way to trade them. And if they couldn't trade their goods, they couldn't get the tea and silk demanded by their countrymen back home. Enter the Americans. When the Americans signed the bonds promising not to import opium, they were given the right to continue trading, which also enabled them to serve as middlemen for the British.

For a healthy fee the Americans would go to the British ships off Hong Kong, pick up their goods, transport them to Canton, make the trades, and bring the purchases back to the British. The Americans also shuttled goods between British India and Canton. These new arrangements worked wonderfully well. As Forbes wrote his wife in August, "The Americans are reaping a rich harvest out of the English & I hope their ships will be kept out of port for a good while."[41] Freighting fees were so high that sometimes an American ship could earn more running goods between the British and Canton than it could transporting goods between America and China. Elliot, who had formerly scolded the Americans for not following the British out of Canton, now commended them for staying. "My dear Forbes," Elliot said at the conclusion of the 1839–40 trading season, "the

Queen owes you many thanks for not taking my advice as to leaving Canton. We have got in all our goods, and got out a full supply of teas and silk."[42] The American windfall didn't sit well with all British traders, however, one of whom remarked, "While we hold the horns, they [the Americans] milk the cow."[43]

It wasn't only tea and silk that the British were getting from the Chinese; there was plenty of silver, too. Lin had done an excellent job of cutting off the opium trade in Canton, and of clamping down on Chinese users in the area. By the summer of 1839 he had arrested sixteen hundred people for opium smuggling or use, and confiscated fifty thousand pounds of the drug along with seventy thousand opium pipes.[44] But he had not succeeded in stopping the opium trade altogether. Instead the British, who sometimes hoisted the American flag for cover, ramped up their operations along the coast, working in concert with smugglers to get the opium landed and the silver brought back to the ships. These smugglers came up against determined and often quite effective opposition from local governments, yet opium continued to flow into China, albeit at reduced levels.[45]

While the Americans were working as middlemen for the British, and the British were trading opium along the coast, events were taking place thousands of miles away that would soon dramatically alter the course of Chinese history, and the China trade.

THROUGHOUT LIN'S CRACKDOWN, Elliot had sent dispatches to Lord Palmerston, the British foreign secretary, and he was urging Palmerston to act. In early April 1839, while still confined at Canton, Elliot wrote to Palmerston, "It appears to me, my Lord, that the response to all these unjust violences should be made in the form of a swift and heavy blow."[46] To move the government in that direction, British merchants in Canton raised twenty thousand dollars to support an extensive lobbying push in London, to present their side of the story, which was essentially that the government should not focus on the moral evils of the opium trade—which were being trumpeted by missionary societies—but rather on the need to protect British citizens, British honor, and British trade with China.[47]

In the late summer of 1839 through early 1840, as reports about the happenings at Canton filtered back to London, press coverage increased. There were demands from merchants that the government compensate them for their loses, not only because Elliot had promised that this would happen, but also because the government had long sanctioned the trade and therefore bore considerable responsibility for its operation. Some argued that now was the time for military action, with one correspondent from Bombay writing to *The Times*, "It is certain that our trade there will never be upon a proper footing until we teach these people to respect us; and the present seems a fitting opportunity." Still other reports focused on the evils of the opium trade, and the urgent moral imperative for Britain to divest itself of this ghastly commerce. "Neither in principle, propriety, nor expediency," thundered *The Times*, "can the trade in opium be defended."[48]

At the same time a number of pamphlets on the state of affairs in China were published in England, one of which was written by the Reverend Algernon Thelwall, titled *The Iniquities of the Opium Trade with China*. Relying primarily on lengthy extracts from published materials, Thelwall railed against the pernicious impact of opium on the Chinese, and lamented that "those who profess and call themselves Christians are systematically and perseveringly engaged in this iniquitous and poisonous traffic." As a result he claimed, Britain's "national character is degraded, and covered with infamy too well deserved, among the nations of the East." Thelwall's hope was that the government, merchants, and all good Christians would oppose this "nefarious traffic."[49] Another pamphlet, this one anonymous—and most likely sponsored by the opium merchants—argued that Britain should demand that the Chinese pay compensation for the destroyed opium, pay reparations for the "insult inflicted upon national honor by the detention and captivity of British subjects," take control of Lintin Island, and compel China to sign a commercial treaty that protected

British residents in that country "from insult and aggression." To achieve these goals the pamphleteer suggested that British envoys to the emperor of China be "backed by a force amply sufficient for leveling the forts at the Bogue, and laying Canton in ashes," if need be.[50]

The one thing that was not clear from all the coverage and pamphlets was how the government was going to respond to the situation in China. Behind the scenes, however, the response was being crafted, with the encouragement of William Jardine, the chief lobbyist for the British opium merchants, who was also a partner in Jardine, Matheson & Company, a firm that had long been heavily involved in the opium trade. Nicknamed "the Iron-Headed Old Rat" by the Chinese on account of his having not flinched after being repeatedly hit on the head while trying to deliver a protest to Chinese officials, Jardine met with Palmerston and tutored the foreign secretary on the events in Canton, the geography and government of China, and the military force he thought would be needed "should Her Majesty's ministers determine on demanding redress," something Jardine fervently hoped they would do—and, of course, he also offered suggestions as to what type of remedy or redress would be appropriate. Jardine was aided in his efforts by letters and protests sent in by firms and merchant associations that wanted the government to take decisive action to protect their employees in Canton, and the China trade itself. If that was not enough of an incentive to act, there was another potent reason—Elliot's promise to the British merchants in Canton. The promise of an official representative of the Crown was not a casual comment Palmerston could easily ignore, especially since the merchants themselves were strongly urging the government to live up to the bargain Elliot had struck. The government, however, was in poor financial shape and would be hard pressed to find the millions of pounds necessary to reimburse the merchants for the opium that was destroyed. Furthermore, trying to convince the British taxpayers, many of whom did not support the opium trade with China, that they should "compensate opium smugglers might result in [Palmerston] . . . being laughed or hooted out of office." But there was a solution,

Palmerston and his fellow cabinet ministers thought: Why not force the Chinese to cover the losses; it didn't matter what they destroyed, the point was they had destroyed British property.[51]

Although the government Palmerston represented—that of the Whig prime minister Lord Melbourne—had formerly maintained a somewhat hands-off policy with regard to the rising tensions over the opium trade, it now decided to take an aggressive stance.[52] In a letter written on February 20, 1840, and addressed to the emperor of China, Palmerston laid out the government's perspective and its course of action. "It seems that the cause . . . [of all the problems] was the contraband trade in Opium, carried on by some British Subjects," he began. "It appears that the Laws of the Chinese Empire forbid the importation of opium into China, and declare that all opium which may be brought into the Country is liable to confiscation." (Palmerston knew this was the case, since he, like every other British politician, was well aware of the stream of edicts China had issued on this subject.) Palmerston then scolded the emperor for not sufficiently enforcing the law on his own subjects before requiring foreigners to comply, stating that the Chinese had "no right to permit its own subjects to violate the Law with impunity, and then to punish foreigners for doing the very same thing." Palmerston claimed that the prohibitions on the trade had long been "allowed to sleep as a dead letter," and that "suddenly, and without sufficient warning" they had been "put in force with the utmost rigor and severity" (this despite the fact that the Chinese had been trying for years, admittedly with minimal success, to clamp down on the opium trade). Palmerston argued that if the Chinese wanted to enforce the law, they "should have begun by punishing [their] own Officers who were the greatest delinquents in this matter," because they were the ones who had encouraged, facilitated, and profited from the trade by allowing the smuggling to proceed with impunity.

Palmerston didn't want the emperor to think, however, that the British condoned the opium trade. "The Queen of England desires that her subjects who may go into foreign countries should obey the laws of those countries; and Her Majesty does not wish to protect them from the just consequences of any offences which they may commit in foreign parts." (This was arrant nonsense. The British government long ignored its merchants' willful violations of Chinese law, while at the same time relishing the money that those violations were pumping into the British economy. As for the queen wanting her subjects to obey other countries' laws, that may have been true in general, but it obviously didn't apply in the case of opium in China.)[53] Palmerston added: "The British Government would not have complained, if the Government of China, after giving due notice of its altered intentions, had proceeded to execute the Law of the Empire, and had seized and confiscated all the opium which they could find within the Chinese territory, and which had been brought into that territory in violation of the Law. The Chinese Government had a right to do so, by means of its own officers, and within its own territory." Instead, Palmerston argued, the Chinese had "seize[d] peaceable British Merchants, instead of seizing the contraband opium," and "imprisoned" them, depriving them of "the assistance of their Chinese servants," and threatening them "with death by starvation." It was this harsh treatment of British citizens and, more importantly, of Elliot, an official representative of the Crown, all in "violation of the Law of Nations," Palmerston contended, that was forcing the British to act. "Her Majesty cannot permit that Her Subjects residing abroad should be treated with violence, and be exposed to insult and injustice; and when wrong is done to them, Her Majesty will see that they obtain redress."

The nature of the "redress" was also clearly spelled out in the letter to the emperor, as well as in the private instructions Palmerston gave Elliot. The main demands were, first, that the Chinese government had to return the opium or pay for what already been destroyed. Second, it had to treat and communicate with the British government's representative, the superintendent of trade, in "a manner consistent with the usages of civilized Nations, and with the respect due to the Dignity of the British Crown." Third, the Chinese had to hand over to the British government one or more islands along the coast to serve "as a place of residence and of commerce for British Subjects; where their persons may be safe from molestation, and where their Property may be secure." Fourth, British subjects were no longer to be restricted to dealing with the hong merchants, and be free to trade with whomever they wanted at multiple ports on the Chinese mainland. Fifth, fixed duties were to be set for all legally imported and exported goods. And, finally, British subjects who committed crimes while in China would be answerable to British law and punishment, not Chinese (an arrangement called extraterritoriality).

Although the British government didn't officially declare war on the Chinese, war it was nonetheless. Palmerston's letter was to be delivered to China by an impressive naval and military force, headed by Charles Elliot's cousin, Adm. George Elliot, and consisting of 16 warships with 540 guns, 4 armed steamers, 27 transports, and 4,000 troops, all departing from India. To ensure that the Chinese complied with the British demands, Admiral Elliot was given the authority to blockade Chinese ports, capture Chinese vessels, and take control of Chinese territory "until everything shall be concluded and executed to the satisfaction of the British Government." As for who would pay for this British invasion, Palmerston's letter to the emperor informed the Son of Heaven that China was expected to cover the cost.

WHILE PALMERSTON WAS devising his government's plan of attack, during late 1839 and early 1840, he intentionally kept Parliament in the dark about what was transpiring behind the scenes. Palmerston's thinking was that it would be best to wait until the expeditionary force was heading for China before engaging in an open debate, especially since the opium issue was a flashpoint for controversy, and bringing it up too early might derail the government's plans. When opposition members in Parliament raised concerns about what the government was up to in China, and requested documents pertaining to the events in Canton, the government's answers remained vague, and the delivery of the documents was repeatedly put off. But by early March rumors of military action started swirling in London, and on the twelfth of the month, a member of the opposition Tory Party asked a government representative in Parliament outright: "Is there any truth in the report very generally believed that war has been declared against China?"[54] The government's answer was that war had not been declared, but instructions had been sent to India to prepare for action should it be necessary.

Over the next couple of weeks, as information leaked out, and the details of those instructions became more widely known, the Tories, sensing the growing public displeasure with the idea of going to war to defend the odious opium trade and compensate opium merchants, decided the time was ripe to move to censure the Whig government for its handling of the situation in China. The debate on the no confidence vote in the House of Commons lasted three evenings, April 7–9, during which time extremely long speeches dragged on for hours.[55] The main line of the Tory attack was that the Whig government had for many years failed to control the rapidly expanding contraband opium trade, or to provide Elliot with the instructions, guidance, or powers necessary for him to deal with the problem; as a result it was government inaction and ineptitude that had brought Britain to this shameful state of affairs, in which hostilities had broken out, the country was on the verge of war, and the legitimate trade with China was threatened.[56]

The question of the morality of the opium trade was raised most eloquently by William Ewart Gladstone, a thirty-year-old Tory member of Parliament and already a silver-tongued orator who would go on to serve as prime minister of Great Britain four times. Gladstone's interest in the opium question was not only professional but personal. His younger sister, Helen, had become addicted to laudanum, after having it prescribed to control pain from a recent illness.

On April 8, 1840, Gladstone delivered a blistering attack on the war. "I am not competent to judge how long this war may last," he told his fellow MPs, "or how protracted may be its operations; but this I can say, that a war more unjust in its origin, a war more calculated, in its progress, to cover this country with permanent disgrace, I do not know, and have not read of." The reason that the sight of the British flag caused every Englishman's spirit to rise, Gladstone argued, is that "it [had] always been associated with the cause of justice, with the protection of the oppressed, with respect for national rights, with honorable commercial enterprise." But, in Canton, at the direction of Lord Palmerston, the British flag had been "hoisted for the purpose of protecting an infamous contraband traffic." While Gladstone agreed that the Chinese were "guilty of much absurd phraseology, of no little ostentatious pride, and of some excess, justice . . . is with them; and that whilst they, the Pagans, and semi-civilized barbarians, have substantial justice on their side, we, the enlightened and civilized Christians, are pursuing objects at variance both with justice and with religion."[57]

The Whigs, however, defended the government's past actions in China, claiming that there was nothing it could have done differently that would have avoided the current situation. As for the Tories' contention that this war was simply an effort to force opium down the throats of the Chinese against their will, Lord Macaulay, the secretary of state for war, responded, "God forbid that an idea so absurd, so atrocious, should have ever entered into the mind of any English minister!"[58] Instead the government steadfastly maintained that its motives were noble. Echoing the themes of Palmerston's letter to Elliot, the government argued that when British envoys and merchants were imprisoned and their lives threatened, when British women and children were forced to flee to the safety of British ships for their own protection, and when British property was seized, the government had no alternative but to take action to protect British honor and dignity. The no-confidence vote was close, narrowly losing by nine votes. The planned invasion of China would proceed.[59]

———

THE BRITISH FORCE arrived in China in June 1840 and left some ships behind to blockade Canton, while the rest of the fleet, along with superintendent Elliot, headed rapidly up the coast, blockading key ports and rivers along the way, and seizing the island of Zhoushan.[60] Admiral Elliot arrived at the mouth of the Beihe (Pei-ho) River in early August, and delivered Palmerston's letter. Once the emperor had become aware of the gravity of the situation, he deputed Qishan (Ch'i-shan), the trusted governor-general of the region, to open negotiations with the British. At the same time the emperor wrote Lin, blaming him for failing to halt the opium trade and for bringing down the wrath of the British upon the Middle Kingdom. "Externally you wanted to stop the [opium] trade, but it has not been stopped," the emperor complained. "Internally you wanted to wipe out the outlaws [opium smugglers and smokers], but they are not cleared away. You are just making excuses with empty words. Nothing has been accomplished but many troubles have been created. Thinking of these things, I cannot contain my rage. What do you have to say now?"[61] Soon thereafter the emperor sacked Lin and about a year later, exiled him to the northwest frontier.

Qishan persuaded the British to return to Canton to negotiate by telling them that since the trouble had begun there, it would be the best place to gather information relating to the dispute. In fact Qishan was only interested in getting the British as far away from the capital as possible. When negotiations broke down over the question of ceding Hong Kong, the British showed their resolve by attacking the forts at Chuanbi on January 7, 1841, inflicting major casualties. Before the British continued their assault farther up the river, negotiations resumed, resulting in a draft agreement—the Chuanbi Convention—whose terms would reopen trade between the British and the Chinese, give Hong Kong to the British, require the Chinese to pay a $6 million indemnity, and make the two countries equals with regard to direct official contacts.

THE BRITISH STEAMER *NEMESIS* DESTROYING CHINESE WAR JUNKS
NEAR THE BOCA TIGRIS, JANUARY 7, 1841, ENGRAVING BY
G. GREATBACH AFTER PAINTING BY G. W. TERRY, 1854.

On January 20, 1841, Elliot publicly announced the draft agreement with Qishan, and when their respective governments found out about it, they couldn't have been angrier. Palmerston learned of it in April, and soon thereafter fired Elliot for not following all of the government's instructions, for not effectively using British force, and for making a lousy deal. The convention, among other things, failed to set fixed duties for goods, abolish the hong system, or establish the principle of extraterritoriality. Palmerston was especially angry at the indemnity, which didn't come close to covering the costs of the opium and the expedition. After being briefed on the campaign by Palmerston, Queen Victoria wrote to her uncle Leopold, the king of Belgium, "The Chinese business vexes us much. . . . *All* we wanted might have been got, if it had not been for the unaccountably strange conduct of Charles Elliot . . . who completely disobeyed his instructions and *tried* to get the *lowest* terms he could."[62] In contrast the emperor thought that Qishan had exceeded his authority by agreeing to the indemnity and ceding Hong Kong. As a result the emperor ordered Qishan to be executed, later lowering the sentence to banishment. The convention was scrapped, and thus began the second stage of the war.

THIS TIME THE BRITISH sent Sir Henry Pottinger as plenipotentiary, backed up by additional naval and military forces, with instructions to negotiate a treaty with the emperor, whose details were much the same as the ones Elliot had been given. Pottinger, who had entered the military in his early teens and distinguished himself during the Napoleonic Wars, arrived in the Pearl River estuary in early August 1841, and discovered that the situation had deteriorated. Between the drafting of the Chuanbi Convention and Pottinger's arrival, Elliot had remained in charge, having officially learned he was fired only when Pottinger handed him the dismissal letter from Palmerston. During those seven months fighting twice broke out between the British and the Chinese, with British forces ultimately destroying more than seventy Chinese war junks, capturing multiple batteries along the Pearl River, and taking control of parts of Canton. The fighting finally ended with the signing of a convention between Elliot and the Chinese authorities, in which the latter paid the British $6 million, in exchange for British forces withdrawing from the city and the river.[63]

Soon after Pottinger arrived in China, he headed north with the bulk of the British fleet. His men handily overpowered their Chinese opponents, in some instances inflicting heavy casualties, and soon the British gained control of multiple ports, including Xiamen, Zhoushan, Zhenhai (Chinhai), Ningbo (Ningpo), Wusong (Woosung), Zhapu (Chapu), and Shanghai. Chinese officials were surprised by these and earlier British successes because they had grossly underestimated Britain's military. Writing to the emperor in 1839, Lin showed his ignorance of Britain's fighting force. "As to their soldiers," Lin claimed, "they do not know how to use fists and swords. Also, their legs are firmly bound with cloth and in consequence it is very inconvenient for them to stretch. Should they land it is apparent that they can do little harm." A year later another Chinese official observed, "The English barbarians are an insignificant and detestable race, trusting entirely to their strong ships and large guns; but the immense distance they have traversed will render the arrival of seasonable supplies impossible, and their soldiers, after a single defeat, being deprived of provisions, will become dispirited and lost." British sailors wouldn't be able to accurately shoot their ship's guns, this cocky official believed, because the guns would be too high off the water and the waves would make them difficult to aim. Thus rendered impotent, the invading ships could easily be destroyed by the guns mounted on the walls of the Chinese forts. If that didn't work, then the Chinese could always

CHINESE SOLDIER WITH BOW, BY JOHN OUCHTERLONY, 1844.

burn the British ships. "Without, therefore, despising the enemy," the official concluded, "we have no cause to fear them."[64]

British success, however, was understandable. There was a dramatic disparity between British and Chinese military forces. British troops were highly trained, superbly commanded, well supplied, and had the most modern guns and field artillery, while the Chinese were less schooled in the art of war, disorganized, often undisciplined, and still fought mainly with bows and arrows, spears, swords, and antiquated matchlock muskets. Although the Chinese war junks were

CHINESE SOLDIERS WITH SPEARS,
BY JOHN OUCHTERLONY, 1844.

sizable, their cannons were small and few in number, and thus were no match for the British warships, bristling with scores of massive cannons. Contributing to the ferocity of the British fleet was the presence of the *Nemesis*, a flat-bottomed paddle steamer made of iron, which had a shallow draught and could therefore get close to the shore, where its thirty-two-pounders and a rocket launcher could be employed with devastating effect. The many cannons at the Chinese forts did not worry the British because in addition to being small, they were bolted down and therefore could shoot in only one direction, a distinct drawback against a moving target.

Adding to the Chinese army's woes was the fact that it was falling apart. Decades of imperial neglect and anemic military budgets, combined with widespread corruption and stagnant wages in the face of rising inflation, left the soldiers not only little to fight with, but also little motivation to fight for the emperor. The Chinese might have been able to compensate for their deficiencies with a huge fighting force, overwhelming their enemies with sheer numbers, but there too they fell short. Despite having an enormous army on paper, purported to comprise eight hundred thousand individuals, the effective fighting force was only a fraction of that size, and those soldiers were widely dispersed throughout the empire and not easily called to duty. Thus, in many engagements with the British the number of Chinese soldiers brought to bear was relatively small. And even when the Chinese outnumbered the British, it was not by enough to help turn the tide in their favor. Making matters worse, was a tendency on many occasions for Chinese forces to run off rather than fight when the British attacked. Taking all this into account, it is not surprising that "During the Opium War," according to the historian Julia Lovell, "Qing politicians of the pro- and anti-war faction could agree on only one thing: that their army was hopeless."[65]

Although Chinese soldiers were not a serious threat to the British, illness was. Once off their ships, and fighting and camping on Chinese soil, exposed to the elements, and lacking fresh provisions, British troops were devastated by malaria, dysentery, and strong fevers. Between July and December 1840, for example, when Britain's first expeditionary force was holding the island of Zhoushan, 5,329 British soldiers were admitted to the infirmary; of those, 448 died.[66]

IN EARLY JULY 1842 the British fleet of seventy-three ships sailed up the Yangtze River, the longest river in China, and third longest in the world, which served as a major artery of life and commerce in the country, winding its way nearly four thousand miles from the glaciers of the Tibetan Plateau through deep gorges and broad farmlands to the East China Sea. An officer on one of the ships marveled at the scene. "It was a beautiful sight. On a signal from Flag for fleet to weigh, in a few minutes you would see a white cloud, three miles in extent, moving up the river. While the seamen went aloft to loose sails, troops manned sheets and halyards. Wind heading, the reverse took place, and a forest of masts succeeded the white cloud."[67] On the twentieth of the month the fleet anchored off the city of Zhenjiang (Chen-chiang). A British force of nearly seven thousand landed, buoyed by confidence from their earlier victories, and expecting little effective resistance. But the roughly three thousand Chinese defenders "behaved with great spirit," Pottinger said, "and disputed every inch of the ramparts," although exposing themselves to slaughter by the technologically superior foe.[68]

After battling for most of the day, the British, who lost thirty men, seized Zhenjiang. Chinese military casualties exceeded one thousand, and once the Chinese in the city realized that all was lost, many of them took their own lives and those of their families. "Some of the Manchus shut the doors of their houses," wrote a contemporary American chronicler, "while through the crevices persons could be seen deliberately cutting the throats of their women, and destroying their children by throwing them into wells. . . . Such was their terror and hatred of the invaders, that every Manchu preferred resistance, death, suicide, or flight, to surrender."[69] The taking of lives was not limited to the residents of the city. Pottinger said that the commanding Chinese general had his servants set his house on fire while he sat in a chair within until he was engulfed in flames.[70]

Zhenjiang was located at the intersection of the Yangtze River and the "Grand Canal," the latter of which was a major transportation route between southern and northern China. In this strategic position the British blocked two of China's main arteries of traffic and communication. The situation became even more desperate for the Chinese when the British fleet continued up the Yangtze to Nanking (Nanjing), the former capital. Intimidated by the relative ease with which the British forces had advanced, and fearful that further bloody defeats might follow and bring the battle closer to Peking, the emperor ordered his representatives to negotiate the terms of peace.[71]

"Negotiate," though, was hardly the correct word for what took place. The terms of the subsequent Treaty of Nanking, which was signed on August 29, 1842, were less negotiated than dictated to the Chinese at the end of a gun. The British achieved their goals. Among the treaty's main provisions, the Chinese would pay a $21 million indemnity to cover the costs of the opium, the war, and debts owed by the hong merchants to British traders; abolish the Cohong (hong merchants') monopoly on trade at Canton; open the ports of Canton,

SHANGHAI, BY UNIDENTIFIED CHINESE ARTIST, CIRCA 1865.

Fuzhou (Foochow), Xiamen, Ningbo, and Shanghai, where the British could trade with whomever they chose "without molestation or restraint"; cede Hong Kong to Britain; establish uniform duties on imports and exports; and require official correspondence to use terms that were not condescending or derogatory but indicated equality between the two countries. The supplementary Treaty of the Bogue, ratified the following year, gave Britain two more major concessions: British subjects involved in criminal cases would be answerable to British, not Chinese, law (extraterritoriality), and Britain was granted most-favored-nation status, meaning that any rights that China granted to other nations in the future would also be granted to Britain.[72]

Although the only mention of opium in the treaty is about China paying for what was destroyed, the broader issue of the opium trade made a cameo appearance in the negotiations. Palmerston had instructed Pottinger to urge the Chinese to legalize opium for three reasons: The Chinese seemed powerless to halt the trade, the British were not going to stop exporting it from India, and if it remained illegal it would only lead to more smuggling and violence. But urge was all Pottinger could do, for, as Palmerston told him, Her Majesty's position was that Britain had "no right" to demand that China legalize opium. If the emperor wanted to prohibit the importation of opium, that was his right, and any British subjects who engaged in "a contraband trade, must take the consequences of doing so."[73]

Pottinger attempted to broach the subject, which he euphemistically called "the great cause that produced the disturbances which led to the war," but the Chinese steadfastly refused until he assured them it would be "a topic of private conversation" rather than part of the formal negotiations. The Chinese wanted to know why the British "would not act fairly towards them, by prohibiting" poppy cultivation in their dominions, and "thus effectually stop a traffic so pernicious to the human race." Pottinger claimed that such a move would not be consistent with British law, and further that even if Britain did so, the trade would not end, for others would simply pick up where the British left off. Then Pottinger shifted the onus to the Chinese. Stopping the opium trade, he said, "rests entirely with yourselves. If your people are virtuous, they will desist from the evil practice; and if your officers are incorruptible, and obey their orders, no opium can enter your country." If, however, the Chinese government could not keep its people from smoking opium, then they would "procure the drug in spite of every enactment." Given that, wouldn't it be better, Pottinger argued, to legalize opium, and eliminate the scourge of smuggling? Hearing this the Chinese negotiators cut off further discussion, stating that the emperor "would never listen to a word upon the subject."[74]

In Britain the war's conclusion brought a welcome sense of relief. There was widespread support for the Treaty of Nanking, and the British seemed less interested in debating the merits of the war than they were in contemplating the rich bounty that would hopefully soon benefit the nation. "It secures a few round millions of dollars and no end of very refreshing tea," the *London Illustrated News* said of the treaty. "It gives an impetus to trade, cedes us one island

THE SILVER DOLLARS THAT THE CHINESE WERE FORCED
TO PAY BRITAIN UNDER THE TREATY OF NANKING, BEING
DELIVERED TO THE BRITISH MINT, 1842.

in perpetuity, and in short puts that sort of climax to the war which satisfies our interests more than our vanity and rather gives over glory a preponderance of gain." A letter writer to *The Times* of London was even more ebullient: "Perhaps no circumstance in the history of Great Britain ever gave such universal satisfaction to all classes of society in this country as the termination of the war with China—an event, the importance of which cannot be overrated, opening up, as it undoubtedly will, that vast empire to the extension of our commerce and manufactures."[75] Even in France, where antipathy for Britain ran deep, there was grudging support for the treaty. One French newspaper, however, *Le Siècle* (The Age), still managed to condemn Britain for starting the war, also making clear its disdain for China's leaders: "The English began the war on grounds purely selfish, for the promotion of their own interests, and from an odious motive; but if they succeed in bringing [the Chinese people] . . . now supinely vegetating under an astute and immoral government, into the improvements of European civilization, a great service will be rendered to the cause of humanity."[76]

THE "OPIUM WAR," AS the conflict between the British and the Chinese is most often known, remains an appropriate appellation. It was certainly opium's devastating impact that set the two nations on a collision course, compelling China's emperor to act. As for Britain, its long-standing encouragement of the trade, enabling British merchants to continue sending opium to China, created the explosive situation that led to the outbreak of hostilities. That the Crown demanded that China pay compensation for the seized opium further implicates the drug.

Many Britons were, like Gladstone, convinced that opium was the key factor in causing the war. The British government at the time, however, maintained that the war was not predominantly about opium, which it regarded merely as an "incident" or "spark." Instead the government pointed to the factors highlighted in Palmerston's instructions to Elliot and Pottinger—namely its desire to preserve its honor, protect its citizens, compel Chinese respect, receive compensation for British goods that were seized, and open China to more trade, or what was called in the parlance of the time, "free trade."[77]

To many in the British government, the Opium War was the culmination of a long history of perceived insults at the hands of the Chinese. On the eve of the war the painful memories of the *Lady Hughes* affair were still fresh, as was the poor reception of Britain's missions to China—the Macartney mission in 1792–93, and the one headed by Lord Amherst in 1816—which had tried but failed to establish broader trade relations between the two countries. Despite a major dust-up over his failure to kowtow before the Son of Heaven, Macartney was granted an audience with the emperor, but he got nothing else except two letters addressed to King George III, in which the emperor rejected all the British requests. One of those letters included a warning that showed just how condescending a tone the Chinese could take toward foreigners. "It behooves you, O King, to respect my sentiments and to display even greater devotion and loyalty in the future, so that, by perpetual submission to our Throne, you may secure peace and prosperity for your country hereafter. . . . Tremblingly obey and show no negligence."[78] Still, Macartney did better than Amherst, who never met with the emperor, as a result of controversy over his refusal to kowtow, as well as the timing of his audience with the Chinese ruler.

Another perceived slight was what came to be known as the "Napier Fizzle." Lord Napier was the first superintendent of trade appointed after the end of the British East India Company's monopoly. When he arrived in Canton during the summer of 1834, he proceeded to ignore the long-standing customs of the Canton System of trade, and instead tried to force the Chinese to treat him as an equal and a representative of the Crown. When things did not go his way, he threatened the Chinese with the use of military force. Napier's impertinent behavior led to a sharp Chinese response, including shutting off trade, placing Napier and his entourage under house arrest, and firing upon British frigates summoned by Napier as they headed up the Pearl River. Finally Napier succumbed to Chinese pressure and left Canton for Macao, where he soon died from a fever he had contracted during the ordeal. Despite the fact that Napier had acted rashly and disregarded his instructions—which included avoiding the use of armed force, and not doing anything else to offend the Chinese—the British government remained upset by the treatment of its representative, and there was even talk of war to avenge Britain's honor.[79]

To the British government these perceived insults reflected a bigger problem. Namely that the Chinese system of trade operated by rules that were, in British eyes, patently unfair and humiliating. Making matters worse was China's insufferable sense of superiority, which galled the British since they didn't see themselves as barbarians but rather as subjects of the most powerful and advanced civilization of the day. As the historian Kenneth Scott Latourette noted, "The British were accustomed to intercourse between nations on the basis of equality. To them the Chinese procedure, grounded in the conviction that all other peoples were tributary to the Emperor, was intolerable."[80]

One of the best contemporary explications of the view that the war was caused primarily by China's attitude toward, and treatment of, the British comes not from a Briton but from John Quincy Adams, who had served as the sixth president of the United States. In November 1841 Adams, then a congressman from Massachusetts, and a vehement opponent of slavery, gave a speech before the Massachusetts Historical Society on the war:

> It is a general, but I believe altogether mistaken opinion that the quarrel is merely for certain chests of opium imported by British merchants into China, and seized by the Chinese government for having been imported contrary to law. This is a mere incident to the dispute; but no more the cause of the war, than the throwing overboard of the tea in Boston harbor was the cause of the North American Revolution. . . . The cause of the war is the kowtow!—the arrogant and insupportable pre-

tensions of China, that she will hold commercial intercourse with the rest of mankind, not upon terms of equal reciprocity, but upon the insulting and degrading forms of the relation between lord and vassal.

Although Adams was too dismissive of the role of opium, as he was of the role of the Boston Tea Party in the Revolution, he was correct about British anger over the state of trade with China. This anger, along with Britain's resentment over the treatment of its citizens and the destruction of its property, were, in the British government's estimation, the main reasons that it went to war.[81]

THE AMERICANS REMAINED not disinterested bystanders during the Opium War. Though it was not their conflict, they could not help but have strong opinions about it. Many of the nation's China traders had hoped that hostilities could be avoided by a unified show of force. The memorial that American traders submitted to Congress in May 1839, in which they declared their opposition to the continuation of the opium trade, also included a plea that Congress send a naval force to China. The presence of American ships, combined with others from Britain and France, would, the memorialists believed, "without bloodshed" result in mutually beneficial trade treaties that would place America's (as well as the other nations') commerce with China "upon a secure footing." Such a combined force never materialized, and once hostilities broke out, many American traders thought that the British actions were warranted, since Chinese attitudes and actions had rankled them as well. These traders' view was that China needed to be taught a lesson, even if they were reluctant about using armed force to do so. There were, however, also many American traders who opposed the war. As one of them commented, "Whatever faults the Chinese may have, & they are not faultless, bad treatment of commercial foreigners is not one of them & they appear to me to have the right side of the question in their quarrel with the English."[82]

Another American trader who opposed the war was Charles William King. Like the firm in which he was a partner—Olyphant & Company—King had long railed against the evils of the opium trade. In a letter to British superintendent Elliot, penned during the detention of foreigners in Canton, King wrote feelingly about the transgressions that appeared to be hurtling Britain toward conflict with China.

> For nearly forty years, the British merchants, led on by the East India Company, have been driving a trade, in violation of the highest laws, and the best interests of the Chinese empire. This course has been pushed so far, as to derange its currency, to corrupt its officers, and ruin multitudes of its people. The traffic has become associated in the politics of the country, with embarrassments and evil omens; in its penal code, with the axe and the dungeon; in the breasts of men in private life, with the wreck of property, virtue, honor, and happiness. All ranks, from the Emperor on the throne, to the people of the humblest hamlets, have felt its sting. To the fact of its descent to the lowest classes of society, we are frequent witnesses; and the Court gazettes are evidence that it has marked out victims for disgrace and ruin even among the Imperial kindred.

King hoped that Britain would choose to "make this crisis" an opportunity to repair its relationship with China, and engage only in respectable trade, devoid of opium. King also warned Elliot that if the British chose to fight, they would not only lose, but they would also further alienate the Chinese people.

> Justice forbids that the steps, taken by the Chinese, to arrest a system of wrongs practiced on them . . . be made the pretence for still deeper injuries. Interest condemns the sacrifice of the lawful and useful trade with China, on the altar of illicit traffic. Still more loudly does it warn against the assumption of arms in an unjust quarrel, against—not the Chinese Government

only—but, the Chinese people. Strong as Great Britain is—in any good cause irresistible—she cannot war with success, or even safety, upon the consciences—the moral sense—of these three or four hundred million people.[83]

American missionaries were of two minds about the war. On the one hand virtually all of them condemned the illicit opium trade and its pernicious impact on the Chinese, viewing it as a serious obstacle to reaching the people and gaining converts. In a report submitted to the American Board of Commissioners for Foreign Missions in late 1839, at about the time that the British evacuated Macao, American missionaries in Canton argued that opium was "an evil scarcely less, perhaps greater, than both slavery and intemperance combined." What was most troubling, the report added, was "the notorious fact that foreigners, enlightened nations, and Christian people, have been the chief agents in providing in administering this drug."

But at the same time some missionaries saw the war as a necessary and even providential step, which, if successful, might force open the doors of China, and allow them to travel far beyond the narrow confines of Canton to spread Christianity throughout the land. "How these difficulties do rejoice my heart!" wrote Henrietta Shuck, the first female American missionary in China, to her father in late August 1839. "I think the English government may be enraged," she continued, "and God, in his power, may break down the barriers which prevent the gospel of Christ from entering China." Soon after, another American missionary, Samuel Wells Williams, wrote of his earnest "hope that the day of China's emancipation is hastening on . . . The first shock of the two nations will be calamitous for China, but a hard knock is necessary to rouse her from her fancied goodness and security." A year later, just as Pottinger's forces were arriving to deliver the final blows of the war, Elijah Coleman Bridgman, an American Protestant missionary and founder of the *Chinese Repository*, was joyfully anticipating the denouement that he was confident was to come. "We are on the eve of a new era," he said, "and a great revolution has commenced. We have long mourned over the evils and the desolations around us. For these the gospel is the only remedy. And now we trust the God of nations is about to open a highway for those who will preach the word."[84]

Americans back home, heavily influenced by missionary tracts about the evils of opium, and by the still-lingering animosity toward Britain as a result of two hard-fought wars, for the most part opposed Britain's actions and believed that opium was the root cause of the conflict. Evidence for this comes from the reaction to Adams's speech. "The view taken in my lecture," Adams wrote in his diary a few days before the event, "is so adverse to the prevailing prejudices of the time and place that I expect to bring down a storm upon my head." Those words proved prophetic. Adams's arguments were widely denounced in the press, although it appears that only one publication—*Niles' National Register*—saw fit to print it whole so that the public could fully consider what he said. The *North American Review*, impressed by the public outcry, reneged on its agreement to publish the speech. After receiving the *Review*'s sheepish rejection, Adams noted, "The excitement of public opinion and feeling by the delivery of this lecture far exceeds any expectation that I had formed."[85]

More in line with American public opinion were the words of Freeman Hunt, editor of the *Merchant's Magazine and Commercial Review*: "The whole enlightened and Christian world ought solemnly to protest against it [the war], as an unwarranted act of arbitrary power, committed in violation of the broad principles of eternal justice." A similarly disposed critic was Caleb Cushing, a Massachusetts congressman who, when asked about the possibility of America joining forces with Britain in the war, roundly dismissed the idea. The Americans in Canton, he said, "have manifested a proper respect for the laws and public rights of the Chinese empire, in honorable contrast with the outrageous misconduct of the English there. . . . God forbid that I should entertain the idea of cooperating with the British government in the purpose—if purpose it have—of upholding the base cupidity and violence, and highhanded infraction of all law, human and divine, which have characterized" their despicable actions with respect to opium in China. Of course, Americans too, including many whom Cushing represented, had been heavily involved in the opium trade for years, and therefore guilty of not respecting the laws and rights of the Chinese empire, but when American voices were raised in opposition to the war they often conveniently left out of the picture the unsavory and indefensible role of their fellow citizens. That extended to Cushing himself, whose family had once profited handsomely from the opium trade, only later to leave it behind.[86]

Whatever their disposition during the war, however, Americans were eager to share in the spoils of Britain's victory. Ever since the *Empress of China* had left the docks, the U.S. government had employed an almost hands-off policy when it came to the China trade. With the exception of imposing favorable duties and appointing relatively powerless consuls, it had done little to further the trade or establish more meaningful relations with China. Now, with the Opium War over and the British having imposed a treaty, U.S. officials wanted a favorable treaty too. To get it President John Tyler sent Cushing to China at the head of a diplomatic mission, America's first to the Middle Kingdom.

BORN IN SALISBURY, Massachusetts, Cushing was a Harvard-trained lawyer, an excellent writer, a true Renaissance man—fluent in French, Italian, and Spanish and well versed in literature, botany, and mineralogy. Before reaching Congress he had served as an editor of a local paper, a state representative and senator from Newburyport, and a counselor-at-law to the Supreme Judicial Court of Massachusetts. In all these positions he had honed his negotiating skills, which would serve him well in his new endeavor.[87]

A couple of months prior to his departure, at a dinner in Boston's Faneuil Hall marking the dedication of a new monument to the Battle

CALEB CUSHING,
ENGRAVED BY
T. DONEY, 1844.

of Bunker Hill, Cushing told the audience of his impending trip: "I have myself been honored with a commission of peace, and am entrusted with the duty of bringing nearer together if possible, the civilization of the old and new worlds. . . . For though, of old, it was from the east that civilization and learning dawned upon the civilized world, yet now by the refluent tide of letters, knowledge was rolled back from the west to the east, and we have become the teachers of our teachers. I go to China . . . on behalf of civilization."[88]

Despite Cushing's exalted and chauvinistic perspective, the mission's actual goals were much simpler. His instructions were basically to get what the British had gotten, if not better. "Your constant aim must be," Daniel Webster, the secretary of state, told his friend, "to produce a full conviction on the minds of the government and the people [of China] that your mission is entirely pacific; that you come with no purposes of hostility or annoyance; that you are a messenger of peace, sent from the greatest power in America to the greatest empire in Asia, to offer respect and good-will, and to establish the means of friendly intercourse." Webster impressed upon Cushing the potential commercial benefits that could accrue to America if it gained access to the same ports that Britain had: "These ports belong to some of the richest, most productive, and most populous provinces of the empire, and are likely to become very important marts of commerce." If American ships were allowed into those ports on an equal footing with the British, Webster believed that it might be possible for American merchants to stop relying so heavily on bills on London or specie to finance their purchases, and instead sell more American manufactures. Cushing was to try to meet with the emperor in Peking; failing that, he was to confer with other high-ranking officials who could speak for the emperor. Cushing was to be polite, respectful, and firm, as befitted an equal, not a tribute bearer. Highlighting the long-standing confusion that some Chinese still harbored about the autonomy of the United States, and America's sensitivity about its place in the world, Webster added, "It can not be wrong for you to make known, where not known, that the United States, once a country subject to England, threw off that subjection years ago, asserted their independence, sword in hand, established that independence after a seven years' war, and now meet England upon equal terms upon the ocean and upon the land."[89] A few months before giving Cushing these instructions, Webster confided to a colleague that he thought the approaching mission "more important" than any that had ever "proceeded from this country, & the more important than any other, likely to succeed it, in our days."[90]

The president gave Cushing two letters for the emperor, one introducing Cushing, and the other a more general note from one head of state to another. In the latter Tyler offered a mix of history, flattery, and hopes for the future. After listing all the states of which he was president, Tyler began: "The twenty-six United States are as large as China, though our people are not so numerous. The rising sun looks upon the great mountains and great rivers of China. When he sets, he looks upon rivers and mountains equally large in the United

States. Our territories extend from one great ocean to the other; and on the west we are divided from your dominions only by the sea." Tyler called America and China "great countries," and hoped that they would "respect" each other. "The Chinese love to trade with our people," Tyler observed, "and to sell them tea and silk, for which our people pay silver, and sometimes other articles." If that trade were to continue, it had to be based on mutually acceptable rules of commerce. The treaty that Tyler wanted Cushing to negotiate with the emperor had to be "just," giving "no unfair advantage to either side." In a nod to the opium trade, the president said that America "shall not take the part of evil-doers," and "shall not uphold them that break your laws." Tyler signed off with the almost folksy, "Your good friend."[91]

CUSHING AND HIS entourage, including Daniel Webster's son Fletcher and four attachés, left from Norfolk, Virginia, on August 5, 1843, and after many delays and mishaps, arrived in China on February 24, 1844. Before departing, Cushing bought every book he could on China, and read them on the voyage over to be fully prepared. Settling into the former governor's mansion on Macao, the mandarinlike emissary, according to an American resident, established a "miniature court" and created "in the colony a profound sensation by the novelty and magnitude of his mission, as well as by his attractive personal qualities." That Cushing and the five young men he had in tow were all handsome bachelors only added to their warm reception and made them a most welcome addition to the foreign community, which included a few single women.[92]

When the Americans arrived it became clear that the Chinese weren't particularly interested in negotiating. As the Chinese saw it there was no need for an American treaty, because an imperial edict had already granted the Americans every right granted the British in theirs. The American merchants in Canton held a similar perspective. As one of them commented:

When at Macao I had the honor of seeing much of his Excellency (Cushing) who has spurs on his heels, and mustachios and imperial, very flourishing! Although I like the man, I most heartily wish he were anywhere else but here and am, as well as every other American merchant here, in great fear. As Americans we are now on the very *best* terms possible with the Chinese; and as the only connection we want with China is a commercial one, I cannot see what Mr. Cushing expects to do. He *cannot* make us better off.[93]

Cushing was rebuffed in his attempts to gain an audience with the emperor. Instead Qiying (Ch'i-ying), the imperial commissioner, would negotiate, but he was in Peking and would not return for more than three months. The interim was not without some excitement, however. Cushing had presented the American consul with a flagpole topped with a weathervane shaped like an arrow. It was duly erected, and then the problems began. At the time many Cantonese suffered from an unidentified malady, and the locals blamed the swinging weathervane for the problem, claiming that the notorious pointing arrow was "causing serious impediment to the felicity and good fortunes of the land." When the Americans took down the offending weathervane on May 6, they were attacked by a group of angry Chinese. Local forces quickly intervened, but the altercation was of sufficient concern to the local gentry and elders that they issued a proclamation to soothe public anger. After commending the Americans for rectifying their "error," the authors hoped that from then on the "people from afar" would be regarded with "compassion."[94]

Some locals clearly didn't get the message. On June 16 a band of "lawless Chinese," as Cushing called them, invaded the American garden and attacked the Americans with clubs, to which they responded with gunfire. During the melee an American shot and killed a Chinese man. Commissioner Qiying, by this time back from the capital and established at a house in the village of Wangxia (Wanghia) on the outskirts of Macao, told Cushing that the locals might demand a life for a life. But Cushing stood strong. He was already negotiating the terms of the American-Chinese treaty with Qiying, and one of the main features he hoped to include was the very same protection against Chinese prosecution afforded by the extraterritoriality clause that the British had obtained. Cushing informed Qiying that the American who had shot the Chinese man would not be handed over but would be tried by a jury of his peers. Neither Qiying nor the local officials interfered, and the trial was held on July 11, whereupon the shooter was found innocent since the killing was deemed to be "a justifiable act of self-defense."[95]

On July 3, 1844, more than a week before Cushing reported the verdict to Qiying, the two men agreed on the terms of the Treaty of Wangxia, aided in their negotiations by the interpreting services of Peter Parker and Elijah Bridgman. Cushing had done well, attaining everything the Americans wanted. The basic structure of the treaty was the same as the one the British forged—with the exception of a land cession like Hong Kong—but the American treaty was much more detailed, and it added a few new twists. Americans residing in one of the five trading ports were allowed to build not only houses but also "hospitals, churches, and cemeteries," thereby laying the groundwork for doctors to tend to the sick, and for missionaries to expand their outreach. No longer would it be a crime for Americans to learn Chinese, since they could now hire Chinese to teach them. The notion of extraterritoriality—that foreigners would be subject to their own laws, not Chinese law—was extended to civil as well as criminal cases. The issue of opium, on which the British were silent, received an article all its own, which said that any Americans who traded in opium would be at the mercy of Chinese laws and justice, and would get no protection from the American government. The article also said that the United States would "take measures" to prevent other countries from using its flag "as a cover for the violation of the laws of the empire." Finally the last article required that the treaty itself be revisited in twelve years' time, and revised if necessary.[96]

THE BRITISH AND AMERICAN treaties were the death knell for what became known as the old China trade. The often exasperating Canton system had now expired, and the city was no longer the only portal through which foreigners could enter China. The symbolic end of the old China trade came on September 4, 1843, with the death of the venerable Howqua at the age of seventy-five. He, more than anyone, had personified the Canton system. The *New-Hampshire Patriot*, in noting Howqua's passing, called him an "honest man" and a "great" merchant, while a British newspaper published in Hong Kong asserted: "We believe the deceased could be favorably contrasted with the most eminent [merchants] that Europe has produced. . . . [S]ound judgment, true prudence, wary circumspection, and a wise economy, were distinguishing traits of his mercantile character."[97]

The Opium War greatly weakened an already tottering Chinese empire. In the five or so decades leading up to the war, China's stability had been rocked by many forces. The enormous and rapidly increasing population, which far outpaced the growth in agricultural lands, placed a tremendous strain on the country's food supplies, leading to shortages, a decline in the standard of living, and a rise in the numbers of the poor. That rise in turn only exacerbated the already deep chasm that existed between the haves and the have-nots, generating anger and dissent among those who were being left behind. Secret societies, gravely unhappy with the ruling Qing Dynasty, launched rebellions that sapped the government's power. Widespread corruption among civil and military officials further reduced government effectiveness and efficiency, and increased cynicism among the populace. Lavish, self-indulgent imperial expenditures, plus the huge amounts of money required to support the military's campaigns against internal rebels, depleted the treasury. The rapid increase in opium consumption and addiction tore at the physical and financial fabric of society. And in the face of these mounting forces stood a relatively timid and weak government bureaucracy, overseen by often ineffective and vacillating emperors who were no match for the troubles buffeting China. Thus the Opium War, rather than initiate a period of decline, only made China's already fragile situation worse.

The treaties that resulted from the Opium War have been called "unequal treaties" because, as the historian Immanuel Chung-Yueh Hsü noted, "they were not negotiated by nations treating each other as equals but were imposed on China after a war, and because they encroached upon Chinese sovereign rights . . . [and] reduced her to semicolonial status." And although the Opium War was the first major clash between the West and China, it wouldn't be the last. Over the next seventy years China would fight other wars with European powers, as well as a war with Japan, and one that pitted China against an alliance of six European nations, along with the United States and Russia (the Boxer Rebellion, 1899–1901). These wars resulted in additional so-called unequal treaties, which further eroded the Qing Dynasty's power and made it ever more susceptible to the widespread internal unrest and rebellions that cropped up during this period and further destabilized Chinese society. All these factors contributed to the ultimate disintegration of the Qing Dynasty in 1911, and its replacement with the Republic of China, thereby ending more than two thousand years of imperial rule.[98]

Although the treaties that followed immediately upon the heels of the Opium War humiliated and angered the Chinese, the Americans were pleased, believing that new trade opportunities would now open up. The signing of the Treaty of Wangxia did launch a new era in the American China trade: one in which the need for speed took center stage.

Nine

RACING THE WIND

*A*T NINE IN THE MORNING ON JANUARY 22, 1845, A LARGE CROWD
gathered at the New York City shipyard of Smith & Dimon to celebrate the christening of the new ship *Rainbow*. A bottle of wine was
first smashed on the ship's prow, then the *Rainbow* slid stern first into
the East River with a tremendous splash. A little more than a week
later, when the *Rainbow* was fully loaded and about to sail, Philip
Hone, the dapper former mayor of New York and a man who had

grown rich auctioning off the goods brought back to the city by merchant ships, toured the *Rainbow* with Samuel S. Howland, one of the ship's owners. In his diary entry for February 1, Hone wrote, "This beautiful ship sailed for Canton this morning . . . [it is] the finest ship in model, symmetry, and finish that ever left this port. She appeared to me like a pilot-boat or a race-horse; she was so long and slim, and everything about her so clean and taper[ed]. If she does not sail fast there are no fish in the sea." The *Rainbow's* destination was not novel. It was following a well-worn path in search of Far Eastern fortune, inaugurated sixty-one years earlier by the *Empress of China*. But the *Rainbow* herself was unique. Those who observed its christening and then watched its departure down the East River were witness to the birth of a new era in America's maritime history—the clipper ship had arrived. In the coming years these "greyhounds of the sea," arguably the most magnificent sailing ships ever built, would help write one of the most colorful chapters in the annals of the China trade.[1]

Speed was key. The *Rainbow* and all the China clippers that followed were designed to get to China and back quickly because of the fragility of tea. No matter how well the tea leaves were prepared, and how tightly the tea chests were sealed, the longer it took to get the tea to market, the greater the risk that the tea's quality would degrade. The lower the quality, the lower the sale price, an outcome that the merchants wanted desperately to avoid. There was yet another reason for speed: Ships that arrived first in port garnered the highest prices, but as more ships arrived, the market for tea fell. Thus every China merchant placed a premium on speed, hoping to be the first back with the freshest tea. Now, with the end of the Opium War and the exciting prospect of expanding the tea trade before them, every China merchant's goal was to build the fastest ships of all. To achieve that goal, the New York firm of Howland & Aspinwall hired the naval architect John Willis Griffiths to design the *Rainbow*.

Griffiths was a man with an exceptional vision. Using his mathematical expertise to draft plans and make models, and water tanks to test his ideas—all of which was quite unusual at that time—Griffiths set out to create a vessel that could slice through the water like none had ever before. The *Rainbow*, however, was not entirely new. As the premier chronicler of clipper ships, Carl C. Cutler, noted, the "development of the American clipper" was "evolutionary rather than revolutionary in character."[2] In designing the *Rainbow*, Griffiths looked to the past for inspiration, focusing on the "rakish topsail schooners" called Baltimore clippers that Americans had been building since the Revolution.[3] The Baltimore clipper he studied the most was the *Ann McKim*, built by the merchant Isaac McKim in 1832 and named after his wife. The *Ann McKim* was a very fast ship, on that all agreed, but based on his calculations and testing, Griffiths thought that some of its design elements actually held it back. Its narrow bow—not blunt like a "cod's head," which was the traditional shape for merchant ships—contributed to its speed, but Griffiths thought that a narrower one would make it faster still. In contrast the *Ann McKim*'s stern, in Griffiths's estimation, was too narrow; if it were made a little rounder, he felt, it would create less drag. As for the downward-sloping keel, there, too, Griffiths thought of an improvement—a flatter keel throughout. Finally, the entire length of the ship could be increased and more gently tapered, with the beam, or widest part of the ship, being closer to the stern.[4]

A ship based on Griffiths's new design began taking shape at the Smith & Dimon yard early in 1843. But controversy surrounded it soon after construction commenced. Traditional boat builders, designers, and mariners mocked the *Rainbow*, arguing that it would sail poorly, if at all. It was too sharp up front, and its concave bow made it look as if it was turned "inside out." Instead of smashing through the waves like the older ships with the "cod's head" bows, some thought the *Rainbow* might cut right into and then under the waves, swamping the ship and sending it—swiftly to be sure—into the abyss. Others claimed that the masts were too high and the yards too wide: With such a broad expanse of sail, the rigging would likely give way during the first strong blow. The *Rainbow*'s harshest critics took to calling it "Aspinwall's Folly."

Griffiths never lost confidence in his design, but the owners were stung by the criticism and were having second thoughts. So they hired naval architects in London as consultants and passed along the proposed changes, but neither Griffiths nor Smith & Dimon would budge, and work resumed on the *Rainbow*, according to Griffiths's plan. The 757-ton ship that resulted was a graceful 159 feet long; 31 feet, 10 inches wide; and 18 feet, 4 inches deep. The height of its masts, unfortunately, has been lost in the mists of time, but they must have soared above the deck.[5]

Identifying the *Rainbow* as the first true clipper, or extreme clipper, as it is sometimes called, raises the question of what gives it that distinction. No specific measurements define what a clipper is; no formula can be applied; the name itself offers no help. According to the maritime author A. B. C. Whipple, "The term 'clipper' was derived from the word 'clip,' meaning 'pace,' as in 'to go at a good clip.' "[6] Thus it is merely synonymous with speed, and since it was also applied to the Baltimore clippers, and to the relatively small opium clippers that the British launched during the late 1820s (which made multiple smuggling runs per year between India and China), it is not useful as a unique identifier. Cutler noted two main characteristics of a clipper. "First, she was 'sharp built'—designed as to hull for speed rather than cargo space—and in the second place, she was extremely heavily sparred, in order to spread a far larger area of canvas than ships of equal size were accustomed to spread."[7] An even better definition comes from a "nautical mechanic," who wrote in 1855 that a clipper was

> clean, long, and smooth as a *smelt*. A sharp, arching head, thin, hollow bow, convex sides, light, round, and graceful stern, defines the hull. Aloft, large built, iron-banded masts, . . . tapering smaller masts, long-proportioned spars, from lower to skysail yards, complete the outline. Above-board she towers up with strong, fibrous arms, spreading a cloud of canvas. . . . Being widened and lengthened in dimensions of hull, she rides

the glassy wave in security, or, proudly oscillating in the crazy sea, flies with life before the swift propelling gale.[8]

Still, such definitions are not very clear, leaving the accurate impression that determining what is and what is not a true clipper is somewhat subjective. That is why mariners and historians have been debating for years which ship should be anointed the first clipper. Some want that title to go to the *Houqua* (with a *u*, not a *w*), a very fast ship that had many similarities with the *Rainbow*, and that sailed from New York to Canton in 1844. A few even think that the *Ann McKim* should wear the crown. But most give the laurel to the *Rainbow*, and that is a fine place for it to be.[9]

The *Rainbow* clearly had what it took to be a clipper on paper and in the docks, but on February 1, 1845, the question still remained— could it go fast? Capt. John Land promptly answered the question, sailing the *Rainbow* to Hong Kong in 102 days and returning in 105, for a round trip, including loading time in China, of seven months and 17 days, setting a new record for the China trade and earning the owners more than twice the twenty-two thousand dollars it cost to build. This passage, however, was plagued by problems. On the trip out Land strained and shattered the topgallant masts in a mighty gale. The timing of the voyage was off, and in both directions the ship faced adverse monsoon winds. On the way back all the sails were reduced to tatters, requiring nearly two weeks to repair the damage.

Land knew he could do better, and he had his chance later in 1845 when the *Rainbow* set off again. This time the trip was ninety-nine days out, and an astounding eighty-four days back, making for a record-setting round trip of six months, sixteen days—an overall time that cut in half the typical duration of such a voyage. So fast did the *Rainbow* scud over the waves that it brought back to New York the first news of its arrival in Canton. The usually modest Land could not restrain himself: "The *Rainbow* was the fastest ship that had ever sailed the seas," he bragged, "and moreover, the ship couldn't be built to beat her."[10] But the *Sea Witch* was soon to prove Land wrong.

———

LAND WAS NOT the only talented captain whom Howland & Aspinwall had in their stable. Robert H. Waterman caught the owners' attention early in 1845 when he sailed their vessel the *Natchez*, loaded with tea, from Hong Kong to New York in a record seventy-eight days (after having taken a fairly long and circuitous route to get to China). No clipper, the *Natchez* was rather a New Orleans–style packet ship, 130 feet long, with a shallow draft, which had benefited on its historic run from exceptionally fine winds. The press ballyhooed the voyage, calling it an "astonishing passage."[11] Howland & Aspinwall were also mightily impressed, and just after the *Rainbow* returned from its first China trip, they decided that Waterman needed to test his mettle with a clipper of his own, so they tapped Griffiths to build the *Sea Witch*.

As the *Sea Witch* took form at Smith & Dimon's shipyard, there were no naysayers grumbling about the unusual design. The *Rainbow*'s initial success had washed such doubts away. On December 8, 1846, when the just-completed *Sea Witch* slid into the East River, a local reporter called her a "splendid ship," and "as fine a specimen of New York shipbuilding as we have seen in a long time."[12] At 907 tons; 170 feet, 3 inches long; 33 feet, 11 inches wide, and 19 feet deep, it was larger than the *Rainbow*, had a sharper bow, sported a mainmast that towered 140 feet toward the sky, and carried "more sails than were normally used by a 74-gun warship three times" its size. Griffiths believed that the figurehead of a ship "stamps an impression on the mind in relation to the entire ship," and the *Sea Witch*'s figurehead— a roaring Chinese dragon with a loosely coiled tail that ended in a daggerlike point—left no doubt: This was an aggressive and powerful vessel, ready to attack and beat back the ocean, no matter the obstacles placed in its way.[13]

When the *Sea Witch* left port a few weeks later, Waterman's main goal was to beat the *Natchez*'s record. He came close on that first voyage, arriving in New York on July 26, 1847, with a return trip of eighty-one days, letting the city's residents know of the ship's return with a peal of cannons. Within two weeks Waterman was off again, this time pushing the *Sea Witch* harder, piling on the sails, and bringing it back from Hong Kong in seventy-seven days, barely beating the *Natchez*'s record, and leading a local newspaper to dub the *Sea Witch* "the fastest vessel in the world." But it hadn't done its best yet. When Waterman returned from China on his third voyage with the *Sea Witch*, on March 25, 1849, a cheer erupted along the New York waterfront. It had made the passage from Hong Kong to New York in seventy-four days and fourteen hours, a record never to be eclipsed by another sailing ship.[14]

The success of the *Rainbow* and the *Sea Witch* spurred other merchants to invest in clipper ships for the China trade, and between 1845 and 1855 a small number of these magnificent vessels were commissioned, perhaps no more than a dozen, and sent to Hong Kong, Canton, Shanghai, and other open ports in the Middle Kingdom. But during the same period hundreds of other clipper ships participated in the China trade, though they were not built for that purpose. These were the famed California clippers, and gold, not tea, spurred them on.

IN HIS ANNUAL message to Congress on December 5, 1848, President James K. Polk told his fellow Americans that the fantastic rumors emanating from California were true. "The accounts of the abundance of gold in that territory," Polk said, "are of such extraordinary character as would scarcely command belief were they not corroborated by authentic reports of officers in the public service."[15] With that, gold fever, which had already infected California, swept the East Coast. Soon hundreds of ships raced from eastern ports, heading around the treacherous waters off Cape Horn to California, depositing in San Francisco tens of thousands of people all hoping to strike it rich. San Francisco, which had formerly been a sleepy little town, swelled to twenty thousand by the end of 1849, and continued growing at an exponential rate. Few of the forty-niners made much money, but the

GOLD RUSH CARTOON SHOWING DOCK CROWDED WITH MEN WITH PICKS
AND SHOVELS, AND MEN JUMPING FROM THE DOCK TO REACH THE DEPARTING
SHIP. A CROWDED AIRSHIP AND A MAN ON A ROCKET FLY OVERHEAD, AND A
MAN WITH A PICK AND SHOVEL PARACHUTES FROM THE AIRSHIP.
LITHOGRAPHY BY N. CURRIER, 1849.

people who supplied their needs certainly did. Since speedy freight
delivery commanded a premium, the gold rush created a golden
opportunity for clipper ships.

The first clipper ships to head for the West Coast were ones
originally built for the China trade. The *Memnon* led the way, leaving
New York on April 11, 1849, and reaching San Francisco 123 days
later, a considerable improvement over the 150–200 days it usually
took for bulkier ships to make the fifteen-thousand-mile trip. Other
China clippers followed in the *Memnon*'s wake, with the *Sea Witch*
making it to San Francisco in July 1850, just 97 days after leaving New
York. More impressive than its time was its profit margin. The *Sea
Witch* cost its owners $84,626 to load, but commanded $275,000 in

San Francisco thanks to gold rush inflation, in which something so prosaic as a shovel that cost one dollar anywhere else could sell for more than ten times that amount.[16]

As the first few clippers dropped anchor in San Francisco, the most astounding scene greeted them. The waterfront had been transformed into a forest of ships, with masts for tree trunks and yards for branches. "The number of vessels entering our harbor is really a matter of wonder," observed the *Pacific News* on November 20, 1850. "Within the forty-eight hours ending on Sunday night, nearly sixty sail entered the Golden Gate. The history of the world presents no comparison. The arrivals yesterday were between twenty and thirty sail."[17] And many of those ships would soon be empty hulks bobbing silently in the water, as their crews ran off to the goldfields.

SINCE THE EXTREMELY small number of China clippers couldn't come close to meeting the demand for swift passages to California, eastern merchants rushed to build new fleets of clippers. Shipyards all along the coast from Maine to Maryland hummed with activity. In the biggest cities, like New York, Boston, and Baltimore, and in the smaller towns like Newburyport, Mystic, Bath, Damariscotta, and Portsmouth, a steady stream of clippers slid down the rails ready to sail. Most of them were loaded in New York, the nation's hub for maritime trade, but many left from Boston as well. The residents of those cities and towns shared a great sense of accomplishment in being part of this new wave of shipbuilding. "New York is one of the great shipyards of the world," boasted a newspaper from that teeming metropolis. "Our clippers astonish distant nations with their neat and beautiful appearance. . . . In the furthest corners of the earth the Stars and Stripes wave over New-York-built vessels."[18]

The most famous of the great shipbuilders who improved the clippers, making them bigger, faster, and sturdier, was Donald McKay. Born in the fishing community of Jordan Falls, Nova Scotia, McKay grew up as at home on the water as he was on land, spending count-

DONALD McKAY,
BY W. G. JACKMAN.

less hours sailing along the coast in the small sailboat he and one of his younger brothers had built. In 1826, at the age of sixteen, he left Jordan Falls for New York to apprentice as a shipwright. After working for some of the best builders in the business, including Isaac Webb and Jacob Bell, and serving briefly as a foreman at the Brooklyn Navy Yard, McKay headed to Massachusetts. There he worked in the Currier yards at Newburyport before connecting with Enoch Train, a successful Boston merchant who loaned McKay money for his own shipyard in East Boston.[19]

McKay drew upon all his experience, as well as his many discussions with his close friend and fellow designer Griffiths, in building his first clipper, the 226-foot-long *Stag Hound*. It took just one hundred days from the laying of the keel until the day of its launch, on December 7, 1850, when the shipyard foreman christened it with a bottle of Medford rum, and yelled, "*Stag Hound*! Your name's *Stag Hound*!"[20] On December 21, just a few days before it sailed for New

York, the *Boston Daily Atlas* reported: "This magnificent ship has been the wonder of all who have seen her. . . . She is longer and sharper than any other vessel of the merchant service in the world. . . . Every element in her has been made subservient to speed."[21] Not everyone was favorably impressed with the *Stag Hound*'s prospects, however. "I would think you would be somewhat nervous in going so long a voyage in so sharp a ship, so heavily sparred," remarked an insurance underwriter to its captain, Josiah Richardson. "No," came the reply, "I would not go in the ship at all if I thought for a moment that she would be my coffin."[22]

As it turned out, the underwriter was onto something. Six days out of New York, the main topmast crashed down, taking with it the three topgallant masts. After repairs the *Stag Hound* still surged around the Horn, arriving at Valparaiso, Chile, on April 8, from which port Richardson wrote the owners that it had made the passage in just sixty-six days, the second-shortest time on record, and would have broken the record if the ship had not been dismasted. "The ship is yet to be built to beat the *Stag Hound*," Richardson boasted. "Nothing we have fallen in with yet can hold her play. I am in love with the ship; a better sea boat, or working ship, or dryer, I never sailed in." The *Stag Hound* continued on to San Francisco, arriving 108 days after leaving New York; all things considered, a very respectable time.[23]

In the years to come McKay went on to become the premier designer and builder of clipper ships. In November 1852 the *Boston Daily Atlas* said of him, "He delights in his noble profession, and considers labor or expense nothing, compared with success. It is his ambition to build the best, most beautiful, and swiftest clippers in the world." On that last count in particular, McKay excelled. Of the thirteen clipper ships that ever sailed more than four hundred miles in a single day, twelve were McKay's.[24]

MCKAY'S EMPHASIS ON speed was exactly what was needed during the rambunctious era of the gold rush. The California clippers, like the

CLIPPER SHIP *FLYING CLOUD*, LOADING CARGO BEFORE ITS MAIDEN
VOYAGE FROM NEW YORK TO SAN FRANCISCO IN JUNE 1851.

China clippers before them, were all about speed, and their captains
constantly strove to log the best time to San Francisco. Each year
California clippers raced with one another, and the owners regularly
placed wagers, often up to ten thousand dollars, to go to the ship
that got to California fastest. The record passage to California was
claimed by McKay's *Flying Cloud*, whose captain, Josiah Perkins
Creesy of Marblehead, Massachusetts, along with his wife, Eleanor,
who served as his highly skilled navigator, guided their ship from
New York to San Francisco in eighty-nine days, eight hours, early in
1854.[25]

Matthew Fontaine Maury, the "Pathfinder of the Seas," who published detailed wind and current charts of all the world's oceans, called
the passage between New York and California "the great race-course

of the ocean. . . . Here the modern clipper ship—the noblest work that has ever come from the hands of man—has been sent, guided by the lights of science, to contend with the elements, to outstrip steam, and astonish the world." Maury's pride in these accomplishments was no doubt amplified by the fact that many clipper ship captains relied on his charts to speed their way.[26]

The California clipper boom had an enormous impact on the China trade. After stopping in San Francisco to discharge their cargo and passengers, most of the clippers continued on to China to pick up tea. Many of them came back to New York, while others were hired by British merchants to go to London, by far the largest tea market in the world. Such a voyage would have been unthinkable only a few years earlier, given that the British Navigation Acts had long allowed only British ships to import tea into the country. Those acts were repealed in 1849, and soon thereafter the American invasion began.

EVER SINCE THE first American clippers arrived in China, British merchants there had been eyeing them with a mixture of admiration, envy, and dread. Britons had long dominated the seas, and were exceedingly proud of their merchant marine, but in this instance the upstart Americans had bested them, producing the fastest ships on the ocean, exceptionally well suited to the tea trade. As soon as the straitjacket imposed by the Navigation Acts was removed, however, the British merchants, with thoughts of profit margins foremost on their minds, started viewing the American clippers in a wholly different light—as potential carriers of choice.

Such was the function of the *Oriental*, which Jacob Bell built in New York in 1849, for A. A. Low & Brother. Intended for the China trade, it cost seventy thousand dollars, and was 185 feet long, 36 feet wide, and 21 feet deep. Its first commander, Nathaniel Palmer of Antarctica fame, sailed it round trip to China in 1849–50, but it was its voyage to China, begun from New York on May 18, 1850, and commanded by Palmer's younger brother Theodore, for which it is remembered. When Theodore brought the *Oriental* into Hong Kong's harbor on August 8, 1850, after a record-breaking passage of 81 days from New York, the British merchants were ready.

Three of the largest British trading firms made Russell & Company, which was acting as agent for the *Oriental*, an astonishing offer. At a time when ships shuttling tea from China to London were routinely getting about three pounds per ton of fifty cubic feet, the Brits were happy to pay six pounds per ton of forty cubic feet to hire the *Oriental*, the higher price being justified by her great speed in getting the tea to market, thereby ensuring a fresher product. The Americans readily accepted, and the *Oriental* was quickly loaded with 1,618 tons of the finest Chinese tea. Departing Hong Kong on August 28, 1850, it arrived at London's West India Docks 97 days later, setting the record for the route, and earning the British merchants a hefty profit. As the clipper-era chronicler Arthur Hamilton Clark observed, "It is not too much to say that the arrival of [the *Oriental*] . . . aroused almost as much apprehension and excitement in Great Britain as was created by the memorable Tea Party held in Boston harbor in 1773."[27]

The curious flocked to see the brilliant new American ship, which towered above all the other vessels at the docks. Once the shock of the *Oriental*'s arrival wore off, *The Times* of London laid out the challenging situation facing Britain's merchant marine:

> The profits derived from [the *Oriental*] . . . thus far will be sure to lead many others in her train. As our ships have precisely the same opportunities, . . . the case of the *Oriental*, though it has gained the whole of its freight at the expense of British vessels in the first instance, should be rather a stimulus than a discouragement. It is simply a trial of speed, and as such is just as open to the British as to the American shipbuilders. . . .
> We must run a race with our gigantic and unshackled rival. We must set our long-practised skill, our steady industry, and our dogged determination against his youth, ingenuity, and ardor. It is the father who runs a race with his son. A fell necessity

constrains us, and we must not be beat. Let our shipbuilders and their employers take warning in time. . . . We trust that our countrymen will not be beaten; but, if they should be, we shall know that they deserve it.[28]

The British Admiralty, aware of the threat posed by the *Oriental*, received permission from the Americans to take its measurements while it lay in dry dock, to serve as a starting point for their own shipbuilding efforts along the same lines. The steadfast British then proceeded to design themselves back into the competition, producing their own line of smaller but still very fast clippers. Until the mid-1850s the American and British clippers shared the extremely lucrative tea runs between China and London. Then the British shoved the Americans aside completely.

THE AMERICAN CLIPPERS in the China trade were massive, most over one thousand tons and many exceeding two thousand. All of them were undeniably gorgeous, especially under full sail, with acres of canvas billowing in the wind and their slender, finely curved bows piercing the waves. The captains of these ships were called "drivers" for good reason, for they drove their crews hard day and night, through good weather and bad, all in the service of the prime directive—speed. Although the *Sea Witch*'s record remained frustratingly beyond reach, the China clippers were all fast, many making the all-important run back to New York in well under one hundred days, and in a few instances attaining sustained speeds of eighteen knots.

The men who owned, designed, and sailed the clippers were extremely proud of their ships, which were the most impressive sailing vessels of the day. These men's chauvinism seemed to capture a brand-new strain of American confidence and exceptionalism, the dramatic success of the clippers coming at the end of America's victory over Mexico and at the beginning of the cra of manifest destiny. Each time a clipper ship sailed from port, the men onboard, called "flying-fish men" by their contemporaries, believed that they were on the fastest, finest craft afloat. A letter written by a crewman on the clipper *Samuel Russell*, published in the *New York Herald* in 1851, beautifully captured their ebullient feelings:

> When I made a voyage to China in that 'ere ship, under command of old Captain Nat. Palmer (a captain, let me tell you, as is a captain), we had [a wonderful experience]. . . . Scores of vessels, on the same tack with ourselves, were overhauled and ran away from with just the same ease as the *America* beat the Royal yachts of England [in the first America's Cup race]. Occasionally, to be sure, some brother Yankee would put up a good ship to her mettle before we could shake her off; but as to anything foreign—whether English, or French, or Dutch, or what not, and we had chances with all sorts of them—why, Lord bless you, sir, it was the merest baby play in the world.[29]

CLIPPER SHIP *RED JACKET*, IN THE ICE OFF CAPE HORN,
N. CURRIER, CIRCA 1855.

Clippers' names often glorified their speed, providing a grace note to American exuberance in the nineteenth century. The *Flying Cloud* was joined by the *Flying Arrow*, the *Flying Eagle*, the *Golden Rocket*, the *Comet*, and the *Lightning*, to name but a few. This trend led an American merchant in the 1850s to comment sarcastically, "The *Wings of the Morning* came in day before yesterday from New York, but the *Utter-most-parts-of-the-Sea* has not been heard from. *Snail*, or *Tortoise*, or *Drone*, I would suggest for the next clipper, just for a change; I am tired of these *always-a-little-faster* clipper names."[30] The conceit that clipper men had for their ships extended even to the fanciful names they gave the various sails that soared high above the main deck: "moonrakers, cloud cleaners, skyscrapers, stargazers, and, atop them all, an angel's footstool."[31]

GIVEN AMERICANS' GENUINE affection and pride for their clippers, it is no surprise that they took umbrage when word filtered back across the Atlantic that the British, having only recently built two new clippers along the lines of the *Oriental*, were already bragging that their clippers were faster than the Americans'. This angered the members of Boston's American Navigation Club, many of whom were China merchants and clipper ship owners. If the British were so sure of themselves, let them prove it. To give them that chance, the club threw down the gauntlet in the summer of 1852, challenging the "ship-builders of Britain to a ship-race with cargo on board from a port in England to a port in China and back." Each side could enter one ship, built, commanded, and crewed entirely by citizens of their own country. The British were given the right to specify "the size of the ships, not under 800 nor over 1200 American registered tons," and "the weight and measurement [of the cargo] which shall be carried each way." The winner would receive ten thousand pounds, courtesy of the club.

The letter outlining the challenge was reprinted in many British publications, but months passed, and nobody stepped forward to answer the call. So the club upped the ante. "As a sort of enticement . . . to our shipbuilders," wrote the editors of the British sporting magazine *Bell's Life* in early October 1852, "the President of the American Navigation Club . . . is authorized, should the present challenge not be accepted within thirty days," to offer new terms. British ships would be given a fourteen-day head start, and also be allowed to pick crews comprised of seamen who were experienced in sailing between British and Chinese ports, while the American ships would have to make do with crews that had only limited familiarity with such trips. And, the editors added, the Americans were willing to increase the stakes to twenty thousand pounds or more, if necessary.

It is hard to understand how the club could possibly think that this new "enticement" would be successful, with terms that were clearly insulting to the British, implying that they couldn't compete without a considerable handicap (perhaps that was the point). Nevertheless the editors of *Bell's Life* concluded their announcement of the modified challenge by telling their readers: "The Americans want a match, and it reflects somewhat upon our chivalry not to accommodate them." The *London Daily News* added its voice to those calling for someone to uphold Britain's honor, but despite all this coaxing and the lucrative terms offered, the challenge expired for lack of interest. This is a bit odd, since during the same year the challenge was made, there were a number of unofficial "tea races" between British and American clippers, from China to London, with considerable sums wagered on the outcome, and in which the British gave the Americans as good as they got. Perhaps the British, who had only recently been defeated by the Americans in the first-ever America's Cup race, were not confident enough to contest the Americans again with the whole world watching.[32]

THE DECADE OF the 1850s was the high point for American clippers. But as gold fever subsided, fewer clippers were needed to rush passengers and freight to California, and the remaining demand for such services was increasingly mct by coal-fired steamships operating in the Atlantic, which took people and cargo to Panama for rail transport across the isthmus to the Pacific, where steamships took them on to California. Many of the clippers that had formerly made the gold-coast run first now bypassed the promised land of the American West altogether and went straight to China to transport tea. This trade, however, diminished as British clippers displaced their American competitors on tea runs to London, and other ships took over the runs to the States. By the end of the 1860s there were very few American clippers left. Quite a few were scrapped after being worn out by the rigors of sailing so fast and so hard. Others had become victims of hurricanes or hidden shoals, or had been burned at sea as a result of lightning strikes, carelessness, or the attacks of Confederate raiders during the Civil War. Most of those still afloat were sold to other countries or converted to carry coal or lumber, an ignominious end for ships that were once the pride of America's merchant marine.

The rise and fall of the American clipper spanned little more than a generation. During that time the broader story of the China trade was one of unfulfilled expectations as well as the horrible inhumanity of man to man.

Ten

FADING FORTUNE

ENRAGED CHINESE COOLIE
ONBOARD THE SHIP *NORWAY.*

*T*HE CONCLUSION OF THE OPIUM WAR AND THE SIGNING OF THE
Treaty of Wangxia in 1844 led many American merchants to become
excited by the prospects of rapidly expanding the trade with China.
Freeman Hunt, the editor of the influential *Merchant's Magazine and
Commercial Review*, reflected a widely held view when he called the

new order established by the treaty "one of the greatest commercial revolutions that ever took place." He compared the opening of the China trade to the "discovery of a new continent" full of "rich, industrious people," and he was hopeful that the Chinese would soon clamor to purchase more American goods.[1]

Hunt's optimism had a familiar ring. Americans had long dreamed of the day when the hundreds of millions of Chinese would generate a tidal wave of profitable consumerism. That dream, however, would not be realized. From 1844 until 1869, America's trade with China did increase, reaching a high of roughly $22 million in 1860, and averaging about $15 million for the rest of that decade. But that was hardly a boom, given that the overall value of America's foreign trade at that time rose nearly threefold. Thus America's trade with China during this period, which averaged roughly $13 million per year, represented only about 2.5 percent of U.S. foreign trade, placing China, most of the time, behind Britain, France, Germany, Canada, Cuba, and Brazil, on the list of America's main trading partners. In the grand scheme of things, therefore, America's China trade from 1844 to 1869, although a significant part of the economy and a source of great wealth to many firms and individuals, was not the economic boon that so many had hoped.[2]

One reason for disappointment was China's not-surprising lack of interest in American products. While America exported an impressive range of domestic goods to China—including iron, whale oil, guns, petroleum, pork, beef, tobacco, glass, shoes, leather, lumber, and even ice cut from ponds and lakes—all were sold in limited quantities.* The majority of America's exports to China consisted of cotton goods, with wheat, flour, ginseng, and coal also posting strong numbers toward the end of this period. On the import side, the situation was similar. Although Americans imported relatively small quantities of many Chinese products—including brass, dyes, rhubarb, coffee, rice, porcelain, ginger, and linseed oil—the only goods imported on

---

* To keep the ice from melting too much, it was covered in sawdust.

a large scale were tea and, to a much lesser extent, silk. Consequently America's trade with China remained constrained, with a continuing trade deficit. In some years, the United States imported more than twice the value of goods it exported, covering much of the difference with bills on London, specie, and bullion.[3]

Robert Hart, a British customs official who worked in China from the late 1860s through the beginning of the twentieth century, neatly summarized part of the problem facing the United States, as well as other countries trading with China—a problem that had been around as long as the West had been trying to tap Chinese markets. "Many regard China as a far-distant land, with an immense population, but so wanting in all that others possess as to be ready to purchase, in unlimited quantities, whatever is offered for sale." But, Hart argued, this was not true. China could do without foreign trade, Hart said, because the "Chinese have the best food in the world, rice; the best drink, tea; and the best clothing, cotton, silk, and fur. Possessing these staples, and their innumerable native adjuncts, they do not need to buy a penny's worth elsewhere."[4] Although Hart's claim that the Chinese were basically self-sufficient was mistaken—as evidenced by the many items they imported—he was correct about China not having unlimited demand, and when it came to the goods that America could provide, China's interest was not that great.

Conflict in the United States was also a reason for the relatively weak performance of the American China trade. The Civil War curtailed the flow of cotton from the South to mills in the North, which in turn constrained exports of finished cotton goods. Confederate raiders destroyed much of America's merchant marine, and many ships involved in the China trade were burned. The cargoes lost in such actions, as well as the impact of the war on commerce in general, had a depressing effect on the trade between America and China.

Yet another reason the China boom failed to materialize was that China was not nearly as rich as many American merchants had imagined. There was a huge polarity in wealth, and apart from a very small percentage of wealthy people, the large majority of Chinese were extremely poor. The decades after the Opium War, during which China was buffeted by internal strife and rebellion on a massive scale, and a string of devastating natural disasters (floods, droughts, and famines), only made China's weak economic situation worse. In such circumstances purchasing foreign goods often took a backseat to survival.[5] The Chinese, however, were not without spendable cash, even during those difficult times. And they used much of that cash to purchase opium.

AFTER THE OPIUM WAR the drug trade took off.[6] The Treaty of Nanking said nothing about opium, and that was just fine with the British, who were soon bringing in record amounts of the drug and employing smugglers all along the Chinese coast. Opium was still an illegal import, but the Chinese authorities had just suffered through a devastating war precipitated by the opium trade, and they were not about to risk another confrontation by attempting to clamp down aggressively on the trade, especially when the Qing rulers were preoccupied with trying to suppress a rebellion. Since the treaty's provision for extraterritoriality made British subjects bound only by British law, they had nothing to fear, legally, from pursuing the trade, which continued to be sanctioned by their government.

Exports of Indian opium to China surpassed fifty thousand chests in the late 1840s, rose to seventy-eight thousand in 1855, and stayed above seventy thousand for the remainder of the decade, with most of the drug coming from British sources. American merchants followed the British lead. Although the Treaty of Wangxia said that Americans caught trading opium would be subject to Chinese justice, and that the American flag would not be used as a cover for smuggling operations, it did not prohibit Americans from engaging in the trade. Two firms in particular, Russell & Company, and Augustine Heard & Company, took full advantage—so much for the Americans' claim on the eve of the Opium War that they had "no wish to see a revival of the opium trade." Most of the opium on American ships now came from India, not Turkey, and as before, British far outstripped American participation, which never amounted to more than around five thousand chests annually, and often much less. Still, depending on the price of opium, the American share in the trade could be as high as $2 million in a single year, which was used to buy Chinese goods.

The dynamics of the opium trade changed as a result of what is often called the second Opium War, which in many ways was an outgrowth of the first. The treaties that ended the first Opium War did not resolve the conflict over the opium trade, nor did they make for better relations between the signatory nations. In the decade or so after the treaties were signed, while Britain, America, and France (another signatory nation) were often greatly angered by the failure of the Chinese to fully implement some of the provisions of the treaties, the Chinese were equally upset about what they perceived to be the extremely unfair and humiliating nature of the treaties themselves, as well as the dramatic expansion of the illegal opium trade. These years were marked by rising tensions and occasional violence on both sides, including multiple riots. When the Western countries pushed China to renegotiate the treaties and include provisions that were even more favorable to foreigners, the Chinese government refused. Among the most controversial of the foreigners' demands came from the British, who wanted China to legalize the opium trade.

TO MANY IN THE WEST it appeared increasingly likely that the only way they were going to get satisfaction was through force. All that was needed, it seemed, was a spark, which was provided in 1856, after Chinese soldiers boarded a purportedly British-flagged Chinese ship, the *Arrow*, searching for men suspected of piracy. This perceived insult to the British flag became a rallying cry for the British government, which sent a military force to bring the Chinese to terms. The British were joined by the French, whose entrance into the war was in part sparked by their own casus belli, the arrest and beheading of a French missionary. The Americans, although officially neutral, rctaliated against a Chinese attack on an American ship by shelling and taking control of Chinese forts at the mouth of the Pearl River, and Americans also lent naval support to British and French troops during another battle.

Once again the Western armies defeated the Chinese, and in the process looted and burned the emperor's vast and opulent summer palace just outside Peking, destroying hundreds of buildings and smashing or carting away priceless pieces of China's cultural history. A British captain who participated wrote to his mother, "You can scarcely imagine the beauty and magnificence of the places we burnt. It made one's heart sore to burn them; in fact, these palaces were so large, and we were so pressed for time, that we could not plunder them carefully. . . . It was wretchedly demoralizing work for an army. Everybody was wild for plunder."[7] Although this vengeful act was in retaliation for the horrific torture of nearly forty British and Indian prisoners of war, half of whom suffered agonizing deaths, it was a tragedy just the same.

When the fighting finally ended in 1860, the resulting treaties, which ultimately applied to the Americans as well, contained many new provisions, including ones that opened additional ports to foreigners, permitted foreigners to travel throughout China as long as they had valid passports, and also legalized and taxed the opium trade. The Westerners viewed these treaties in a favorable light, but to the Chinese they were but a second round of unequal treaties, which once again trampled on their rights and sovereignty, illustrating the inability of the imperial government to defend its realm. The legalization of opium was particularly harmful, since it allowed the drug to flow into China unimpeded. As a result opium imports from the 1860s through the 1870s spiked as high as 93,000 chests per year, only adding to the expanding volume of opium being cultivated in China.

America's involvement in the opium trade diminished to insignificance soon after legalization, largely as a result of increased competition from foreign merchants with lower operating costs. And by 1880 Americans exited the trade entirely. But between the end of the first

Opium War and 1860, when the Americans were still significant players in the opium trade, the trade itself possibly served as a brake on the sale of American goods, since the amount of money that the Chinese spent on opium diverted a considerable quantity of Chinese capital, some of which might otherwise have been used to purchase Western manufactures. As Robert Bennet Forbes remarked, "Could the opium trade be abolished, there is no doubt that a compensation would be found in the increased sale of manufactured goods, because there would be more ready cash, and more industry in the country [China] to pay for them." Thus, although the American opium trade generated silver American merchants needed to buy Chinese goods, and also made a few American firms rich, it did nothing to help sell American products in China.[8]

Exporting opium to China was not the only nefarious activity in which American merchants participated after the end of the first Opium War. Far more gruesome was their role in the coolie trade.

THE PLANTATION ECONOMIES of Latin America, which had begun in the late sixteenth century, faced a serious problem by the mid-1800s. For hundreds of years the massive amounts of labor required to plant, grow, and harvest crops such as sugar and tobacco had been provided by African slaves, who had been forcibly taken from their homelands and transported into a living hell. International opprobrium for the practice of slavery had set in by the early 1800s, when the leading slave-trading countries, among them Great Britain, France, Portugal, the Netherlands, Spain, and the United States, banned the trade. While these actions didn't halt slavery, they reduced the flow of slaves across the Atlantic, especially since Britain aggressively used its diplomatic and maritime muscle to enforce the new restrictions. In the ensuing decades many countries decided to emancipate the slaves living in their dominions. The bans on slavery, combined with emancipation efforts, caused a severe labor shortage in much of Latin America at the same time as the demand for plantation-grown crops was increasing. The search for new laborers thus intensified, leading to the rise of the coolie trade.[9]

The origins of the term "coolie" are a bit mysterious. Some say it is derived from the name of a Hindu tribe, the Kholees, who were used as unskilled labor, or "bearers of burdens," in India. Others contend that it is a variation of the Chinese word *ku-li*, meaning "hard laborer" or "rented muscles." Either way, the label was first applied to Indian laborers imported into the British colony of Mauritius, off the southeast coast of Africa, in the 1830s to work the sugar fields. But the term is most often associated with the Chinese brought to Latin America. By one estimate, between 1847 and 1874, 250,000 Chinese coolies were sent to Latin America on ships flying the flags of nineteen nations, including Britain, Spain, Portugal, France, the Netherlands, and the United States. The vast majority of those coolies ended up in Cuba and Peru.[10] Chinese coolies were in great demand because they were hard workers. "Of all laborers who have come under my obser-vation," a veteran sugar plantation owner wrote in 1848, "I know of none who can in any way be compared to the Chinese, for enterprise, energy, sobriety, intelligence, application, physical power, determined perseverance, cheerfulness, and prudent economy combined."[11]

On paper, coolies were contract laborers, volunteers who agreed to work for a certain number of years (usually eight) at a specified rate of pay before being released from their contract, free to return to their homeland. In reality, however, they were not much more than slaves by another name. Their journey began with recruitment. Although the emperor prohibited emigration, the Chinese recruiters, called crimps, had little difficulty gathering their human cargoes. Ignored by local officials, or in cahoots with them, the crimps had many ways of transforming Chinese men, and a very small number of women, into coolies.

Early on, the crimps relied on simple persuasion and deceit. Widespread drought and famine, along with the ravages of war and internal unrest, had created an almost incalculable stream of refugees who flooded from the interior of the country to the coastal cities looking for relief. By offering food, clothes, and lodging, the crimps lured the desperate to come to the barracoons, or holding pens. With the added incentive of a small advance, the crimps then persuaded these marginalized refugees to sign on as coolies, telling them that the opportunities that awaited them abroad were decidedly better than those available in China. In return for their service, the crimps were paid a fee-per-coolie, or capitation fee, by an emigration agent or the captain of the ship that would be transporting the coolies to their destination.

As the demand for coolies rose, capitation fees increased to amounts that equaled the yearly salary for an average Chinese laborer. This created a huge motivation for crimps, but no longer could they rely on the older methods to fulfill their quotas, so they became more creative in their duplicity. Holding out the promise of lucrative employment or the possibility of learning a trade, crimps lured potential coolies from the interior. It was an easy sell, since economic distress created an enormous underclass who would jump at the chance to improve their condition. In many instances the crimps' pitch was made more compelling since they were friends or family members of the people being targeted. Once the hopeful migrants reached the ports, however, the crimps informed them that the jobs had inexplicably disappeared. The crimp then offered to arrange for loans or advances from the local emigration agents to the crestfallen job seekers. No sooner had the loans been proffered, of course, than the agent called them in, and knowing that they couldn't be repaid, he helpfully urged his victims to "volunteer" to become coolies to cover their debt, which many of them reluctantly did.

Crimps also used the Chinese love of gambling as a snare. Cavernous gambling ships would be docked in the harbors of major ports, where runners circulating through the city would drum up business among the poor, encouraging them to visit the ships and promising them money to gamble. After the unlucky men had lost their stake, which the crimp had generously supplied, they, too, became coolies to repay their debt. Some coolies were prisoners from clan wars who were then sold to crimps. And there were others who were simply kidnapped, or "shanghaied," into service.[12]

Over time the barracoons became de facto jails with armed guards who regularly beat the detainees. The Chinese called the barracoons *zhuzai guan*, or "pigpens," on account of their filth, and while waiting to be taken away on ships more than a few coolies died from disease or by suicide. The suffering of the Chinese in the barracoons only intensified on the next stage of their journey. After being herded onto the ships, they were stowed like chattel in the between-deck, where they stayed for much of the voyage. Although they were not shackled like the Africans of the notorious "Middle Passage," the coolies endured inhuman conditions, with many hundreds, and sometimes more than a thousand of them sharing the same hot, cramped, dimly lit, poorly ventilated, foul space. The coolies slept on rows of extremely narrow wooden shelves that ran the length of the ship, and had no sides or partitions to separate them. The food, often putrid, was provided in quantities that barely sustained life. Iron grates over the hatchways restricted the coolies' movements, and also kept them from gaining access to provisions in the hold. The living quarters of the captain and crew on the upper deck were walled off by a massive barricade, from behind which the heavily armed crew kept a wary eye on the passengers. The coolies were allowed on the main deck for limited periods of time, and floggings were commonly used to keep them in line.[13]

Having left all they knew behind, and terrified of the future, some coolies lost all hope and flung themselves into the sea. Others reacted more violently. Mutinies occurred on 68 of the 736 voyages between 1847 and 1874 that brought coolies to Latin America, leaving more than four thousand Chinese dead, along with twelve ships' captains and at least two hundred sailors.[14] One of the most tragic mutinies occurred on the American ship *Waverly*.

BOUND FOR PERU with 450 coolies on board, the *Waverly* arrived at Manila, in the Philippines, on October 25, 1855. The captain had died of dysentery just a few days before, and the first mate, a Mr. French, didn't want to continue the voyage without another officer, hence the layover. The local authorities, fearing that dysentery might have spread, quarantined the ship and then sent it for observation to Cavite, about fifteen miles from Manila. On October 27, according to French, the coolie cooks refused to work until they got their wages. French made an unsatisfactory response, upon which "all the coolies came aft." French ordered his men to grab their arms, and in the ensuing melee four or five coolies were shot and the rest forced below. Later that day French discovered that the coolies had taken provisions and also broken into the cistern. Enraged, he shot a Chinese for being "impudent." Soon thereafter the coolies tried to break through the forward hatch, but French and his men beat them back and then battened down all the hatches. During the night French had hot water poured through the seams of the hatches on the coolies below "to frighten them."

The next day a representative of the *Waverly*'s agents came on board and ordered French to open the hatches. Nearly three hundred Chinese were dead. French claimed that the coolies had "murdered one another," but in truth they had suffocated. French and the rest of the crew were thrown into jail pending an investigation, while the remaining coolies were herded onto a German ship to continue their journey to Peru.[15]

Even more infamous and dramatic was the mutiny that took place on the American ship *Norway*.[16] With sixty crewmen onboard, the three-thousand-ton *Norway* arrived in Hong Kong in 1857, after sailing from New York and delivering a load of coal to the U.S. Naval Squadron in the China Seas. For the better part of a year the *Norway* waited in the harbor to collect a full load of coolies, and in the meantime being retrofitted to accommodate its new cargo of human passengers. The *Norway*, like all coolie ships, was anchored a couple of miles offshore so as to minimize the potential for escape, and therefore the 1,037 coolies had to be ferried from the mainland in sampans. Within twenty-four hours of leaving port, two coolies

COOLIES BOARDING
THE *NORWAY*.

committed suicide; one was strangled; and fights broke out, followed
by floggings.

The third day out the guards broke up another fight below, but
not before one man had been severely slashed with a cleaver stolen
from one of the cooks. The injured man, along with the four who had
sparked the altercation, was brought to the main deck, and while the
former was being tended by the ship's surgeon, he asked to speak to
the captain privately. With the interpreter's assistance, the injured
man told the captain that some Chinese were planning to seize the
ship, and that they had fought over who would lead the mutiny. The
interpreter feared the story was true, but the captain dismissed "the
idea as absurd."

Two days passed quietly, but around midnight on the third: "Suddenly a bright gleam of flame shot up from the forecastle, and a yell

like that of ten thousand demons burst on the still night." The crewmen scrambled to arm themselves and lock the main hatch. When the Chinese managed to force the hatch ajar, a crewman shot the leader and sent him tumbling back, whereupon the hatch was closed again, this time more securely. "The foiled wretches, maddened at defeat in the very outset, rushed with furious yells from one hatch to another, swinging lighted fire-brands or striving to wrench away the iron bars that covered them, or hurling bolts and clubs at every face that peered down from above."

The crewmen placed tarpaulins over some of the hatches and pumped saltwater into the deck below to extinguish the fire. As the fire smoldered, thick smoke forced the Chinese to crowd around the uncovered hatches, but when they came into view the crewmen shot at them and sent them scurrying for safety. Throughout the night the fire was reignited and doused. At daybreak the captain demanded that the leaders of the mutiny be turned over. The Chinese responded by passing up a note written in blood, listing their demands: "Three hundred coolies to be allowed on deck at one time. They shall navigate the ship, and take her to Siam, where a certain number may leave her, after which she shall be allowed to proceed on her course. No signals of any kind shall be made to attract attention of other vessels." If these terms were not agreed to, the Chinese threatened to burn the ship.

The captain flatly refused, prepared the ship's boats to be ready

A COOLIE ATTEMPTING
TO BREAK THROUGH ONE
OF THE HATCH GRATES
ON THE *NORWAY*.

for a quick escape, and warned the Chinese that if they burned the ship they would be "smothered" and burned with it. The next day passed uneventfully, but at night the Chinese again raged below, starting another small fire out of paper and rushing the hatchways trying to force their way out. A day later, their spirit broken and their hope of taking control of the ship gone, the Chinese "sued for pardon," and the *Norway* continued on its violent journey to Cuba, the bodies of seventy Chinese men killed during the failed mutiny dumped over the ship's rails and swallowed up by the ocean.

MUTINIES WERE NOT the only tragedies that befell coolie ships. Accidents also took their toll. The *Flora Temple*, an American clipper ship, left Macao in October 1859, with 850 coolies who soon mutinied. The captain acted quickly and harshly to quell the uprising. The next day, hit by fierce gales, the *Flora Temple* foundered on a reef. The ship's lifeboats could barely hold the crew of fifty, who started out for the coast three hundred miles away. Looking back at the *Flora Temple*, they saw it listing badly, with waves washing over the starboard quarter and the Chinese passengers crowding the upper decks. Fourteen days later two of the five boats arrived at Touren, a French settlement in Cochin China (Vietnam). The captain urgently requested that the admiral of a French squadron search for the missing boats, and also rescue the Chinese. When the French found the reef there was no trace of the passengers, and only a small piece of the *Flora Temple* was visible.[17]

The greatest killer of Chinese coolies as they were taken to Latin America was not mutinies or accidents, however, but disease. It is estimated that dysentery, scurvy, and other maladies claimed twenty-six thousand lives. Added to deaths from other causes, these amounted to a shipboard mortality rate approaching 12 percent (the rate for African slaves on the Middle Passage in the nineteenth century was around 10 to 15 percent)—earning the coolie ships the well-deserved label "floating coffins."[18]

————

ONCE THE COOLIES disembarked at their final destination, their situation did not improve. A report by Chinese officials sent to Cuba in 1874 to investigate the treatment of its citizens paints a picture of pain and suffering, compiled from more than one thousand depositions and eighty-five petitions provided by coolies.

> Eight-tenths of the entire number of Chinese in Cuba declared that they had been kidnapped or decoyed; . . . that on arrival at Havana they were sold into slavery [at from $100 to $500 a head], a small proportion being disposed of to families and shops, while the large majority became the property of sugar-planters; that the cruelty displayed even towards those of the former class is great, and that in the latter it assumes proportions which are unendurable. The labor, too, on the plantations is shown to be excessively severe, and the food insufficient. The hours of labor are too long, and the chastisement by rods, whips, chains, stocks, &c, productive of suffering and injury. . . . A large number have been killed by blows, or died from the effects of wounds, and have hanged themselves, cut their throats, poisoned themselves with opium, and thrown themselves into wells and sugar caldrons. Personal inspection verified the accounts of wounds inflicted by others, fractured and maimed limbs, blindness, heads covered with sores, teeth knocked out, ears mutilated, and the skin and flesh lacerated, proofs of cruelty patent to all eyes.[19]

Although sugar and tobacco plantations in Cuba and sugar and cotton plantations in Peru absorbed the great majority of Chinese coolies, they also ended up elsewhere. Thousands were sent to the Chincha Islands, about thirteen miles off the Peruvian coast, to mine guano. For eons the three small, mostly granite, uninhabited islands had been home to an untold number of birds, among them cormorants, boobies, gannets, and gulls. Over time their feces and urine accumulated into mounds of guano—a Peruvian Indian word for "droppings of seabirds"—some of which were more than 150 feet thick. Being extremely rich in phosphorous, nitrogen, and other nutrients, guano was an excellent fertilizer; and beginning in the 1840s an increasing number of ships, mainly from Europe and America, sailed to the Chinchas to fill their holds with the malodorous cargo, reeking of ammonia, and take it back to their countries, where farmers swore by it as an essential ingredient for healthy crops. During the boom years, from 1850 through the early 1870s, more than ten million tons of guano, valued at hundreds of millions of dollars, were ultimately transported from the Chinchas, and for most of that time guano was the single most important Peruvian export. As the industry expanded, more laborers were needed, which is where the coolies came in.[20]

Mining guano, even compared with sugar, tobacco, and cotton

MOUNTAIN OF GUANO ON THE CHINCHA ISLANDS, OFF PERU, 1862.
THE LINES ON THE SIDE OF THE MOUNTAIN ARE STAIRCASES THAT THE
WORKERS CARVED SO THAT THEY COULD CLIMB UP AND HACK
OFF CHUNKS OF GUANO, WHICH WOULD COLLECT BELOW AND BE
CARTED TO WAITING SHIPS.

plantation labor, was especially hellish. George Washington Peck, a correspondent for the *New York Times*, visited the Chinchas in 1853, and recorded his observations. "The labor is severe—much more so than that of the Negroes on our Southern plantations. They are kept at hard work, in the hot sun, throughout the day." Each coolie, "strong and weak alike," had to dig five tons of guano per day, and transport it by wheelbarrow up to a quarter mile away and dump it into chutes leading into the holds of the ships. Because it never rained on the islands, the guano was "compact, like hard, clay-like loam, and as dusty, when dug, as ashes," which choked the coolies and burned their eyes, throats, and lungs. "Negro drivers," who used whips to

GUANO BEING SENT DOWN CHUTES TO BOATS THAT WILL TRANSFER IT
TO THE SHIPS WAITING OFFSHORE, 1858.

maintain order, oversaw the nearly naked coolies, who were forced to work every day. This existence was so unbearable, Peck said, that every week a few coolies committed suicide "to escape their fate."[21]

Many coolies were literally worked to death. It is estimated that 50 percent of the coolies in Cuba, and more than two-thirds of those on mainland Peru, died before their contracts were up. For those working on the Chincha Islands the numbers were higher still. As to what happened to those coolies who survived until their contract expired, many plantation owners or bosses ignored the contracts entirely, forcing the coolies to continue working as they had before. Some coolies were made to sign new contracts or face arrest. Others simply ran away and were never found. Very few ever saw their homeland again.[22]

AMERICA WAS INDIRECTLY involved in the coolie trade from its inception. Americans built some of the "slaver" ships, which "were renowned the world over for their beauty and speed," and America was a major market for sugar and guano. Direct involvement didn't begin, however, until 1852, when the *Ohio* sailed with three hundred Chinese from China to Peru. Over the next ten years sixty-two ships flying the American flag engaged in the coolie trade, one estimate claiming that during the first six of those years, American ships carried forty thousand Chinese, earning the shipowners millions of dollars.[23]

Many of the American coolie ships were clippers, like the *Flora Temple*. That these swift vessels, once the royalty of America's merchant marine, had been demoted to participation in the coolie trade was a function of supply and demand. The surge of British clippers in the tea trade, in addition to the fading fortunes in California's goldfields, had left many American clippers idle. Rather than have their clippers remain at the docks, the owners, never renowned for their idealism, sent them into the coolie trade. Thus it became the misfortune of these graceful ships, such as the *Westward Ho, Winged*

Racer, Challenge, Bald Eagle, and the *Sea Witch*, to have their names tainted by association with such a shameful and inhuman traffic.[24]

Both before and after the Americans became directly involved in the coolie trade, a broad cross-section of the American public and its elected officials railed against the practice, with much of the fervor coming from the abolitionists, who were better known for their fight against the African slave trade. Peter Parker, who became United States commissioner to China in 1855, spoke for a great many when he chose in his first official communication from his new office to attack the coolie trade. "The history of the traffic in Chinese coolies," Parker began, "as carried on in vessels of the United States, and under other flags, during the past few years, is replete with illegalities, immoralities, and revolting and inhuman atrocities, strongly resembling those of the African slave trade in former years, some of them exceeding the horrors of the 'Middle Passage.'" Coolies had, Parker continued, "not merely [been] seduced under false pretences, ignorant of their destination, but some forcibly abducted and violently borne to countries unknown to them, never to return," despite the fact that the Chinese government prohibited the trade and threatened those who participated in it with death. Parker then called upon "all citizens of the United States to desist from this irregular and immoral traffic," which the U.S. government disapproved of, and he warned any who persisted in the trade that they would forfeit all governmental protection and be subject to any penalties that might arise.[25]

Parker's plea, plus the broader efforts of the government and widespread support in the press, spurred legislative efforts to end America's involvement in the coolie trade. Particularly compelling were the many articles that followed Parker's lead and equated the coolie trade with the African slave trade. The *New York Times* urged the government to "do something towards suppressing this abominable trade [in coolies]. The excuses which have been urged on its behalf are precisely those which were made for the African slave-trade. It is said that the coolies are victims of horrible oppression at home—that their condition is improved by their transportation to other countries,

&c. But common sense has long since branded these apologies as they deserve." The most damning commentaries were provided by publications that pointed out that most of the coolie ships were not owned by firms operating in the slave-holding states of the South, but rather by merchants who lived in the North, where antislavery sentiments burned hot. Were those merchants hypocrites, or worse, Southern sympathizers, that they could participate in this "new slave trade," as the abolitionist *Liberator* called it.[26]

On February 19, 1862, Congress finally passed, and President Abraham Lincoln signed, "An Act to prohibit the 'Coolie Trade' by American Citizens in American Vessels," thereby making the United States the first Western nation to prohibit the trade. The broader coolie trade to Latin America continued until the 1870s, when the Chinese government, in conjunction with key Western nations, most notably Portugal and Spain, finally took effective steps to end it.[27]

NOT LONG AFTER the first Chinese coolies set foot in Latin America, another group of Chinese, almost all of whom were men, headed to the United States, lured there by the discovery of gold in California.[28] Like other dreamers from around the world, the tens of thousands of Chinese who made their way to San Francisco hoped to strike it rich in the land that they called *Gam Saan*, or "Gold Mountain." Their contemporaries almost uniformly called these Chinese "coolies." But the Chinese who came to California were very different from the coolies who went to Latin America. Most of the Chinese gold seekers came voluntarily. While it is true that the advertisements used to entice them to California were often deceptive, holding out the prospects of an easy path to quick wealth, the Chinese who did come typically were not subjected to the strong-arm recruiting tactics used regularly by the crimps looking for bodies to send to Latin America. Instead most of the Chinese heading to California either paid their way or came on the "credit-ticket" system, in which their passage was paid for by another person, usually a Chinese merchant in Hong

Kong or San Francisco, whom the emigrant agreed to pay back out of the wages he earned laboring in America. Once their debts were paid these Chinese emigrants were free to return to China or stay in the United States and pursue other forms of employment, as most of them did. Some of the latter panned for gold on their own account, and the few who struck it rich and went back to China to live like kings only increased the desire of their peers to take their chances in California too. One exception to this largely voluntary emigration of Chinese was the "sex trade," in which Chinese women were tricked or coerced into going to California by crimps, or in some instances by their families, who sold them. Once in California the women were auctioned to the highest bidder and forced into prostitution.

This is not to say that the Chinese who came to work in the gold-fields had an easy time of it. The trip to America was often miserable, with crowding, wretched food, and death from disease not uncommon, and on at least one voyage a violent mutiny erupted. Chinese merchants in California who brought in the workers at times treated them viciously, even physically abusing them to keep them in line. Although the Chinese were for the most part at least tolerated during the earliest years of the gold rush, when they supplied much-needed cheap labor, their situation rapidly deteriorated as the goldfields gave out and they came to be viewed as competition by white workers. Before long the Chinese were subjected to a cavalcade of abuses. They were ostracized, underpaid, overtaxed, denied many basic civil rights, and often persecuted and beaten either by their employers or rabble rousers. They were routinely demonized in the press and by unscrupulous politicians as aliens who would—if given a chance—put American laborers out of work, mongrelize the white population through intermarriage, and spread their religion to the detriment of Christianity. Similar problems and arguments arose when Chinese provided the labor necessary to build the transcontinental railroad in the 1860s. During this period, from the 1850s through the early 1880s, animosity toward the Chinese in America reached a fever pitch. It culminated with the passage of the Chinese Exclusion Act in

1882, which banned Chinese laborers from entering the country for ten years, and in the process became the first American law barring entry to the country based on a person's race or nationality—a kind of law that would be enacted in various forms in the decades to come.

But the treatment of the Chinese who came to America during this time, as reprehensible as it often was, was not the same as the much more abominable treatment accorded to the coolies who were sent to Latin America. Female prostitutes excepted, the Chinese who came to the United States were not forced into a system that was akin to slavery. They did not view themselves as slaves but rather as free laborers seeking to better their condition and provide support for the families they left behind. They were not bought and sold and traded as goods, as the coolies were. It is because of all the differences between the coolie trade and the emigration of Chinese to America that the former is part of the broader story of the China trade, while the latter is not.

THE HAMMERING OF the ceremonial golden spike at Promontory Summit, Utah, on May 10, 1869, to celebrate the completion of the transcontinental railroad marked another turning point in America's trade with China. Part of the change came from the railroad itself and the opportunity it would soon provide to move goods quickly across the continent. Americans had long believed that the opening of such an avenue for commerce would transform America's trade with China. Among the first to envision this new world was Asa Whitney, who had grown rich in the China trade, and had been an early proponent of a transcontinental railroad. In 1845 he proposed a rail line from Lake Michigan to the mouth of the Columbia River. In trying to persuade Congress to grant public land for his project, Whitney calculated that the entire trip from New York City to Xiamen, China—first across the continent, then over the ocean—was 9,200 miles. "With a railroad to the Pacific, and thence to China by steamers," Whitney argued, this trip "can be performed in thirty days, being now a sailing distance of

ALLEGORY OF THE LINKING OF THE TRANSCONTINENTAL
RAILROAD AT PROMONTORY SUMMIT, UTAH, IN
FRANK LESLIE'S ILLUSTRATED NEWSPAPER (MAY 29, 1869).

nearly seventeen thousand miles, and requiring from one hundred to one hundred fifty days for its performance. Then the [cotton] drills and sheetings of Connecticut, Rhode Island, and Massachusetts, and other manufactures of the United States, may be transported to China in thirty days; and the teas and rich silks of China, in exchange, come back to New Orleans, to Charleston, to Washington, to Baltimore, to Philadelphia, New York, and to Boston, in thirty days more."[29]

Over the years many others added their voices to Whitney's, among them Senator Thomas Hart Benton of Missouri, long a promoter of western expansion and fervent believer in America's manifest destiny. In advocating his own plan to build a railroad to the Pacific, he too leaned heavily on expanded trade with China as a reason for supporting the venture:

The trade of the Pacific Ocean, of the western coast of North America, and of eastern Asia, will all take its track; and not only for ourselves, but for posterity. . . . The American road to India will also become the European track to that region. The

European merchant, as well as the American, will fly across our continent on a straight line to China. The rich commerce of Asia will flow through our centre. And where has that commerce ever flowed without carrying wealth and dominion with it? . . . In no instance has it [the Asiatic trade] failed to carry the nation, or the people which possessed it, to the highest pinnacle of wealth and power.[30]

The completion of the transcontinental railroad was only one of the reasons why this time was a turning point in the China trade. Whitney referred to the other key element in his speech, namely steamers or steamships. At the moment that the golden spike was struck, the age of sail was coming to a close, as steamships were increasingly replacing sailing vessels in commerce throughout the world. It wasn't a clean break, however. Sailing ships would continue to be employed for many more years transporting goods between

THE 360-FOOT, 3,800-TON STEAMSHIP *CHINA*, LAUNCHED BY THE PACIFIC MAIL STEAMSHIP COMPANY IN 1867, TOOK PASSENGERS AND FREIGHT FROM SAN FRANCISCO TO YOKOHAMA AND HONG KONG, AND BROUGHT BACK TEA, RICE, SILK, AND OTHER ASIAN GOODS, AS WELL AS MANY THOUSANDS OF JAPANESE AND CHINESE IMMIGRANTS. LITHOGRAPH BY ENDICOTT & COMPANY, NEW YORK, CIRCA 1867.

China and the United States, but the trend was undeniable. Steamships, which had the virtue of being able to travel at fairly high rates of speed regardless of the weather, were the wave of the future. By the mid-1870s steamships—which often used sails as an auxiliary source of propulsion—accounted for nearly half of all the Chinese tea imported to the States, and tea was still far and away the single most important import from China.

Like Whitney, many people felt that the combination of rail and steam was unbeatable, and that with both of these carriers available for use, the China trade would, after years of steady growth, finally explode. The hoped-for boom did not materialize, however. Instead, although America's trade with China trade rose considerably during the balance of the 1800s, overall foreign trade grew at a faster clip. As a result, the China trade fell to less than 2 percent of America's international commerce; and the trade balance between the United States and China remained decidedly in the latter's favor.[31] But that story, as well as an account of how America's trade with China evolved during the twentieth and twenty-first centuries, is a tale for another book.

Epilogue

ECHOES OF THE PAST

FORBES HOUSE MUSEUM, MILTON, MASSACHUSETTS. THIS GREEK-
REVIVAL MANSION WAS BUILT IN 1833 FOR MARGARET PERKINS FORBES
BY HER SONS, ROBERT BENNET FORBES AND JOHN MURRAY FORBES.

*T*HERE ARE MANY WAYS OF LOOKING AT HISTORY. I FIND TWO OF
the most illuminating to be considerations of how the past influences
the present, and how that present is different from the past. On the
first count it is clear that the period of history chronicled in this book
continues to have relevance today. Throughout America evidence
abounds of our early trade relations with China. A large number of
art and history museums contain exquisite objects brought over from

the Middle Kingdom. Innumerable Americans have among their most prized possessions Chinese items that can trace their origins back to the nineteenth century, and even earlier. Mansions built by the leading China merchants dot the landscape, especially in New England, among them the Forbes House Museum in Milton, Massachusetts, and Chateau-sur-Mer, in the rarefied setting of Newport, Rhode Island. Some of these grand homes are open to the public and offer brilliant reminders of just how lucrative the China trade was. All these tangible assets showcasing the beauty of China have contributed to a much broader appreciation of how the trade influenced America's aesthetic and cultural sensibilities.

The China trade was an early engine of American investment. Many of the most prominent China merchants plowed their millions into a wide array of business ventures that helped build America's nineteenth-century economic and industrial might. High on the list of favored investment opportunities were the railroads that crisscrossed the continent and joined the nation together. John Murray Forbes, Robert Bennet's brother, and a prominent China merchant, for example, contributed to the creation and management of the Michigan Central and the Chicago, Burlington, & Quincy railroads. Both Forbes brothers, as well as other China merchants and business titans of their day, including the Whitneys, Sturgises, Astors, Browns, Cushings, Delanos, Perkinses, Russells, and Lows, to name a few, spread their capital throughout the expanding economy, investing in, among other things, real estate, banks, mining, textiles, and insurance companies.[1] Those investments left an indelible mark on the country, both in terms of creating infrastructure and building fortunes.

Many China merchants invariably became philanthropists, leaving behind lasting legacies, none more impressive than the one created by Stephen Girard, who died during the Jacksonian Age in 1831. In his will he left the bulk of his $7.5 million estate to a wide array of causes, including the support of the downtrodden and disabled, and the beautification and improvement of his beloved Philadelphia. Two million dollars of his fortune—up to that time the largest single private charitable donation in American history—went to establishing a school for "poor white male orphans," which has since morphed into Philadelphia's Girard College, a full-scholarship private boarding school for male and female students (grades 1 through 12) of all races who come from families of limited means headed by a single parent or guardian.[2]

But these American fortunes, and all their good works, must be weighed against the damage that was done in acquiring them. As we have seen, many of America's China traders earned a significant portion of their wealth from the morally and legally indefensible opium trade. And though the Opium Wars were not American wars, Americans still bear a heavy responsibility for having nurtured the drug trade.

Despite this indelible stain on American history, the vast majority of Americans know almost nothing about the Opium Wars. Such ignorance, however, should be a concern, for in China the wars are not forgotten history, and the anger relating to them still resonates very loudly. The wars, especially the first, are common knowledge in China and part of a shared identity among the Chinese. Commissioner Lin is regarded as a hero not only for standing on principle, but also for standing up to foreigners. From a broader perspective, the wars are widely viewed in China as an egregious example of Western imperialism, and of Western nations' disregard for the country's rights and sovereignty. Although there is evidence that perspectives are changing, and that a growing number of Chinese no longer view China merely as a victim in the wars, but as bearing some responsibility for the outbreak of hostilities, as well as for the defeats, the wars are still perceived largely as humiliating attacks on China and its people.[3]

The Opium Wars continue to affect the way China views and responds to the West. When Western nations take actions that the Chinese perceive to be overbearing, dictatorial, or even imperialistic in nature, China's responses are influenced by this tragic period in its history. It behooves Westerners, therefore, to be familiar with the

Opium Wars so that they can be more sensitive to Chinese concerns, and better evaluate and respond to Chinese actions.

WHILE THE ERA recounted in this book has clearly influenced the present, it is also instructive to look at just how much things have changed in America's relationship with China. For one thing, the relationship has grown much more critical. Although the China trade was important to the United States up through the 1860s, especially in the early years, it was fairly limited in terms of economic value and the scope of the products traded. The situation today could hardly be more different. China is the United States' second-largest trading partner behind Canada, accounting for roughly 14 percent of America's foreign trade. The China trade, once measured in the tens of millions of dollars, is now worth hundreds of billions per year. Rather than two products dominating imports—tea and silk—China now sells America a vast array of goods that have an enormous impact on how Americans live.[4] Whereas one can imagine American society from the dawn of the Republic through the end of the Civil War surviving without the goods China provided, it is virtually impossible to imagine contemporary America without Chinese products. Thus the phrase "Made in China," once denigrated as a sign of poor quality, is currently emblazoned on much of what we consider absolutely necessary for modern life.

In the early to mid-nineteenth century the China trade was not a major focus of American policy. Although the American government did not ignore the trade, especially when issues such as the Opium Wars and the coolie trade fairly compelled attention, neither did it make trade relations with China a central policy concern (hardly an indefensible position, given the limited importance of the China trade to America's overall economic well-being).

Today, however, the China trade is one of the most important policy issues facing the United States. Of special concern is the United States' enormous trade deficit with China. Whether that concern is justified is debatable, but it is noteworthy that this one aspect of the China trade is currently as it was in the beginning: America imports from China much more than it exports. Thus to some extent the old dream of China becoming a vast, almost limitless market for American goods remains unrealized.[5]

While today's trade deficit has parallels in the past, other economic realities are totally new. No longer connected only by imports and exports, America's and China's economies are now bound by an increasingly strong nexus of investments, including the cross-border flow of businesses, manufacturing plants, and capital. As with the trade deficit, these expanded economic ties have caused considerable consternation in the United States, particularly with respect to the amount of American debt China owns, and the loss of jobs when American companies relocate overseas. Nevertheless the United States and China are now closer and more dependent upon each other than ever before.

That closeness underscores yet another difference in America's relationship with China. In the early years of the China trade Americans knew relatively little about the Chinese or their culture. That is no longer the case. Decades of commercial intercourse, joint ventures, and cross-cultural exchanges have greatly increased both sides' mutual understanding, making the recently forged connections much stronger than those of the past. Although America and China still often view each other unfavorably, and many issues still profoundly divide the two nations, perhaps a respective (and respectful) backward glance over our historic shoulders to see where we have been will enable us to focus more clearly on how far we have come since we first met—and to travel more hopefully into the future.

ACKNOWLEDGMENTS

EVERY BOOK IS A JOURNEY, AND ON THIS ONE MANY PEOPLE HELPED me along the way. Foremost on that list are all the writers and historians who took the time to record history as it was happening, or chronicle it after the fact. Without them this book couldn't have been written, and the endnotes and bibliography reflect their enormous contributions.

The people who reviewed and commented on the manuscript provided valuable guidance that greatly improved the book. For that I wish to thank Bruce and Ann Belason, Robert Booth, Joan Druett, Caroline Frank, Ruth Rooks, and Lixing Sun. Any errors, of course, are mine.

Bob Weil, my editor at Liveright, puts an incredible amount of time and energy into making his writers and their books better, and I am grateful for his efforts. He proved once again to be a master at molding my prose, and forcing me to dig deeper to make the story come alive. His confidence in the book and in me is sincerely appreciated. Bob's assistants, Philip Marino and Will Menaker, helped me navigate the many steps that went into preparing this book, and made the process run smoothly.

Managing editor Nancy Palmquist oversaw the editing and indexing processes, and selected Sue Llewellyn to copyedit the book, a task she performed—as she did on *Leviathan* and *Fur, Fortune, and Empire*—with great skill and humor. Don Rifkin, the project editor, made sure that the text was as flawless as possible. Albert Tang, the art director, created a beautiful cover. I also thank David Cain of Able Illustrator for producing the magnificent maps of eastern China and the Canton/Macao region that appear in the book.

My agent, Russ Galen, continues his unbroken streak of giving me invaluable advice and guidance on the art of writing, pitching, and publishing books. I thoroughly enjoy being one of his clients, knowing that I have access to his wisdom and can count on his support.

Other people whom I would like to thank for helping turn this book into a reality, include Christine Bertoni, Dawn Bonner, Ellen McCallister Clark, Susan Drinan, Elizabeth Frengel, Jeanne Gambel, Pilar Garro, Keith Gervase, Alan Gehret, Florence Gillich, Frederic D. Grant, Jr., Carrie Hamel, Marie Henke, Elizabeth Laurent, George Lovely, Mary Elizabeth Nora, Lawrence Officer, Peter Parker V, Steve Potash, Rhys Richards, Joann Sacco, Doug Smith, Neva Sullaway, Robin M. Tagliaferri, Rodney Taylor, Giema Tsakuginow, Kathleen Wall, Louisa Watrous, and Samuel Williamson.

I would also like to thank the staffs of the Phillips Library at the Peabody Essex Museum, the Massachusetts Historical Society, and the Abbot Public Library, as well as Beth Hall and Lauren Edwards at Adam Matthew Digital, who were gracious enough to give me access to their online data archive—*China: Trade, Politics and Culture, 1793–1980.*

Writing is a solitary act, but I couldn't do it without my family. My folks, Stan and Ruth, never tire of hearing about my latest project, and are always there with encouraging feedback. My children, Lily and Harry, keep me smiling, and I love it when they visit me in the basement office, or "the cave," as they call it, forcing me to focus on something other than a screen. As for my wife, Jennifer, there really are no words to describe how important she is, certainly for my writing but, more important, for my life. She is my first reader, and the one I want to please the most. She does so many things that enable me to write, I couldn't imagine being a writer without her. In short, she is simply the best.

$\mathcal{N}OTES$

Chapter One: "THE ADVENTUROUS PURSUITS OF COMMERCE"

1. Philip Chadwick Foster Smith, *The Empress of China* (Philadelphia: Philadelphia Maritime Museum, 1984), 3–6, 74, 78; Samuel Shaw, *The Journals, The First Consul at Canton, with a Life of the Author by Josiah Quincy* (Boston: WM. Crosby and H. P. Nichols, 1847), 133–34, 137; and David M. Ludlum, *Early American Winters, 1604–1820* (Boston: American Meteorological Society, 1966), 64–67.

2. "New-York, February 26," *Salem Gazette* (March 4, 1784); and Smith, *The Empress*, 6.

3. "Charlestown (South-Carolina) July 5," in *Continental Journal* (August 21, 1783).

4. John J. McCusker and Russell R. Menard, *The Economy of British America: 1607–1789* (Chapel Hill: University of North Carolina, 1991), 108, 130, 174.

5. Charles Rappleye, *Robert Morris: Financier of the Revolution* (New York: Simon & Schuster, 2010), 7–10, 12; and Theodore Thayer, "Town into City, 1746-1765," in *Philadelphia: A 300-Year History* (New York: W. W. Norton, 1982), 79.

6. Rappleye, *Robert Morris*, 13–14, 21–26.

7. Marla R. Miller, *Betsy Ross and the Making of America* (New York: Henry Holt & Company, 2010), 170; and Rappleye, *Robert Morris*, 71–74.

8. Rappleye, *Robert Morris*, 93–94, 227–77; Clarence L. Ver Steeg, *Robert Morris, Revolutionary Financier* (New York: Octagon Books, 1972), 58–59, 65–77, 198–99; and Thomas M. Doerflinger, *A Vigorous Spirit of Enterprise: Merchants and Economic Development in Revolutionary Philadelphia* (Chapel Hill: University of North Carolina Press, 1986), 236–40.

9. Ellis Paxson Oberholzer, *Robert Morris: Patriot and Financier* (New York: Macmillan Company, 1903), 91.

10. Ver Steeg, *Robert Morris*, 13–14, 29.

11. Ibid., 186–88; and Mary A. Y. Gallagher, "Charting a New Course for the

China Trade: The Late Eighteenth-Century American Model," *American Neptune* (Summer 1997), 204.

12. Jared Sparks, *Memoirs of the Life and Travels of John Ledyard, from his Journals and Correspondence* (London: Henry Colburn, 1828), 1, 8, 12, 21–24, 30, 38–39, 46–47; James Zug, *American Traveler: The Life and Adventures of John Ledyard, the Man Who Dreamed of Walking the World* (New York: Basic Books, 2005), 1–34; Bill Gifford, *Ledyard: In Search of the First American Explorer* (Orlando, FL: Harcourt, 2007), 3–55.

13. James Cook and James King, *The Voyages of Captain James Cook*, vol. 2 (London: William Smith, 1842), 263.

14. Ibid., 232, 258–64; and John Ledyard, *A Journal of Captain Cook's Last Voyage to the Pacific Ocean, and In Quest of a North-West Passage Between Asia and America, Performed in the Years 1776, 1777, 1778, and 1779* (Hartford, CT: Nathaniel Batten, 1783), 70.

15. William Sturgis, "The Northwest Fur Trade," *Merchant's Magazine* (June 1846), 534; and James L. Bodkin, "Sea Otter (*Enhydra lutris*)," in *Wild Mammals of North America: Biology, Management, and Conservation*, edited by George A. Feldhamer, Bruce Carlyle Thompson, Joseph A. Chapman (Baltimore: Johns Hopkins University Press, 2003), 736.

16. Cook and King, *The Voyages of Captain James Cook*, vol. 2, 532.

17. Ledyard, *A Journal*, 70.

18. Zug, *American Traveler*, 129. See also Tyler Dennett, *Americans in Eastern Asia: A Critical Study of United States' Policy in the Far East in the Nineteenth Century* (New York: Macmillan Company, 1922), 3.

19. Sparks, *Memoirs*, 173–74. See also Gifford, *Ledyard*, 129–33; Zug, *American Traveler*, 132–33; Smith, *The Empress*, 14–18.

20. Smith, *The Empress*, 26–27; Howard I. Chapelle, *The History of American Sailing Ships* (New York: Bonanza Books, 1949), 134, 138; and "A New York Item," *Maryland Journal and Baltimore Advertiser* (March 5, 1784).

21. "Salem, August 21," *Salem Gazette* (August 21, 1783); "Salem, August 21," *Providence Gazette* (August 30, 1783); Smith, *The Empress*, 23–26.

22. Robert Morris to John Jay, November 27, 1783, in William Jay, *The Life of John Jay*, vol. 2 (New York: J. & J. Harper, 1833), 139. See also Smith, *The Empress*, 20–30, 43–50; and "Appendix I, Early Records of Robert Morris's Involvement in American Trade with China," in *The Papers of Robert Morris, 1781–1784: May 5–December 31, 1783*, edited by Elizabeth M. Nuxoll and Mary A. Gallagher, vol. 8 (Pittsburgh: University of Pittsburgh Press, 1995), 857–64.

23. Sparks, *The Life of John Ledyard*, 197.

24. Smith, *The Empress*, 63, 87, 154–55, 239.

25. Niall Ferguson, *The Ascent of Money: A Financial History of the World* (New York: Penguin Press, 2008), 25–26. See also James R. Fichter, *So Great a*

Proffit: How the East Indies Trade Transformed Anglo-American Capitalism (Cambridge: Harvard University Press, 2010), 31–32.

26. C. Toogood Downing, *The Fan-Qui in China, in 1836–1837*, vol. 2 (London: Henry Colburn, 1838), 146. See also Pierre Jartoux, "Of a Tartarian Plant called Ginseng, etc.," in *The Philosophical Transactions (From the Year 1700, to the Year 1720)*, abridged and compiled by Henry Jones, vol. 4, part 2 (London: W. Innys et. al., 1749), 314; and Kristin Johannsen, *Ginseng Dreams: The Secret World of America's Most Valuable Plant* (Lexington: University of Kentucky Press, 2006), 16–17, 29–30.

27. Jonathan Edwards to Mr. McCulloch, November 24, 1752, in *The Works of Jonathan Edwards, A. M., With an Essay on His Genius and Writings*, by Henry Rogers, revised by Edward Hickman, vol. 1 (London: William Ball, 1839), 195. See also Johannsen, *Ginseng Dreams*, 6; Smith, *The Empress*, 34–35; and "Philadelphia, July 27," *New-York Weekly Journal* (August 21, 1738).

28. Smith, *The Empress*, 31–42.

29. Oscar V. Armstrong, "Opening China," *American Heritage* (February/March 1982), 42.

30. Smith, *The Empress*, 53. See also ibid., 151–55; and Sheldon S. Cohen, *Yankee Sailors in British Gaols: Prisoners of War at Forton and Mill, 1777–1783* (Newark: University of Delaware Press, 1995), 51, 173, 200–202.

31. Shaw, *The Journals*, 110–11. See also Smith, *The Empress*, 60.

32. John Fiske, *The Critical Period of American History, 1783-1789*, 7th ed. (Boston: Houghton, Mifflin and Company, 1891), 114–15; Smith, *The Empress*, 6; Mandell Creighton, *History of Rome* (New York: D. Appleton & Company, 1875), 23; and Society of the Cincinnati Web site, http://www.societyofthc cincinnati.org/history.htm, accessed by author on December 1, 2010.

33. "New-York, July 5," *Virginia Journal* (July 29, 1784). See also Smith, *The Empress*, 23–25; William Weeden, *Economic and Social History of New England, 1620–1789*, vol. 2 (Boston: Houghton, Mifflin and Company, 1894), 820–21; and Gallagher, "Charting a New Course for the China Trade," 211.

34. "Friday, January 30, 1784," *Journals of the American Congress, from 1774 to 1788*, vol. 4 (Washington, DC: Way and Gideon, 1823), 333–34.

35. John Green, "A Journal of an Intended Voyage on Board the Ship *Empress of China*, Bound from New York to Canton in India," entry for February 22, 1784, quoted in Smith, *The Empress*, 78; ibid., 6–7; Shaw, *The Journals*, 133–34. James Riker, "'*Evacuation Day,' 1783, Its Many Stirring Events: With Recollections of Capt. John Van Arsdale* (New York: Printed for the author, 1883), 14–18; and "Extract from a Letter from New York, dated November 26," *New-Jersey Gazette* (December 9, 1783).

36. "New-York, Feb. 23," *New-York Packet and the American Advertiser* (February 23, 1784).

37. Samuel W. Woodhouse, "The Voyage of the *Empress of China*," *Pennsylvania Magazine of History and Biography*, vol. 63, no. 1 (January 1939), 24.

38. Philip Freneau, *The Poems of Philip Freneau, Poet of the American Revolution*, edited by Fred Lewis Pattee, vol. 2 (Princeton: University Library, 1903), 262–63.

39. Woodhouse, "The Voyage of the *Empress of China*," 25–27. See also Smith, *The Empress*, 103; and "Journal of the Ship *Empress of China*," edited by William Bell Clark, *American Neptune* (April 1950), 83–84, 89–90.

40. Quote from Shaw, *The Journals*, 153. See also ibid., 155; and Green's journal in Smith, *The Empress*, 137–38.

Chapter Two: THE MIDDLE KINGDOM

1. Adam Smith, *An Inquiry into the Nature and Causes of the Wealth of Nations*, vol. 1, 5th ed. (London: A. Strahan and T. Cadell, 1789), 20. See also William J. Bernstein, *A Splendid Exchange: How Trade Shaped the World* (New York: Grove, 2008), 8.

2. James Yates, *Textrinum Antiquorum: An Account of the Art of Weaving Among the Ancients*, part 1 (London: Taylor and Walton, 1843), 183. See also E. Jane Burns, *Sea of Silk: A Textile Geography of Women's Work in Medieval French Literature* (Philadelphia: University of Pennsylvania Press, 2009), 9; "A Silk Dress," in *Harper's New Monthly Magazine* (July 1885), 240; Edward Gibbon, *The History of the Decline and Fall of the Roman Empire*, edited by William Smith, vol. 5 (Boston: Little, Brown, and Company, 1854), 57a; and Frances Wood, *The Silk Road: Two Thousand Years in the Heart of Asia* (Berkeley: University of California Press, 2002), 29.

3. *The Natural History of Pliny*, translated by John Bostock and H. T. Riley, vol. 2 (London: George Bell & Sons, 1890), 36. See also Wood, *The Silk Road*, 29; and *Cyclopaedia of India and of Eastern and Southern Asia*, edited by Edward Balfour, 2d ed., vol. 5 (Madras: Lawrence and Adelphi Press, 1873), 330–31.

4. Silvio Farago, "Sericulture," in Mary Schoeser, *Silk* (New Haven: Yale University Press, 2007), 60, 65; Premamoy Gosh, *Fibre Science and Technology* (New Delhi: Tata McGraw Hill, 2004), 97.

5. Colin Thubron, *Shadow of the Silk Road* (New York: Harper Perennial, 2006), 4; Harry G. Gelber, *The Dragon and the Foreign Devils* (New York: Walker and Company, 2007), 36; *Summary of the Principal Chinese Treatises upon the Culture of the Mulberry and the Rearing of Silk Worms*, translated by Stanislaus Julien (Washington, DC: Peter Force, 1838), 77–78; and Schoeser, *Silk*, 17.

6. *Summary of the Principal Chinese Treatises*, 86–87, 99–102, 105, 113–14, 122. See also *The British Cyclopaedia of Natural History*, edited by Charles F. Partington, s.v. "silkworm" (London: W. S. Orr & Co., 1837), vol. 3, 685.

7. James Mease, "Letter from James Mease, Transmitting a Treatise on the Rearing of Silk-Worms by Joseph De Hazzi," Doc. 226, 20th Cong., 1st Sess., H.R., February 2, 1828 (Washington, DC: Gales & Seaton, 1828), 10–14; Linus Pierpoint Brockett, *The Silk Industry in America* (New York: Privately published for the Silk Association of America, 1876), 18–23; Schoeser, *Silk*, 20, 24; and Robert Browning, *Justinian and Theodora* (Piscataway, NJ: Gorgias Press, 2003), 154–56. For the view that the story about Justinian and silk might be apocryphal, see Schoeser, *Silk*, 26.

8. Robert Temple, *The Genius of China: 3,000 Years of Science, Discovery, and Invention* (New York: Simon & Schuster, 1986), 91–94; Wood, *The Silk Road*, 14, 26–27, 80; and Jean McClure Mudge, *Chinese Export Porcelain for the American Trade, 1785–1835* (Newark: University of Delaware Press, 1962), 47–48.

9. A. C. Moule and Paul Pelliot, *Marco Polo: The Description of the World* (London: George Routledge & Sons, 1938), 40, 192, 326. See also Laurence Bergreen, *Marco Polo: From Venice to Xanadu* (New York: Alfred A. Knopf, 2007), 3–8, 92–97, 123, 141, 144–49, 157, 163–64, 168–69, 206–7, 224–28.

10. Henry Yule, *Cathay and the Way Thither, Being a Collection of Medieval Notices of China*, vol. 1 (London: Hakluyt Society, 1866), cxxiv. See also Bergreen, *Marco Polo*, 132, 326–32; Jacques Gernet, *A History of Chinese Civilization*, translated by J. R. Foster and Charles Hartman, 2d ed. (Cambridge, UK: Cambridge University Press, 1996), 331–38, 347–48; S. Wells Williams, *The Middle Kingdom: A Survey of the Geography, Government, Education, Social Life, Arts, Religion, &c. of the Chinese Empire and its Inhabitants*, vol. 2 (New York: Wiley and Putnam, 1848), 217; and Robert Temple, *The Genius of China: 3,000 Years of Science, Discovery, and Invention* (New York: Simon & Schuster, 1986), 16–23, 42–44, 58–62, 81–86, 89–94, 98, 103–19, 139, 149–51, 224–29.

11. Gelber, *The Dragon*, 12–13, 33, 123–24; and John King Fairbank, *China: A New History* (Cambridge: Harvard University Press, 1992), 69.

12. Quote from John King Fairbank, *The United States and China*, 4th ed. (1948; reprint, Cambridge: Harvard University Press, 1979), 159–60. See also Gelber, *The Dragon*, 24, 33–34, 36.

13. First quote from Daniel J. Boorstin, *The Discoverers* (New York: Random House, 1983), 192; second quote from Gelber, *The Dragon*, 89. See also Boorstin, *The Discoverers*, 186–201; Gelber, *The Dragon*, 88–90; Bernstein, *A Splendid Exchange*, 99–103; and Fairbank, *The United States and China*, 149–51.

14. Boorstin, *The Discoverers*, 139–78; and Hosea Ballou Morse, *The Chronicles of the East India Company trading to China, 1635–1834*, vol. 1 (Cambridge: Harvard University Press, 1926), 1–2.

15. Boorstin, *The Discoverers*, 156–78, 259–66; Morse, *The Chronicles*, vol. 1,

3–7, 9–11; William H. Ukers, *All About Tea*, vol. 1 (New York: Tea and Coffee Trade Journal Company, 1935), 23–29, 67–69; Caroline Frank, *Objectifying China, Imagining America: Chinese Commodities in Early America* (Chicago: University of Chicago Press, 2011), 5, 38–42; John King Fairbank, *Trade and Diplomacy on the China Coast: The Opening of the Treaty Ports, 1842–1854* (Cambridge: Harvard University Press, 1953), 35–36; and Jack Turner, *Spice: The History of a Temptation* (New York: Alfred A. Knopf, 2004), 108–10.

16. Charles Patrick Fitzgerald, *China: A Short Cultural History* (New York: Frederick A. Praeger, 1950), 474–87; Gelber, *The Dragon*, 94–98; Morse, *The Chronicles*, vol. 1, 14–30; and Giles Milton, *Nathaniel's Nutmeg, or, The True and Incredible Adventures of the Spice Trader Who Changed the Course of History* (New York: Farrar, Straus & Giroux, 1999), 318–42.

17. William C. Hunter, *The 'Fan Kwae' at Canton Before Treaty Days, 1825–1844, by An Old Resident* (London: Kegan Paul, Trench & Co., 1882), 63–64. See also Gelber, *The Dragon*, 87–98; John Barrow, *Travels in China* (Philadelphia: W. F. McLaughlin, 1805), 402; and Henry Ellis, *Journal of the Proceedings of the Late Embassy to China* (London: John Murray, 1817), 405.

18. Robert Burts, *Around the World: A Narrative of a Voyage in the East India Squadron, under Commodore George C. Read, by an Officer of the U.S. Navy*, vol. 2 (New York: Charles S. Francis, 1840), 288–90. See also Fitzgerald, *China*, 478, 552–53; and Amasa Delano, *A Narrative of Voyages and Travels, in the Northern and Southern Hemispheres: Comprising Three Voyages Around the World* (Boston: E. G. House, 1817), 530–31; and Paul A. Van Dyke, *The Canton Trade: Life and Enterprise on the China Coast, 1700–1845* (Hong Kong: Hong Kong University Press, 2007), 9, 16.

19. Quotes from Hunter, *The 'Fan Kwae,'* 53–54, 65, 99. See also Jacques M. Downs, *The Golden Ghetto: The American Commercial Community at Canton and the Shaping of American China Policy, 1784–1844* (Bethlehem, PA: Lehigh University Press, 1997), 19–25, 74; Van Dyke, *The Canton Trade*, 19–33; Samuel Wells Williams, *The Chinese Commercial Guide* (Hong Kong: A. Shortrede & Co., 1863), 158; "Ship Anchorage at Whampoa," *American Penny Magazine, and Family Newspaper* (May 3, 1845), 202; and letter from Robert Morrison to Dr. Staughton, October 12, 1809, in *Panoplist, and Missionary Magazine United* (October 1810), 227.

20. Hunter, *The 'Fan Kwae,'* 28–30; and Jonathan D. Spence, *The Search for Modern China* (New York: W. W. Norton, 1990), 121.

21. John Ayto, *Dictionary of Word Origins* (New York: Arcade Publishing, 1990), 374; Peter Ward Fay, *The Opium War: 1840–1842* (Chapel Hill: University of North Carolina Press, 1997), 3–5; and Martin Booth, *Opium: A History* (New York: St. Martin's Press/Thomas Dunne Books, 1996), 4–7.

22. John Scarborough, "The Opium Poppy in Hellenistic and Roman Medi-

cine," in *Drugs and Narcotics in History*, edited by Roy Porter and Mikuláš Teich (Cambridge: Cambridge University Press, 1995), 4. See also Booth, *Opium*, 11, 15–19; Pierre-Arnaud Chouvy, *Opium: Uncovering the Politics of the Poppy* (Cambridge: Harvard University Press, 2009), 3–4; and Carl A. Trocki, *Opium, Empire and the Global Political Economy: A Study of the Asian Opium Trade 1750–1950* (London: Routledge, 1999), 14–17.

23. Xu Boling, quoted in Zheng Yangwen, *The Social Life of Opium in China* (Cambridge: Cambridge University Press, 2005), 11. See also ibid., 12; Booth, *Opium*, 103–5; and Chouvy, *Opium*, 4–5.

24. Hunt Janin, *The India-China Opium Trade in the Nineteenth Century* (Jefferson, NC: MacFarland & Company, 1999), 41. See also Yangwen, *The Social Life of Opium in China*, 25–40, 46; Bernstein, *A Splendid Exchange*, 287–88; Fay, *The Opium War*, 7–9; and Charles C. Mann, *1493: Uncovering the New World Columbus Created* (New York: Alfred A. Knopf, 2011), 164.

25. Duncan McPherson, *Two Years in China: Narrative of the Chinese Expedition from Its Formation in April, 1840, to the Treaty of Peace in August, 1842* (London: Saunders and Otley, 1843), 245–46. See also Fay, *The Opium War*, 8–9; and *Encyclopaedia Britannica*, 9th ed., s.v. "opium."

26. "The Opium Trade," *Museum of Foreign Literature, Science and Art* (December 1839), 529. See also Nathan Allen, *The Opium Trade: Including a Sketch of Its History, Extent, Effects, Etc., as Carried on in India and China* (Lowell, MA: James P. Walker, 1853), 34.

27. McPherson, *Two Years in China*, 248–49.

28. Frank Dikötter, Lars Laaman, and Zhou Xun, *Narcotic Culture: A History of Drugs in China* (London: C. Hurst & Co., 2004), 33–34. See also Yangwen, *The Social Life of Opium in China*, 41–55; and Jack Beeching, *The Chinese Opium Wars* (New York: Harcourt Brace Jovanovich, 1975), 23–24.

29. Ukers, *All About Tea*, vol. 1, 1–7; Beatrice Hohenegger, *Liquid Jade: The Story of Tea from East to West* (New York: St. Martin's Press, 2006), 4–8; and Alan Macfarlane and Iris Macfarlane, *The Empire of Tea: The Remarkable History of the Plant That Took Over the World* (New York: Overlook Press, 2004), 41–42.

30. Lu Yü, *The Classic of Tea*, translated by Francis Ross Carpenter (Boston: Little, Brown, and Company, 1974), 60, 77–111. See also Ukers, *All About Tea*, vol. 1, 4–5, 11–20; and Hohenegger, *Liquid Jade*, 12–13.

31. William H. Ukers, *All About Tea*, vol. 2 (New York: Tea and Coffee Trade Journal Company, 1935), 484; and Kakuzō Okakura, *The Book of Tea* (London: G. P. Putnam's Sons, 1906), 34–35.

32. Joseph M. Walsh, *Tea: Its History and Mystery* (Philadelphia: Published by the author, 1892), 10. See also Ukers, *All About Tea*, vol. 1, 5.

33. Carole Manchester, *Tea in the East* (New York: William Morrow, 1996), 54–55; Mary Lou Heiss and Robert J. Heiss, *The Story of Tea: A Cultural*

History and Drinking Guide (Berkeley, CA: Ten Speed Press, 2007), 187–89; Bernstein, *A Splendid Exchange*, 81–83; Ukers, *All About Tea*, vol. 1, 23–29; and Ukers, *All About Tea*, vol. 2, 108.

34. Ukers, *All About Tea*, vol. 1, 38–39; and Ukers, *All About Tea*, vol. 2, 294.

35. Ukers, *All About Tea*, vol. 1, 29, 41–46; and John Phipps, *A Practical Treatise on the China and Eastern Trade* (London: William H. Allen, and Co., 1836), 98.

36. Ukers, *All About Tea*, vol. 1, 29–32; Hohenegger, *Liquid Jade*, 69; and Robert Finlay, *The Pilgrim Art: Cultures of Porcelain in World History* (Berkeley: University of California Press, 2010), 129.

37. Ukers, *All About Tea*, vol. 1, 41–46; Ukers, *All About Tea*, vol. 2, 389–96; Macfarlane and Macfarlane, *The Empire of Tea*, 80–82; John Keay, *China: A History* (New York: Basic Books, 2009), 456; and Reginald Hanson, *A Short Account of Tea and the Tea Trade* (London: Whitehead, Morris & Lowe, 1876), 51–52.

38. Samuel Johnson, "Review of a Journal of Eight Days Journey from Portsmouth to Kingston Upon Thames," in *The Works of Samuel Johnson*, vol. 2 (London: Luke Hansard & Sons, 1806), 390; and Benjamin Woods Labaree, *The Boston Tea Party* (London: Oxford University Press, 1964), 3, 5–6.

39. Ukers, *All About Tea*, vol. 1, 269–96; Ukers, *All About Tea*, vol. 2, 123–24; Hohenegger, *Liquid Jade*, 94–95; Robert Fortune, *Three Years' Wanderings in the Northern Provinces of China* (London: John Murray, 1847), 186–208; and Luke Hebert, *The Engineer's and Mechanic's Encyclopedia*, vol. 2 (London: Thomas Kelly, 1836), 763–64.

40. Keay, *China*, 456. See also Ukers, *All About Tea*, vol. 1, 32, 77; Ukers, *All About Tea*, vol. 2, 397, 436–48; Henry Hobhouse, *Seeds of Change: Six Plants That Transformed Mankind* (Berkeley, CA: Shoemaker & Hoard, 2005), 112, 134–38; Heiss and Heiss, *The Story of Tea*, 338; Jane Pettigrew, *The Tea Companion: A Connoisseur's Guide* (Philadelphia: Running Press Books, 2004), 47–53; Bernstein, *A Splendid Exchange*, 266–71; *Eighteenth-Century English Porcelain in the Collection of the Indianapolis Museum of Art*, edited by Jean Kane (Indianapolis: Indianapolis Museum of Art, 1987), 191; and Rodris Roth, "Tea Drinking in 18th-Century America: Its Etiquette and Equipage," *United States National Museum Bulletin* 225 (1961), 84.

Chapter Three: CHINA DREAMS

1. Washington Irving, *The Sketch Book of Geoffrey Crayon, Gent.*, vol. 2 (London: John Murray, 1822), 360–61. See also Washington Irving, *A History of New York From the Beginning of the World to the End of the Dutch Dynasty* (London: John Murray, 1820), 179–82; Elisabeth Paling Funk, "Netherlands' Popular Culture in the Knickerbocker Works of Washington Irving,"

in *New World Dutch Studies: Dutch Arts and Culture in Colonial America, 1609–1776*, edited by Roderic H. Blackburn and Nancy A. Kelley (Albany, NY: Albany Institute of History and Art, 1987), 88; Jane Pettigrew and Bruce Richardson, *The New Tea Companion: A Guide to Teas Throughout the World* (London: National Trust Enterprise, Ltd., 2005), 22–23; Ukers, *All About Tea*, vol. 1, 49; Esther Singleton, *Dutch New York* (New York: Dodd, Mead & Company, 1909), 115, 132–33; and David Sanctuary Howard, *New York and the China Trade* (New York: New-York Historical Society, 1984), 20–21.

2. Israel Acrelius, *A History of New Sweden: or, The Settlements on the River Delaware*, translated by William M. Reynolds (Philadelphia: Publication Fund of the Historical Society of Pennsylvania, 1874), 158. See also T. H. Breen, *The Marketplace of Revolution: How Consumer Politics Shaped American Independence* (Oxford, UK: Oxford University Press, 2004), 304–5; Ukers, *All About Tea*, vol. 1, 49–51; and Frank, *Objectifying China*, 97–98.

3. Justin Winsor, *The Memorial History of Boston, Including Suffolk County, Massachusetts, 1630–1880*, vol. 2 (Boston: James R. Osgood and Company, 1881), 454.

4. Ukers, *All About Tea*, vol. 1, 50–51; Edward Hagaman Hall, *The Catskill Aqueduct and Earlier Water Supplies of the City of New York* (New York: Mayor's Catskill Aqueduct Celebration Committee, 1917), 32; Gilbert Barkly, *"The Memorial of Gilbert Barkly, merchant, in Philadelphia, in North America, who resided there upwards of sixteen years, and who is well acquainted with the consumption of that country, particularly in the article of Teas, &c.,"* in Francis S. Drake, *Tea Leaves: Being a Collection of Letters and Documents Relating to the Shipment of Tea to the American Colonies in the Year 1773, by the East India Tea Company* (Boston: A. O. Crane, 1884), 200; Bernstein, *A Splendid Exchange*, 241; Hohenegger, *Liquid Jade*, 229; and U.S. Bureau of the Census, *Historical Statistics of the United States, Colonial Times to 1957* (Washington, DC: U.S. Department of Commerce, 1960), 756.

5. Frank, *Objectifying China*, 1–4, 55–59, 116–26, 133–42. See also Breen, *The Marketplace of Revolution*, 35, 40, 52–53, 185, 304.

6. John Trusly, letter to the editor, *New-York Weekly Journal* (April 22, 1734). See also Breen, *The Marketplace of Revolution*, 171; John Kuo Wei Tchen, *New York Before Chinatown: Orientalism and the Shaping of American Culture, 1776–1882* (Baltimore: Johns Hopkins University Press, 1999), 6; and *The Grove Encyclopedia of Decorative Arts*, edited by Gordon Campbell (Oxford, UK: Oxford University Press, 2006), s.v. "chinoiserie," vol. 1, 237–39.

7. Tchen, *New York Before Chinatown*, 4–8; and Susan Gray Detweiler, *George Washington's Chinaware* (New York: Harry N. Abrams, 1982), 30.

8. Frank, *Objectifying China*, 27–55; Breen, *The Marketplace of Revolution*, 88; Kenneth Scott Latourette, *The History of Early Relations Between the United States and China, 1784–1844* (New Haven: Yale University Press, 1917), 11;

and Donald Johnson, *The United States in the Pacific: Private Interests and Public Policies, 1784–1899* (Westport, CT: Praeger Publishers, 1995), 3.

9. Breen, *The Marketplace of Revolution*, 88; Jonathan Goldstein, *Philadelphia and the China Trade, 1682–1846: Commercial, Cultural, and Attitudinal Effects* (University Park: Pennsylvania State University Press, 1978), 17–19; Labaree, *The Boston Tea Party*, 7; Bernstein, *A Splendid Exchange*, 241; Benjamin Labaree, *America's Nation-Time, 1607–1789* (New York: W. W. Norton, 1976), 98; John J. McCusker and Russell R. Menard, *The Economy of British America, 1607–1789* (Chapel Hill: University of North Carolina Press, 1986), 77–78.

10. Quotes, respectively, from Andrew Coe, *Chop Suey: A Cultural History of Chinese Food in the United States* (Oxford, UK: Oxford University Press, 2009), 23; Jean Baptiste Du Halde, *The General History of China*, 3d ed., vols. 1 (London: J. Watts, 1741), preface (unnumbered) and 2; and M. de Voltaire, *A Philosophical Dictionary*, vol. 2, 2d ed. (London: John and H. L. Hunt, 1824), 151. See also Fairbank, *The United States and China*, 156–7.

11. George Anson, *A Voyage Round the World, in the Years 1740, 41, 42, 43, 44*, compiled by Richard Walter under Anson's direction, vol. 2 (1748; reprint, Edinburgh: Campbell Denovan, 1781), 231–32, 255. See also ibid., 118–38; Gelber, *The Dragon*, 158–59; and Spence, *The Search for Modern China*, 120–21.

12. Charles-Louis de Secondat, baron de La Brède et de Montesquieu, *The Spirit of Laws*, vol. 1 (Dublin: G. and A. Ewing, 1751), 156. See also ibid., 153–55; and Gunn, *First Globalization*, 146–48.

13. Charles Thomson, *Transactions of the American Philosophical Society, Held at Philadelphia, for Promoting Useful Knowledge*, vol. 1, 2d ed. (Philadelphia: Aitken & Son, 1789), xvii, xix. See also Ellis Paxson Oberholzer, "Franklin's Philosophical Society," *Popular Science Monthly* (March 1902), 432.

14. Alexander Hamilton, *The Papers of Alexander Hamilton*, vol. 1, edited by Harold C. Syrett and Jacob E. Cooke (New York: Columbia University Press, 1961), 384; and Tchen, *New York Before Chinatown*, 17–18.

15. "Colonist's Advocate: X," *Public Advertiser*, Feb. 19, 1770, in *Benjamin Franklin's Letters to the Press, 1758–1775*, edited by Verner W. Crane (Chapel Hill: University of North Carolina Press, 1950), 206; and Frank, *Objectifying China*, 109.

16. Much of the following discussion, encapsulated in the question "Why tea?" is based on Fichter, *So Great a Proffit*; Breen, *The Marketplace of Revolution*; Frank, *Objectifying China*; and Labaree, *The Boston Tea Party*.

17. "To Our Ladies," *Boston News-Letter*, in *Songs and Ballads of the American Revolution*, by Frank Moore (New York: D. Appleton & Company, 1856), 48–50; Thomas O'Connor, *The Hub, Boston Past and Present* (Boston: Northeastern University Press, 2001), 55; Labaree, *The Boston Tea Party*,

50, 73, 80; Breen, *The Marketplace of Revolution*, 300; Roth, *Tea Drinking in 18th-Century America*, 66–67; and Fichter, *So Great a Proffit*, 18.

18. Sydney Greenbie and Marjorie Barstow Greenbie, *Gold of Ophir: The China Trade in the Making of America* (New York: Wilson-Erickson, 1937), 18.

19. Edmund Burke, "Speeches in the Trial of Warren Hastings," in *Speeches of the Managers and Counsel in the Trial of Warren Hastings*, vol. 1, edited By E. A. Bond (London: Longman, Brown, Green, Longmans, & Roberts, 1859), 15.

20. Labaree, *The Boston Tea Party*, 90–103; Bernstein, *A Splendid Exchange*, 242; Breen, *The Marketplace of Revolution*, 298–301; and Ukers, *All About Tea*, vol. 1, 52–53, 78.

21. A Mechanic, "To the Tradesmen, Mechanics, &c. of the Province of Pennsylvania," broadside, December 4, 1773, viewed by author at Library of Congress American Memory Web site, on January 19, 2011: http://memory.loc.gov /ammem/index.html. See also Frank, *Objectifying China*, 188; Labaree, *The Boston Tea Party*, 58–79, 89–91; and Bernstein, *A Splendid Exchange*, 242.

22. Breen, *The Marketplace of Revolution*, 306.

23. Fichter, *So Great a Proffit*, 17. See also ibid., 18–30.

24. Breen, *The Marketplace of Revolution*, 300, 304. See also ibid., 305–31; and Ukers, *All About Tea*, vol. 1, 57–65.

Chapter Four: THE "NEW PEOPLE"

1. Green, quoted in Smith, *The Empress*, 159. See also Shaw, *The Journals*, 162, 211–12.

2. Anson, *A Voyage Round the World*, vol. 2, 186. See also *The Modern Part of An Universal History From the Earliest Accounts to the Present Time*, vol. 8 (London: C. Bathurst, 1781), 120; Greenbie and Greenbie, *Gold of Ophir*, 160–61; and Christopher Kelly, *A New and Complete System of Universal Geography* (London: Weed and Riden, 1819), 39.

3. Shaw, *The Journals*, 163–64.

4. Pierre le Poivre, *Travels of a Philosopher: Or, Observations on the Manners and Arts of Various Nations in Africa and Asia* (Glasgow: Robert Urie, 1770), 139–42.

5. Quotes from Hunter, *The 'Fan Kwae,'* 108–9; and Shaw, *The Journals*, 178–79. See also Downs, *The Golden Ghetto*, 26–33; *The Chinese Traveller, Containing A Geographical, Commercial, and Political History of China*, vol. 1 (London: E. And C. Dilly, 1772), 37–38; Charles Tyng, *Before the Wind: The Memoir of an American Sea Captain, 1808–1833* (New York: Viking, 1999), 33–34; Clarke Abel, *Narrative of a Journey in the Interior of China, and of a Voyage to and from that Country, in the Years 1816 and 1817* (London: Longman, Hurst, Rees, Orme, and Brown, 1818), 281; Samuel Shaw, "The Drone,"

New-York Magazine or Literary Repository (January 1796), 3, 5; Charles Toogood Downing, *The Fan-Qui in China, in 1836–7*, vol. 1 (London: Henry Colburn, 1838), 211–12, 307–8; and Richard J. Cleveland, *A Narrative of Voyages and Commercial Enterprises*, vol. 1 (Cambridge, UK: John Owen, 1843), 46.

6. Shaw, *The Journals*, 179–80, 183, 199–200.

7. Swift, quoted in Smith, *The Empress*, 154. See also ibid., 155; and "Extract of a letter from a Swedish Supra Cargo, at Canton, to his friend in London, dated 25th Feb. 1785, per True Briton," *Independent Ledger and the American Advertiser* (February 13, 1786).

8. Shaw, *The Journals*, 176–77, 185.

9. All the quotes are from Hosea Ballou Morse, *The Chronicles*, vol. 2 (Cambridge: Harvard University Press, 1926), 99–105. See also Shaw, *The Journals*, 186–95, 339; Letter from Thomas Randall to Alexander Hamilton, August 14, 1791, in *The Papers of Alexander Hamilton*, vol. 9, edited by Harold C. Syrett (New York: Columbia University Press, 1965), 50; "East India Intelligence," *Gentleman's Magazine* (August 1785), 655–56; and "Riot At China," *The Times* (July 8, 1785).

10. Morse, *The Chronicles*, vol. 2, 99–105.

11. Shaw, *The Journals*, 195.

12. Li Chen, "Law, Empire, and Historiography of Modern Sino-Western Relations: A Case Study of the *Lady Hughes* Controversy in 1784," *Law and History Review* (Spring 2009), accessed by the author at the following Web site on February 1, 2011: www.historycooperative.org/journals/lhr/27.1/chen.html.

13. Smith, *The Empress*, 172–73; Shaw, *The Journals*, 200–213; and "New-York, May 12," *Connecticut Courant* (May 16, 1785).

14. Shaw, *The Journals*, 337, 341.

15. Dennet, *Americans in Eastern Asia*, 7–8.

16. Thomas Jefferson to Count de Vergennes, October 11, 1785, in *Memoir, Correspondence, and Miscellanies from the Papers of Thomas Jefferson*, edited by Thomas Jefferson Randolph, vol. 1 (Charlottesville, VA: F. Carr, and Co., 1829), 337–38.

17. Although the very complicated backstory to the *Empress of China*'s return—which includes financial and legal battles among the backers, threats and recriminations, and years of litigation—is interesting, it is not relevant to this book's narrative or to the ultimate impact the voyage had on American history. To learn more about this story, see Smith, *The Empress of China*, 84–88, 115–26, and 220–50.

18. "Elizabeth Town, May 18," *Political Intelligencer and New-Jersey Advertiser* (May 18, 1785). See also "New-York, May 14," *Independent Journal* (May 14, 1785); "Philadelphia, May 13," *Pennsylvania Evening Herald* (May 14, 1785); Shaw, *The Journals*, 218; and Robert Morris to John Jay, May 19,

1785, in William Jay, *The Life of John Jay*, vol. 1 (New York: J. & J. Harper, 1833), 191; "India Goods," *Political Intelligencer* (May 25, 1785); "Hyson Tea," *Columbian Herald* (July 6, 1785); and "Theodosius Fowler," *Connecticut Courant* (July 11, 1785).

19. "Extract of a letter from an English gentleman in New-York to his friend in England, Jun 2," *London's New-York Packet* (January 16, 1786).

Chapter Five: CHINA RUSH

1. James Fenimore Cooper, *Notions of the Americans: Picked up by a Traveling Bachelor*, vol. 1 (London: Henry Colburn, 1828), 16; and Alexis de Tocqueville, *Democracy in America*, translated by Henry Reeve (New York: George Adlard, 1838), 402.

2. "From the New-York Gazetteer Reflections on a Trade to India," *The United States Chronicle, Political, Commercial and Historical* (August 25, 1785); and John Adams to John Jay, November 11, 1785, in *The Diplomatic Correspondence of the United States of America, From the Signing of the Definitive Treaty of Peace, 10th September 1783, to the Adoption of the Constitution, March 4, 1789*, vol. 2 (Washington, DC: Blair & Rives, 1837), 533–34.

3. Greenbie and Greenbie, *Gold of Ophir*, 34.

4. Rhys Richards, "United States Trade with China, 1784–1814," special supplement to *American Neptune* 54 (1994), 9–66; and Rhys Richards, "Re-Viewing Early American Trade with China, 1784–1833," in *Mains'l Haul: A Journal of Pacific Maritime History* (Spring 2003), 18–19.

5. Henry Carter Adams, "Taxation in the United States, 1789–1816, vols. V–VI," in *Johns Hopkins University Studies in Historical and Political Science*, edited by Herbert B. Adams (Baltimore: N. Murray, 1884), 70.

6. *Independent Chronicle*, quoted in Hamilton Andrews Hill, *The Trade and Commerce of Boston, 1630–1890* (Boston: Damrell & Upton, 1895), 89–90.

7. Thomas Randall to Alexander Hamilton, August 14, 1791, in *The Papers of Alexander Hamilton*, edited by Harold C. Syrett, vol. 10 (New York: Columbia University Press, 1965), 54.

8. Fichter, *So Great a Profit*, 22–27, 39–45; Dennet, *Americans in Eastern Asia*, 7–8; Nancy Ellen Davis, *The American China Trade, 1784–1844: Products for the Middle Class* (Washington DC: Ph.D. diss., George Washington University, February 15, 1987), 10–11; Alexander Hamilton, "Trade with India and China," February 10, 1791, in Alexander Hamilton, *The Works of Alexander Hamilton*, vol. 3, edited by John C. Hamilton (New York: John F. Trow, 1850), 188–89; John Steele Gordon, *An Empire of Wealth: The Epic History of American Economic Power* (New York: HarperCollins, 2004), 66; and John K. Fairbank, *Chinese-American Interactions: A Historical Summary* (New Brunswick, NJ: Rutgers University Press, 1975), 11–12.

9. Kenneth Wiggins Porter, *John Jacob Astor, Business Man*, vol. 1 (New York: Russell & Russell, 1966), 129–63; Washington Irving, *Astoria; or, Enterprise Beyond the Rocky Mountains* (Paris: Baudry's European Library, 1836); Eric Jay Dolin, *Fur, Fortune, and Empire: The Epic History of the Fur Trade in America* (New York: W. W. Norton, 2010), 189–222; and Nathaniel Philbrick, *Sea of Glory: America's Voyage of Discovery, The U.S. Exploring Expedition* (New York: Penguin, 2004), 4.

10. John Bach McMaster, *The Life and Times of Stephen Girard, Mariner and Merchant*, vol. 1 (Philadelphia: J. B. Lippincott Company, 1918), 1–48; Greenbie and Greenbie, *Gold of Ophir*, 144–48; Goldstein, *Philadelphia and the China Trade*, 35; Jonathan Goldstein, *Stephen Girard's Trade with China 1787–1824: The Norms Versus Profits of Trade* (Portland, ME: MerwinAsia, 2011), 40; and Jean Gordon Lee, *Philadelphians and the China Trade, 1784–1844* (Philadelphia: Philadelphia Museum of Art, 1984), 104.

11. Robert E. Peabody, *The Logs of the Grand Turks* (Boston: Houghton Mifflin Company, 1926), 1–104; Freeman Hunt, "Elias Hasket Derby," in *Lives of American Merchants*, vol. 2 (New York: Derby & Jackson, 1858), 17–56; Shaw, *The Journals*, 204, 208–9; Joseph B. Felt, *Annals of Salem*, vol. 2 (Salem, MA: W. & S. B. Ives, 1849), 292; *Maritime Salem in the Age of Sail* (Washington, DC: National Park Service in cooperation with the Peabody Museum of Salem, 2009), 17; Doug Stewart, "Salem Sets Sail," *Smithsonian Magazine* (June 2004), accessed by the author on February 15, 2011, at http://www.smithsonianmag.com/history-archaeology/salem.html; Samuel Eliot Morison, *The Maritime History of Massachusetts, 1783–1860* (Boston: Houghton Mifflin Company, 1961), 45–46, 85, 175; "New-York, January 28," *Independent Journal* (January 28, 1786); and "New-York, February 17," *Gazette of the United States* (February 17, 1790).

12. Malcolm Gladwell, *Outliers: The Story of Success* (Boston: Little, Brown, and Company, 2008), 56–61. See also Robert E. Peabody, "The Derbys of Salem: A Study of 18th Century Commerce Carried on by a Family of Typical New England Merchants," *Historical Collections of the Essex Institute* 44 (July 1908), 217–18; and Axel Madsen, *John Jacob Astor: America's First Multimillionaire* (New York: John Wiley & Sons, 2001), 1.

13. Quotes from Rappleye, *Robert Morris*, 507, 512. See also ibid., 490–515; Oberholzer, *Robert Morris, Patriot and Financier*, 224; and Walter Lefferts, *Noted Pennsylvanians* (Philadelphia: J. B. Lippincott Company, 1913), 54.

14. Fichter, *So Great a Proffit*, 27, 112–13; Edwin J. Perkins, "Financing the War of 1812," in *Encyclopedia of the War of 1812*, edited by David S. Heidler and Jeanne T. Heidler (Annapolis, MD: Naval Institute Press, 1997), 182–84; Jerry Markham, *A Financial History of the United States*, vol. 1 (Armonk, NY: M. E. Sharpe, 2002), 122; and Edward S. Kaplan, *The Bank of the United States and the American Economy* (Westport, CT: Greenwood Press, 1999), 44.

15. "New-York, April 24," *Worcester Magazine* (May 1787), 64; Paul E. Fontenoy, "An 'Experimental' Voyage to China, 1785-1787," *American Neptune* 55 (1995), 289, 294–95; "New-York, December 26," *Pennsylvania Mercury and Universal Advertiser* (December 30, 1785); and Richards, "United States Trade with China, 1784-1814," 6.

16. All quotes from Amasa Delano, *A Narrative of Voyages and Travels in the Northern and Southern Hemispheres*, 23, 25. See also ibid., 21–40; William Hackett, *Papers Relating to the Building of the Ship Massachusetts, at Braintree, 1787* (Salem, MA: Reprinted from the Essex Institute Historical Collections, 1938); "For Canton, in China," *Independent Chronicle* (January 7, 1790); and "Ship News," *Massachusetts Centinel* (March 31, 1790).

17. Quote from Goldstein, *Stephen Girard's Trade with China*, 13. See also Timothy Pitkin, *A Statistical View of the Commerce of the United States of America* (New York: James Eastburn & Co., 1817), 247–48; John Macgregor, *Commercial Statistics*, vol. 3 (London: Whitaker and Co., 1847), 816–17; and Goldstein, *Philadelphia and the China Trade*, 2.

18. Carl L. Crossman, *The Decorative Arts of the China Trade* (Suffolk, NY: Antique Collector's Club, 1991), 215–16; and Milton Esterow, "The Many Faces of George Washington," *ARTNews* (October 2009), accessed by the author on June 8, 2011 at the following Web site: http://www.artnews.com/issues/article.asp?art_id=2760.

19. Fichter, *So Great a Proffit*, 1, 26, 56–81; and Gordon S. Wood, *Empire of Liberty: A History of the Early Republic, 1789-1815* (Oxford: Oxford University Press, 2009), 620.

20. William Milburn, *Oriental Commerce; Containing a Geographical Description of the Principal Places in The East Indies, China, and Japan*, vol. 2 (London: Black, Parry, and Co., 1813), 485.

21. Wood, *Empire of Liberty*, 202. See also Pitkin, *A Statistical View of the Commerce of the United States of America*, 248; Macgregor, *Commercial Statistics*, 816; and Downs, *The Golden Ghetto*, 65–67.

22. Nathaniel Portlock, *Voyage Round the World; But More Particularly to the Northwest Coast of America: Performed in 1785, 1786, 1787, and 1788, in the King George and Queen Charlotte, Captains Portlock and Dixon* (London: John Stockdale and George Goulding, 1789), 37, 42. See also Michael A. Jehle, *From Brant Point to the Boca Tigris: Nantucket and the China Trade* (Nantucket: Nantucket Historical Association, 1994), 52–54; Edouard A. Stackpole, *The Sea Hunters: The New England Whalemen During Two Centuries, 1635-1835* (Philadelphia: J. B. Lippincott Company, 1953), 183–88; James Kirker, *Adventures to China: Americans in the Southern Oceans, 1792-1812* (New York: Oxford University Press, 1970), 9–11.

23. James Fenimore Cooper, *The Sea Lions; or, The Lost Sealers*, vol. 1 (New York: Stringer & Townsend, 1849), 46. See also R. Henry, "Seals as Naviga-

tors," *Transactions and Proceedings of the New Zealand Institute, 1900*, 33 (1901), 439.

24. Delano, *A Narrative of Voyages and Travels*, 306; and Ebenezer Townsend, "The Diary of Mr. Ebenezer Townsend, Jr., the Supercargo of the Sealing Ship 'Neptune,' on Her Voyage to the South Pacific and Canton," in *Papers of the New Haven Colony Historical Society*, vol. 4 (New Haven: Printed for the Society, 1888), 35–36.

25. Kirker, *Adventures in China*, 74–75. See also ibid., 52–91; and Townsend, "The Diary of Mr. Ebenezer Townsend, Jr.," 47–48.

26. Kirker, *Adventures in China*, 8–9, 71–72, 167. See also Delano, *A Narrative of Voyages and Travels*, 306–07; Edmund Fanning, *Voyages to the South Seas, Indian and Pacific Oceans, China Sea, North-West Coast, Fiji Island, South Shetlands, &c & c.* (New York: William H. Vermilye, 1838), 341; Briton Cooper Busch, *The War Against the Seals: A History of the North American Seal Fishery* (Kingston, ON: McGill-Queens University Press, 1985), 8, 20–36; James R. Gibson, *Otter Skins, Boston Ships, and China Goods: The Maritime Fur Trade of the Northwest Coast, 1785–1841* (Seattle: University of Washington Press, 1999), 252–53; Benjamin Morrell, *A Narrative of Four Voyages, to the South Sea, North and South Pacific Ocean, Chinese Sea, Ethiopic and Southern Atlantic Ocean, Indian and Antarctic Ocean* (New York: J. & J. Harper, 1832), 130, 393–404; and Richard Ellis, *The Empty Ocean* (Washington, DC: Island Press, 2003), 155.

27. Sparks, *Memoirs*, 193, 196–97, 201–5; and Gifford, *Ledyard*, 153.

28. David Lavender, *Land of Giants, The Drive to the Pacific Northwest, 1750–1950* (New York: Doubleday & Company, 1958), 23.

29. Mary Malloy, *"Boston Men" in the Northwest Coast: The American Maritime Fur Trade 1788–1844* (Kingston, ON: Limestone Press, 1998), 26; and William Sturgis, "The Northwest Fur Trade," 536. See also Gibson, *Otter Skins*, 36–61, 299–318; Morison, *The Maritime History of Massachusetts*, 53; Dolin, *Fur, Fortune, and Empire*, 139–43; and Adele Ogden, *The California Sea Otter Trade, 1784–1848* (Berkeley: University of California Press, 1941), 2.

30. McCracken, *Hunters of the Stormy Sea* (New York: Doubleday, 1957), 38–39, 55–58; and Agnes C. Laut, *Pioneers of the Pacific Coast, A Chronicle of Sea Rovers and Fur Hunters* (Toronto: Glasgow, Brook & Company, 1915), 36–37.

31. "The Fur Trade Between the N.W. Coast of America and China," *Niles' National Register* (March 18, 1843), 40. See also William Sturgis, "The Northwest Fur Trade," 536; Gibson, *Otter Skins*, 57–58, 199–203, 317; Ogden, *The California Sea Otter Trade*, 32–65; Glenn Farris, "Otter Hunting by Alaskan Natives Along the California Coast in the Early Nineteenth Century," *Mains'l Haul* (Summer/Fall 2007), 20–33; Rodney J. Taylor, "The Log of the Brig *Betsy*, 1799–1801," in *Mains'l Haul* (Summer/Fall 2007),

70–87; and John Boit, Jr., *Log of the Union, John Boit's Remarkable Voyage to the Northwest Coast and Around the World, 1794–1796*, edited by Edmund Hayes (Boston: Massachusetts Historical Society, 1981), xviii–xxiv, 88.

32. The following sources, in addition to those cited in the text, were used as background for the section on sandalwood: Fanning, *Voyages to the South Seas*, 54, 57–63, 121–23; Kirker, *Adventures in China*, 111–43; Ernest S. Dodge, *Islands and Empires: Western Impact on the Pacific and East Asia* (Minneapolis: University of Minnesota Press, 1976), 60–65; Gibson, *Otter Skins*, 253–58; Latourette, *The History of Early Relations*, 43–44; Hosea Ballou Morse, *The Chronicles of the East India Company trading to China, 1635–1834*, vol. 3 (Cambridge: Harvard University Press, 1926), 3–4, 174–75, 219; Ernest Dodge, *New England and the South Seas* (Cambridge: Harvard University Press, 1965), 53–54, 86; Ronald Albert Derrick, *A History of Fiji*, vol. 1 (Suva: Government Press, 1957), 39–46; and Gavan Daws, *Shoal of Time: A History of the Hawaiian Islands* (Honolulu: University of Hawaii Press, 1968), 49–50.

33. Quotes, respectively, from Fanning, *Voyages to the South Seas*, 61–62; and Alan Gurney, *The Race to the White Continent: Voyages to the Antarctic* (New York: W. W. Norton, 2000), 29.

34. Garrett Hardin, "The Tragedy of the Commons," *Science* (December 13, 1968), 1243–48; Dodge, *Islands and Empires*, 59–64; Malloy, *"Boston Men" in the Northwest Coast*, 37–39; Ann Fabian, *The Skull Collectors: Race, Science, and America's Unburied Dead* (Chicago: University of Chicago Press, 2010), 134; Gibson, *Otter Skins*, 315; and Sturgis, "The Northwest Fur Trade," 536.

35. Michael Greenberg, *British Trade and the Opening of China, 1800–1842* (Cambridge: Cambridge University Press, 1969), 6–9; Morse, *The Chronicles*, vol. 1, 67–68, 291; Trocki, *Opium*, 42–43; Immanuel Chung Yueh Hsü, *The Rise of Modern China* (New York: Oxford University Press, 1995), 156; and George Staunton, *An Authentic Account of an Embassy from the King of Great Britain to the Emperor of China*, vol. 1 (Philadelphia: Robert Campbell, 1799), 23.

36. Edmund Backhouse and John O. P. Bland, *Annals & Memoirs of the Court of Peking, from the 16th to the 20th Century* (Boston: Houghton Mifflin Company, 1914), 325–26.

37. Joanna Waley-Cohen, *The Sextants of Beijing: Global Currents in Chinese History* (New York: W. W. Norton, 1999), 92–97.

38. Teemu Ruskola, "Canton Is Not Boston: The Invention of American Imperial Sovereignty," in *American Quarterly* (September 2005), 868.

39. Greenberg, *British Trade and the Opening of China*, 104–10.

40. Morse, *The Chronicles*, vol. 1, 215–16; Hosea Ballou Morse, *The Chronicles*, vol. 2 (Cambridge: Harvard University Press, 1926), 77; Hosea Ballou Morse,

The International Relations of the Chinese Empire: The Period of Conflict, 1834–1860 (New York: Longman's, Green and Co., 1910), 209; Charles Clarkson Stelle, *Americans and the China Opium Trade in the Nineteenth Century* (New York: Arno Press, 1981), 3, 5; Trocki, *Opium*, 44–45, 48–52, 81; Shaw, *The Journals*, 238; Van Dyke, *The Canton Trade*, 125–27; Booth, *Opium*, 113; Downs, *The Golden Ghetto*, 108–9, 116; Beeching, *The Chinese Opium Wars*, 26; and R. M. Dane, "Historical Memorandum," Appendix B in *Final Report of the Royal Commission on Opium, Proceedings*, vol. 7 (London: Eyre and Spottiswoode, 1895), 61.

41. Morse, *The Chronicles*, vol. 2, 326–27, 344–46. See also Morse, *The Chronicles*, vol. 3, 127–29.

42. Downs, *The Golden Ghetto*, 108–9, 114–17, 121–25; Dane, "Historical Memorandum," 61; James B. Lyall, "Note on the History of Opium in India and of the Trade in it with China," Appendix A, in *Final Report of the Royal Commission on Opium, Proceedings*, vol. 7, 18; Bernstein, *A Splendid Exchange*, 288–90; Greenberg, *British Trade and the Opening of China*, 10, 110–12; and Van Dyke, *The Canton Trade*, 120–34.

43. Fairbank, *Chinese American Interactions*, 15. See also, Morse, *The Chronicles*, vol. 1, 215; Morse, *The Chronicles*, vol. 2, 77–78, 326–27; Hsin-pao Chang, *Commissioner Lin and the Opium War* (Cambridge: Harvard University Press, 1964), 219; and Henry Moses, *Sketches of India: With Notes on the Seasons, Scenery, and Society of Bombay, Elephanta, and Salesette* (London: Simpkin, Marshall & Co., 1750), 67–69.

44. Paul E. Fontenoy, "The Opium Trade in China: An Early American Connection," part 1, *Mains'l Haul* (Winter 1996), 23.

45. Downs, *The Golden Ghetto*, 115. See also Goldstein, *Philadelphia and the China Trade*, 54; Stelle, *Americans and the China Opium*, 19–20; and Morse, *The Chronicles*, vol. 3, 72–73.

46. Timothy Pitkin, *A Statistical View of the Commerce of the United States of America* (New Haven: Durrie & Peck, 1835), 303; Richards, "Re-Viewing Early American Trade with China," 15–18; Shü-Lun Pan, *The Trade of the United States with China* (New York: China Trade Bureau, 1924), 9; Downs, *The Golden Ghetto*, 105–7; and Lawrence H. Officer, *Between the Dollar-Sterling Gold Points: Exchange Rates, Parity, and Market Behavior* (Cambridge, UK: Cambridge University Press, 1996), 19–20, 147.

47. Edward Sanderson, "Rhode Island Merchants in the China Trade," in *Federal Rhode Island: The Age of the China Trade, 1790–1820* (Providence: Rhode Island Historical Society, 1978), 44; and Gertrude Selwyn Kimball, "The East-India Trade of Providence, from 1787 to 1807," in *Papers from the Historical Seminary of Brown University*, vol. 6, edited by J. Franklin Jameson (Providence: Preston and Rounds, 1896), 5–6.

48. Gabriel Franchère, "Narrative of a Voyage to the Northwest Coast of America

in the Years 1811, 1812, and 1813, or the First Settlement on the Pacific," in *Early Western Travels 1748–1846*, vol. 6, edited by Reuben Gold Thwaites (1854; reprint, Cleveland: Arthur H. Clark Company, 1904), 289–92; Washington Irving, *Astoria; or, Enterprise Beyond the Rocky Mountains* (Paris: Baudry's European Library, 1836), 64–70; and James P. Ronda, *Astoria & Empire* (Lincoln: University of Nebraska Press, 1990), 235–37.

49. Quote from James Jackson Jarvis, *History of the Hawaiian Islands* (Honolulu: Charles Edwin Hithcock, 1847), 76–77. See also Hiram Bingham, *A Residence of Twenty-One Years in the Sandwich Islands; or the Civil, Religious, and Political History of Those Islands* (Hartford, CT: Hezekiah Huntington, 1847), 39–40; Townsend, "The Diary of Mr. Ebenezer Townsend, Jr., 59–60; Daws, *Shoal of Time*, 33–34; and Kirker, *Adventures in China*, 148–50.

50. Gibson, *Otter Skins*, 156.

51. John R. Jewitt, in collaboration with Richard Alsop, *Narrative of the Adventures and Sufferings of John R. Jewitt* (Middletown, CT: Seth Richards, 1815), 114. See also Gibson, *Otter Skins*, 159–75; Malloy, *"Boston Men" in the Northwest Coast*, 35; and Dolin, *Fur, Fortune, and Empire*, 156–61.

52. Sturgis quoted, respectively, in Charles G. Loring, *Memoir of the Hon. William Sturgis* (Boston: John Wilson and Son, 1864), 24; and Gibson, *Otter Skins*, 158. See also William Sturgis, *"A Most Remarkable Enterprise," Lectures on the Northwest Coast Trade and Northwest Coast Indian Life by Captain William Sturgis*, edited by Mary Malloy (Marston's Mills, MA: Parnassus Imprints, 1997), 77.

53. Quotes, respectively, from Robert Bennet Forbes, *Personal Reminiscenses* (Boston: Little, Brown, and Company, 1882), 392–93; and William Elliot Griffis, "Our Navy in Asiatic Waters," in *Harper's New Monthly Magazine* (October 1898), 739. See also *Other Merchants and Sea Captains of Old Boston* (Boston: State Street Trust Company, 1919), 51–53; Edmond S. Meany, "Book Review, *The Northwest Fur Trade and the Indians of the Oregon Country*, by William Sturgis," *Washington Historical Quarterly* (October 1920), 304–5; and Downs, *The Golden Ghetto*, 61.

54. Dodge, *Islands and Empires*, 60–65.

55. Fanning, *Voyages to the South Seas*, 59.

56. Dodge, *Island and Empires*, 64; Derrick, *A History of Fiji*, 43–46; Peter Dillon, *Narrative and Successful Result of a Voyage in the South Seas, Performed by Order of the Government of British India, to Ascertain the Actual Fate of La Pérouse's Expedition*, vol. 1 (London: Hurst, Chance, and Co., 1829), 1–19, 27; and Kirker, *Adventures in China*, 132–37.

57. Delano, *A Narrative of Voyages and Travels*, 139. See also Stackpole, *The Sea-Hunters*, 240–44; and Thomas Boyles Murray, *Pitcairn: The Island, the People, and the Pastor* (London: Society for Promoting Christian Knowledge, 1859), 104–6.

58. Phineas Bond to Lord Carmarthen, May 17, 1787, in *Annual Report of the American Historical Association for the Year 1896*, vol. 1 (Washington, DC: Government Printing Office, 1897), 535; and Phineas Bond to Lord Carmarthen, July 2, 1787, in ibid., 540–42. See also Phineas Bond to Lord Carmarthen, December 29, 1787, in ibid., 555–56; Phineas Bond to Lord Carmarthen, October 2, 1788, in ibid., 578; Phineas Bond to Lord Carmarthen, December 2, 1788, in ibid., 590; and Greenbie and Greenbie, *Gold of Ophir*, 83–86.

59. Edmund Burke, *Burke's Speech on Conciliation with America*, edited by Charles R. Morris (New York: Harper & Brothers, 1945), 14, 21–23, 103. See also Stanley Ayling, *Edmund Burke, His Life and Opinions* (New York: St. Martin's Press, 1988), 80.

60. Quotes, respectively, from Samuel Shaw to John Jay, December 21, 1787, in *The Diplomatic Correspondence of the United States of America, from the Signing of the Definitive Treaty of Peace, 10th September, 1783, to the Adoption of the Constitution, March 4, 1789*, vol. 7 (Washington, DC: Francis Preston Blair, 1834), 469; and A. Owen Aldridge, *The Dragon and the Eagle: The Presence of China in the American Enlightenment* (Detroit: Wayne State University Press, 1993), 127.

61. Townsend, "The Diary of Mr. Ebenezer Townsend, Jr.," 87–88.

62. Richard Henry Lee to Samuel Adams, May 20, 1785, in *The Letters of Richard Henry Lee*, vol. 2, edited by James Curtis Ballagh (New York: Macmillan Company, 1914), 360; "Dublin, May 31," *Providence Gazette and Country Journal* (August 4, 1787); William Bentley, *The Diary of William Bentley D.D., Pastor of the East Church Salem, Massachusetts*, vol. 2, edited by Joseph Gilbert Waters, Marguerite Dalrymple, and Alice G. Waters (Salem, MA: The Essex Institute, 1907), 192; and "Extract of a letter from an American gentleman in London, to his friend in Philadelphia," *Public Advertiser* (September 18, 1807).

63. Dennett, *Americans in Eastern Asia*, 45, 56; Morse, *The Chronicles*, vol. 2, 184, 193, 205, 256, 266, 278, 294, 311, 322, 348, 358, 389, 401; Morse, *The Chronicles*, vol. 3, 2, 27, 55, 77, 101, 131, 158, 175, 206; Tench Coxe to Alexander Hamilton, August 1791, in *The Papers of Alexander Hamilton*, vol. 10, edited by Harold C. Syrett (New York: Columbia University Press, 1965), 143; Milburn, *Oriental Commerce*, 486; Foster Rhea Dulles, *The Old China Trade* (Boston: Houghton Mifflin Company, 1930), 209–11; and Pitkin, *A Statistical View of the Commerce of the United States of America* (1817), 247–49.

64. Greenbie and Greenbie, *Gold of Ophir*, xiii. The number for the value of the China trade relative to overall United States trade is based on my calculations, using the following sources: Pitkin, *A Statistical View of the Commerce of the United States of America* (1835), 302–6; and *Historical Statistics of the United States: Earliest Times to the Present, Millennial Edi-*

tion, vol. 5, edited by Susan B. Carter, Scott Sigmund Gartner, Michael R. Haines, Alan L. Olmstead, Richard Sutch, and Gavin Wright (Cambridge: Cambridge University Press, 2006), 534–44. See also Fichter, *So Great a Profit*, 207; Morse, *The Chronicles*, vol. 3, 27, 77, 131; and *Documents Relating to the Finances of the United States*, Doc. no. 31, U.S. Senate, 19th Cong., 1st sess. (February 6, 1826), 9.

65. Adam Johann von Krusenstern, *Voyage Round the World in the Years 1803, 1804, 1805, & 1806*, vol. 1, translated from the German by Richard Belgrave Hoppner (London: John Murray, 1813), 332–33; Gibson, *Otter Skins*, 28–35; Latourette, *Early Relations Between the United States and China*, 46–47.

66. Benjamin W. Labaree, William M. Fowler, Jr., Edward W. Sloan, John B. Hattendorf, Jeffrey J. Safford, and Andrew W. German, *America and the Sea: A Maritime History* (Mystic, CT: Mystic Seaport, 1998), 198; and Robert Leckie, *The Wars of America* (New York: Harper & Row, 1968), 230–31.

67. The background for this section on Pinqua Wingchong (whose name is also spelled "Winchung" in some places) comes from the following sources, unless otherwise noted: Porter, *John Jacob Astor*, vol. 1, 142–50; and Greenbie and Greenbie, *Gold of Ophir*, 103–8.

68. "Washington City," *National Intelligencer* (July 25, 1808).

69. Thomas Jefferson to Albert Gallatin, July 25, 1808, in Thomas Jefferson, *The Writings of Thomas Jefferson*, edited by Albert Ellery Bergh, vol. 11 (Washington, DC: Thomas Jefferson Memorial Association, 1907), 106–7.

70. Quotes, respectively, from, Porter, *John Jacob Astor*, vol. 1, 147; and Madsen, *John Jacob Astor*, 70. See also untitled article, *The North American and Mercantile Daily Advertiser* (July 28, 1808).

71. "The Ship *Beaver* and the Mandarin," *New-York Commercial Advertiser* (August 13, 1808).

72. "Notice to Mandarins," *New-York Gazette & General Advertiser* (August 13, 1808). See also untitled article, *The North American, and Mercantile Daily Advertiser* (August 13, 1808).

73. Walter Barrett, *The Old Merchants of New York City* (New York: Carleton, 1866), 9–10.

74. Thomas Jefferson to Albert Gallatin, August 15, 1808, in Thomas Jefferson, *The Writings of Thomas Jefferson*, edited by Albert Ellery Bergh, vol. 11 (Washington, DC: Thomas Jefferson Memorial Association, 1907), 133–34. See also Albert Gallatin to Thomas Jefferson, August 5, 1808, in *The Writings of Albert Gallatin*, edited by Henry Adams, vol. 1 (Philadelphia: J. B. Lippincott & Co., 1879), 400.

75. Untitled article, *Portland Gazette and Maine Advertiser* (August 19, 1808).

76. Frances Ruley Karttunen, *The Other Islanders: People Who Pulled Nantucket's Oars* (New Bedford: Spinner Publications, 2005), 146.

77. For another take on this episode—that Wingchong might have been a low-

level merchant seeking to secure payment for debts owed him by Shaw and Randall—see Tchen, *New York Before Chinatown*, 41–42.

78. Labaree et al., *America and the Sea*, 207.

79. Milburn, *Oriental Commerce*, vol. 2, 486; Richards, *United States Trade with China*, 9, 49–58, and Latourette, *The History of Early Relations*, 52.

80. Peter Auber, *China: An Outline of the Government, Laws, and Policy: And of the British and Foreign Embassies to, and Intercourse with, That Empire* (London: Parbury, Allen, and Co., 1834), 241–42. See also Morse, *The Chronicles*, vol. 3, 214–19.

81. The quotes are Girard speaking, and they come from McMaster, *The Life and Times of Stephen Girard*, 216–17. See also ibid., 214–15, 218–20; and Stephen Simpson, *Biography of Stephen Girard, with his Will Affixed* (Philadelphia: Thomas L. Bonsal, 1832), 122.

Chapter Six: THE GOLDEN GHETTO

1. Robert Waln, Jr., from Mudge, *Chinese Export Porcelain*, 123; "A Review of Charles Gutzlaff's, *A Sketch of Chinese History, Ancient and Modern: comprising a retrospect of the Foreign Intercourse and Trade with China*," in *American Quarterly Review* (March 1835), 140. Figures for the value of America's China trade calculated by me, based on the following sources: J. Smith Homans, *An Historical and Statistical Account of the Foreign Commerce of the United States* (New York: G. P. Putnam & Co., 1857), 181; *Historical Statistics of the United States*, vol. 5, 534–44; and Pitkin, *A Statistical View of the Commerce of the United States of America* (1835), 299–301. See also Downs, *The Golden Ghetto*, 348–57; John Tyler, "Sandwich Islands and China: Message from the President of the United States," H. doc. 35, 27th Cong., 3d sess. (December 31, 1842), 3; and Yen-P'ing Hao, "Chinese Teas to America—A Synopsis," in *America's China Trade in Historical Perspective: The Chinese and American Performance*, edited by Ernest R. May and John K. Fairbank (Cambridge: Harvard University Press, 1986), 22–23.

2. S. doc. 31, Committee on Finance, 19th Cong., 1st sess. (February 6, 1826); Downs, *The Golden Ghetto*, 143–220, 364–66; Goldstein, *Philadelphia and the China Trade*, 61; Goldstein, *Stephen Girard's Trade with China*, 85–91; and John Denis Haeger, *John Jacob Astor: Business and Finance in the Early Republic* (Detroit: Wayne State University Press, 1991), 230–31; and Howard, *New York and the China Trade*, 27–28.

3. "The Discovery," *The American* (September 22, 1820).

4. Busch, *The War Against Seals*, 22–25; Dulles, *The Old China Trade*, 92–93; Stackpole, *The Sea Hunters*, 355–60; J. A. Allen, "Fur-Seal Hunting in the Southern Hemisphere," *Proceedings of the Tribunal of Arbitration, Convened*

at Paris Under the Treaty Between the United States of America and Great Britain, Concluded at Washington February 29, 1892, vol. 1 (Washington, DC: Government Printing Office, 1892), 398; and "The Discovery," *The American* (September 22, 1820).

5. Quotes from John Randolph Sears, *Captain Nathaniel Brown Palmer: An Old-Time Sailor of the Sea* (New York: Macmillan Company, 1922), 42–75. See also Philbrick, *Sea of Glory*, 14–16; William H. Goetzmann, *New Lands, New Men: America and the Second Great Age of Discovery* (New York: Viking, 1986), 253–56; Busch, *The War Against the Seals*, 23–24; Stackpole, *The Sea Hunters*, 355–68.

6. David Starr Jordan, *The Fur Seals and Fur-Seal Islands of the North Pacific Ocean*, pt. 3 (Washington, DC: Government Printing Office, 1899), 313.

7. Gibson, *Otter Skins*, 315.

8. David Porter, *Journal of a Cruise Made to the Pacific Ocean by Captain David Porter in the United States Frigate Essex in the Years 1812, 1813, and 1814*, 2d ed., vol. 2 (New York: Wiley & Halsted, 1822). See also I. C. Campbell, *A History of the Pacific Islands* (Berkeley: University of California Press, 1989), 61–62.

9. In addition to the sources cited in the text, this section on sandalwood in Hawaii is based on the following: Dodge, *New England and the South Seas*, 81–83; Dodge, *Islands and Empires*, 61–62; Walter Muir Whitehall, *George Crowninshield's Yacht*, Cleopatra's Barge (Salem, MA: Peabody Museum, 1959), 3, 5, 7, 11–13; Ralph Simpson Kuykendall, *The Hawaiian Kingdom, 1778–1854*, vol. 1 (Honolulu: University of Hawaii, 1938), 88–89; Norris W. Potter, Lawrence M. Kasdon, and Ann Rayson, *History of the Hawaiian Kingdom* (Honolulu: Bess Press, 2003), 26–28; William Ellis, *Narrative of a Tour Through Hawaii, or, Owhyhee* (London: H. Fisher, Son, and P. Jackson, 1826), 375–76; Ralph S. Kuykendall and A. Grove Day, *Hawaii: A History from Polynesian Kingdom to American State* (Englewood: Prentice-Hall, 1961), 41–43; and Morison, *The Maritime History of Massachusetts*, 262.

10. Yunte Huang, *Charlie Chan: The Untold Story of the Honorable Detective and his Rendezvous with American History* (New York: W. W. Norton, 2010), 13.

11. Paul Forsythe Johnston, "A Million Pounds of Sandalwood: The History of *Cleopatra's Barge* in Hawaii," *American Neptune* (Winter 2002), 5–10.

12. Walter A. McDougall, *Let the Sea Make a Noise: A History of the North Pacific From Magellan to MacArthur* (New York: Basic Books, 1993), 181.

13. Quoted in Gibson, *Otter Skins*, 61. See also William Sturgis, "The Northwest Fur Trade," *Hunt's Merchant Magazine* (June 1846), 536; and Latourette, *The History of Early Relations Between the United States and China*, 54–55.

14. Dodge, *Islands and Empires*, 290; Goldstein, *Philadelphia and the China Trade*, 50–51; Phipps, *A Practical Treatise*, 313; Stelle, *Americans and the*

China Opium, 32; Robert Bennett Forbes, *Remarks on China and the China Trade* (Boston: Samuel N. Dickinson, 1844), 27; and Downs, *The Golden Ghetto*, 124–28.

15. Dennett, *Americans in Eastern Asia*, 120. See also "China, Cohong Address," *Literary Panorama, and National Register*, vol. 8 (London: Stimpkin and Marshall, 1819), 463–64; "On Further Interferences with the East-India Company's Privileges of Exclusive Trade," *Asiatic Journal* (December 1821), 526; and "Murder & Piracy," *Boston Palladium* (December 18, 1817).

16. Downs, *The Golden Ghetto*, 119.

17. In addition to the sources cited in the text, this account of the Terranova affair is based on the following: Jacques M. Downs, "The Fateful Case of Francis Terranova: An Incident of the China Trade," *Mains'l Haul* (Spring 2003), 4–13; "Account of the trial and fate of the sailor belonging to the American ship *Emily*, executed by the Chinese of Canton," *Republican Chronicle* (April 3, 1822); and "Execution of an Italian at Canton," *North American Review* (January 1835), 58–68.

18. "Account of the trial and fate of the sailor belonging to the American ship *Emily*."

19. Dennett, *Americans in Eastern Asia*, 87.

20. "Opium Trade with China," *Providence Patriot* (December 21, 1822); and Dennett, *Americans in Eastern Asia*, 121.

21. Morse, *The Chronicles of the East India Company Trading to China, 1635–1834*, vol. 4 (Cambridge: Harvard University Press, 1926), 26.

22. Phyllis Forbes Kerr, *Letters from China: The Canton-Boston Correspondence of Robert Bennet Forbes, 1838–1840* (Mystic, CT: Mystic Seaport Museum, Inc., 1996), 14–15; Maurice Collis, *Foreign Mud: The Opium Imbroglio at Canton in the 1830's and the Anglo-Chinese War* (1946; reprint, New York: W. W. Norton, 1968), 22; Downs, *The Golden Ghetto*, 120–21; and Robert Bennet Forbes, et al., "Memorial of R. B. Forbes and Others" (January 9, 1840), House Doc. 40, 26th Cong., 1st sess., 2.

23. John Tyler, "Sandwich Islands and China: Message from the President of the United States," House doc. 35, 27th Cong., 3rd sess. (December 31, 1842), 8–10; S. doc. 31, Committee on Finance, 19th Cong., 1st sess. (February 6, 1826); and Forbes, *Remarks on China*, 27–28.

24. "Sea Cucumber," *International Wildlife Encyclopedia*, edited by Maurice Burton (Tarrytown, NY: Marshall Cavendish Corporation, 2002), 2271–72; and Charles Darwin, *The Voyage of the Beagle* (New York: P. F. Collier & Son Company, 1909), 468. Unless otherwise noted, the background for this section on the bêche-de-mer trade comes from the following sources: Dodge, *New England and the South Seas*, 86–100; William S. Cary, *Wrecked on the Feejees* (Nantucket: 1887; reprint, Inquirer and Mirror Press, 1949), 46–53; and Mary Wallis, *The Fiji and New Caledonia Journals of Mary Wallis,*

1851–1853, edited by David Routledge (Salem, MA: Institute of Pacific Studies, 1994), xviii–xx.

25. Frederick J. Simons, *Food in China: A Cultural Historical Inquiry* (Boca Raton, FL: CRC Press, 1991), 435.

26. James Oliver and William Giles Dix, *Wreck of the* Glide *with Recollections of the Fijis* (New York: Wiley & Putnam, 1848), 34–36.

27. Almost all the background information, and the quotes for the following section on the *Glide*, come from Oliver and Dix, *Wreck of the* Glide, 13, 27–38, 45–46, 67–71, 75–79, 84–90, 202–3. See also Dodge, *New England and the South Seas*, 96–98.

28. Homans, *An Historical and Statistical Account of the Foreign Commerce of the United States*, 181; Pitkin, *A Statistical View of the Commerce of the United States of America* (1835), 303; Dennett, *Americans in Eastern Asia*, 73; Hao, "Chinese Teas to America," 24–25; Freeman Hunt, "Commerce of China," *Hunt's Merchant Magazine* (December 1840), 476; Downs, *The Golden Ghetto*, 108–12; and "Exchange in China," *Farmer's Register* (March 1834), 618.

29. Quote from Robert B. Marks, *The Origins of the Modern World: Fate and Fortune in the Rise of the West* (Lanham, MD: Rowman & Littlefield, 2007), 144. See also Paul E. Fontenoy, "Ginseng, Otter Skins, and Sandalwood: The Conundrum of the China Trade," *Northern Mariner* 7, no. 1 (1997), 1–4; letter to the editor, *The Patron of History* (July 19, 1820); and "Trade Beyond the Cape of Good Hope," *New-York Columbian* (February 6, 1819).

30. Hunt, "Commerce of China" (December 1840), 477–79; and Tyng, *Before the Wind*, 75.

31. Walter Barrett, *The Old Merchants of New York City*, vol. 1 (New York: Thomas R. Knox & Co., 1885), 39–45.

32. Downs, *The Golden Ghetto*, 85.

33. Fairbank, *Chinese-American Interactions*, 14.

34. All the quotes, and much of the information for this section on Forbes, come from the following source, except where otherwise noted in the text: Robert Bennet Forbes, *Personal Reminiscences* (Boston: Little, Brown, and Company, 1878), 1–5, 14–27, 30–31, 81, 124, 131–41.

35. Margaret C. S. Christman, *Adventurous Pursuits: Americans and the China Trade, 1784–1844* (Washington, DC: Smithsonian Institution Press, 1984), 113.

36. All quotes from Hunter, *The 'Fan Kwae' at Canton*, 43–44. See also Downs, *The Golden Ghetto*, 41–43, 76; and Greenberg, *British Trade and the Opening of China*, 61.

37. Hunter, *The 'Fan Kwae' at Canton*, 48; Downs, *The Golden Ghetto*, 80–82; Christman, *Adventurous Pursuits*, 85.

38. Abeel, *Journal of a Residence in China*, 88–89.

39. Quote from George B. Stevens, *The Life, Letters, and Journals of the Rev. and Hon. Peter Parker, M.D.* (Boston: Congregational Sunday-School and Publishing Society, 1896), 106–7. See also Downs, *The Golden Ghetto*, 44–45; and Latourette, *The History of Early Relations*, 81–82.

40. Hunter, *The 'Fan Kwae' at Canton*, 25–26; and Aldridge, *The Dragon and the Eagle*, 106–7.

41. "China and the Chinese," *Southern Quarterly Review* (July 1847), 17. See also Christman, *Adventurous Pursuits*, 95.

42. Downs, *The Golden Ghetto*, 49–50.

43. All the quotes in this section attributed to Harriet Low come from the following: Harriet Low, *My Mother's Journal: A Young Lady's Diary of Five Years Spent in Manila, Macao, and the Cape of Good Hope*, edited by Katherine Hillard (Boston: George H. Ellis, 1900), 28, 32–33, 44, 38, 64–65, 77–85, 119–20, 236. See also Christman, *Adventurous Pursuits*, 96–105.

44. Wang Ping, *Aching for Beauty: Footbinding in China* (Minneapolis: University of Minnesota Press, 2000), 3–12; and Tiffany Marie Smith, "Footbinding," in *Encyclopedia of Gender and Society*, edited by Jodi O'Brien, vol. 2 (Thousand Oaks, CA: Sage Publications, 2009), 331–32.

45. Wang Ping, *Aching for Beauty*, 3–12, 55; Spence, *Search for Modern China*, 39; Eileen H. Tamura, Linda K. Menton, Noreen W. Lush, and Francis K. C. Tsui, *China: Understanding Its Past* (Honolulu: University of Hawaii Press, 1997), 14–15; and Smith, "Footbinding."

46. Robert Bennet Forbes to Rose Forbes, November 22, 1838, in Kerr, *Letters from China*, 70; and Stevens, *The Life, Letters, and Journals of the Rev. and Hon. Peter Parker*, 88, 118–32. See also Christman, *Adventurous Pursuits*, 127–40; and Chi-Chao Chan, Melissa M. Liu, and James C. Tsai, "The First Western-Style Hospital in China," *Archives of Ophthalmology* (June 2011), 791–97.

47. "China and the Chinese," *Southern Quarterly Review* (July 1847), 15. See also Downs, *The Golden Ghetto*, 29.

48. Downs, *The Golden Ghetto*, 48; and Hunter, *The 'Fan-Kwae' at Canton*, 47–48.

49. The background for this section on the fire comes from the following: "China: Chinese Proclamation Respecting the Late Fire in Canton in 1822," *Asiatic Journal* (July 1823), 99; "An Account of the Fire of Canton, in 1822," in *Memoirs of the Life and Labours of Robert Morrison, Compiled by His Widow*, vol. 2 (London: Longman, Orme, Brown, Green, and Longmans, 1839), Appendix, 33–39; Morse, *The Chronicles*, vol. 4, 64–66; John Francis Davis, *The Chinese: A General Description of the Empire of China and its Inhabitants*, vol. 1 (London: Charles Knight, 1836), 110–11; and "Great Fire in Canton," *New England Farmer* (March 22, 1823).

50. "An Account of the Fire of Canton, in 1822," appendix, 34–35.

51. "China: Chinese Proclamation Respecting the Late Fire in Canton," 99.

52. W. W. Wood, *Sketches of China* (Philadelphia: Carey & Lea, 1830), 65.

53. George Nugent Temple Grenville, *Considerations Upon the Trade with India; and the Policy of Continuing the Company's Monopoly* (London: T. Cadell, 1807), 115; and John Crawford, *History of the Indian Archipelago: Containing an Account of the Manners, Arts, Languages, Religions, Institutions, and Commerce of its Inhabitants*, vol. 3 (London: Hurst, Robinson, and co., 1820), 252.

54. "East-India Trade," *Columbian Centinel* (October 2, 1813).

55. Greenberg, *British Trade and the Opening of China*, 55, 175, 185–86; Morse, *The Chronicles*, vol. 2, 344–45; Morse, *The Chronicles*, vol. 4, 20–22, 67–68, 84–86, 99–100, 118–19, 139–40, 158–59, 181–82, 195–96, 248–49, 271–72, 339–40, 369–70; "British and India Trade," *Louisiana Advertiser* (May 27, 1820); "East India Trade," *New-York Daily Advertiser* (March 29, 1820); "Opening of the China Trade—Government of India," *Salem Gazette* (May 7, 1833); and "China Trade," *St. Louis Inquirer* (December 18, 1819).

56. Letter from Meriwether Lewis to Thomas Jefferson (September 23, 1806), in *The Original Journals of the Lewis and Clark Expedition*, Edited by Reuben Gold Thwaites as Published in 1905, vol. 7, part 2, app. 61 (Scituate, MA: Digital Scanning Inc., 2001), 335–36. See also Dolin, *Fur, Fortune, and Empire*, 152–54, 284–85, 292–93; and Latourette, *The History of Early Relations*, 55–57.

57. John Floyd, "Occupation of the Columbia River," in *Abridgment of the Debates of Congress, from 1789 to 1856*, vol. 7, ed. by Thomas Hart Benton (New York: D. Appleton & Company, 1858), 392, 394. See also ibid., 78; and Hubert Howe Bancroft, *The Works of Hubert Howe Bancroft*, vol. 27 (San Francisco: A. L. Bancroft & Company, 1884), 419–20.

58. Fred Wilbur Powell, "Hall Jackson Kelley—Prophet of Oregon," *Quarterly of the Oregon Historical Society* (June 1917), 174, n15.

59. Latourette, *The History of Early Relations*, 57; Foster Rhea Dulles, *China & America: The Story of Their Relations Since 1784* (Princeton: Princeton University Press, 1946), 32–34; Newman, *Empire of the Bay*, 510–11; Robert H. Ferrell, "Oregon Controversy," in *The New Encyclopedia of the American West*, 833–34; Constance L. Skinner, *Adventures of Oregon: A Chronicle of the Fur Trade* (New Haven; Yale University Press, 1921), 262–64.

Chapter Seven: CHINA THROUGH AMERICAN EYES

1. Ezra Stiles, "Dr. Stiles' Election Sermon, 1783: The United States Exalted to Glory and Honor," in *The Pulpit of the American Revolution: or, the Political Sermons of the Period of 1776*, edited by John Wingate Thornton (Boston: Gould and Lincoln, 1860), 463–64.

2. John Rogers Haddad, *The Romance of China: Excursions to China in U.S. Culture: 1776–1876*, chap. 2 (New York: Columbia University Press, 2008), accessed April 12, 2011, through Gutenberg e-book, posted at the following Web site: http://www.gutenberg-e.org/haj01/index.html. See also Ping Chia Kuo, "Canton and Salem: The Impact of Chinese Culture upon New England Life during the Post-Revolutionary Era," *New England Quarterly* (January 1930), 435–41.

3. Wood, *Sketches of China*, viii. See also Shaw, *The Journals*, 167–68. For another take on the limited perspective that foreigners had of China, see Robert Waln, Jr., *China: Comprehending a View of the Origin, Antiquity, History, Religion, Morals, Government, Law, Population, Literature, Drama, etc.* (Philadelphia: Published by the author, 1823), 133.

4. Delano, *A Narrative of Voyages and Travels*, 542. See also Latourette, *The History of Early Relations*, 124; Greenbie and Greenbie, *Gold of Ophir*, 178–79; Downs, *The Golden Ghetto*, 76–83; and Frederick W. Drake, "Bridgman in China in the Early Nineteenth Century," *American Neptune* (Winter 1986), 34–42.

5. Wood, *Sketches of China*, x–xi; Haddad, *The Romance of China*, chap. 2; and Thomson et al, *Sentimental Imperialists*, 25.

6. Tchen, *New York Before Chinatown*, 25. See also James C. Thomson, Jr., Peter W. Stanley, and John Curtis Perry, *Sentimental Imperialists: The American Experience in East Asia* (New York: Harper Torchbooks, 1981), 13–15.

7. Tchen, *New York Before Chinatown*, 25–26. See also Jacques M. Downs, "Fair Game: Exploitive Role-Myths and the American Opium Trade," *Pacific Historical Review* (May 1972), 143.

8. Shaw, *The Journals*, 183–84.

9. Wood, *Sketches of China*, 232. See also "Article III: Negotiations with China," *Chinese Repository* (January 1835), 417–28; and "Glimpses of Society and Manners, by a Cosmopolitan," *New-England Magazine* (April 1835), 275.

10. "For the Port Folio—On China," *The Port Folio* (February 1819), 111; and Goldstein, *Philadelphia and the China Trade*, 72–73. See also "Military skill and power of the Chinese; actual state of the soldiery, forts, and arms; description of the forts on the river of Canton; army and navy of China; modes of warfare; offensive and defensive arms," *Chinese Repository* (August 1836), 177–78; and Miller, *The Unwelcome Immigrant*, 33–34.

11. Edmund Roberts, *Embassy to the Eastern Courts of Cochin-China, Siam, and Muscat; in the U.S. Sloop-of-War Peacock, David Geisenger, Commander, During the Years 1832-3-4* (New York: Harper & Brothers, 1837), 159.

12. Downs, *The Golden Ghetto*, 33, 36; William Samuel Waithman Ruschenberger, *A Voyage Round the World: Including An Embassy to Muscat and Siam, in 1835, 1836, and 1837* (Philadelphia: Carey, Lea & Blanchard, 1838), 430; Tyng, *Before the Wind*, 32; and Roberts, *Embassy to the Eastern Courts*, 151.

13. Jessica Lanier, "The Post-Revolutionary Ceramics Trade in Salem, Massachusetts, 1783–1812" (M.A. thesis, Bard College, 2004), 114.

14. Abeel, *Journal of a Residence in China*, 85–86, 133–36; "The Food of Various Nations," *American Masonick Record and Albany Saturday Magazine* (October 10, 1829), 291; Haddad, *The Romance of China*, chap. 3; John N. Reynolds, *Voyage of the United States Frigate Potomac* (New York: Harper & Brothers, 1835), 340–41; and Stuart Creighton Miller, *The Unwelcome Immigrant: The American Image of the Chinese: 1785–1882* (Berkeley: University of California Press, 1969), 27–28, 67–68.

15. Stevens, *The Life, Letters, and Journals of the Rev. and Hon. Peter Parker*, 107; Abeel, *Journal of a Residence in China*, 86–88; Fitch W. Taylor, *The Flag Ship: Or A Voyage Around the World, in the United States Frigate Columbia*, vol. 2 (New York: D. Appleton & Co., 1840), 175–76; and Howard Malcolm, *Travels in South-Eastern Asia, Embracing Hindustan, Malaya, Siam, and China*, vol. 2 (Boston: Gould, Kendall, and Lincoln, 1839), 150–51.

16. "China," in *Twenty-Second Annual Report of the American Tract Society* (Boston: Perkins & Marvin, 1836), 73; Thomson, Stanley, and Perry, *Sentimental Imperialists*, 15–16; Downs, "Fair Game," 142; Murray A. Rubinstein, "American Board Missionaries and the Formation of American Opinion Toward China, 1830–1860," in *America Views China: American Images of China Then and Now*, edited by Jonathan Goldstein, Jerry Israel, and Hilary Conroy (Bethlehem, PA: Lehigh University Press, 1991), 77; and Miller, *The Unwelcome Immigrant*, 57–82.

17. Downs, "Fair Game," 141n21, 142. See also Collis, *Foreign Mud*, 178.

18. Untitled article, *Independent Chronicle & Boston Patriot* (June 4, 1823). See also Iris Chang, *The Chinese in America: A Narrative History* (New York: Penguin, 2003), 103. According to some sources, the first known Chinese to come to the United States were three men—Ashing, Achun, and Accun—who were part of the crew of the *Pallas*, a Baltimore ship that came back from China in 1785. What happened to these men after landing is not clear. See Him Mark Lai, Joe Huang, and Don Wong, *The Chinese of America, 1785–1980* (San Francisco: Chinese Culture Foundation, 1980), 12.

19. Tchen, *New York Before Chinatown*, 97–99.

20. Ibid., 106.

21. Untitled article from the *Boston Patriot*, reprinted in the *Baltimore Patriot & Mercantile Advertiser* (August 21, 1829).

22. Irving Wallace and Amy Wallace, *The Two: The Story of the Original Siamese Twins* (New York: Simon & Schuster, 1978), 59.

23. "The Siamese Boys," *Boston Galaxy*, reprinted in the *Newburyport Herald* (September 15, 1829).

24. Wallace and Wallace, *The Two*, 15, 127–29.

25. Ibid., 301–2; Tchen, *New York Before Chinatown*, 106–13; and J. N. More-

heid, *Lives, Adventures, Anecdotes, Amusements, and Domestic Habits of the Siamese Twins* (Raleigh, NC: E. E. Barclay, 1850), 9–15.

26. Haddad, *The Romance of China*, chap. 3; Krystyn R. Moon, *Yellowface: Creating the Chinese in American Popular Music and Performance, 1850s–1920s* (Piscataway, NJ: Rutgers University Press, 2005), 59–62; "The Chinese Lady," *New Hampshire Patriot and State Gazette* (November 11, 1834); and Tchen, *New York Before Chinatown*, 101–6.

27. Untitled reprint from the *New York Gazette, New Hampshire Patriot and State Gazette* (November 24, 1834).

28. Haddad, *The Romance of China*, chap. 3.

29. Moon, *Yellowface*, 60–62.

30. M. L. E. Moreau de Saint-Méry, *An Authentic Account of the Embassy of the Dutch East-India Company, to the Court of the Emperor of China in the Years 1794 and 1795; (Subsequent to that of the Earl of Macartney) Containing a Description of Several Parts of the Chinese Empire, Unknown to Europeans; Taken from the Journal of André Everard Van Braam*, vol. 1 (London: Lee and Hurst, 1798), 238–39. See also Lee, *Philadelphians and the China Trade*, 81–82; and Haddad, *The Romance of China*, chap. 1.

31. Saint-Méry, *An Authentic Account of the Embassy*, xiii, 298–324.

32. Haddad, *The Romance of China*, chap. 1; William W. H. Davis, *History of Bucks County, Pennsylvania*, vol. 1 (New York: Lewis Publishing Company, 1905), 97; and Lee, *Philadelphians and the China Trade*, 82.

33. Caroline Howard King, quoted in Walter Muir Whitehill, *The East India Marine Society and the Peabody Museum of Salem: A Sesquicentennial History* (Salem, MA: Peabody Museum, 1949), 44–46. See also ibid., 3; and Mary Malloy, *Souvenirs of the Fur Trade: Northwest Coast Indian Art and Artifacts Collected by American Mariners, 1788–1844* (Cambridge: Harvard Peabody Museum of Archaeology and Ethnology, 2000), 61–63.

34. Charles Coleman Sellers, *Mr. Peale's Museum: Charles Willson Peale and the First Popular Museum of Natural Science and Art* (New York: W. W. Norton, 1980), 273.

35. Brantz Mayer, "A Nation in a Nut Shell," *Baltimore Literary Monument* (October 1839), 275.

36. Haddad, *The Romance of China*, chap. 4.

37. Nathan Dunn, *"Ten Thousand Chinese Things:" A Descriptive Catalogue of the Chinese Collection in Philadelphia* (Philadelphia: Printed by Nathan Dunn, 1839), 3.

38. Mayer, "A Nation in a Nut Shell," 273.

39. Dunn, *"Ten Thousand Chinese Things,"* 13, 75–76.

40. Enoch Cobb Wines, *A Peep at China, in Mr. Dunn's Chinese Collection* (Philadelphia: Printed for Nathan Dunn, 1839), vii–viii.

41. "China and the Chinese," *Southern Quarterly Review* (July 1847), 7–8. See

also Spence, *The Search for Modern China*, 132–36; and Paul A. Cohen, *China Unbound: Evolving Perspectives on the Chinese Past* (London: Routledge Curzon, 2003), 49–50.

42. Dunn, "Ten Thousand Chinese Things", 119.

Chapter Eight: THE OPIUM WAR

1. Hunter, *The 'Fan Kwae' at Canton*, 136–37. See also Arthur Waley, *The Opium War Through Chinese Eyes* (New York: Macmillan Company, 1958), 12–20; Fay, *The Opium War*, 128–29, 138–39, 142; "Crisis in Opium Traffic," *Chinese Repository* (April 1839), 610; and W. Travis Hanes III and Frank Sanello, *The Opium Wars: The Addiction of One Empire and the Corruption of Another* (Naperville, IL: Sourcebooks, 2002), 37.

2. Hosea Ballou Morse, who probably knew as much about the history of the China trade as anyone else, offered the following less than satisfying statement on the opium trade in China. "Every statement regarding the quantities of opium consumed in China appears to differ from every other statement." Morse, *The International Relations of the Chinese Empire*, 211. I have relied on the following sources for these numbers: ibid., 209–10; and Chang, *Commisioner Lin and the Opium War*, 223. See also Spence, *The Search for Modern China*, 129, 149.

3. Fay, *The Opium War*, 58–60; Greenberg, *The British Trade and the Opening of China*, 124–31; Charles William King, *A Letter Addressed to Charles Elliot, Esq.* (London: Edward Suter, 1839), 53–54; and Samuel Warren, *The Opium Question* (London: James Ridgway, 1840), 52.

4. "War with China, and the Opium Question," *Blackwood's Edinburgh Magazine* (March 1840), 381. See also Robert Bennet Forbes, *Remarks on China and the China Trade* (Boston: Samuel N. Dickinson, 1844), 50–51; Samuel Warren, *The Opium Question* (London: James Ridgway, 1840), 125; Phipps, *A Practical Treatise on the China and Eastern Trade*, viii; Hanes and Sanello, *The Opium Wars*, 157; Collis, *Foreign Mud*, 262; and H. B. Morse, "The History and Economics of the Trade of China," *Journal of the American Asiatic Association* (April 1910), 83.

5. R. K. Newman, "Opium Smoking in Late Imperial China: A Reconsideration," *Modern Asian Studies* (October 1995), 765–94; Bernstein, *A Splendid Exchange*, 289; Chang, *Commissioner Lin*, 34–36; Hsü, *The Rise of Modern China*, 171–72; Fay, *The Opium War*, 129; Trocki, *Opium*, 90–91; "Remarks on the Opium Trade, being a rejoinder to the second letter of a Reader, published in the Repository for March, 1837," *Chinese Repository* (April 1837), 565; Allen, *An Essay on the Opium Trade*, 22; and Wood, *Sketches of China*, 206–7.

6. Spence, *The Search for Modern China*, 149; Chang, *Commissioner Lin*, 41;

Trocki, *Opium*, 98; "Commerce and Finances," *De Bow's Review* (August 1853), 206–7; and Waley, *The Opium War Through Chinese Eyes*, 25.

7. "Memorial recommending that tea, rhubarb, and silk, be sold to foreigners at fixed prices: imperial reply to the same," *Chinese Repository* (October 1838), 313.

8. Wood, *Sketches of China*, 206.

9. "Memorial from Hwang Tseotsze, soliciting increased severity in the punishments of the consumers of opium; and the imperial reply," *Chinese Repository* (September 1838), 271–80.

10. Hunter, *The 'Fan Kwae' at Canton*, 72–73.

11. Forbes, *Personal Reminiscences*, 144–45. See also "Art. II. American influence on the destinies of Ultra-Malayan Asia, From a Correspondent. (Conclusion of Article ii. No. 1, vol. vii.)," *Chinese Repository* (June 1838), 80–81.

12. Robert Bennet Forbes to Rose Greene Smith Forbes, March 10, 1839, in Kerr, *Letters from China*, 101.

13. Jan Pottker, *Sara and Eleanor: The Story of Sara Delano Roosevelt and her Daughter-in-Law, Eleanor Roosevelt* (New York: St. Martin's, 2005), 15; and Geoffrey C. Ward and Frederic Delano Grant, Jr., "A Fair, Honorable, and Legitimate Trade," *American Heritage* (August/September 1986), 49–64.

14. Fairbank, *Trade and Diplomacy*, 133; Booth, *Opium*, 35–46; and *A New Family Encyclopedia*, edited by Charles A. Goodrich (Philadelphia: T. Belknap, 1831), 146–47.

15. Downs, *The Golden Ghetto*, 335.

16. King, *A Letter Addressed to Charles Elliot*, 60–61; Collis, *Foreign Mud*, 255–56; and "The Opium Trade with China," *The Times* (August 7, 1839).

17. William C. Hunter, *Bits of Old China* (London: Kegan Paul, Trench, & Co., 1885), 1–3.

18. Fay, *The Opium War*, 129. See also ibid., 119–27.

19. The following discussion of the December 12 riot is based on these sources: Hunter, *The 'Fan Kwae' at Canton*, 73–77 (all quotes come from this source); Collis, *Foreign Mud*, 186–90; Fay, *The Opium War*, 133–34; "China: The Opium Traffic," in *Asiatic Journal and Monthly Register* (May 1839), 40–41; "Captain Elliot to Viscount Palmerston (December 13, 1838)," in *Correspondence Relating to China, Presented to Both Houses of Parliament, by Command of Her Majesty* (London: T. R. Harrison, 1840), 324; and Kerr, *Letters from China*, 76–77.

20. "Crisis in Opium Traffic," *Chinese Repository* (April 1839), 610.

21. Waley, *The Opium War Through Chinese Eyes*, 23–25.

22. Ibid., 28–31, 93. See also Fay, *The Opium War*, 143, 206; "Letter to the Queen of England from the Imperial commissioner and the provincial authorities requiring interdiction of opium," *Chinese Repository* (May 1839), 9–12; "Letter to the queen of England, from the high imperial commissioner

Lin, and his colleagues," *Chinese Repository* (February 1840), 497–503; and "The High Commissioner's Second Letter to the Queen of England," *The Times* (June 11, 1840).

23. "Crisis in Opium Traffic," 610–19.

24. The background for the following section on the conflict between Lin and the foreigners up until the opium is destroyed is from these sources, in addition to those cited in the text: Fay, *The Opium War*, 142–61; Spence, *The Search for Modern China*, 150–52; Waley, *The Opium War Through Chinese Eyes*, 35–49; Hunter, *The 'Fan Kwae' at Canton*, 136–45; Forbes, *Personal Reminiscences*, 145–49; and Downs, *The Golden Ghetto*, 135–37; Henry Charles Sirr, *China and the Chinese: Their Religion, Character, Customs, and Manufactures*, vol. 2 (London: William S. Orr, 1849), 332–33; and King, *A Letter Addressed to Charles Elliot*, 17–25.

25. Collis, *Foreign Mud*, 205–7. See also "Chinese Affairs," *London Quarterly Review* (March 1840), 301.

26. Fay, *The Opium War*, 140; Forbes, *Letters from China*, 98; and Samuel Warren, *The Opium Question* (London: James Ridgway, 1840), 5.

27. Forbes, *Personal Reminiscences*, 148.

28. Hunter, *The 'Fan Kwae' at Canton*, 143–44.

29. Forbes, *Remarks on China and the China Trade*, 49.

30. Waley, *The Opium War Through Chinese Eyes*, 44–46, 49.

31. Letter from Russell & Co., quoted in Downs, *The Golden Ghetto*, 136.

32. Robert Bennet Forbes et al., "Memorial of R. B. Forbes and Others," 2. See also Downs, *The Golden Ghetto*, 261–62.

33. Forbes, *Personal Reminiscences*, 149–50.

34. The background for the following section on increasing tensions between the British and the Chinese, up through the Battle of Chuanbi, is based on these sources, in addition to those cited in the text: Morse, *The International Relations of the Chinese Empire*, 230–57; Captain Elliot to Viscount Palmerston, November 5, 1839, in *A Digest of the Despatches [sic] on China* (London: James Ridgway, 1840), 168–71; 9–10; Fay, *The Opium War*, 165–79; Collis, *Foreign Mud*, 229–50; and Chang, *Commissioner Lin*, 189–208.

35. "Journal of Occurrences," *Chinese Repository* (August 1839), 223.

36. "Proclamation calling on the people to arm themselves, to resist parties of English landing on their Coasts," *British and Foreign State Papers, 1840–1841*, vol. 29 (London: James Ridgway and Sons, 1857), 1067.

37. "Captain Elliot to the Officers at Kowloon," *British and Foreign State Papers, 1840–1841*, vol. 29, 1057.

38. Chang, *Commissioner Lin*, 203.

39. Captain Elliot to Viscount Palmerston, November 5, 1839, in *A Digest of the Despatches*, 169.

40. Morse, *The International Relations of the Chinese Empire*, 257.

41. Kerr, *Letters from China*, 162, 168.

42. Forbes, *Personal Reminiscences*, 155.

43. Fay, *The Opium War*, 176.

44. Spence, *The Search for Modern China*, 151.

45. Fay, *The Opium War*, 168–69; and Charles Clarkson Stelle, *Americans and the China Opium Trade in the Nineteenth Century* (New York: Arno Press, 1981), 83.

46. Fay, *The Opium War*, 192–93.

47. Spence, *The Search for Modern China*, 154; Harry G. Gelber, "China as 'Victim'? The Opium War that Wasn't," Center for European Studies, Harvard University, Working Paper Series #136, accessed at the following Web site on June 29, 2011: http://www.ces.fas.harvard.edu/publications/docs/pdfs/Gelber136.pdf.

48. The quotes from, respectively, "Private Correspondence," *The Times* (November 1, 1839); and "The Opium Trade With China," *The Times* (September 27, 1839). See also Julia Lovell, *The Opium War: Drugs, Dreams, and the Making of China* (London: Picador, 2011), 103–5; "Iniquities of the Opium Trade with China," *The Times* (August 15, 1839); "Opium Trade With China," *The Times* (August 7, 1839); and "London, Wednesday, October 23, 1839," *The Times* (October 23, 1839).

49. Algernon S. Thelwall, *The Iniquities of the Opium Trade with China* (London: William H. Allen and Co., 1839), 173, 177.

50. *Brief Observations Respecting the Pending Disputes with the Chinese, and a Proposal for Bringing Them to a Satisfactory Conclusion* (London: James Ridgway, 1840), 1–15; "London, Wednesday, December 25, 1839," *The Times* (December 25, 1839); and "Chinese Affairs, Art. VIII," in *London Quarterly Review* (March 1840), 294–319.

51. Quotes from, respectively: Alain Le Pichon, *China Trade and Empire: Jardine Matheson & Co., and the Origins of British Rule in Hong Kong, 1827–1843* (Oxford: Oxford University Press, 2006), 387; and Collis, *Foreign Mud*, 256–57. See also Fay, *The Opium War*, 190–93; Collis, *Foreign Mud*, 250–56; Beeching, *The Chinese Opium Wars*, 41, 107; Chang, *Commissioner Lin*, 192–93; and "The Opium Trade with China," *The Times* (August 7, 1839).

52. For all the quotes from Palmerston's letters, see Morse, *The International Relations of the Chinese Empire*, 621–30.

53. H. G. Gordon to different East India Associations in Great Britain, June 3, 1839, in John Slade, *Narrative of the Late Proceedings and Events in China* (Canton: Canton Register Press, 1839), 142.

54. Collis, *Foreign Mud*, 259. See also ibid., 256–57; and "Express from India, Declaration of War Against China," *The Times* (March 12, 1840).

55. *The Mirror of Parliament*, Session of 1840, vol. 3, edited by John Henry

Barrow (London: Longman, Orme, Brown, Green & Longmans, 1840), 2385–424, 2431–70, 2485–545.

56. Collis, *Foreign Mud*, 260–61; Lovell, *The Opium War*, 107.

57. *The Mirror of Parliament*, Session of 1840, vol. 3, 2460–61. See also ibid., 2485–543; "The Opium War," *Tait's Edinburgh Magazine* (July 1840), 474–75; "The Opium War with China," *The Times* (April 25, 1840); and Hanes and Sanello, *The Opium Wars*, 78.

58. *The Mirror of Parliament*, Session of 1840, vol. 3, 2407.

59. Ibid., 2401–8, 2494, 2527–43; Collis, *Foreign Mud*, 274; "War with China, and the Opium Question," *Blackwood's Edinburgh Magazine* (March 1840), 372; Gelber, "China as 'Victim'?"; "The Opium Trade," *Museum of Foreign Literature, Science and Art*, 533–34; and "House of Commons, Thursday, April 9," *The Times* (April 10, 1840).

60. The background for this section on the first phase of the Opium War comes from the following sources, unless otherwise noted in the text: Morse, *The International Relations of the Chinese Empire*, 255–83; Spence, *The Search for Modern China*, 154–56; Fay, *The Opium War*, 213–76; and Li Chien-Nung, *Political History of China, 1840–1928* (Stanford, CA: Stanford University Press, 1956), 37–38.

61. Chang, *Commissioner Lin*, 212.

62. "Queen Victoria to the King of the Belgians," April 13, 1841, in *The Letters of Queen Victoria: A Selection from Her Majesty's Correspondence Between the Years 1837 and 1861*, vol. 1, edited by Arthur Christopher Benson and Viscount Esher (London: John Murray, 1908), 26.

63. Morse, *The International Relations of the Chinese Empire*, 280–91; Fay, *The Opium War*, 277–307; and Hanes and Sanello, *The Opium Wars*, 134.

64. Quotes are, respectively, from Collis, *Foreign Mud*, 180; and John Francis Davis, *China, During the War and Since the Peace*, vol. 1 (London: Longman, Brown, Green, and Longmans, 1852), 11–12.

65. Lovell, *The Opium War*, 115. See also ibid., 111–15, 184–91, 205; Fay, *The Opium War*, 261, 344–47; Haines and Sanello, *The Opium Wars*, 31; Hunt Janin, *The India-China Opium Trade in the Nineteenth Century* (Jefferson, NC: McFarland & Company, 1999), 109–10; and Fairbank, *Trade and Diplomacy*, 86.

66. John Ouchterlony, *The Chinese War: An Account of all the Operations of the British Forces From the Commencement to the Treaty of Nanking* (London: Saunders and Otley, 1844), 53–54.

67. Sir Henry Keppel, *A Sailor's Life under Four Sovereigns*, vol. 1 (London: Macmillan and Co., 1899), 269.

68. Alexander Murray, *Doings in China: Being the Personal Narrative of an Officer Engaged in the Late Chinese Expedition, from the Recapture of Chusan in 1841, to the Peace of Nankin in 1842* (London: Richard Bentley, 1843), 244.

69. Samuel Wells Williams, *The Middle Kingdom: A Survey of the Geography, Government, Education, Social Life, Arts, Religion, &c. of the Chinese Empire and its Inhabitants*, vol. 2 (New York: Wiley and Putnam, 1848), 562. See also Ouchterlony, *The Chinese War*, 394–406.

70. "China," *Niles' National Register* (December 31, 1842). See also Demetrius Charles Boulger, *The History of China*, vol. 2 (London: W. Thacker & Co., 1898), 130; Morse, *The International Relations of the Chinese Empire*, 295–96; and Fay, *The Opium War*, 351–53.

71. Morse, *The International Relations of the Chinese Empire*, 288–97; and Spence, *The Search for Modern China*, 156–57.

72. Morse, *The International Relations of the Chinese Empire*, 298–318; Spence, *The Search for Modern China*, 158–62; and Hsü, *The Rise of Modern China*, 190.

73. Lord Palmerston to Henry Pottinger (May 31, 1841), in Morse, *The International Relations of the Chinese Empire*, 658–59.

74. Granville G. Loch, *The Closing Events of the Campaign in China: The Operations in the Yang-Tze-Kiang; and the Treaty of Nanking* (London: John Murray, 1843), 173–74.

75. Fay, *The Opium War*, 366–67; and "The Chinese Treaty," *The Times* (November 26, 1842).

76. "London, Friday, November 25, 1842," *The Times* (November 25, 1842).

77. Morse, *The International Relations of the Chinese Empire*, 253–54; Gelber, *The Dragon*, 188; and Collis, *Foreign Mud*, 260–74; Fairbank, *Trade and Diplomacy*, 74; Hsü, *The Rise of Modern China*, 192; Ouchterlony, *The Chinese War*, 35–37; "The Chinese Question and the British," *New Hampshire Sentinel* (May 6, 1840); "Chinese Affairs," *The London Quarterly Review*, 295, 312–13, 316–17; "The Chinese Question," *New Hampshire Sentinel* (May 8, 1840); and Lord Macaulay, "China," in The *Mirror of Parliament*, Session 1840, vol. 3, 2407.

78. Backhouse and Bland, *Annals & Memoirs of the Court of Peking*, 331.

79. Morse, *The International Relations of the Chinese Empire*, 119–44; Fay, *The Opium War*, 67–79; and Collis, *Foreign Mud*, 108–72.

80. Kenneth Scott Latourette, *The Chinese: Their History and Culture* (New York: Macmillan Company, 1962), 277. See also Fairbank, *Trade and Diplomacy*, 72–73; "China," *The Mirror of Parliament*, Session of 1840, vol. 3, 2432–33; and "The Chinese Trade," *The Corsair: A Gazette of Literature, Art, Dramatic Criticism, Fashion, and Novelty* (January 4, 1840), 684–85.

81. John Quincy Adams, "Lecture on the War with China, delivered before the Massachusetts Historical Society, December, 1841," *Chinese Repository* (May 1842), 281, 288. See also Dulles, *The Old China Trade*, 182–83; Gelber, *The Dragon*, 188; and Dennett, *Americans in Eastern Asia*, 106–8.

82. Augustine Heard, quoted in Downs, *The Golden Ghetto*, 140. See also

Downs, *The Golden Ghetto*, 261; Robert Bennet Forbes, et al., "Memorial of R. B. Forbes and Others," 2–3; Fay, *The Opium War*, 337–38; and Miller, *The Unwelcome Immigrant*, 97–100.

83. King, *A Letter Addressed to Charles Elliot*, 49, 51.

84. The quotes from, respectively, Michael C. Lazich, "American Missionaries and the Opium Trade in Nineteenth-Century China," *Journal of World History* (June 2006), 205–6; Jeremiah Bell Jeter, *A Memoir of Mrs. Henrietta Shuck: The First American Missionary to China* (Boston: Gould, Kendall, & Lincoln, 1849), 145–46; William Wells Williams, "Letter from Mr. Williams, Dated at Macao, Aug. 29th, 1839," *Missionary Herald* (April 1840), 115–16; and "Recent Intelligence, China," *Missionary Herald* (January 1841), 43. See also Latourette, *The History of Early Relations*, 120; Fay, *The Opium War*, 331. Miller, *The Unwelcome Immigrants*, 100–2; Stevens, *The Life, Letters, and Journals of the Rev. and Hon. Peter Parker*, 168; and Murray A. Rubinstein, "The Wars They Wanted: American Missionaries' Use of *The Chinese Repository* before the Opium War," *American Neptune* (Fall 1988), 271–82.

85. John Quincy Adams, *Memoirs of John Quincy Adams, Comprising Portions of His Diary from 1795 to 1848*, vol. 11, edited by Charles Francis Adams (Philadelphia: J. B. Lippincott & Co., 1876), 30–31. See also John Quincy Adams, "Lecture on the War With China," *Niles' National Register* (January 26, 1842), 326–30; Downs, *The Golden Ghetto*, 268–71; "J. Q. Adams and the Opium War," *Pittsfield Sun* (December 2, 1841); and "Mr. Adams and the Opium War," *Baltimore Sun* (December 20, 1841). Not all coverage of Adams's speech was negative. See, for example, "Hon. John Quincy Adams," *The Daily Atlas* (November 24, 1841). See also Fay, *The Opium War*, 337–38; Dennett, *Americans in Eastern Asia*, 102; and Howard Malcolm, *Travels in South-Eastern Asia, Embracing Hindustan, Malaya, Siam, and China*, vol. 1 (Boston: Gould, Kendall, and Lincoln, 1839), 159–60; and "The Opium Trade," *Farmer's Cabinet* (April 10, 1840).

86. Freeman Hunt, "The Opium Trade—England and China," *Merchant's Magazine, and Commercial Review* (May 1840), 413; and "Twenty-Sixth Congress—1st Session," *Niles' National Register* (March 21, 1840), 46. See also "The Opium Trade"; Dulles, *The Old China Trade*, 180–81; "China and the Chinese," *The Southern Literary Messenger* (February 1841), 151–52; Downs, *The Golden Ghetto*, 260–62; Beeching, *The Chinese Opium Wars*, 106; Miller, *The Unwelcome Immigrant*, 96; and Dennett, *Americans in Eastern Asia*, 105.

87. John Tyler, "Sandwich Islands and China, Message From the President of the United States, December 31, 1842," House Document no. 35, United States Congress, 27th Congress, 3rd Session; and *A Memorial of Caleb Cushing from the City of Newburyport* (Newburyport: Published by Order of the City Council, 1874), 101–4.

88. "The Dinner at Faneuil Hall, on the 17th Instant," *Niles' National Register* (July 1, 1843).

89. Daniel Webster to Caleb Cushing, May 8, 1843, in *The Diplomatic and Official Papers of Daniel Webster* (New York: Harper & Brothers, 1848), 361–62, 364.

90. Robert V. Remini, *Daniel Webster: The Man and His Time* (New York: W. W. Norton & Company, 1997), 578.

91. John Tyler, "The President's Letter to the Emperor," in *The Diplomatic and Official Papers of Daniel Webster*, 367–68.

92. Stevens and Markwick, *The Life, Letters, and Journals of the Rev. and Hon. Peter Parker*, 249–50. See also Downs, *The Golden Ghetto*, 290.

93. Dennett, *Americans in Eastern Asia*, 143.

94. "The American Flag-Staff," *Chinese Repository* (May 1844), 276–77. See also John Watson Foster, *American Diplomacy in the Orient* (Boston: Houghton, Mifflin and Company, 1903), 91–92; Downs, *The Golden Ghetto*, 296; and "The Hon. Caleb Cushing, Commissioner to China," *Daily Atlas* (May 24, 1843).

95. First quote: Caleb Cushing to Ch'i-ying, June 22, 1844, in *Chinese Repository* (October 1845), 491. Second quote: Caleb Cushing to Ch'i-ying, July 22, 1844, in *Chinese Repository* (November 1845), 531. See also Morse, *The International Relations of the Chinese Empire*, 327–28.

96. Treaty with China, in *The Public Statutes at Large of the United States of America, from the Organization of the Government in 1789 to March 3, 1845*, vol. 8, edited by Richard Peters (Boston: Charles C. Little and James Brown, 1846), 592–600.

97. "Howqua,—The Hong Merchant," *New-Hampshire Patriot* (May 23, 1844); and *The Friend of China and Hong Kong Gazette*, quoted in "Howqua, The Senior Hong Merchant," *Merchant's Magazine* (May 1844), 459–61.

98. Hsü, *The Rise of Modern China*, 192. See also ibid., 123–35; Spence, *The Search for Modern China*, 139–48, 165–67; and Gelber, *The Dragon*, 154.

Chapter Nine: RACING THE WIND

1. Philip Hone, *The Diary of Philip Hone, 1828–1851*, edited by Bayard Tuckerman, vol. 2 (New York: Dodd, Mead and Company, 1889), 242. See also *Federal Writer's Project, Maritime History of New York* (1941; reprint Brooklyn: Going Coastal, 2004), 139–40; and "New Ships," *The New York Herald* (January 22, 1845).

2. Carl C. Cutler, *Greyhounds of the Sea: The Story of the American Clipper Ship* (Annapolis, MD: Naval Institute Press, 1984), 50.

3. Howard Irving Chapelle, *The Baltimore Clipper, Its Origin and Development* (Salem: Marine Research Society, 1930), 3.

4. Addison Beecher Colvin Whipple, *The Clipper Ships* (Alexandria, VA: Time-Life Books, 1980), 23–24; and "Early History of Shipbuilding in New York," *U. S. Nautical Magazine and Naval Journal* (September 1857), 438–39.

5. Whipple, *The Clipper Ships*, 25–27; Basil Lubbock, *The China Clippers* (London: Century Publishing, 1984), 24; Robert Carse, *The Moonrakers: The Story of the Clipper Ship Men* (New York: Harper & Brothers, 1961), 43–44; and Arthur H. Clark, *The Clipper Ship Era: An Epitome of Famous American and British Clipper Ships, Their Owners, Builders, Commanders, and Crews* (New York: G. P. Putnam's Sons, 1910), 66.

6. Whipple, *The Clipper Ships*, 21.

7. Cutler, *Greyhounds of the Sea*, 44.

8. Mirror, "Dock Rambles of a Nautical Mechanic," *Monthly Nautical Magazine and Quarterly Review* (February 1855), 353.

9. Clark, *The Clipper Ship Era*, 61–62; Arthur H. Clark, "A Glimpse of the Clipper-Ship Days," *Harper's Monthly Magazine* (June 1908), 93; Whipple, *The Clipper Ships*, 23–29; Cutler, *Greyhounds of the Sea*, 112–13; Lubbock, *The China Clippers*, 24; and Leo Block, *To Harness the Wind: A Short History of the Development of Sails* (Annapolis, MD: Naval Institute Press, 2003), 101.

10. Cutler, *Greyhounds of the Sea*, 115, 120; Octavius T. Howe and Frederick C. Mathews, *American Clipper Ships: 1833–1858*, vol. 2 (Mineola, NY: Dover Publications, 1986), 501; Whipple, *The Clipper Ships*, 29–30; and Lubbock, *The China Clippers*, 24.

11. "Very Late from China—Astonishing Voyage," *Weekly Herald* (April 5, 1845); and Whipple, *The Clipper Ships*, 30.

12. Cutler, *Greyhounds of the Sea*, 121.

13. Whipple, *The Clipper Ships*, 31, 61. See also Howe and Mathews, *American Clipper Ships*, 569.

14. "The Fastest Vessel in the World," *Northern Standard* (July 15, 1848). See also "Eighty One Days From China," *Constitution* (August 4, 1847); "One Week Later from China," *Daily Picayune* (April 3, 1849); Whipple, *The Clipper Ships*, 34, 36, 41; and Cutler, *Greyhounds of the Sea*, 137–38.

15. James K. Polk, Fourth Annual Message to Congress, December 5, 1848, in *A Compilation of the Messages and Papers of the Presidents, 1789–1897*, vol. 4, edited by James D. Richardson (Washington, DC: Published by Authority of Congress, 1899), 636.

16. "Ho! For California," *Weekly Herald* (January 13, 1849); Carse, *The Moonrakers*, 70; Cutler, *Greyhounds of the Sea*, 143–44; Clark, *The Clipper Ship Era*, 102–5; and Whipple, *The Clipper Ships*, 48–51.

17. Cutler, *Greyhounds of the Sea*, 148.

18. Frank Moss, *The American Metropolis, from Knickerbocker Days to the Present Time: New York City Life in All Its Various Phases* (New York: Peter Fenelon Collier, 1897), 251.

19. Whipple, *The Clipper Ships*, 51–54.

20. Lubbock, *The China Clippers*, 41.

21. "The New Clipper Ship *Stag Hound*, of Boston," *Boston Daily Atlas* (December 21, 1850).

22. F. C. Mathews, "The Clipper Ship *Stag Hound*," *Pacific Marine Review* (March 1922), 153.

23. Ibid., 153–54.

24. "The New Clipper Ship *Bald Eagle*, of Boston," *Boston Daily Atlas* (November 17, 1852); and Whipple, *The Clipper Ships*, 51–54.

25. David W. Shaw, *Flying Cloud: The True Story of America's Most Famous Clipper Ship and the Woman Who Guided Her* (New York: William Morrow, 2000), 259–62; Octavius T. Howe and Frederick C. Mathews, *American Clipper Ships: 1833–1858*, vol. 1 (1926; reprint, Mineola, NY: Dover Publications, 1986), 190–95; Priscilla Sawyer Lord and Virginia Clegg Gamage, *The Spirit of '76 Lives Here: Marblehead* (Radnor, PA: Chilton Book Company, 1972), 176–78; "The Clipper Race," *New-Hampshire Gazette* (October 21, 1851); "Magnificent Clipper Race," *Sun* (May 17, 1853); "Clipper Race," *Weekly Alta California* (December 1, 1854); and Clark, *The Clipper Ship Era*, 212–13.

26. Matthew F. Maury, *The Physical Geography of the Sea* (New York: Harper & Brothers, 1855), 263–64; and Whipple, *The Clipper Ships*, 41–45.

27. Clark, *The Clipper Ship Era*, 97–98. See also Spears, *Captain Nathaniel Brown Palmer*, 207–208; and Howe and Mathews, *American Clipper Ships*, vol. 2, 461–63.

28. "London, Thursday, December 5, 1850," *The Times* (December 5, 1850).

29. Cutler, *Greyhounds of the Sea*, 125. See also Carse, *The Moonrakers*, 78.

30. George Francis Train, *An American Merchant in Europe, Asia, and Australia* (New York: G. P. Putnam, 1857), 446.

31. Whipple, *The Clipper Ships*, 21.

32. Clark, *The Clipper Ship Era*, 202–5; Whipple, *The Clipper Ships*, 103; and "Challenge from American Ship-Builders," *The People's Illustrated Journal*, July 10, 1852, 175.

Chapter Ten: FADING FORTUNE

1. Freeman Hunt, "Monthly Commercial Chronicle," *Hunt's Merchants' Magazine* (January 1845), 79–80. See also James Christy Bell, *Opening a Highway to the Pacific, 1838–1846* (New York: Columbia University, 1921), 129–30 n4, and Dennett, *Americans in Eastern Asia*, 74.

2. The calculations are mine, based on the following: Homans, *An Historical and Statistical Account of the Foreign Commerce of the United States*, 64, 181; *Historical Statistics of the United States*, vol. 5, 534–44; and Pan, *The Trade of the United States with China*, 22, 32. See also Peter Schran, "The Minor

Significance of Commercial Relations Between the United States and China, 1850–1931," in *America's China Trade in Historical Perspective*, 237–58.

3. Statements about the range of exported and imported goods are based on data culled from multiple reports, from the 1840s through the 1860s, issued by the secretary of the treasury or the director of the U.S. Bureau of Statistics, reporting on the commerce and navigation of the United States for particular years. For example, *Report of the Secretary of the Treasury, Transmitting a Report from the Register of the Treasury of the Commerce and Navigation of the United States, for the Year Ending June 30, 1860* (Washington, DC: George W. Bowman, 1860), 7–51. See also, Pan, *The Trade of the United States with China*, 20 43, 205 9, 329 31; Hao, "Chinese Teas to America," 16–31; Kang Chao, "The Chinese-American Cotton-Textile Trade, 1830–1930," in *America's China Trade in Historical Perspective*, 104–5.

4. Robert Hart, *"These From the Land of Sinim": Essays on the Chinese Question* (London: Chapman & Hall, 1901), 60–61.

5. Hsü, *The Rise of Modern China*, 221–56; Latourette, *The Chinese*, 280–87; and Whipple, *The Clipper Ships*, 112–13.

6. The background for this section comes from the following sources, unless otherwise noted: Spence, *The Search for Modern China*, 179–81; Hsü, *The Rise of Modern China*, 196–219; Morse, *The International Relations of the Chinese Empire*, 367–437, 539–56; Gelber, *The Dragon*, 192–203; Stelle, *Americans and the China Opium Trade*, 87, 106–34; Fairbank, *Trade and Diplomacy*, 240–43; Hunt Janin, *The India-China Opium Trade in the Nineteenth Century* (Jefferson, NC: McFarland & Company, 1999), 70; "The War in China," *The Times* (December 15, 1860); and Hanes and Sanello, *The Opium Wars*, 3–12.

7. Demetrius C. Boulger, *The Life of Gordon* (London: T. Fisher Unwin, 1896), 46.

8. Forbes, *Remarks on China*, 56. See also Stelle, *Americans and the China Opium Trade*, 96–97, 106–9, 135–40; Gideon Nye, "Tea: And the Tea Trade," *Hunt's Merchants' Magazine and Commercial Review* (January 1850), 20; "Tea—Its Consumption and Culture," *Merchant's Magazine and Commercial Review* (February 1863), 118; Nathan Allen, *An Essay on the Opium Trade* (Boston: John P. Jewett, 1850), 12–13; Trocki, *Opium*, 109–10; R. Alexander, *The Rise and Progress of British Opium Smuggling* (London: Judd and Glass, 1856), 40–54; United Nations Office on Drugs and Crime, "A Century of International Drug Control," *Bulletin on Narcotics* 49 (2007), 18–20; and "The Opium Question," *Church Missionary Intelligencer*, vol. 8 (London: Seeley, Jackson and Halliday, 1857), 89–90.

9. Arnold J. Meagher, *The Coolie Trade: The Traffic in Chinese Laborers to Latin America 1847–1874* (diss., University of California, Davis, 1975; reprint, Bloomington, IN: XLibris, 2008), 27–41.

10. "The Word Coolie," *Notes and Queries on China and Japan*, June 29, 1867), 77; "Coolie," in *Mission Life; or, The Emigrant and the Heathen*, vol. 4, edited by J. J. Halcombe (London: J. E. Adlard, 1867), 19; Chang, *The Chinese in America*, 30; and Jean Pfaelzer, *Driven Out: The Forgotten War Against Chinese Americans* (New York: Random House, 2007), 25. See also Meagher, *The Coolie Trade*, 24–25, 29–30, 140–44, 148, 169–70; Tchen, *New York Before Chinatown*, 49–50; and Evelyn Hu-Dehart, "Chinese Coolie Labor in Cuba in the Nineteenth Century: Free Labor of Neoslavery," in *Black Studies* (1994), 39.

11. Leonard Wray, *The Practical Sugar Planter* (London: Smith, Elder and Co., 1848), 83–84. See also Meagher, *The Coolie Trade*, 50–51; and "The Cuban Slave Trade," *Charleston Mercury* (December 23, 1856).

12. Meagher, *The Coolie Trade*, 52–91; "The Chinese Puzzle," *Chambers's Journal of Popular Literature* (August 8, 1863), 96; William Fred Mayers, N. B. Dennys, and Charles King, *The Treaty Ports of China and Japan* (London: Trubner and Co., 1867), 228; "Coolie Slaves," *Anglo-American Times* (July 21, 1866), 9; Lisa Yun, *The Coolie Speaks: Chinese Indentured Laborers and African Slaves of Cuba* (Philadelphia: Temple University Press, 2008), 1–2, 8, 18, 21; and "The Coolie Trade," *Charleston Mercury* (October 9, 1856).

13. Meagher, *The Coolie Trade*, 153–62; and Chang, *The Chinese in America*, 30–31.

14. Meagher, *The Coolie Trade*, 179, 190.

15. U.S. Senate, *Report of the Secretary of State in Compliance with a Resolution of the Senate of April 24, Calling for Information Relative to the Coolie Trade, Index to the Executive Documents, 1855–1856*, doc. 99 (Washington, DC: A. O. P. Nicholson, 1856), 8–10; "The Coolie Trade," *De Bow's Review* (July 1857), 33–34.

16. All the background and the quotes for this section on the *Norway* are from Edgar Holden, "A Chapter on the Coolie Trade," in *Harper's New Monthly Magazine* (June 1864), 1–10. See also "Revolt of the Chinese Coolies," *Sun* (May 18, 1857).

17. "The Ship *Flora Temple*: Shipwreck, and Loss of Eight Hundred and Fifty Lives," *New York Times* (February 6, 1860); and "Later from China," *San Francisco Bulletin* (February 6, 1860).

18. Meagher, *The Coolie Trade*, 163, 168–73; Hu-Dehart, "Chinese Coolie Labor in Cuba in the Nineteenth Century," 45; and Sharon A. Roger Hepburn, "Disease," in *Encyclopedia of the Middle Passage*, edited by Toyin Falola and Amanda B. Warnock (Santa Barbara, CA: Greenwood, 2007), 138.

19. G. Fitz-Roy Cole, "John Chinaman Abroad," *Fraser's Magazine* (October 1878), 451–52. See also Meagher, *The Coolie Trade*, 140–43.

20. Meagher, *The Coolie Trade*, 222; Paul R. Ehrlich, David S. Dobkin, and Darryl Wheye, *The Birder's Handbook: A Field Guide to the Natural History*

of North American Birds (New York: Simon & Schuster, 1988), 263; Gregory T. Cushman, "The Most Valuable Birds in the World: International Conservation Science and the Revival of Peru's Guano Industry, 1909–1965," *Environmental History* (July 2005), 477–509; David Hollett, *More Precious than Gold: The Story of the Peruvian Guano Trade* (Madison, NJ: Fairleigh Dickinson University Press, 2008), 82; W. M. Mathew, "Peru and the British Guano Market, 1840–1870," *The Economic History Review* (April 1970), 112–28; and Richard J. King, "'The Most Valuable Bird in the World': A Maritime History of the Cormorant," *Log of the Mystic Seaport* (2002–3), 24–25.

21. George Washington Peck, "Chincha Islands," *Littell's Living Age* (January 28, 1854), 213–14. See also George Washington Peck, *Melbourne and the Chincha Islands: With Sketches of Lima, and a Voyage Around the World* (New York: Charles Scribner, 1854), 209; and "Chinese Immigration and the Guano Trade," *Anti-Slavery Reporter*, vol. 3 (London: Peter Jones Bolton, 1855), 39–42.

22. Lisa Yun, *The Coolie Speaks: Chinese Indentured Laborers and African Slaves of Cuba* (Philadelphia: Temple University Press, 2008), 28–32; Hu-Dehart, "Chinese Coolie Labor in Cuba in the Nineteenth Century," 46–47; Meagher, *The Coolie Trade*, 98, 100; W. W. Wright, "The Coolie Trade, or, the Encomienda System of the Nineteenth Century," *De Bow's Review* (January 1859), 296–322; and Charles Dickens, "The Coolie Trade in China," *All the Year Round* (July 18, 1860), 365.

23. Basil Lubbock, quoted in Tchen, *New York Before Chinatown*, 49. See also ibid., 50; Meagher, *The Coolie Trade*, 145, 148; and Daniel Henderson, *Yankee Ships in China Seas: Adventures of Pioneer Americans in the Troubled Far East* (New York: Hastings House, 1946), 185.

24. Meagher, *The Coolie Trade*, 145; George Francis Train, *An American Merchant in Europe, Asia, and Australia* (New York: G. P. Putnam & Co., 1857), 78–79; and Lubbock, *The China Clippers*, 28–31.

25. Stevens, *The Life, Letters, and Journals of the Rev. and Hon. Peter Parker, M.D.*, 306–7. See also Meagher, *The Coolie Trade*, 283–84; U.S. House, Committee of Commerce, "Coolie Trade," 36th Cong., 1st sess., Report No. 443 (April 16, 1860), 7.

26. Editorial, *New York Times* (April 21, 1856); Moon-Ho Jung, *Coolies and Cane: Race, Labor, and Sugar in the Age of Emancipation* (Baltimore: Johns Hopkins University, 2006), 24; "A New Slave Trade Protected by the Stars and Stripes," *New York Herald* (September 2, 1856); "The White Slave Trade," *Pittsfield Sun* (April 17, 1856); "The Coolie Trade," *The Charleston Mercury* (October 9, 1856); and U.S. House, Committee of Commerce, "Coolie Trade," 5.

27. Meagher, *The Coolie Trade*, 144–45, 278–94; "An Act to Prohibit the

'Coolie Trade' by American Citizens in American Vessels," in *The Columbia Documentary History of the Asian American Experience*, edited by Franklin Odo (New York: Columbia University, 2002), 24; and Najia Aarim-Heriot, *Chinese Immigrants, African Americans, and Racial Anxiety in the United States, 1848–82* (Champaign: University of Illinois Press, 2003), 77–79.

28. This next section on the Chinese in California is based on the following sources: Chang, *The Chinese in America*, 1–132; Tchen, *New York Before Chinatown*, 170–75; Pfaelzer, *Driven Out*, 3–6, 24–29; David Haward Bain, *Empire Express: Building the First Transcontinental Railroad* (New York: Viking, 1999), 205–9; Meagher, *The Coolie Trade*, 136–39; "An Act to Execute Certain Treaty Stipulations Relating to the Chinese (a.k.a. Chinese Exclusion Act), May 6, 1882," in *The Columbia Documentary History of the Asian American Experience*, 62; Shih-Shan Henry Tsai, *The Chinese Experience in America* (Bloomington: Indiana University Press, 1986), 6–10; Stephen E. Ambrose, *Nothing Like it in the World: The Men Who Built the Transcontinental Railroad, 1863–1869* (New York: Simon & Schuster, 2000), 149–52; and "The Chinese Coolie Question," *San Francisco Bulletin* (December 16, 1859).

29. Asa Whitney, "House of Representatives, January 28, 1845," in *The Congressional Globe, Containing Sketches of the Debates and Proceedings of the Second Session of the Twenty-Eighth Congress*, vol. 14 (Washington, DC: *Globe*, 1845), 218; and Robert V. Hine and John Mack Faragher, *The American West: A New Interpretive History* (New Haven: Yale University, 2000), 280.

30. Thomas Hart Benton, "Speech of Mr. Benton," in *Niles' National Register* (March 14, 1849), 171. See also William H. Seward, "Colonization in North America," (January 25, 1853), in *Appendix to the Congressional Globe for the Second Session, Thirty-Second Congress*, vol. 27 (Washington, DC: John C. Rivers, 1853), 127; and Bruce Cummings, *Dominion from Sea to Sea: Pacific Ascendancy and American Power* (New Haven: Yale University Press, 2009), 70–72.

31. "Mail Communication with China," *The Congressional Globe* (February 16, 1865), 828–31; U.S. House, "Causes of the Reduction of American Tonnage," 41st Cong., 2d sess., Report No. 28 (February 17, 1870), 48; Seth Low, "Tea," in *Johnson's Universal Cyclopedia: A Scientific and Popular Treasury of Useful Knowledge*, edited by Frederick A. P. Barnard and Arnold Guyot (New York: A. J. Johnson, 1878), 751; "The New Route of Commerce to the Eastern World," *New York Times* (January 1, 1867); "America and China," *New York Times* (December 2, 1869); "Report of the Secretary of the Treasury (December 1, 1868), in *Message From the President of the United States to the Two Houses of Congress at the Commencement of the Third Session of the Fortieth Congress* (Washington, DC: Government Printing Office, 1869), 32; "The Pacific Railroad," *Engineering* (May 14, 1869), 324; Schran, "The

Minor Significance of Commercial Relations Between the United States and China," 238–47; Pan, *The Trade of the United States with China*, 30–43, 330–31; and *Historical Statistics of the United States*, vol. 5, 534–44.

Epilogue: ECHOES OF THE PAST

1. Henrietta M. Larson, "A China Trader Turns Investor—A Biographical Chapter in American Business History," *Harvard Business Review* vol. 12 (1933–34), 345–58; Downs, *The Golden Ghetto*, 236–41.

2. Richard B. Westbrook, *Girard's Will and Girard College Theology* (Philadelphia: Published by the author, 1888), 145–72; and the Girard College Web site, accessed on June 15, 2011: http://www.girardcollege.edu/page.cfm?p=359.

3. Lovell, *The Opium War*, 8–15, 333–61. Soon after *When America First Met China* went into editing, Julia Lovell's new book on the Opium Wars was published. She provides a fascinating and thought-provoking new perspective on the Opium Wars, especially the first, and analyzes how China viewed and reacted to the wars, and how those views and reactions have changed from the nineteenth to the twenty-first centuries. It is important to note that the Chinese interpretation of the Opium Wars is wrapped up in a much larger debate that involves China's history through the present, and includes the so-called century of humiliation—the period from the first Opium War up through 1949, when the Communist Party took over in China, during which time China was repeatedly defeated in wars with foreign powers, and forced to accept more so-called unequal treaties. The wars that took place during that period are not, with the exception of the second Opium War, covered in *When America First Met China*, and neither is the Chinese government's interpretation of how those wars contributed to modern Chinese nationalism, which tends to view the Opium Wars as part of a continuum of imperialistic attacks on China that subjugated China until the Communist Party liberated the nation and lifted it to glory.

4. U.S. Census Bureau, "Foreign Trade Statistics, Top Trading Partners—Total Trade, Exports, Imports: Year-to-Date December 2011," Web site accessed on February 26, 2012: http://www.census.gov/foreign-trade/statistics/highlights/top/top1112yr.html.

5. As John King Fairbank once commented, "American commercial interest in China has always had a large admixture of imagination and hope." Fairbank, *The United States and China*, 324.

SELECT BIBLIOGRAPHY

*T*HIS BIBLIOGRAPHY CONTAINS BUT A SMALL FRACTION OF THE
sources cited in this book. It is intended as a starting point for the general reader
who wants to learn more about the history of the early trade between the United
States and China. For more information about specific topics covered in the text,
please refer to the endnotes.

Bernstein, William J. *A Splendid Exchange: How Trade Shaped the World*. New
York: Grove, 2008.
Booth, Martin. *Opium: A History*. New York: St. Martin's Press/Thomas Dunne
Books, 1996.
Breen, T. H. *The Marketplace of Revolution: How Consumer Politics Shaped American Independence*. Oxford, UK: Oxford University Press, 2004.
Busch, Briton Cooper. *The War Against the Seals: A History of the North American
Seal Fishery*. Kingston, ON: McGill-Queen's University Press, 1985.
Carse, Robert. *The Moonrakers: The Story of the Clipper Ship Men*. New York:
Harper & Brothers, 1961.
Chang, Hsin-pao. *Commissioner Lin and the Opium War*. Cambridge: Harvard
University Press, 1964.
Chang, Iris. *The Chinese in America: A Narrative History*. New York: Viking, 2003.
Christman, Margaret C. S. *Adventurous Pursuits: Americans and the China Trade,
1784–1844*. Washington, DC: Smithsonian Institution Press, 1984.
Clark, Arthur H. *The Clipper Ship Era: An Epitome of Famous American and British Clipper Ships, Their Owners, Builders, Commanders, and Crews*. New York:
G. P. Putnam's Sons, 1910.
Cutler, Carl C. *Greyhounds of the Sea: The Story of the American Clipper Ship*.
Annapolis: U.S. Naval Institute Press, 1984.
Dennett, Tyler. *Americans in Eastern Asia: A Critical Study of United States' Policy in
the Far East in the Nineteenth Century*. New York: Macmillan Company, 1922.

Dodge, Ernest S. *Islands and Empires: Western Impact on the Pacific and East Asia*. Minneapolis: University of Minnesota Press, 1976.

Downs, Jacques M. *The Golden Ghetto: The American Commercial Community at Canton and the Shaping of American China Policy, 1784–1844*. Bethlehem, PA: Lehigh University Press, 1997.

Dulles, Foster Rhea. *The Old China Trade*. Boston: Houghton Mifflin Company, 1930.

Fairbank, John King. *Trade and Diplomacy on the China Coast: The Opening of the Treaty Ports 1842–1854*. Cambridge: Harvard University Press, 1953.

Fay, Peter Ward. *The Opium War: 1840–1842*. Chapel Hill: University of North Carolina Press, 1997.

Fichter, James R. *So Great a Profit: How the East Indies Trade Transformed Anglo-American Capitalism*. Cambridge: Harvard University Press, 2010.

Forbes, Robert Bennet. *Personal Reminiscences*. Boston: Little, Brown, and Company, 1878.

Frank, Caroline, *Objectifying China, Imagining America: Chinese Commodities in Early America*. Chicago: University of Chicago Press, 2011.

Gelber, Harry G. *The Dragon and the Foreign Devils*. New York: Walker and Company, 2007.

Gibson, James R. *Otter Skins, Boston Ships, and China Goods: The Maritime Fur Trade of the Northwest Coast, 1785–1841*. Seattle: University of Washington Press, 1999.

Goldstein, Jonathan. *Philadelphia and the China Trade, 1682–1846: Commercial, Cultural, and Attitudinal Effects*. University Park: Pennsylvania State University Press, 1978.

Greenberg, Michael. *British Trade and the Opening of China, 1800–1842*. Cambridge, UK: Cambridge University Press, 1969.

Greenbie, Sydney, and Marjorie Barstow Greenbie. *Gold of Ophir: The China Trade in the Making of America*. New York: Wilson-Erickson, 1937.

Hohenegger, Beatrice. *Liquid Jade: The Story of Tea from East to West*. New York: St. Martin's Press, 2006.

Hsü, Immanuel Chung Yueh. *The Rise of Modern China*. New York: Oxford University Press, 1995.

Hunter, William C. *The 'Fan Kwae' at Canton Before Treaty Days, 1825–1844 by An Old Resident*. London: Kegan Paul, Trench & Co., 1882.

Kirker, James. *Adventures to China: Americans in the Southern Oceans, 1792–1812*. New York: Oxford University Press, 1970.

Labaree, Benjamin Woods. *The Boston Tea Party*. London: Oxford University Press, 1964.

Latourette, Kenneth Scott. *The History of Early Relations Between the United States and China, 1784–1844*. New Haven: Yale University Press, 1917.

Lee, Jean Gordon. *Philadelphians and the China Trade, 1784–1844.* Philadelphia: Philadelphia Museum of Art, 1984.

Lovell, Julia. *The Opium War: Drugs, Dreams and the Making of China.* London: Picador, 2011.

Malloy, Mary. *"Boston Men" in the Northwest Coast: The American Maritime Fur Trade 1788–1844.* Kingston, ON: Limestone Press, 1998.

May, Ernest R., and John K. Fairbank, ed. *America's China Trade in Historical Perspective: The Chinese and American Performance.* Cambridge: Harvard University Press, 1986.

Meagher, Arnold J. *The Coolie Trade: The Traffic in Chinese Laborers to Latin America 1847–1874.* Ph.D. diss., University of California, Davis, 1975; reprint, Bloomington, IN: XLibris, 2008.

Morse, Hosea Ballou. *The International Relations of the Chinese Empire: The Period of Conflict, 1834–1860.* New York: Longman's, Green & Co., 1910.

Rappleye, Charles. *Robert Morris: Financier of the Revolution.* New York: Simon & Schuster, 2010.

Richards, Rhys. "United States Trade with China, 1784–1814." Special Supplement to vol. 54, *American Neptune* (1994), 9–66.

———. "Re-Viewing Early American Trade with China, 1784–1833." *Mains'l Haul: A Journal of Pacific Maritime History* (Spring 2003), 14–19.

Smith, Philip Chadwick Foster. *The Empress of China.* Philadelphia: Philadelphia Maritime Museum, 1984.

Spence, Jonathan D. *The Search for Modern China.* New York: W. W. Norton, 1990.

Tchen, John Kuo Wei. *New York Before Chinatown: Orientalism and the Shaping of American Culture, 1776–1882.* Baltimore: Johns Hopkins University Press, 1999.

Temple, Robert. *The Genius of China: 3,000 Years of Science, Discovery, and Invention.* New York: Simon & Schuster, 1986.

Waley, Arthur. *The Opium War Through Chinese Eyes.* New York: Macmillan Company, 1958.

Whipple, Addison Beecher Colvin. *The Clipper Ships.* Alexandria, VA: Time-Life Books, 1980.

Wood, Frances. *The Silk Road: Two Thousand Years in the Heart of Asia.* Berkeley: University of California Press, 2002.

Yangwen, Zheng. *The Social Life of Opium in China.* Cambridge: Cambridge University Press, 2005.

Zug, James. *American Traveler: The Life and Adventures of John Ledyard, the Man Who Dreamed of Walking the World.* New York: Basic Books, 2005.

ILLUSTRATION CREDITS

Page iv: (map) Courtesy Library of Congress, Geography and Map Division; (natives swimming) *The Treasures of the Deep* (London: T. Nelson and Sons, 1876)

Page xv: Courtesy Library of Congress

Page 3: Courtesy Library of Congress

Page 6: Courtesy © Independence National Historic Park

Page 9: Courtesy Ledyard National Bank

Page 10: Courtesy John James Audubon Museum, Henderson, KY

Page 14: Newark Museum / Art Resource, NY

Page 17: Samuel Shaw, *The Journals, The First Consul at Canton, with a Life of the Author by Josiah Quincy* (Boston: Wm. Crosby and H. P. Nichols, 1847)

Page 24: Courtesy bpk, Berlin/Kunstbibliothek, Staatliche Museen, Berlin, Germany / Dietmar Katz / Art Resource, NY

Page 26: Thomas Allom and George Newenham Wright, *China, in a Series of Views, Displaying the Scenery, Architecture, and Social Habits, of That Ancient Empire*, vol. 3 (London: Fisher, Son & Co., 1843)

Page 29: Courtesy Peabody Essex Museum, Salem, MA, E80322.A-C

Page 36: Courtesy Library of Congress, Geography and Map Division

Page 43: Lithograph after W. S. Sherwill, reproduced in Benjamin Broomhall, *The Truth About Opium Smoking* (London: Hodder & Stoughton, 1882)

Page 45: Stapleton Collection / Art Resource, NY

Page 47: Robert Sears, *The Wonders of the World, in Nature, Art, and Mind* (New York: Robert Sears, 1843)

Page 56: Courtesy Library of Congress

Page 58: Courtesy Peabody Essex Museum, Salem, MA, E81592.10

Page 67: Courtesy © The British Library Board

Page 70: Courtesy Library of Congress

Page 72: Courtesy © Mystic Seaport Collection, Mystic, CT, 1938.77

Page 73: Thomas Allom and George Newenham Wright, *China, in a Series of Views, Displaying the Scenery, Architecture, and Social Habits, of That Ancient Empire*, vol. 2 (London: Fisher, Son & Co., 1843)

Page 74: Courtesy Peabody Essex Museum, Salem, MA, M4468

Page 76: "Some Account of the City of Canton," *Saturday Magazine* (April 1837)

Page 77: Robert Elliot, *Views in the East: Comprising India, Canton, and the Shores of the Red Sea*, vol. 1 (London: H. Fisher, Son & Co., 1833)

Page 85: *Political Intelligencer and New-Jersey Advertiser* (June 1, 1785)

Page 88: Edmund Fanning, *Voyages to the South Seas, Indian and Pacific Oceans, China Sea, North-West Coast, Fiji Island, South Shetlands, &c* (New York: William H. Vermilye, 1838)

Page 92: Courtesy Library of Congress

Page 94: Courtesy Peabody Essex Museum, Salem, MA, gift of the Derby Family, 1824, M353

Page 101: Courtesy Nantucket Historical Association

Page 104: Courtesy Mike Boylan, United States Fish and Wildlife Service

Page 105: Edmund Fanning, *Voyages Round the World; with Selected Sketches of Voyages to the South Seas, North and South Pacific Oceans, China, etc.* (New York: Collins & Hannay, 1833)

Page 108: George Henry Mason, *Costumes of China: Illustrated by sixty engravings; with explanations in English and French* (London: W. Miller, 1804)

Page 111: Courtesy Rare Books and Special Collections Division of the Library of Congress

Page 113: Elizabeth Twining, *Illustrations of the Natural Orders of Plants with Groups and Descriptions*, vol. 2 (London: Sampson Low, Son, and Marston, 1868)

Page 119: Lithograph after W. S. Sherwill, reproduced in Benjamin Broomhall, *The Truth About Opium Smoking* (London: Hodder & Stoughton, 1882)

Page 136: Courtesy Peabody Essex Museum, Salem, MA, E78680

Page 144: Courtesy Girard College History Collections, Philadelphia, PA

Page 146: William C. Hunter, *The 'Fan Kwae' at Canton Before Treaty Days, 1825–1844 by An Old Resident* (London: Kegan Paul, Trench, & Co., 1882)

Page 147: Courtesy Collection of New-York Historical Society

Page 152: Otto von Kotzebue, *Voyage of Discovery in the South Sea and the Behring's Strait* (London: J. and C. Adlard, 1821)

Page 161: Christian Horace B. Alfred Moquin-Tandon, *The World of the Sea* (London: Cassell, Petter, and Galpin, 1869)

Page 162: Courtesy of the author

Page 163: *The Treasures of the Deep* (London: T. Nelson and Sons, 1876)

Page 169: Courtesy Rhode Island Historical Society, RHi X3 7352

Page 172: Courtesy Forbes House Museum, photograph by Benjamin Wight

Page 174: Courtesy Forbes House Museum, photograph by Benjamin Wight

Page 175: Courtesy Peabody Essex Museum, Salem, MA, E75256

Page 177: Courtesy Peabody Essex Museum, Salem, MA, museum purchase, 1931 A. Heard Collection, M3793

Page 179: Courtesy Peabody Essex Museum, Salem, MA, museum purchase with partial funds donated by Lee and Juliet Folger Fund and Joan Vaughan Ingraham, 2001, M18709

Page 180: Courtesy Forbes House Museum, photograph by Benjamin Wight

Page 183: Thomas Allom and George Newenham Wright, *China, in a Series of Views, Displaying the Scenery, Architecture, and Social Habits, of That Ancient Empire*, vol. 2 (London: Fisher, Son & Co., 1843)

Page 184: Courtesy Peter Parker V

Page 185: Courtesy Peabody Essex Museum, Salem, MA, museum purchase with funds donated anonymously, M22764

Page 193: Courtesy Museum of the City of New York

Page 199: Courtesy Library of Congress

Page 208: Thomas Allom and George Newenham Wright, *China, in a Series of Views, Displaying the Scenery, Architecture, and Social Habits, of That Ancient Empire*, vol. 3 (London: Fisher, Son & Co., 1843)

Page 209: Lithograph after W. S. Sherwill, reproduced in Benjamin Broomhall, *The Truth About Opium Smoking* (London: Hodder & Stoughton, 1882)

Page 210: Alexander Murray, *Doings in China* (London: Richard Bentley, 1843)

Page 212: John Francis Davis, *The Chinese: A General Description of the Empire of China and Its Inhabitants*, vol. 2 (New York: Harper & Brothers, 1836)

Page 224: Courtesy Peabody Essex Museum, Salem, MA, M4806

Page 241: William Freke Williams, *England's Battles by Sea and Land: From the Commencement of the Great French Revolution to the Present Time* (London: London Printing and Publishing Company, 1854)

Page 243: John Ouchterlony, *The Chinese War: An Account of All the Operations of the British Forces from the Commencement to the Treaty of Nanking* (London: Saunders and Otley, 1844)

Page 244: John Ouchterlony, *The Chinese War: An Account of All the Operations of the British Forces from the Commencement to the Treaty of Nanking* (London: Saunders and Otley, 1844)

Page 247. Courtesy Peabody Essex Museum, Salem, MA, gift of Mr. Robert J. Clark, 1960, M10565

Page 249: *Illustrated London News* (November 12, 1842)

Page 258: Courtesy Historical Society of Old Newbury

Page 265: Courtesy Peabody Essex Museum, Salem, MA, M5162

Page 272: Courtesy Library of Congress

Page 274: Courtesy Library of Congress

Page 276: Courtesy Library of Congress

Page 280: Courtesy Library of Congress

Page 284: Edgar Holden, "A Chapter on the Coolie Trade," in *Harper's New Monthly Magazine* (June 1864)

Page 295: Edgar Holden, "A Chapter on the Coolie Trade," *Harper's New Monthly Magazine* (June 1864)

Page 296: Edgar Holden, "A Chapter on the Coolie Trade," in *Harper's New Monthly Magazine* (June 1864)

Page 299: Courtesy © Mystic Seaport, Photography Collection, Mystic, CT, 1994.107.1.20

Page 300: "The Chincha Guano Islands," *National Magazine* (June 1858)

Page 306: Courtesy Library of Congress

Page 307: Courtesy Pacific Mail Steamship Company Collection of Stephen J. and Jeremy W. Potash (steve@PotashCo.com)

Page 309: Courtesy Forbes House Museum, photograph by Benjamin Wight

Color Insert

1. Courtesy © British Library Board
2. Courtesy Library of Congress
3. Courtesy Peabody Essex Museum, Salem, MA, Museum Purchase, 1993, M25794
4. Courtesy LuEsther T. Mertz Library, NYBG / Art Resource, NY
5. Courtesy Peabody Essex Museum, Salem, MA, E80322.A-C
6. Courtesy Mount Vernon Ladies' Association Collection
7. Courtesy Museum of Fine Arts, Boston, gift of Joseph W. Revere, William B. Revere, and Edward H. R. Revere
8. Courtesy © Independence National Historic Park
9. Courtesy © Dumbarton Oaks Research Library and Collection, Rare Book Collection
10. Courtesy Philadelphia History Museum at the Atwater Kent, Historical Society of Pennsylvania Collection
11. Courtesy Philadelphia Museum of Art, purchased with Thomas Skelton Harrison Fund, 1970
12. Courtesy Historic New England, gift of Constance McCann Betts, Helena W. Guest, and Frasier W. McCann, 1942.4655
13. Courtesy New Britain Museum of American Art, gift of Caroline N. Dealy, Frank P. Dealy, Darilyn H. Dealy, and Wensley A. Dealy, 2008.74
14. Courtesy National Portrait Gallery, Smithsonian Institution / Art Resource, NY
15. Courtesy Girard College History Collections, Philadelphia, PA
16. Courtesy Peabody Essex Museum, Salem, MA, gift of the Derby Family, 1824, M353
17. Courtesy Peabody Essex Museum, Salem, MA, M8255
18. Courtesy Peabody Essex Museum, Salem, MA, gift of Mr. Russell Sturgis Paine, 1958, M9751.1
19. Courtesy Peabody Essex Museum, Salem, MA, M4468
20. Courtesy Peabody Essex Museum, Salem, MA, E79708

21. Courtesy Peabody Essex Museum, Salem, MA, E78680
22. Courtesy Peabody Essex Museum, Salem, MA, museum purchase, 1931 A. Heard Collection, M3793
23. Courtesy Forbes House Museum, photograph by Benjamin Wight
24. Courtesy Forbes House Museum, photograph by Benjamin Wight
25. Courtesy Peabody Essex Museum, Salem, MA, gift of Miss Amy Curtis and Miss Clare Curtis, 1952, E82553
26. Courtesy Peabody Essex Museum, Salem, MA, gift of Mrs. Emory W. Johnson, 1923, E19144.12
27. Courtesy Peabody Essex Museum, Salem, MA, E81592.10
28. Courtesy Peabody Essex Museum, Salem, MA, museum purchase with funds donated anonymously, M22764
29. Courtesy Peabody Essex Museum, Salem, MA, museum purchase with partial funds donated by Lee and Juliet Folger Fund and Joan Vaughan Ingraham, 2001, M18709
30. Courtesy Peter Parker V
31. Philadelphia Museum of Art, gift of Mrs. Joseph H. Gaskill, 1970
32. J. Elliot Bingham, *Narrative of the Expedition to China, from the Commencement of the War to Its Termination in 1842*, vol. 1 (London: Henry Colburn, 1843)
33. Courtesy Seaman's Bank for Savings Collection, South Street Seaport Museum Foundation
34. Courtesy © Mystic Seaport Collection, Mystic, CT, Coll. 112, Box 1, Folder 14
35. Courtesy Peabody Essex Museum, Salem, MA, 124724
36. Courtesy Peabody Essex Museum, Salem, MA, gift of Mr. Louis Pappas, 1961, E82881
37. Courtesy Pacific Mail Steamship Company Collection of Stephen J. and Jeremy W. Potash. (steve@PotashCo.com)

I N D E X

Page numbers in *italics* refer to illustrations.
Page numbers beginning with 317 refer to notes.

ERIC JAY DOLIN, who grew up near the coasts of New York and Connecticut, graduated from Brown University, where he majored in biology and environmental studies. After getting a master's degree in environmental management from the Yale School of Forestry and Environmental Studies, he received his Ph.D. in environmental policy and planning from the Massachusetts Institute of Technology.

Dolin has worked as a program manager at the U.S. Environmental Protection Agency, an environmental consultant stateside and in London, an intern at the National Wildlife Federation and on Capitol Hill, a fisheries policy analyst at the National Marine Fisheries Service, and an American Association for the Advancement of Science Mass Media Science and Engineering Fellow at *Business Week*.

Much of Dolin's writing reflects his interest in wildlife, the environment, and American history. His books include *Fur, Fortune, and Empire: The Epic History of the Fur Trade in America* (W. W. Norton), *Leviathan: The History of Whaling in America* (W. W. Norton), the *Smithsonian Book of National Wildlife Refuges, Snakehead: A Fish Out of Water*, and *Political Waters*, a history of the degradation and cleanup of Boston Harbor. *Leviathan* was chosen as one of the best nonfiction books of 2007 by the *Los Angeles Times*, the *Boston Globe*, and the *Providence Journal*. It also won a number of awards, including the 2007 John Lyman Award for U.S. Maritime History and the twenty-third annual L. Byrne Waterman Award, given by the New Bedford Whaling Museum, for outstanding contributions to whaling research and history. *Fur, Fortune, and Empire* was chosen as one of the best books of 2010 by the *Seattle Times*, and one of the top ten books of 2010 by the Rocky Mountain Land Library. It also won the 2011 James P. Hanlan Book Award, given by the New England Historical Association, and was awarded first place in the Outdoor Writers Association of America, Excellence in Craft Contest.

Dolin and his family reside in Marblehead, Massachusetts.